CHRISTIANA HERRINGHAM

and the Edwardian Art Scene

CHRISTIANA HERRINGHAM

and the Edwardian Art Scene

MARY LAGO

LUND HUMPHRIES PUBLISHERS
LONDON

First published in Great Britain in 1996 by
Lund Humphries Publishers Ltd.
Park House
1 Russell Gardens
London NW11 9NN

British Library Cataloguing in Publication Data
A catalogue record for this book is available
from the British Library

ISBN 0 85331 680 5

Designed by Kristie Lee

Printed and bound in the United States
of America by Thomson-Shore Inc.

Typefaces: Minion, Trajan, Nuptual Script

To Jane and Tim

CONTENTS

ILLUSTRATIONS

PREFACE

MY FIRST ENCOUNTER with Christiana Herringham's name occurred in 1967, when I began to edit the thirty-year correspondence of the English painter Sir William Rothenstein and the Bengali poet Rabindranath Tagore. In order to annotate that account, I had to learn something about Lady Herringham, for she played a crucial part in the development of Rothenstein's interest in India, which led directly to his successful efforts to introduce Tagore and his work to readers in the West. This meant that, indirectly, she, too, had a part in the enlargement of Tagore's reputation. From her letters to William Rothenstein and his wife Alice, and to the English painter and critic Roger Fry and his wife Helen, I learned that Christiana Herringham was an expert copyist of quattrocento tempera paintings, that she visited India three times, and that two of those visits were for the purpose of copying the deteriorating wall paintings in the Buddhist caves at Ajanta.

These activities seemed notable in themselves, but from almost everyone to whom I addressed questions about her, the response was "Christiana *who?*" Nevertheless, I had learned enough to know that this was a woman about whom I must know more.

The early trail led from records at Somerset House, London, the national repository for probated wills, to a helpful family solicitor in Lymington, Hampshire, who introduced me to Mrs. Robert Hole, elderly widow of Robert Herringham Hole, the nephew who became the heir of Sir Wilmot and Lady Christiana Herringham. Mrs. Hole could not tell me a great deal, for during most of her years with the family, Christiana had been "away." There was, however, a family story to the effect that after her last return from India in 1911 she had believed herself to be pursued by vengeful Indians: an intriguing clue, but not to be fully explained until much later. Mrs. Hole could, however, lend me some of Sir Wilmot Herringham's letters and other papers. They were interesting and helpful but did not yet explain why Christiana Herringham's achievements seemed so thoroughly forgotten.

My next promising clue was a book that I found in London, at a Bayswater secondhand bookshop: *Twenty-Five Years of the National Art Collections Fund,* edited by D. S. MacColl and published in 1928. I bought it because Rothenstein and MacColl were both members of the New English Art Club, but from it I learned that Christiana Herringham was not only a member of the National Art Collections Fund but a very important one. She had revived a forgotten suggestion that Britain was in desperate need of an organized effort to stem the tide of artworks that were leaving British private collections for foreign owners. She gave the money that launched the organization.

I went to the Fund's headquarters, at that time in the Wallace Collection in Manchester Square. How appropriate a location this was became clear to me much later. Still, no one there could tell me anything about Lady Herringham, and there were only a few impersonal references to her in the minutes of some of the Fund's early meetings.

Other work intervened, and I laid the subject aside, but for another twenty years, as I went to libraries and interviewed persons connected with other projects, I asked in every likely quarter about Christiana Herringham. I found a letter here, a fragmentary reference there, all of which I stored away. Friends occasionally happened upon helpful bits of information and forwarded them to me. Mrs. Hole died, and Mrs. Jean Vernon-Jackson, her daughter and Sir Wilmot's grandniece, took an interest in my search. Each time I returned to England, I got in touch with her, and sometimes she had found something of interest to be added to the file, but everything that we had discovered did not add up to a connected account.

At last, when I had finished other work in hand, I returned to Christiana Herringham. I went back to the National Art Collections

Fund, which had moved its offices to Millbank, near the Tate Gallery. Again, no one I spoke to there knew anything about her. But I had a lead that proved extremely valuable: the papers of the Fund's first chairman, David Lindsay, twenty-seventh Earl of Crawford and tenth Earl of Balcarres, were on deposit in the John Rylands Library in Manchester. The present Earl, his grandson, gave permission for access to them, and I began to read them there; but before I could finish, the Crawford Papers were transferred to the National Library of Scotland. I followed them to Edinburgh.

Now a more complete narrative emerged. When I added information from the Rothenstein Papers at Harvard University to that from the Crawford Papers, I had a much more substantial part of Christiana's story and the beginning of an explanation for the mystery of her near oblivion. Mrs. Vernon-Jackson traced documents that completed still more of the Herringham side of the narrative. The late Mr. Peter G. Warren, of the London firm of which Christiana's father, Thomas Wilde Powell, was an earlier partner, gave me access to materials that illuminated her paternal ancestry. Some parts of her story only Christiana could have told, and those died with her in 1929. But enough remains to complete a portrait of a woman who was far seeing, courageous, and utterly devoted to the welfare of art.

Still, it seems that an unkind fate was determined to wipe out all traces of Christiana Herringham. Mr. Warren took me to Piccard's Rough, the Powell home at Guildford, Surrey, which had represented all that both Christiana and her father held to be primary among principles of art. It had been a beautiful house, a famous house—*had been,* because in 1958, after the building had passed out of the Powell family's ownership, a heedless "planning" commission had allowed demolition of its splendid central hall. That left the two wings as separate residences, both very handsome but never again to be as Richard Norman Shaw, the designer, and Thomas Powell, its owner, had intended. Back in London, I went to Wimpole Street to see Number 40, the house where Christiana and her husband, Dr. Wilmot Herringham, had lived. As soon as I turned the corner, I guessed what had happened. A German bomb had fallen there (in the mews at the rear, I learned). Neighboring houses survived to be restored, but even from a distance the modern construction at Number 40 stands out bleakly, a squared-off red-brick obstruction to a vista of gracious old dwellings.

I took the mutilation at Piccard's Rough and the incongruity in Wimpole Street as a challenge. Whatever that unkind fate had intended, I would do my best to reconstruct Christiana's story. For background, I have taken as precedent two books that I admire; they survey the attitudes that shaped Christiana Herringham's artistic environment: Walter Houghton's *The Victorian Frame of Mind* and Samuel Hynes's *The Edwardian Turn of Mind.* For her own story, I have borrowed a suggestion from the title of David Robertson's *Sir Charles Eastlake and the Victorian Art World,* for many circumstances of that world, the good as well as the worse, were carried over to the more circumscribed Edwardian art scene. Christiana Herringham had no prominent public position to match that of Sir Charles Lock Eastlake, a great Director of the National Gallery; indeed, no woman then served on a body that made official policy for art administration and preservation. That exclusion did not keep her from taking action in areas where something that could be done for art had not been done. Her work on the Edwardian scene was a crucial part of the effort to find a new way, for the new century, to preserve the national art heritage not only of Britain but of India as well.

A project that continues for twenty-five years comes to involve a great many individuals and institutions. It has brought me many new friends and associates—so many that it is impossible to thank all by name. I hope that all will accept my thanks for their help and, very often, for generous hospitality. I want them to know that they have not only assisted my research; they have enriched my life.

Some individuals, however, I must mention by name. First are the late Mrs. Robert Herringham Hole and her daughter, Mrs. Jean Vernon-Jackson. I must also gratefully acknowledge the late Mr. A. W. N. Cowper, solicitor, of Lymington, Hampshire, who was my first link to the Herringham family.

My link to the family of Thomas Wilde Powell was Mr. Thomas Luckock, who directed me to three descendants of that family: Mrs.

Bridget St. John, Mrs. Charlotte Fulford, and Miss Jennifer Hobbs. They have taken the most cordial interest in my research, as did the late Mr. Peter G. Warren, who wrote the history of the stockbroking firm of which Thomas Powell had been a partner.

Two major manuscript collections contain substantial numbers of Herringham letters as well as illuminating collateral correspondence. One of these collections is Sir William Rothenstein's papers in the Houghton Library at Harvard University. Since 1967, when I began to edit the Rothenstein-Tagore correspondence, I have had the most generous help and hospitality from all of the Rothenstein family, and most particularly from the late Sir John Rothenstein and Lady Rothenstein, and then from the late Mr. Michael Rothenstein, the succeeding executor. Many scholars besides myself are indebted to Sir William, who took care to preserve letters that he felt certain would have future value.

The aforementioned Crawford Papers are the second major collection. Their author and compiler, David Lindsay, preserved and arranged the papers with the most meticulous care. They include records of the years of Christiana Herringham's greatest involvement in the National Art Collections Fund. I wish to acknowledge the kindness of his grandson, Robert Alexander Lindsay, the present Earl, in allowing me repeated access to those volumes as well as permission to quote from his grandfather's letters.

For permission to quote from letters for which they hold executor's responsibility, I wish to thank the following: the present Lord Aldenham (for Lord Aldenham), Miss Felicity Ashbee (for C. R. Ashbee), Mr. David Benson (for Robert H. Benson), Dr. Rama Coomaraswamy (for Ananda Kentish Coomaraswamy), Miss Julia Ionides (for Euterpe Ionides Craies), Viscount Scarsdale (for Lord Curzon), Mrs. Annabel Cole (for Roger Fry), Mrs. Sonia Wilson (for Ernest B. Havell), the late Mr. Leonard Elton (for D. S. MacColl), Mrs. Geoffrey Hermges (for Mrs. William Marshall), Miss Riette Sturge Moore (for Charles Ricketts), Mrs. Ruth Sebag-Montefiore and the Mr. L. H. L. Cohen (for Isidore Spielmann). And I am also grateful for permission to quote from the letters of Sir Charles Read, granted by courtesy of the Trustees of the British Museum;

and for permission to quote from the Charles Ricketts Diary, British Library, granted by Miss Riette Sturge Moore. For records from Barnwood House Institution, I wish to thank Mr. B. R. Church, Trust Secretary, Gloucestershire County Archives, and Mrs. Jean Vernon-Jackson, who granted permission for my access to them. I also wish to thank Mrs. Ruth Sebag-Montefiore for permission to quote from her Magnus Lecture to the Jewish Historical Society, London, 9 July 1992.

In a few cases I have been unable to trace present executors. I hope that the brief passages quoted from letters will cause no offense. In several cases I am advised that no executors survive and that estates are closed.

I can mention here only some of the many institutions whose directors, librarians, and archivists have provided information and have suggested additional avenues of research. I must particularly thank the following: Bedford College (now combined with the Royal Holloway College), Egham, Surrey; Old Vic Archives, Bristol University Theatre Collection; British Library and British Museum, London; University Library, Cambridge; India Office Library and India Office Records, London; Western Manuscripts Collection, King's College Library, University of Cambridge; South Asia Centre, University of Cambridge; Houghton Library, Harvard University; Special Collections, University of Illinois Library, Urbana; London Library; Manchester University Library; National Art Collections Fund, London; National Gallery Archives, London; National Library of Scotland, Edinburgh; National Portrait Gallery, London; Newnham College, University of Cambridge; Public Record Office, Kew, Richmond, Surrey; Ruskin Gallery, Sheffield; Harry Ransom Humanities Research Center, University of Texas at Austin; Indian Section, Victoria and Albert Museum, London; Wallace Collection, London; Wren Library, Trinity College, University of Cambridge.

My long-standing indebtedness continues, to Martha Alexander, Director of the Ellis Library at the University of Missouri–Columbia. She and her staff, most particularly those who administer Interlibrary Loan, have helped me in a multitude of ways. Three colleagues, Professors Winifred Horner, Elaine Lawless, and Martha Townsend, have broadened the context of my study by their special interest in this example of an Edwardian woman whose initiatives brought her into conflict with established procedures and institutions.

I wish to thank the *Burlington Magazine* for its interest in this history and for its publication in March 1993 of an earlier version of the material that became Chapters 4 and 5. I am grateful also to Professor Norman Land, who read Chapter 3 in manuscript, and to Dr. Partha Mitter, who read Chapters 6 and 7, for their very helpful comments and corrections.

Two Cambridge University colleges have contributed to the progress of this work by giving me accommodations and thus the opportunity to add to Christiana Herringham's story as I went about other work in progress. St. Edmund's House (now College) gave me a visiting fellowship in 1982–1983; and Selwyn College appointed me a visiting bye-fellow in 1991–1992. For travel and other research expenses I had assistance from the University of Missouri through a Weldon Spring Humanities Seminar Grant, 1984, and from the university's Research Council in 1991–1992 and 1994.

Finally, I wish to thank the Director and staff of the University of Missouri Press for their sustained and lively interest in this book, and Catherine F. McKenzie for her patient and ever-helpful copyediting. With the greatest pleasure I have placed this text in their capable hands.

CHRISTIANA HERRINGHAM

and the Edwardian Art Scene

1

INTRODUCTION TO AN ARTIST

The introduction of the Fine Arts into every country, and their subsequent cultivation, have at all periods afforded materials for chronological history, highly interesting to the lover of art and to the man of letters. Occurrences connected therewith spring up in succession, and though more or less important in themselves, they often pass unheeded, and from a want of proper notice sink back into the general mass of oblivion, which swallows up all that belongs to human nature. Inquiry succeeds at some future period when it is probably too late, and such is at best followed up with a greater or less degree of certainty, as governed by casual circumstance.

William James Buchanan, *Memoirs of Painting* (1834)[1]

IN THE EDWARDIAN YEARS, Christiana Jane Powell Herringham (1852–1929) played an important part in the cultivation of new attitudes toward the fine arts in Britain and in Britain's Indian Empire. She is also one of those who "from a want of proper notice" have sunk back into "the general mass of oblivion." Casual circumstance has been unkind and unjust. Some uncertainties remain about her and her work, but now is that "future period," not quite too late, for restoring her to active memory.

In 1899 she translated *Il libro dell' arte o trattato della pittura* (1390), Cennino Cennini's manual, standard throughout the fifteenth century, for painters in tempera and fresco. In 1901 she was the moving force of a new society dedicated to the revival of tempera as a medium and the acceptance of quattrocento painting as more than a stopping place on the path to perfectibility in art. In 1903 she gave the money that launched Britain's National Art Collections Fund, which acquires or assists with acquisition of artworks for the nation. In the winters of 1909–1910 and 1910–1911 she went to India to make copies of the Buddhist wall paintings in the caves at Ajanta, which for at least six centuries past had been left to deteriorate in dark and damp.

We may wonder now why these activities were necessary. Quattrocento painting is appreciated as one of the great eras in the history of art, and tempera is taken seriously as a medium. Every major gallery and museum has a "Friends of" group that rallies round when help is needed. Ajanta's paintings are considered a national treasure, on the itinerary of scholars and tourists interested in India's fine arts. But in the late-Victorian years none of that was true. Nineteenth-century standards for art, art education, and art administration still prevailed. Progress, in the arts as in the sciences, meant moving on, improving upon the past, and looking back principally to measure how far behind one had left the predecessors. Quattrocento painters, not to mention those long-dead Buddhist artists at Ajanta, were still "primitives," their work unrealistic and devoid of correct perspective. Truly great art was thought to have begun only with Raphael. Tempera's particular difficulties made it useful for disciplinary exercises, but its austerities could not compete with oil's lushness and variety of tone: this was a shibboleth of Victorian art instruction.

Britain's National Gallery was in trouble. Gifts from wealthy individuals and general bequests from collectors were its only means of supplementing the Treasury's utterly inadequate annual appropriation. In fact, the nation's entire art heritage was in trouble. New taxes, a stubborn agricultural depression, and high death duties pressed hard upon the owners of the great private collections. As they found themselves in need of cash, and masterworks began to appear in dealers' rooms, the competition among foreign buyers drove art prices steadily upward, and inherited treasures of fine art departed for France, Germany, and America. Many worried about the exodus, but no one had done anything substantive toward stopping it. The administrators of the national collections could do little, in view of the Treasury's parsimony and their own old habit of elitist management.

"Boards have hitherto consisted largely of the lordly type," wrote the dissident art critic D. S. MacColl. "As a class lords have their virtues, one of which is a certain aloofness or you-bedamnedness which prevents them from attaching undue importance to anything that appears in print. . . . [But] they bring with them a House-of-Lords atmosphere, which means obstruction as a half-conscious habit on general principle."[2] Behind the opulent façade was a great deal of personal and public anxiety.

That the British public, ostensible owner of the national collections, might welcome an opportunity to share the financial responsibility for acquisitions was a new and startling idea. Would not a National Art Collections Fund attempt to dictate acquisition policy? Administrators and boards had decided what the public ought to see, and the public came and saw it. That was as far as democracy ought to go in a gallery.

Democracy did not yet include votes for women, and women rarely participated in bodies that made or substantially affected public policy. "The presence of too many women on a public body could actually embarrass the men in their very essential duties. . . . Women are, as a whole, too indifferent to what happens outside their domestic life to take a too prominent part in public work."[3] That was the general attitude. When the National Art Collections Fund became a reality in 1903, Christiana Herringham became ill at ease about her being the only woman on its executive committee. The present Earl of Crawford and Balcarres, grandson of the Fund's first chairman, commented on the reasons for her misgivings.

> I must say that I can understand her sense of awe in being of their company in committee because they certainly were a worldly group comprising the most eminent connoisseurs and directors that it is possible to imagine. They would have been intimidating for any man to work with—let alone a woman at that time. Some of them certainly do not appear to have gone out of their way to make her feel welcome and at home in their midst.[4]

Her discomfort on the Fund's executive committee was an extension of the social disabilities with which she had grown up. They affected any late-Victorian woman who aspired to a serious career in art. Christiana knew that she was not a great painter, but she wanted to be more than the mere "sketcher" upon whom Florence Nightingale heaped scorn in 1852.

> Here and there a solitary individual, it is true, makes a really careful study. . . . But, in general, a "lady" has too many sketches on hand. She has a sketch of society, a sketch of her children's education, sketches of her "charities," sketches of her reading. She is like a painter who should have five pictures in his studio at once, and giving now a stroke to one, and now a stroke to another, till he had made the whole round, should continue his routine to the end. . . . When shall we see a woman making a *study* of what she does?[5]

In 1857 Philip Gilbert Hamerton, editor of the *Art-Journal,* made the same point when he welcomed a new organization, the Society of Female Artists. Hamerton's was "a rare male voice of reason and insight," a reformer robustly impatient with the static condition of British art.[6] This new society's exhibition, he wrote, should "satisfy even the most incredulous." But if incredulity was the male reaction to women's art, prejudice and the art establishment were to blame, for women had few opportunities for serious study. They were not excluded from the lectures at the Royal Academy of Arts, Hamerton continued, "but few are bold enough to attend them," and the Academy's segregated classes for women offered only inferior instruction. This was why women's pictures were so often only "pretty and graceful." The wonder was not that they fell short of men's professional standards but that they persevered at all. "Separate but unequal is the leitmotif" is a modern comment on that situation.[7] The Royal Academy excluded women from its mixed classes until 1860, when Laura Herford gained admission on the strength of an entry drawing signed only "L. Herford," so that the examiners assumed it to be a man's work. It was a triumph, but it was also demeaning, and throughout the nineteenth century the Academy excluded women from classes in drawing from the nude, considered an essential part of an academic training.[8]

When women finally obtained admission to the Academy's mixed classes, the double standard still prevailed, and for blatantly sexist reasons. G. D. Leslie, a product of its classes and later himself a professor of painting, told more than he realized about male attitudes when he confessed that he was "glad that the female invasion took place after I had left the schools," for he feared the distraction of a pretty girl in the class. Pretty girls seemed to do the best work because they received "decidedly more attention" than plainer girls, which "is not quite fair, but I am afraid it is inevitable." In the end, women artists whether plain or pretty could not equal male artists because "for the most part, they lack the self reliant conceit which so often characterises the brightest genius of the male sex."[9]

A woman could not win. Without modesty she was not a womanly woman; without conceit she was not a true artist. When Elizabeth Thompson Butler painted impressive military scenes and subjects, critics praised her work but could not understand how she could paint "from a thoroughly manly point of view." If she painted masculine subjects so well, how was she a "true woman"? Ruskin admired one of her paintings in 1875 but added a caveat about loss of womanliness, for "it is amazon's work this."[10] Quite extraneous factors could determine a woman's status in the art world. In 1876 Royal Academician William Frith warned Elizabeth Butler "with a long face" that she must continue to submit to the Academy's exhibitions if she wanted to be the third woman member since it was founded in 1768. But when her name was proposed, a terrible crisis of protocol arose. If a lone woman appeared at the Academicians' annual banquet and if a royal personage attended, should the president of the Academy escort her or the royal personage; or would the personage escort the lady and leave the president to tag along behind? Elizabeth Butler missed election by two votes. "Luckily," wrote Leslie, "the danger passed away. . . ."[11]

Christiana Herringham did not aspire to Royal Academy membership or, so far as we know, to instruction in its classes. She intended to become an expert copyist. How, then, did she get instruction? Only scraps of information survive about her training. As a girl in Blackheath Park, South London, she attended a school conducted by a Miss Lydia Hale. Its great virtue was that Miss Hale brought in a special teacher of drawing. Christiana then went to a school in Brighton, perhaps a Miss Abbott's school, which her mother had attended. We do know, however, that she was "happy and exceedingly interested in her schoolwork, particularly in her having masters (the only *master* at Miss Hale's was for drawing)." What or how much she learned at either school we do not know. However, her mother died in 1871, and soon Christiana, not yet twenty years old, took charge of a large and complicated household that included her busy and successful stockbroker father, three brothers, five sisters, and an appropriate staff of servants. Her father wrote that "dear Chrissie took up her new burdens with wonderful strength and ability."[12] If she had hoped to continue formal instruction in art, her plans were probably shelved at that time. However, there was always the National Gallery, and there she joined the ranks of earnest students and amateur copyists. The gallery became her classroom.

Stereotypes of the "true woman" pursued the copyist as well as the aspiring artist. Dante Gabriel Rossetti wrote to William Allingham in 1856 about a Mrs. Burr, a copyist "with a tendency to poetic travelling" who was "refined and very nearly beautiful, energetic withal to an extraordinary degree in Ruskin's style, but quite mild and feminine. . . ."[13] Extraordinary! A lady who was "refined and very nearly beautiful" could also be purposeful and energetic; she could be "mild and feminine" instead of strident and masculine.

Copying was considered safe for women because, supposedly, it eliminated the emotional strain imposed by original artistic creation. Women's emotions must be kept safe and steady for the domestic sphere. Original work came under public judgment as copies did not. "The more public the medium, the greater the menace," Anne Higonnet says of the social assumptions arrayed against the French painter Berthe Morisot, who was not only a successful artist and an accepted member of the impressionist circle but also an attractively successful wife and mother.[14] Yet even Morisot conformed to expectations by painting domestic subjects and remaining an amateur until she was thirty-three. "In novel after novel the cultural ban on women's artistic careers is given its ideological structure," says Higonnet. She cites Hawthorne's *The Marble Faun*, in which the aggressive talent of the sculptor Miriam endangers the "angelic purity" of Hilda the copyist. "Your powerful magnetism would be too much for me," Hilda says to Miriam. "The pure, white atmosphere, in which I try to discern what things are good and true, would be discoloured." An elderly German painter warns Hilda that even when copying, a woman who put her heart and soul into it would find the old masters "a tyrannous race! . . . too mighty a spirit to be dealt with, for long together, by the slender hand, the fragile mind, and the delicate heart of a young girl."[15]

Christiana Herringham was fragile and feminine in appearance, but she did not find the quattrocento masters tyrannous. They became her colleagues and instructors, and Cennini's manual was her textbook. She made copying the tempera masters her profession. She did not exhibit at the Royal Academy; whether she submitted works that were rejected is not known. She seems not to have belonged to the women's group whose name had inched slowly forward from Society of Female Artists (gender-designated), to Society of Lady Painters (socially qualified), to Society of Women Painters (at last, professionally identified). She was an independent agent.

Her independence supported her particular genius for perceiving something crucial but undone for the welfare of art, and for setting a solution in motion. Her nonacademic training, if a handicap in one respect, was an advantage in another, for her view of the English art world was not bounded by its policymakers: the Royal Academy, the National Gallery, the government's South Kensington Schools of Art. Still, she was not outside the circle, for her father was an art collector, and one of his business partners was a trustee of the National Gallery. Therefore, Christiana spoke the language of the connoisseurs, and she had access to an established network of contacts in influential places. The readiest responses to her initiatives came from individuals like D. S. MacColl, whose views already stood at an angle to contemporary thinking about art and art administration. Thus she was often part of a very small minority obliged to fight for its position and even, in some instances, for a hearing. Their experience provides further illustration of how entrenched in the Edwardian years were the attitudes and habits of the Victorian era, and how difficult it was to encourage those in charge to take a deep breath, as it were, and to move forward.

She had two crucial advantages. First, she had money inherited from her father; and second, she inherited his philosophy for using it in a way that created initiatives and encouraged self-respect. We must, therefore, know more about this very Victorian gentleman, himself a successful inheritor of nineteenth-century optimism, who believed quite simply that if society took a wrong turning, philanthropy and the energetic goodwill of individuals could set it right.

Thomas Wilde Powell (1818–1897) was a native of Leeds, forty-one years old when Samuel Smiles's *Self-Help* appeared in 1859. Like many other enterprising Yorkshiremen, Powell was already practicing what Smiles was to preach so effectively: the importance of character, thrift, duty, and perseverance as keys to self-help and advancement in the new environment created by the Industrial Revolution. Thomas Powell began as a law clerk in Leeds and in 1841 had just returned there from London after passing the examinations to qualify as a solicitor. He promptly opened offices, with his father, who had retired after thirty-two years as chief clerk of the Leeds "Old Bank," as his bookkeeper. James Powell's influence on his son, and indirectly on his granddaughter Christiana, was profound. He and his family resided in a house adjacent to the bank's building, and Thomas Powell, who was born there, the eldest of eight children, grew up intensely conscious of his father's responsibility, day and night, for other people's money. The whole family

> knew that the Bank's cash, at all times large enough to tempt the most high-flying and desperate thieves, was kept in the cellars under the Bank, and we used to imagine all sorts of possibilities of schemes and plots of original first-class hands to get at such a booty—in short, it is not too much to say that the never-ceasing feeling of care and charge of the Bank and its treasure threw a perpetual atmosphere around the whole family.

The son had deep respect and admiration for his father's utter integrity. He grew up admiring "force of character" and wary of persons who were "energetic but without ballast."[16] To his mind, virtue might not invariably guarantee success, but success without virtue was not worth having.

By 1845, when Samuel Smiles was still busy formulating his principles of self-help as a series of lectures to young artisans in Leeds, Thomas Powell had already begun "a little share business, and this business increased more than the law business." He was prospering nicely when "the panic of 1845 came down upon us—a panic indeed!" At once he showed the kind of mettle that Smiles applauded. He sent his distraught partner home to recover for a few days while he "managed the ship." Another rule of conduct inherited from his father was "that whatever my income should be I should make a little less serve." ("Prudence," advised Smiles, "requires that we shall pitch our scale of living a degree below our means, rather than up to them. . . .")[17] Therefore, in 1845 Thomas Powell had enough on hand to buy out his partner and, with his father, to purchase shares in a new gas company, the Western, in London. In 1848 a representative of the Leeds shareholders asked him to take a seat on its board and to initiate "a radical reform, for the company was in bad hands." With dispatch he and the other directors, who responded to him with "frank and cordial cooperation," replaced the chairman, the company solicitor, and the engineer, who was plainly not conversant with the new technology and had to give way to a "good, practical man."[18] Thomas Powell's brief summary of these events is a capsule profile of the urgency and force of the revolution in progress, as younger men with faith in the technological future replaced an older, more cautious generation. Proof of the efficacy of the Smiles ethos, Thomas Powell's thrift had made him one of the new entrepreneurs who rode the wave of prosperity that began in the 1850s, tempered the severity of subsequent nineteenth-century economic recessions, and, for the moment at least, belied Friedrich Engels's predictions of catastrophes to come from capitalism's inner contradictions.

The months spent in London to correct the gas company's affairs also settled the future course of Powell's domestic life. He met Mary Elizabeth Marten, daughter of one of his London agents, Charles Marten of the stockbroking firm of Marten and Heseltine. Thomas Powell's method in courtship was no less expeditious than that in business. He decided quickly that she was the wife he wanted, but prudently waited and had "even then to make my opportunity."

After several visits to the Marten home and a "long afternoon" at the Crystal Palace, "I moved forwards pretty fast."[19] Thomas Powell may have been one of the modern men, but he took care to observe the old standards of decorum that still represented social stability. He wrote to Mary Marten:

> I scarcely dare to hope in my own mind that He who has already given me more blessings than I can ever deserve, or be sufficiently grateful for, should crown them all with a helpmate in every way worthy of someone possessing qualifications such as I have not to boast of. . . . Till I hear from you I am in a tumult of suspense—yet I dread to have my suspense terminated lest my hopes be terminated also.

To which Mary Marten very properly replied that she had "referred the matter to Papa, from whom you will probably hear." However, she kept her own door open in a manner that would later characterize her daughter Christiana: "But on second thoughts I felt it best to write at least this line in acknowledgement myself."[20]

The courtship involved a stipulation that would reoccur, in a somewhat different form, when the time came for Christiana Jane Powell to decide upon marriage. Thomas Powell had

> for years held to a fixed principle as a guiding star, *viz.*, that I would not take to myself any woman of whom I could not feel sure that we both held earnestly the same Christian faith, the same hopes of eternal life in our Lord and Master, "the Way, the Truth and the Life." Before I made her acquaintance she had gone through doubts and troubles of mind; she had had Dr. Binney for friend and comforter and helper; she escaped into belief and happiness, and came to know Him in whom she believed.[21]

But Mary Marten's experience had been more complicated than that. She had a restless and inquiring mind that cast about for a direction amid a multitude of ideas new to her. Her education was provided by "a sort of nursery governess" and, later, local ladies' schools at Camberwell, Brighton, and finally Clapham. In her last year at Camberwell she embarked on an adolescent regime of self-denial and "longed to brace up nature up to the masculine hardihood which I admired." She wished for an education on a level with a man's university training. In 1847, when she was seventeen, her father thought of trying to find "some young ladies of your own age and acquirements to form a class with the instruction of a first-rate professor." This seems not to have come about, nor did she attend a school at Hackney that was considered but that proved to have a "rawness" about it.[22]

At this point her crisis of religious doubts commenced. For a year she read nothing but the Bible and "often longed and prayed to die; then she began to doubt." When Dr. Thomas Binney, a Presbyterian turned Congregationalist who leapt with gusto into ecclesiastical controversy, was recommended as spiritual therapist, she went straight to fundamentals. She wanted to know "whence come all the different opinions and religions that divide the world? Why do I take it for granted that the one I was born into was right?" Binney simply referred her back to the Bible and treated her objections "as if they implied that Christ and all who helped to further Christianity must be impostors if it be not true." Her conscience rebuked her for selfishness, because she had "longed for distinction and cared for nothing but study." She wished she could be a Unitarian, for then she "could love God so much more and Jesus too if he were human than if he be an anomalous kind of thing." Six months later she was calmer and could pray again but still could not "have opinions about anything." Binney's counsel wound up (or down) with this anodyne but destructive advice: "Then don't have opinions; be good and lovely, do God's will."[23]

In a family memoir, one of her daughters wrote: "It is a pity there was no Newnham [College] in those days. There she would have found wholesome food for her mind, converse with other minds as keen and candid as her own, and her natural desire after truth and wisdom would not have seemed half criminal. After a time study would have taken its proper rank as only a part of life. As it was she promised she would put her books away and try to be good."[24]

She must have backslid, for we find her continuing her studies in Latin, Greek, and German. When she met Tennyson in 1848, he did little to resolve her confusion when he told her how he disliked "tremendous duty women" who "push everybody about in an inconvenient way to find or discharge" what they think is their mission. When Mary understood one of his Latin quotations, he told her, "I think you are a learned lady—I am beginning to be afraid of you." She laughed and said she "was not learned and was very sorry for it." He did not mind learned ladies, he said, "but I hate pedantic women. I don't like the blue stocking."[25]

Nevertheless, she solicited advice from all who would give it, on subjects such as the "Geo-theological question." She read *Modern Painters,* which, she said, "worked quite a change in my mind" and made her think it "a great thing to be an artist." But "alas!," she concluded, "in this too I have been fickle." It is small wonder that her friends thought her solemn and depressed and that she feared "nervous maladies." She was wiser than she knew. Of her depression she wrote, "It was that I wanted to love someone."[26]

And so she did. Charles Marten died in 1851. Thomas Powell and Mary Marten were married in 1852, and the firm became Heseltine and Powell. By 1872 Powell was the senior partner, and the firm was Heseltine, Powell and Company. Thomas Powell continued in his faith in the goodness of God and the growing goodness of England. He agreed with Thomas Macaulay that if some leisureliness and coziness had disappeared with the old ways, the achievements of his own day were far preferable. He devoured Macaulay's *History of England* "like a novel—nay, it is better than any novel. . . . I am inclined to say with him, that it is a mistake to talk of the good old times. . . . I rejoice to think that England is advancing socially, morally, religiously."[27]

At one point, however, Heseltine and Powell did not advance economically. In 1877 Thomas Powell had a second experience of a business on the brink of the abyss. Heseltine and Powell handled bonds for two subsidiaries of the New York and Erie Railroad and the Pennsylvania Railroad: the Buffalo and Huron and the Marietta and Cincinnati lines, major accounts that were failing. Charles Marten, Thomas Powell's brother-in-law, wrote of that time, "A great deal of offence was taken and many hard things said."[28] Once again Powell was dispatched to correct the consequences of mismanagement while his family rented out their comfortable home at Blackheath Park, and

Mary and their growing family moved in with relations for a long year of separation and anxiety.

In conditions often reminiscent of Frances Trollope's sojourn among the Americans, Thomas Powell struggled to reorganize the failing companies, pacify unpaid strikers, and arrange more stable financing. By the end of 1878 the depression had abated, the two railways were on a better footing, the Powells were back at Blackheath Park, and Heseltine and Powell was on the mend. The experience only fortified Thomas Powell's convictions about the importance of thrift, prudence, and responsibility for other people's money. "Why was I so easily tempted by interested statements?" he wrote to his wife. "Why did I lay the temptation before others relying on an amount of prudence in me which I ought to have known I did not possess? . . . Is it not well sometimes to be alone in trouble? To have none but God to turn to?"[29]

"The business man gets into a rut," Smiles warned, "and often does not look beyond it. If he lives for himself only, he becomes apt to regard other human beings only in so far as they minister to his ends."[30] Thomas Powell avoided that rut by building. If he built splendidly for himself and his family, he built also for the community. Even in the midst of his American troubles he had thought of building a small church at Zaleski, Ohio. While he enlarged the Blackheath house, his family lived at Charlton, and he had a workmen's institute built at Lower Charlton. During the suburban Queen Anne revival of the 1870s he had Richard Norman Shaw design a splendid house called Piccard's Rough; the choice of architect was certainly influenced by Powell's partner, John Postle Heseltine, son of the firm's senior member and himself a partner, whose London house was Shaw's first important residential design there. Piccard's Rough sits high on Hog's Back above Guildford and commands a long, sloping panorama of gardens and lawns. At nearby St. Catherine's, Powell built nine workmen's cottages and a village hall to go with them. He forestalled indiscriminate development of a fine local meadow by buying it and erecting four cottages there, and at Littleton he built a cottage to serve as his children's holiday house and as a convalescent home for London children.

In Guildford, Powell contributed toward restoration and new classrooms of the Guildford Grammar School and new premises for the Guildford Institute. He also had the Chapel Street Mission fitted up as a gymnasium, for he could not bear "the sight of groups of lads idling away their time in the street." And he saw to the erection of Wycliffe Buildings with a hall designated for "undenominational evangelistic services." Liquor, gambling, and political meetings were prohibited there, and he "gave instructions that the hall should be open daily as a reading room for both men and women." Although he was a faithful Congregationalist, he gave liberally to all the Guildford denominations, but most particularly to the Congregationalists, whose schools he admired. One of his daughters wrote that she could not remember her father when he was not engaged in some kind of building, even if it were only a garden wall.[31]

Money not spent directly for bricks and mortar went for a different kind of building. It was in this that his daughter Christiana was most nearly to follow his example. He gave seed money for enterprises that promised responsible direction and worthy results. He knew that many a self-made man had had a hand up at the beginning, and his first principle was that such giving fostered self-respect and enthusiasm for self-help, whereas continued out-and-out charity produced only abject dependence. In 1882, when Scotland's Married Woman's Property Act of 1881 was extended to England, Ireland, and Wales, he settled large sums on each of his six daughters and specified with care that the money was for their free and independent use. He had already provided for his three sons. In a long letter to all his children he expressed the hope that they would emulate his method of giving. The letter begins:

> When my children become owner after me of the property I may leave them in addition to what I have given them while I live, I hope they will neither forget nor neglect to give now and then, or often, the sort of charity which I like to exercise out of my plenty: being the giving of substantial gifts to those who need a hand to help them, but to help whom it so ever occurs to the wealthy, because forsooth they seem to be in comfortable circumstances and wear goodlooking clothes.

His guiding principle for such giving was that "many people can walk far if helped over stiles." He wanted his children "to be even as I: (and I have every reason to expect that they will) viz: that though they may have from me property which to them may seem wealth, they will continue habits of personal simplicity and inexpensiveness, while using their means with modest liberality. . . . With your money make yourselves friends who when ye fail may receive you with everlasting habitations." He concluded by repeating his faith in their ability and willingness to continue in his ideals.

> I might leave my children my money charged with no wish of this sort, giving as I list in my lifetime, and more largely in my lifetime if I could not trust them to be liberal if I leave them in easy pecuniary circumstances—but I prefer to give them their inheritance charged with an inheritance of such kindness and thoughtful liberality as I have indicated. I believe they will fulfil my wish, and so believing I have pleasant anticipations in imagining them administering the income of the money I hope to leave them. Often have I thought what a pleasure it would have been to me that my wife should have lived to enjoy the abundance that God has multiplied on me since her death: for while she lived she was the centre of all I had and did—but God knows best. He took away, but I must not forget that he gave.[32]

Christiana, the eldest child, received thirty-one thousand pounds in 1882. When her father died in 1897, she received an additional twelve thousand pounds. This was the source of the money with which she helped the National Art Collections Fund over the stile, met her considerable share of the costs of the Ajanta expeditions, and supported other causes in ways that continue to come to light. Thus, in principle and in practice, Thomas Wilde Powell was the true progenitor of the Fund and of all of Christiana's enterprises thereafter.

2

CHRISTIANA JANE HERRINGHAM

WHEREAS THOMAS POWELL'S career as a stockbroker had followed a straight line from client to partner, the early career of Christiana's future husband, Wilmot Parker Herringham (1855–1936), had followed a less certain course. It wavered at first, then took one wrong turning before finding its true direction. Along the way, his obligations to the Christian faith, and eventually faith itself, came into question. This was awkward, for his father was an Anglican clergyman. When Wilmot arrived at the age of decisions, the Reverend William Walton Herringham, after a curacy in Surrey and a parish in Nottinghamshire, was rector of St. Andrew's Church in Old Cleeve, Somerset, and a prebendary of Wells Cathedral. There could not have been a greater contrast, or one more representative of the times, than that between Thomas Powell's Leeds, which rode the wave of the future, and Somerset, where much of the industrial and commercial revolution in the North was distant news.

Wilmot was the elder of two sons in a family of four children. He was sent to Winchester, which gave him a sound classical education. He was diligent and thorough and won his share of prizes. In a memoir written many years later, he saw himself as a reserved and somewhat solitary schoolboy who lacked self-confidence. He had, he thought, "felt himself of no importance in the school. Some boys are weighty and serious, but I certainly was not. Some grow up later than others, & I was very late growing. I don't think I was in any way 'considerable', until I was well over thirty." When he measured himself against that early assessment, he added, "But I have had weight since then." He admitted that he had "never found friendship easy, and I had no great friend" at Winchester.[1] His letters show, however, that he had school friends who, like himself, were to become men of consequence.

In 1873 he went from Winchester to Keble College, Oxford. The choice suggests a paternal ambition. Keble was then only five years old, founded by subscription in 1868 as a memorial to John Keble, initiator of the effort to restore formality and discipline to the Church of England, an effort that would become known as the Oxford Movement. The college was designed to provide an academic education at economical cost and also a training based upon the principles of the Church of England. It quickly became a favorite choice of clergymen for sons who they hoped would follow them into the ministry. Thus Wilmot Herringham may be said to be a second-generation child of the Oxford Movement.

Wilmot remembered himself at Oxford, as at Winchester, as diffident and somewhat solitary. "I liked people well enough, but I never wanted to talk intimately, or to sit in another man's room. I don't know whether it is a good thing or a bad thing to be of a lonely disposition, but I think I have been of that kind."[2] Nevertheless, letters to his father are filled with names of friends and accounts of fun and football, London theater parties, and a reading and climbing party in Wales during which he and his companions "drink a good deal of beer & otherwise improve ourselves." He belonged to an essay club in which he read a paper on Elizabethan literature, and he experimented with contradictions in his philosophical and political views. In a debate he took a wobbling anti-Gladstone position, "my line being that the intrusion of sentiment into politics is a mistake. I don't know the least what I think upon the matter: rather the other way I think; but that's what I'm going to say." Then he decided that he admired "a splendid idea of Gladstone" on the subject of Jews as the " 'custodians of the idea of sin.' I think it's awfully grand when you come to look at it." But when he looked again at some time-honored systems of thought, he decided that he hated "the beastly details of all the old systems (of which the Baconian form is one) which are no real good, being all refuted and dead long ago: I like the more abstract part of the business very much better." Then he added: "However of course the other must be done too to get the true abstract view. It is like the difference between looking at a great town from a balloon & getting the spirit of it, and then having to go down & poke about in all the little streets to see what they really are in detail."[3]

He worked hard at drawing and paid systematic visits to the London galleries. His opinions ran to the literal but sometimes struck an aesthetic truth. He disliked intensely Gustave Doré's work and saw "nothing really grand about it: & it is as I read it the embodiment of sensationalism. . . . I think his own affect [*sic*] is merely tremendous contrasts of light & shade & there is no repose about it: it is nothing like Shakespeare & far more like Victor Hugo as one would expect. . . . I do think if you can't paint an angel without making him either a ghost or a human being, that the human being is a truer idea than the ghost." At the National Gallery he observed wisely that "in such a little time you can't know any picture at all of course, it can only be the precursor to looking again." Then without looking again, he decided on the spot that he "hated Rubens most" and the *Rape of the Sabine Women* in particular, which struck him as grotesque. How could "any man carry off the huge sacks of flesh which stand for women in the picture & however anxious he might be to have something to love honour & cherish: it's a mere physical impossibility."[4] How his father received these opinions we cannot know, but the freedom with which Wilmot poured them out suggests that his efforts at self-education were at least tolerated at home.

In 1877 Wilmot took his degree, but it was only a second class, which no doubt disappointed his father and made Wilmot feel that there was no point in aiming at a career in the church. He began at once to study law at Lincoln's Inn but gave it up after a few months. "It was as well," he wrote. "I had not the logical power that is needed at the Bar. I'm sure I would have failed there." He considered that he had left Oxford "woolly-minded." More than likely he was suffering the effect of overexposure to Oxford Movement theology, for in his subsequent career he was by no means woolly minded.[5] He left the law for medicine and entered the medical school of St. Bartholomew's

Hospital. At first he hated London for the contrast to Oxford. "The bustle, & the bother, & the row, & the feeling that you're alone in a crowd crush one's idealism most completely, for the present."[6]

When he met Christiana Jane Powell, Wilmot Herringham was still in the process of finding himself. That process had begun with the W. Wright Smiths, a couple who owned Parkhill, a handsome country house (now the Parkhill Hotel) near Lyndhurst, Hampshire. How he met them is unknown, but it is certain that they offered him a kind of senior-to-junior relationship that preserved enough informality for a relaxed openness that was new to Wilmot. To Mr. Smith, whom he called "the Skipper" and "the Squire," he owed his "idea of a true gentleman, more than to any other man." Mrs. Smith was an ardent Unionist, and to both, Wilmot owed the beginnings of a more varied political outlook. Mrs. Smith he addressed as "Mrs. Jo," and it is plain that he could talk with her as never with his mother. When he had known the Smiths for three years and was on the eve of marriage, he wrote to Mrs. Jo:

> You began to be kind to me when I was raw and wild & boyish. I feel myself a great deal more than 3 years older since that time, but though our relations naturally changed with the change of nature, there is still the same bond of good will and friendship between us. . . . You were the first people in ordinary life, who became my friends for myself's own sake, and that[,] in the days when I was young and foolish and despairing, did more than I can tell you to put me in heart for my life. I can scarcely recall to myself the abject hopelessness with which I left Oxford, & to find people really caring about me outside my own family was almost a new insight into life.[7]

It was a clear instance of a young person of orthodox education who does not realize, until outsiders point it out by contrast, the narrowness of his accustomed horizons. The W. Wright Smiths became his lifeline. With them, for the first time, he heard "good talk": stimulating, wide-ranging conversation and argument. He did not encounter its like until he became acquainted with the Powell family.[8] In short, the Smiths and the Powells brought home to him for the first time the fact that his world had been not only conventional but boring.

Wilmot Herringham and Christiana Jane Powell first met in the summer of 1878, when a mutual friend invited him to Blackheath for tennis. Then twenty-six, she impressed him as feminine but not frilly, self-contained but not self-centered. She had had principal charge of the household for seven years, and her air of seriousness appealed to Wilmot. "My lady came in whilst we were playing," he wrote in his memoir, "& I remember her first appearance in a brown straw hat & a greenish dress with a little basket in her hand. I liked her face and was struck with a curious reserve & solitude in her, which made me wish to overcome her & make her my friend." His first impression was accurate. Her father remembered her as a serious, often solemn child easily upset by displays of emotion in others and "not quick at apprehending a joke."[9] Wilmot saw in her one who might understand his own reserve and solitude, but he did not meet her again until October. She was then living in London, at Number 20 Harley Street, for the Powells were in transit. They had left Blackheath and awaited the completion of Piccard's Rough, their new home at Guildford.

Piccard's Rough was one of that series of Norman Shaw's Home Counties mansions for wealthy businessmen and their families. Those houses proclaimed position and wealth; Piccard's Rough cost ten thousand pounds. The Queen Anne revival style used tradition to declare a transition to modernity without relinquishing a selective hold on the past. It substituted a secular and domestic idiom for Victorian Gothic and its connotations of ecclesiastical grandeur. In the suburbs it anchored family life in a period of English history that when compared with the frantic contemporary life of the polluted city suggested a golden age of prosperity and contentment. A Shaw house in the suburbs stated that a London business was now so well established that its owner could acquire a setting in which to live graciously and from which to commute to London by the newly expanded Woking-Guildford railway line.[10] It implied that, however humble the family's beginnings, they cherished their solid Englishness. Indeed, the Powells traced their own origins back to the mid-sixteenth century. Thomas Powell intended to knit himself and his family into the life and history of Guildford. He waited impatiently for the end of the Harley Street interlude.

Wilmot called on Christiana in Harley Street, and they went skating and took walks about London. But Wilmot soon discovered another cause for concern about himself: he did not know how to tell whether he was in love. "Never having been in love before, . . . I was hardly able to judge whether I were in love or no, but it was a great trouble to me, for I knew there was something amiss & doubted whether I could cure it." The clinical terminology—the sense of something amiss, the need for diagnosis, and a solution conceived as "cure"—suggests not only that he did not yet recognize the signs of love, but also that the physician's inability to diagnose and prescribe for his own condition shook his confidence in his medical powers. Here were symptoms, but where was the textbook that explained the pathology? Then he fell back on instinct, and his confidence veered around again. "Of my lady's feelings I could not tell anything, but I had a sort of knowledge that I could make her love me if I chose, & I did not doubt her answer if I should ask her."[11] Before he got around to proposing marriage, however, he asked her to come for an evening walk alone with him on the Thames Embankment and got an unsettling shock to what he had assumed was his liberation from convention—not because she refused, but because she accepted his invitation.

Wilmot had underestimated the relative independence of a new generation of women, especially of one who had carried the responsibilities of a large household for so long. He was upset when Christiana accepted, as if he had prescribed a test and she had failed it. However, two days before Christmas in 1878 he asked her to come alone for an early tea with him. There he dismissed misgivings and proposed marriage. On Monday the twenty-ninth they agreed to become engaged. The Powells were greatly surprised, but the Herringhams were "much distressed at the news." Wilmot recalled with chagrin that in his unworldliness he had never considered his situation as a poor medical student with several years of training still ahead. Nor had he considered the enormous gap between Thomas Powell's wealth and the two hundred pounds that his clergyman father, away in rural Somerset, could afford as Wilmot's annual allowance. He did have *something* "and therefore did not suppose the matter hopeless."[12] After all, it was an annual income, which certified respectability, and not wages, which connoted subordination and instability.

The W. Wright Smiths had educated Wilmot on social and political issues. Now the Powells began to educate him aesthetically. No doubt under the influence of John Postle Heseltine, who was a trustee of the National Gallery and a well-known connoisseur and collector, Thomas Powell was acquiring pictures and fine decorative objects, and Ruskin's aesthetic influence reigned. "The Powells under Chrissie's influence were full of it," Wilmot wrote. "Their house, built by Norman Shaw, was to me a revelation of beauty, & Chrissie herself was the best copyist of early Italian paintings that I have ever seen."[13]

The house was a revelation also to Henry Newbolt, an Oxford contemporary of Christiana's brother Herbert. Newbolt first saw Piccard's Rough about 1882. For him, it was not only an eye-opener but an admonition with respect to hasty conclusions about art. At Oxford he had scorned the self-conscious aesthetes with their Morris wallpapers, Liberty silks, Rossetti poems, and attempts to imitate the inimitable Oscar Wilde. The moment he entered Piccard's Rough he knew that he had "come into the Modern Age—what was then called the 'Esthetic Period.' "

> All this we had learned to laugh at as the mark of the "Greenery-Yallery Grosvenor-Gallery foot-in-the-grave young man" though we had no right to laugh. . . . But it had not entered into our minds that there could be a house like Piccard's Rough, built by an architect with an eye for the beauty of everyday life, and decorated by experts in colour, whose every scheme satisfied the senses before surprising them. And it is still true after nearly fifty years that I have never known another house of the same scale and quality.

The Powells themselves were another revelation, and Wilmot certainly must have felt as Newbolt did among them. Newbolt had the sensation of having been dropped into "a long and well-written novel in the style of Tolstoy, with a crowd of interesting characters and some heart-rending events." This family was "an example—its customs, manners, laws, and government were all distinctive: not widely but subtly different from those of other houses. They made up, as family habits often do, a special kind of civilisation, miniature but complete, and not to be exactly paralleled." Their attraction, for Newbolt, "lay not only in their individual talents but in their family temperament." The first article of their creed was "independence, its second a devotion to reason and to scientific truth, its third an equally devoted faith in artistic craftsmanship. . . . The total effect was one of a new outlook, a new England, gained by a revival rather than a revolution." The secret was "the self-governing group, its kaleidoscopic variety, and its fundamental harmony."[14]

Newbolt perceived that the laws of this autonomous state "were the rare but authoritative decrees of Thomas Wilde Powell, our white-haired host, into whose existence we only penetrated at intervals." He reappeared each evening from London "with the same calm and august beneficence, to walk about his garden or inspect his latest purchase of old cottages, saved from the local builders. The government of his house he left for the most part to his elder daughters: he knew them to be perfectly competent, but he could intervene forcibly at times in matters of policy." Piccard's Rough was four years old before he permitted a dance there, "and even then he came into the hall at 1 a.m. and drove us quietly some to the door, some to our beds, turning out the lights with his own hands; and all this was done with the inexorable stillness of Natural Law."

Newbolt's word for Thomas Powell was "Olympian," not only in his conduct at home but in "the scale and unexpectedness of his public dispensations: he preserved, built, or bought, beautiful things with a curiously distant appreciation of their beauty: his eye was quick, but seemed to have no personal desire to answer to it. If he had anything that deserved the name of acquisitiveness it could only have been satisfied by the continual formation of national collections."[15] This was certainly J. P. Heseltine's influence, and a northern influence also was at work. In Manchester, Thomas Agnew and Sons had been art dealers since the 1850s for the newly rich of the industrializing counties. It was no accident that the great 1857 British Art Treasures Exhibition, displaying works from British private collections, took place in Manchester, not only because of Agnew's presence but also because new money was more and more available to the self-made men of the northern counties. Frank Herrmann says:

> What is of interest to us in the history of collecting is that the substantial English landowners who were the great collectors of the eighteenth century in this country had relatively little ready cash, and that the purchase of paintings and antiquities meant the outlay of much more than the mere price paid might indicate today. . . . After 1840 it was the new generation of industrialists and merchants who had the money available for the immediate purchase of works of art.[16]

Therefore, "the distasteful concept of investment was openly acknowledged."[17] That concept survived in Thomas Powell when he entered the circle of wealthy London collectors for whom old masters were considered less an investment than a gauge of cultural attainment. Both were important to Powell, and Newbolt's observations are especially perceptive. Newbolt also implied some fundamental similarities and differences between Christiana and her father. Both loved beautiful things, but whereas his appreciation was "curiously distant," hers was intense and intensely personal, a gospel by which to live. Both cared deeply about the national collections, but to Thomas Powell they were an investment in a national heritage; for Christiana, they *were* the national heritage.

Wilmot and Christiana were already married when Newbolt first went to Piccard's Rough. But at the time of Wilmot's earlier version of the scene—Christiana observant in her little straw hat and green dress, and vigilant for the domestic harmony that she had helped to foster—Wilmot was observant but also a little bewildered at the exuberance and variety of interests, conversations, activities. The bewilderment had not quite worn off by the time he took Christiana to Old Cleeve to meet the Herringhams for the first time.

The ideological distance between Piccard's Rough and the Somerset rectory was even greater than the financial one between Mr. Powell's income and Wilmot's annual allowance. "To my sorrow," Wilmot recalled, "Chrissie's stay for 4 days at home only rendered them [the Herringhams] more set against the affair and on my return I came as near quarrelling with them as I ever had in my life." Their objections were "partly social, and partly personal, and both were fresh to me & had to be answered. And although I had been for some years accustomed to liberal opinions, yet I had never really had such questions brought home to me as now. If it had not happened so, I might to the end of my life have continued to be the slave of prejudice, instilled into me chiefly by my mother, while yet claiming freedom of thought, in all matters."[18] The influences of the Smiths and the Powells had done their work.

The Herringhams' social objections were probably their understandable fears that they could never match Mr. Powell's munificence and, understandably, that Wilmot was entering a sophisticated, materialist environment that would separate him from them and their more conservative values. The personal objections may have been the result of an initial impression, for Christiana was not what might have been expected as the choice of a clergyman's son. Her natural reserve and the years of responsibility at Piccard's Rough had bred an air of independence that perhaps struck them as unbecoming, not to say threatening. Furthermore, she intended to continue in her profession of painter. Her father's wealth and position made her a "lady"; a conventional lady might pursue artistic interests so long as they were for her own amusement or for charity, but not for payment. To Christiana, such a lady was nothing more than the sketcher whom Florence Nightingale scorned; she, however, intended to be fully professional and to accept payment for her work. Like Victorian author Margaret Oliphant's character Lucinda Marjoribanks, she knew that somehow she must have her own "sphere," for "when a woman has an active mind, and still does not care for parish work, it is a little hard for her to find a 'sphere.' "[19] Christiana had not the slightest interest in conventional parish work. She had found her sphere, and Wilmot understood that without a purposeful art she would not be Christiana.

To the Herringhams, perhaps she represented another of Wilmot's failures to measure up to parental hopes. He had done well but had not shone at Winchester, and his Oxford degree was only a second class. He had sidestepped the ministry and then tried and abandoned the law. Now, although full of idealism about medicine, he had a considerable way to go before qualifying, not to mention establishing a practice. His parents may well have doubted whether Christiana, a rich man's daughter, would stay the course.

The question of Christian faith was a ground on which it seemed that Wilmot and his parents might stand together. On that issue Christiana stood alone and apart. In Wilmot's memoir notes of 1880 we find him saying, "I was distressed to find that my wife's attitude to religion was different from my own. I was always thinking, speculating, and longing for a belief, of which I had not a vestige. She was content to live nobly in the present and afraid to allow herself to embark in speculations which had before been ruinous to her peace of mind."[20] Had Christiana read her mother's diary, with the account of that earlier religious crisis? She says nothing about this, but it was a known part of the family archive. Christiana's subsequent development shows how much her aspirations resembled her mother's; it shows also how positively she turned away from her mother's final acquiescence in orthodox Christianity. Christiana, too, had undergone a crisis of faith but had found the struggle "ruinous," had resolved to keep all such speculations at bay, and left Wilmot in no doubt as to her position on the subject.

Wilmot, earnest and anxious, still very much the rector's son, wanted an understanding on the issue, and if his parents had tried to catechize Christiana during the unfortunate visit to Old Cleeve, that, too, could have been a cause of their disapproval. Meanwhile, Wilmot "had to wait, & not only to wait but as far as I could to avoid talking to Chrissie about the state of my mind. And this latter duty I did not at first perceive, & then did not I fear very scrupulously perform." In other words, he had been unable to stop himself (and perhaps his parents as well) from pressing her about Christian beliefs. He felt that he must fight this good fight but did not realize at the time that his own, not Christiana's, faith was the one more at issue. He kept laying out his doubts, turning them over, looking for cracks and crevices that might admit a little light to illumine his darkness. His misery wanted company, and Christiana declined to join him. This last phase of Wilmot's maturing had strong Oxford Movement overtones. "Unless you have some work in hand, unless you are struggling, unless you are fighting with yourselves," declared John

Henry Newman, "you are no followers of those who 'through many tribulations entered into the Kingdom of God.' A fight is the very token of a Christian."[21] So Wilmot fought on and, like his future father-in-law, still considered a mutual declaration of Christian faith an obligatory preface to marriage.

Predictably, there was a crisis. It came, presumably, soon after the visit to Old Cleeve. "We were fond of one another," Wilmot wrote, "& we did not ever disagree, but I knew that I was incapable in my then method of thought, of preserving that simple, pure, & earnest position which could alone entitle me to her love, & the means to which by the mercy of God she herself was to put before me." It did not yet occur to him that he was only repeating the litany of nineteenth-century domestic ideals: simplicity and purity at home, to keep at bay the world's temptations; earnestness in all things; and a wife who maintains the moral atmosphere that shapes and guards the man who will become qualified to love her. He did not realize how unwilling she was to be cast in the role of angel in her home. He was miserably aware that something was wrong. She was unhappy, ill at ease, and since they did not air their disagreement, he could not fathom the reason for her constraint. A year later he was able to wipe from his memory most of "that unhappy time," but he remembered enough to confirm that "never once did any disagreement of suspicion or quarrel come between us. I felt merely that somehow I was losing hold on her heart, and saw no way to remedy it."[22]

Walter Houghton has observed that "the pain of religious doubt was often, in fact, the pain of a potential or actual breaking of the family bond in a period when family life was exalted." What Wilmot was actually in process of losing was the old bond with his parents; conventional religious belief was an integral part of that bond, and being a clergyman's son made it all the more difficult. Thus loyalty as well as faith was the issue. And did he, perhaps, unconsciously use the religious issue to avoid answering his parents' social and personal objections to Christiana? If so, the dodge implied cowardice, and he would have known it. In fact, he had already slipped more seriously than he wished his parents (and himself) to know. In March 1879 he was reading Newman's *Grammar of Assent* and told Mrs. Jo that "it's just what I believe myself. Only I doubt its validity. However, we'll see." In May he wrote to her to say "what a bore it is, telling a lie." His parents kept asking whether he was going regularly to church, and he went now and then to make himself honest.[23]

Wilmot and Christiana met in the Harley Street dining room and agreed to break off their engagement and not to meet for an indefinite period, only trusting that they were doing the right thing. Wilmot diagnosed his feeling with professional detachment. He decided that he did not yet feel too unhappy because the wound was still fresh, and he was buoyed up by the thought that he had sacrificed nobly on the high altar of principle. Thus anesthetized, he parted from Christiana the following day after they had exchanged rings "in token of affection" and attended Communion services together at All Saints Church in nearby Margaret Street—which suggests itself as Wilmot's idea. That that particular church should have been so conveniently close to Harley Street is a bit of biographical serendipity, for a conflict between aesthetic and theological beliefs had figured in its history, and that aesthetic would be fundamental to Christiana's career as a copyist.

From 1838 to 1845 All Saints was the charge of the Reverend Frederick Oakeley, who in 1827 had turned away from evangelicalism to align himself with the Oxford Movement. He had a "strong aesthetic sense and a great love of music." Although "impeded by episcopal dictates and harrassed by bigots," he eventually made All Saints "a centre for Tractarian worship, a mystical soul-elevating haven from the rigid severity of the Protestant church." Inevitably, in July 1845 Oakeley was suspended, and in October, he was received into the Roman Catholic Church. Newman followed in October 1846. In 1850 Edward Pusey himself laid the cornerstone for a new church, to be "the model church of the ecclesiologists."[24] Wilmot Herringham may have been unaware of Oakeley's history of heresy—All Saints was simply the Anglican church closest to the Powells' residence in Harley Street—but his own Oxford Movement orientation hung in the balance.

In 1849 further aesthetic controversy had joined the theological when the artist William Dyce began to design a splendid reredos for All Saints. His interest in fresco and the techniques of the early Renaissance Italians had long been collateral to his concerns about improvements in art education, design, and the decoration of public buildings. He preached a gospel of simplicity and sincerity in art. But not even Dyce, whom his biographer calls "The Leader of the Frescanti," was inventive enough to overcome modern environmental conditions, and his All Saints reredos had faded seriously before Wilmot and Christiana exchanged rings there in 1879.[25] Whether or not she knew the history of Dyce's efforts at All Saints, Christiana was already committed to his revivalist mission. If she had adopted anything in place of an orthodox religious faith, art was that faith. She intended to apply it to ways of making tempera, that other early Renaissance medium whose simplicity and sincerity she so admired, both viable and acceptable for modern use.

In 1879, however, the theological problem was paramount. Wilmot's memoir makes it clear that neither he nor Christiana brought it out for frank discussion. Had they been able to do so, their situation might have been less harrowing. Christiana left no record of her thoughts at the time, but the reaction set in on Wilmot at once. "I remember thinking whether I could bear to see her as another man's wife & it was very hard." Still, "I decided that it was my duty to break it off & then went to sleep." The next day he discovered that his duty cure had been miraculously effective, and "in some wonderful way I came to know that it was my want of pure & holy strength which had led to her losing her love for me and by the great mercy of God I was enabled for the first time in my life to feel His love . . . in a state of ecstasy." This overnight epiphany served as refuge for just three months—until he heard that Christiana had typhoid. Then there was no more self-deception; he only feared losing her forever. He shed complacency and convention and emerged feeling that he could be "more tolerant of others, more able to learn," more open-minded, and less self-centered.[26] It had been a crisis of faith, but a crisis of faith in himself. He had fought the obligatory fight, but the outcome was not quite what Newman had had in mind. So far as Wilmot was concerned, it had been Anglican orthodoxy's last stand. He and Christiana were ready to get on with their lives.

3

MAKING A PLACE FOR HERSELF

WILMOT AND CHRISTIANA were married in September 1880 and settled at Number 22 Bedford Street, near the Strand. In 1881 he took his degree, and they went to Vienna for six months. Wilmot studied and Christiana copied in the galleries. He feared that she was having "a very dull time" and even worried that he was selfishly failing to make her happy. Not Wilmot but Vienna society bored her. The all-afternoon meals took time from gallery work and in any case were unutterably tedious. The women were extremely stylish but were shallow and useless. "Fancy me guzzling in the middle of the day," she wrote to Mrs. Jo. "The women lace most frightfully here, and consequently make themselves high-shouldered and awkward-looking." If they sat in low chairs, they had difficulty getting up again. She wondered how the empress managed to be a good horsewoman, for "she is so pinched that it is a wonder she can ride at all." Houses seemed effeminate, all with "a sort of boudoir look about them." Useless, too, were the men, who spent "several hours of every afternoon in [the cafés]—partly transacting business with one another and partly amusing themselves."[1] Utilitarian England, dowdy by comparison with sparkling Vienna, was where one did real work.

In England, however, a woman artist who wished for work more substantial than what society and the male art establishment allowed her had to find and fortify a place for herself, and this meant rejection of the stereotype of woman as the weaker sex—weaker intellectually because weaker physically. "The hey-day of this special characterization of women's art as biologically determined or as an extension of their domestic and refining role in society, quintessentially feminine, graceful, delicate and decorative, is without doubt the nineteenth century," say Rozsika Parker and Griselda Pollock when they ask why we have no term for women artists equivalent to "old masters." With its unfortunate connotations, "old mistresses" will not do. Women are incapable of mastering serious art, said Ruskin in a statement much quoted of late by feminist writers. The nineteenth century took his prejudice for fact.

> Now their separate characters are briefly these. The man's power is active, progressive, defensive. He is eminently the doer, the creator, the discoverer, the defender. His intellect is for speculation and invention; his energy for adventure, for war, and for conquest, wherever war is just, wherever conquest necessary. But the woman's power is for rule, not for battle,—and her intellect is not for invention or creation but for sweet ordering, arrangement and decision. . . . Her great function is Praise; she enters into no contest, but infallibly adjudges the crown of contest.[2]

Nineteenth-century assumptions being what they were, male control of the official apparatus of art training made a great deal of women's art inevitably second-rate. "By keeping women's creativity at an inconsequential level," says Pamela Gerrish Nunn, "by keeping women's art invisible (or, if that proved impossible, ghettoised as second-rate) men would claim their [own] work to be true Art or Philosophy (or whatever)." And not only art, but art history was ghettoized. With a few notable exceptions such as Anna Jameson, women were shut out of scholarship in art history because they were already ghettoized as artists, and art history, says Linda Nochlin, has remained a male preserve. "Yet a dispassionate, impersonal, sociologically- and institutionally-oriented approach would reveal the entire romantic, elitist, individual-glorifying and monograph-producing substructure upon which the profession of art history is based, and which has only recently been called into question by a group of younger dissidents within it."[3]

Inside the ghetto, enterprising women devised their own substitutes for certified art education, such as the cooperative women's classes organized from the late 1840s by the novelist Elizabeth Gaskell's younger friend Eliza Fox. Those took place in the library of the house she shared with her father, a prominent Unitarian reformer who believed in education for women but disapproved of a professional career in art for his daughter. Nevertheless, such classes "became a meeting-place for egalitarian feminists and a springboard for the campaign against the Royal Academy," and in 1859 a number of those students signed a letter to the *Athenaeum* protesting the Royal Academy's treatment of women artists—Eliza among them, a month after she married the artist William Lee Bridell and became Eliza Bridell-Fox. "Linked by professional interest and a network of friendship, this group of women organised the first feminist campaign for art education for women." Whitney Chadwick argues that such expedient enterprises had value, for they encouraged "the deep friendships and community of purpose that developed among women."[4] "Networking" is the currently fashionable term, awkward but useful, for one way in which creative women, then and now, have sustained themselves and one another while they gather strength and strategies for a concerted effort. The women who organized the Society of Female Painters in 1857 might be said to have ghettoized themselves. But the reality was that if they did not encourage one another, only a rare stalwart like Philip Hamerton was likely to do so. Men had consortiums and clubs where they devised their business and social strategies, and that did not necessarily make them ungentlemanly. Women could be as ladylike as any gentleman could wish and at the same time make contacts with one another and learn how to organize and publicize their purpose effectively. They could serve as mentors for women who were about to make their own first moves toward identity as artists, and they could become a center from which a broader movement could grow.

When Christiana Herringham set out to reconstitute tempera as a medium for modern use, she became the center of the small group of similarly interested artists, men and women both, who were to organize formally in 1901 and would begin to exhibit as the Society of Painters in Tempera. First, however, she had to find a satisfactory balance between art and marriage. In 1882 her first child,

Christopher, was born, and in 1883 Geoffrey, her second. Wilmot advanced steadily through the levels of hospital appointments and took pride in his contributions to professional journals. In 1885 they moved to Number 13 Upper Wimpole Street, where he opened his practice. His religious misgivings became sublimated to ideals of service to friends and of becoming a skilled physician. "Meanwhile there remains the unending pleasure of medicine," he told his friend Henry Babington Smith in 1890. "The growth of this understanding is really I believe the most economical of pleasures"—an attitude that he thought was probably incomprehensible to "the unsympathetic onlooker."[5]

Above all, Christiana had assuaged the awful loneliness that Wilmot had felt as a student in London. He certainly thought her more beautiful than ever before, and he dared to think that marriage to him had made her happier. He made no claim to Christiana's money—indeed, he went out of his way not to do so—and she took care not to flaunt it or to overdo the extra comforts it made possible. However, Wilmot was not always as liberal as he had thought himself or as he was to become. Although he knew that art was essential to Christiana, a comment in his memoir suggests some difficult passages in her effort to balance the demands of husband, family, and "sphere" in art. He told himself that they were so happy and so entirely in each other's confidence that "regrets for art of necessity deserted in some measure, are weak and foolish. Life is greater than art, in my thinking. . . ."[6]

Christiana made her own adjustments. She went on with copying and collected pictures and beautiful objects for their home. "I never knew any one who had a surer judgement of what was beautiful," Wilmot wrote many years later, "and I may say here that I simply cannot express what I owe to her for surrounding my life with beauty." They had congenial friends in common, in medical and artistic circles, and they found a way of dealing with those who did not appeal to both. For instance, Wilmot reserved the company of one of his friends for fishing trips because Christiana disliked his views on art and, even more, his "patronising way with women which she resented extremely." She had no interest in that "hidden world of Art" that Elizabeth Gaskell, who struggled daily to find or make time to write in peace, recommended to her young friend Eliza Fox as a refuge from overcrowded domestic and public lives. Art was a welcome shelter when one was "too much pressed upon by daily small Lilliputian arrows of peddling cares; it keeps them from being morbid, as you say; and takes them into the land where King Arthur lies hidden, and soothes them with its peace."[7] Christiana, however, required of art that it be an excitement and a challenge. She was not interested in art as refuge or therapy. Ironically, it would be through art as personal therapy that she came to be publicly identified with the revival of interest in the tempera techniques of the Italian quattrocento.

In 1891 Christopher Herringham, then nine years old, began a stubborn intermittent fever that was finally diagnosed as acute rheumatoid arthritis. Residence in Egypt's dry climate was prescribed, and Wilmot took a house in Helouan so that Christopher might escape the English winter. Early in 1892 the boy and his mother left for Egypt in hopes of at least a small miracle. There was brief improvement, but when Wilmot met them at Marseilles upon their return in July, although Christopher did not seem critically ill, arthritis had so disabled him that he had trouble turning himself in bed. Christiana was exhausted. "It was about time I joined," Wilmot told Mrs. Jo, "for poor Chrissie was utterly broken up. The responsibility and anxiety told terribly upon her, & she takes everything in such fearful earnest that it makes what would be hard for anyone, perfectly crushing for her. I don't know what the devil will happen next winter."[8]

He kept the Helouan house, and Christiana and Christopher returned there for the winter of 1892–1893. Wilmot engaged a woman to accompany them and relieve some of the strain of nursing, for it was important that Christiana should be free to keep up the boy's spirits. "It is this continually having to be cheerful which is such a hard job for Chrissie to whom it isn't natural, and this is what she wants taking off her hands." Again Christopher seemed to improve, but in May 1893 the fever returned. Wilmot thought at first that it might be "something of the nature of ague & finding that ague recurs there in the summer," he planned for Christiana and Christopher to go, escorted by a physician, to Aix-les-Bains.[9] He and Geoffrey were to join them there in August. Christopher never reached France. He died of uremic poisoning on 19 August, the day he and his mother were to leave Egypt.

"The end was quite sudden," Wilmot told his father, "& was due to the kidney disease. . . . the voyage home will be terrible" for Christiana. Wilmot could not even join her for the journey, for there was no outbound sailing before the twenty-sixth, and she would already be on her way home. "I am glad to think," Wilmot wrote, "that the dear boy had many months of glad & happy life. I wish I could have seen him so." Christiana had asked that no one wear mourning, and Wilmot asked his parents to respect her wishes.[10]

Wilmot's work helped him to bear the loss. He became a fierce crusader for more rigorous quarantine regulations in orphanages and hospitals, and as the years passed, he became noted as an active advocate of programs for improvement in medical education. He had always before him the fact that medicine as he and his contemporaries knew it had not saved Christopher; nor could it save his favorite sister, Kathleen Herringham Hole, who died of complications that followed the birth of her son, or her husband, Robert Hole, who died only a year later.[11]

Christopher's death devastated Christiana. The "fearful earnest" with which she took serious matters only deepened her distress. Her natural intensities lost their focus, and until 1897, Wilmot thought she remained really unwell. Always slight of figure, she now lost weight to only a little over ninety-three pounds. She was painfully restless and had fits of violent longing for a return to the country and an ideal life like that of Piccard's Rough. Had the polluted city killed Christopher? Perhaps Surrey's purer air might save Geoffrey; in 1893 he was at the same age as Christopher when Christiana took Christopher to Egypt for the first time. Wilmot wrote that she would come to him "almost screaming," so that he even considered giving up medicine altogether for some rural or suburban occupation. Although he doubted that the country could satisfy her for very long, they took a cottage near Piccard's Rough. As he had expected, she soon tired of it, and they gave it up. A few years later they tried again and took Piccard's Cottage at St. Catherine's. There Christiana occupied herself with renovations and additions. She often lost her temper violently, and Wilmot "once had to go down to the kitchen to quiet a disturbance with the hired man." She was plainly on the crumbling edge and in need of some handhold by which to pull herself back to solid ground.[12]

Study of quattrocento tempera and fresco became that handhold. Like Elizabeth Gaskell, who after the death of a small son commenced the career of serious publication that began with *Mary Barton*, Christiana began, probably in 1896, to translate *Il libro dell' arte o trattato della pittura*, which was written about 1390 by D'Andrea Cennino Cennini. Translation concentrates the mind wonderfully, and for Christiana it was art scholarship as therapy.

The *trattato* (treatise) was certainly not unknown in the 1890s. An Italian version by Giuseppe Tambroni appeared in 1821 but later proved unsatisfactory, for it was based on an eighteenth-century copy. In 1844 Mary Philadelphia Merrifield made the first English translation, and in 1858 came Victor Mottez's French translation, both derived from Tambroni. An improved Italian version by Carlo and Gaetano Milanesi appeared in 1859, and Christiana Herringham worked from that; she also found Albert Ilg's German translation of 1871 "a most valuable book of reference in translating difficult passages."[13] Daniel V. Thompson, who translated Cennini in 1933 as *The Craftsman's Handbook*, drew upon all of these in addition to another German translation, made by Willibrord Verkade in 1916. Of his own translation, Thompson says:

> Though my publication of the Italian text represents no such major improvement as the Milanesi's [*sic*] wrought over Tambroni's, it seems to me a sounder basis for translation than has hitherto been available.
>
> The Milanesi edition rendered obsolete Mrs. Merrifield's translation from Tambroni; and Lady Herringham's *Book of the Art*, incorporating the Milanesi's [*sic*] improvements, became the standard English version of Cennino's work. I venture to criticize it here, not in dispraise of her translation, for it has shown its merit, but rather to justify a new one.[14]

Thompson notes several types of errors in the Herringham translation: some departures from the original, "sometimes through misconception based on Mrs. Merrifield's version, sometimes through carelessness"; inconsistencies of technical terms; and omissions of some crucial sentences. When and how well Christiana learned Italian is unknown, but as Thompson observes, "the real business of translation is a 'laboratory' matter, involving a knowledge of each rule in practice. This knowledge Lady Herringham possessed in some degree."[15] She possessed also—what is almost as important—a wish to experience sympathetically the ambience of those fifteenth-century masters' shops. When she made Cennini her instructor, she accepted wholeheartedly the master-to-pupil relationship characteristic of the quattrocento workshop studio. Studying under Cennini re-created the excitement of being the pupil carried along not only by new knowledge but also by the instructor's personality and enthusiasm.

Cennini, the master of the *trattato,* follows the pleasant conventions of old instructional manuals. In his text he speaks directly to the student, and it leaves no doubt that the student has his instructor's entire attention. "Now then," he says, "you of noble mind, who are lovers of this good, come at once to art and adorn yourselves with this vesture,—namely, love, reverence, obedience, and perseverance." The aspiring pupil must stay as long as possible with the master selected, for "if you copy to-day from this master and tomorrow from the other, you will not acquire the manner of either; and you will necessarily become fantastic, for each manner will distract your mind."[16]

Advice on this and related themes is threaded throughout the *trattato,* and Cennini never claims that his manual is the complete key to success. Do not, he warns, believe those who say they "have learned the art without having been with a master. Do not believe them, for I give you this very book as an example: even studying it day and night, if you do not see some practice with some master, you will never be fit for anything; nor will you be able with a good face to stay among the masters." He offers as confirmation his own artistic pedigree. He had been for twelve years with Agnolo Gaddi, who learned from his father, Taddeo Gaddi, who learned from Giotto himself, and all three were intensely aware of their places in the Giottesque apostolic succession. Cennini returns again and again to the importance of feeling oneself in the line of a great tradition. He stresses also his philosophy of quality, and he preaches it in small things and in great. Never skimp on materials, he says, for there is true economy and there is a false economy that will betray your future reputation. For example, avoid a red called dragon's blood but get cinnabar red from the apothecary "and pay for it."[17] As he discusses materials and their preparation, he creates a setting that the reader easily visualizes as a pleasant, well-lighted place full of delightful and inviting things: elegant minever brushes and airy sheets of beaten gold, containers all ready for the ingredients and mixing of colors—new pipkins, little tubs, covered strainers, glazed basins, neat little porringers, small baking pans—all kept perfectly clean and in order.

Running through the *trattato* is the idea that the finest materials and even the finest instruction are unavailing if there is no joy in the work. This, too, depends upon the manner of working. Painting can become tedious, and then "it is time to leave your work and to rest yourself for a short space, and then return to the work on your panel. You should always take pleasure in your work."[18] Christiana Herringham took this lesson to heart.

> Much of the painting of the fifteenth century has that intrinsic beauty which comes when we enjoy the material we work with, and feel that we have in our hands the means of success, and are not desirous of other means.[19]
>
> Whatever its nature one thing is certain, namely, that in decorative art which claims to offer objects for admiration, or to make them pleasanter to look at no one will compass this particular beauty who does not love the material employed even in its limitations, using it as a friend and a guide, handling it with both respect and admiration.[20]

Tempera's colors are tempered, or emulsified, with a natural binding agent, usually egg yolk, and applied to a prepared dry surface such as a wood panel. For true fresco—*buon fresco*—the colors are mixed with water and applied to a wet plaster surface, and colors and plaster fuse as they dry. Both tempera and fresco dry very rapidly, so that an even spread of color may become difficult. Therefore, only so much of the medium as is needed can be prepared for one session of work; and unless proportions and ingredients are exactly correct and identical in each mixing, and unless the artist employs the greatest skill in joining one day's work to the next, the finished painting or fresco will have a telltale patchwork appearance. Oil, Christiana believed, can create a luscious surface but encourages bad habits because it dries slowly and can be reworked repeatedly, so that one must sometimes regret oil's convenience. "It too readily lends itself to false finish and smugness. It is only the best artists who ask from it anything more difficult than it can do without effort."[21] Only the truly virtuoso painter can manage tempera or fresco successfully.

Of the two, Christiana valued above all the "bloomy quality" of tempera's colors. That quality was the source of its unique beauty, "a wonderful luminousness and purity" missing from surfaces painted in oil. The secret of creating tempera's beauties had been so long forgotten that in the first volume of *Modern Painters* we find Ruskin puzzling over evidence that the early Dutch painters in tempera had created skies

> which there is no matching in modern times; one would think angels had painted them, for all is now clay and oil in comparison. It seems as if we had totally lost the art, for surely otherwise, however little our painters might aim at it or feel it, they would touch the chord sometimes by accident; but they never do, and the mechanical incapacity is still more strongly evidenced by the muddy struggles of the unhappy Germans,

who had traces of the genuine feeling enough to "bring out the tone if they had the mechanical means and technical knowledge."[22]

Those Germans were the Nazarenes, the Brotherhood of St. Luke (Lukasbrüder), who drew together at the Vienna Academy of Painting in 1809 because they saw themselves as painters in the tradition of the medieval illustrators. Their classmates dubbed them Nazarenes because they affected biblical dress and hairstyles and had a particular fondness for biblical subjects. The leaders, Friedrich Overbeck and Franz Pforr, with a small group of followers from the Vienna Academy, settled in an abandoned monastery at Rome in 1810, where Peter von Cornelius joined them in 1811. Study of the early Renaissance painters and the early Raphael turned them to fresco as their path to truth and purity in art, and also as their protest against Vienna's neoclassical academic tradition, which they thought placed a premium on superficial virtuosity. The comparatively muted colors of fresco reinforced their gospel of simplicity and unpretentiousness in both life and art, for they called upon the viewer to respond less to brilliance and sensuousness of color and more to abstract beauties of design and a sense of oneness with a living continuity in art. They obtained several important commissions for frescoes that attracted the attention of William Dyce during his successive study visits to Rome, and Ford Madox Ford carried Nazarene influence back to England as an inspiration for the English Pre-Raphaelites.[23]

The beliefs and the work of the Nazarenes constituted an episode in the romantic revivalism that sought to counteract the rising industrialism of the nineteenth century. By 1829 all but Overbeck had returned to Germany, where Cornelius had already become prominent through his advocacy of frescoes to embellish the walls of public buildings with literal or allegorical depictions of scenes and events from national history. What was more natural than that the German Prince Albert, when he sat as chairman in 1842 of the new Royal Fine Arts Commission, which was overseeing decorations for the Palace of Westminster, rebuilt after the fire of 1834, should turn to the German Cornelius for guidance with respect to wall paintings? Cornelius, when invited to advise and to execute frescoes himself, was said to have pointed to the homegrown fresco revivalist William Dyce as one who might lead the project at Westminster. Cornelius is said also to have changed his mind about that. But both the prince and Charles Lock Eastlake, secretary to the Commission, believed that English painters should execute English subjects, and Julius Schnorr von Carolsfeld, another of the Nazarenes, agreed with them. Eastlake said, "That the English painters are qualified (except in fresco) to cope with the Germans I have no doubt and fresco, I have as little doubt, is easily learnt. . . . It is not fair to make the Germans more expert than they are."[24] Fresco, as experience would prove, was *not* easily learned, and the artists' eventual discovery that they were less expert than they had thought themselves was as great a threat to the work as any German influence from the Nazarenes or from Prince Albert's German loyalties.

The Westminster project bore directly upon a contradiction inherent in revivalism, which implies successive stages in a history. That is, to what purpose is the revival to be put: a nourishing continuity with the past, or a self-indulgent aggrandizement of the present? The nineteenth century, with its enthusiasms (and sometimes illusions) about the meaning of progress, was particularly susceptible to the latter. Walter Houghton observes that the Victorians, with "relief and joy," regarded progress as "liberation from the burden of the past." The Victorian optimist had a "happy sense of superiority to one's foolish or timid neighbors" who had not yet realized the speed with which times had changed.[25] Revivalist researches in art, archaeology, and literature helped to create the happy sense of a secure place in the forward march of history. At the same time, the catalogue of stages left behind could be used to show how far society had come in its progress toward technological, social, and aesthetic perfection. The frescoes project at Westminster did both. It was a reminder that (where time and lack of care had not obliterated them) England, too, had an ancient tradition of wall painting. And although the painters of early Renaissance Italy were now classified as "primitives," English artists of the 1840s would bring their art up to date by using it to glorify the history and achievements of modern Britain.[26] Instead of endlessly repeated depictions of saints and Virgin, Westminster would get "Boadicea Inciting Her Army," "Trafalgar," the Red Cross Knight, King Lear, and—William Dyce's special assignment—an Arthurian series. All were intended as a permanent reminder of a historical past now made useful in an idealized form.

However, the artists needed some technical guidance. In 1846 Mary Philadelphia Merrifield published at her own expense a book on the art of painting in fresco. The Westminster frescoes, she predicted, would usher in "an epoch in the fine arts, and, will probably, be the means of forming a great school of painting in this country, and lead to the improvement of the sister arts of sculpture and architecture." She touched a spring of popular enthusiasm when she pointed out other parallels with sixteenth-century Florence. "The same wealth and splendour of our nobles and merchants, the same commercial prosperity, and above all, the same spirit of inquiry, which characterised Italy at the period I have mentioned, is applicable to England at the present moment. The advantage is on the side of England."[27]

These noble sentiments encountered reality when the Westminster decorators' work began to decay even before they had finished it. The artists were dismayed to find that as "men of this age of science and industry" they must "accept that a technique mastered by monks in fifteenth-century Italy required all their ingenuity, skill, and inventiveness."[28] They were not ingenious enough to know that the very foundation of their frescoes was wrong. " 'The frescoes were painted on lime and plaster spread on a framework of laths, and there was a space at the back, of some inches, to separate them from the outer wall of stone; and in this space the damp accumulated, and had no exit or ventilation.' By 1861 M.P.'s were bandying jests about the peeling and unrecognisable features of Cordelia *et al.*"[29] Ruskin was quite right about the importance of "mechanical means and technical knowledge."

The artists' difficulties only proved the wisdom of Cennini's doctrine that a painter's understanding must grow along with his skill in handling his medium. Nineteenth-century artists accustomed to oil's amenability and exasperated by what seemed to be fresco's sheer cantankerousness were unlikely to cultivate with patience the "love, reverence, obedience, and perseverence" that Cennini had enjoined. William Dyce, who sincerely sought the spirit of the great age of fresco, persevered despite all the difficulties. At the other extreme was William Etty, who was invited to paint a fresco for the Buckingham Palace Pavilion. He "found the discipline of completing one section of the wall at a time on wet plaster—which he could not then retouch without starting from the beginning again—too much for him. 'Fresco! oh that word!' he declared, 'for the future it will be a "word of fear" . . . I think neither fear nor favour will induce me to take another.' "[30]

Between those two extremes was a variety of motivations for the artists' trying fresco: novelty of the medium, favor from a royal commission, simple patriotism, enthusiasm for the possibilities of decorative art for public buildings. Whatever their motivations, most of those accustomed to the ease of retouching a surface in oil found, like Etty, that fresco seemed perversely and unnecessarily difficult. It is understandable that the failures at Westminster and also at All Souls Margaret Street dampened the enthusiasm for reviving early Renaissance techniques. Paintings in fresco were a product that had failed to come up to standard.

Still another long-lasting influence contributed to the widespread belief that the work of the "primitives" had best be regarded as material for study and not for living art. Two extremely important books, both published in 1847, reinforced the idea that the history of art proceeds invariably according to a principle of perfectibility, and that true art had begun with the refinement and general adoption of oil, instead of water or egg yolk, as a base for colors. One of these books was James Ludovic Lindsay's three-volume *Sketches of the History of Christian Art.* He accepted as a turning point Jan van Eyck's use of oil as base, an improvement "tantamount to the discovery [of a new era in painting]. So complete and satisfactory was the new process, that the old was abandoned at once and for ever, and John [Jan] Van Eyck was universally recognised as the solver of a problem which had puzzled all preceding generations."[31]

Jan van Eyck's solution, Lord Lindsay believed, was a major step in the redemption of both art and man, who was "created in this perfection, but Adam fell, and with the Fall the original harmony ceased, the elements of being lost their equipoise; Spirit, Sense and Intellect, with the two elements of Intellect, Reason and Imagination, have ever since been at variance, and consequently every production of man partakes of the imperfection of its parent." However, the moral sense, "comparatively deadened," still survives, a witness to what is pure, holy, and fitting; painting, when it entered the age of Christendom, proved the existence of "an immortal Spirit, conversing with its God." And to emphasize the fact of "continuous progress toward perfection," each of the three arts matches one of the three principal epochs, each preceded in "rise, progress and decline by an antecedent correspondent development of its elder sister or sisters": Greek sculpture by architecture, European painting by architecture and sculpture. Hence the "superiority for Christian over Classic Art in all her three departments." Art cannot rise above the religious and moral sentiments of the age, and "herein lies our vantage—not in our merit, not our genius, but in that we are Christians, that we are raised by communion with God to a purer atmosphere." Christian artists achieve greater grandeur and sublimity than any predecessors. "No work of genius has ever been produced apart from that influence."[32]

Well on in his second volume, Lord Lindsay arrives at Cennini, whom he sees as a retrograde influence on the forward progress of art because he "adhered with fond affection to the antiquated rules and practice of his master, Angelo [*sic*] [Gaddi]." Indeed, Cennini's loyalty to his " 'tres grandi' . . . the Lares of his veneration, Giotto, Taddeo Gaddi, and Angelo [*sic*]," had set art back by a full century. His *trattato* is admittedly a useful historical and atmospheric document, for it "admits the reader into the bottega of the artist, invites him within the screen by which the painters of those early days fenced themselves and their mysteries off from the uninitiated eye." But however charming this glimpse of old days in the studio, it does not make up for the fact that Cennini was "superseded in his profession by artists of the new school, and unable or unwilling to accommodate his practice to theirs with the facility of his contemporaries." The *trattato* is in the last analysis a "dying legacy of the man who, in his amiable but blind idolatry of the past, might be fitly styled the Last of the Giotteschi."[33]

Lord Lindsay concludes with a "Postscriptum," a plea to the Italian government to begin at once to preserve "the grand old frescoes." To what purpose is this preservation? That nineteenth-century painters might gauge thereby their own progress toward perfection.

> It is not by studying art in its perfection—by worshipping Raphael and Michael Angelo exclusively of all other excellence—that we can expect to rival them, but to re-ascending to the fountain-head . . . in a word by studying Duccio and Giotto we may paint like Taddeo di Bartolo and Masaccio, Taddeo di Bartolo and Masaccio that we may

> paint like Perugino and Luca Signorelli, Perugino and Luca Signorelli that we may paint like Raphael and Michael Angelo. . . . For with genius and God's blessing nothing is impossible.[34]

The second of the influential commentaries was Charles Lock Eastlake's *Methods and Materials of Painting of the Great Schools and Masters.* It was especially important, not only because he was the influential secretary of the Royal Fine Arts Commission that oversaw the decorations at Westminster, but also because in 1843 he had been appointed Keeper of the National Gallery. His book was written specifically "to promote the objects of the Commissioners on the Fine Arts," who were in charge of the Westminster project. Eastlake, born in 1793, had resolved early to become a historical painter. After study with Benjamin Haydon, he entered the Royal Academy Schools. From 1816 to 1830 he lived and worked in Rome. His romantic *banditti* pictures exhibited in England in 1823 attracted notice, but his articles for London journals had already established his reputation for thoroughness and method. He declined invitations and commissions that interfered with painting, until Sir Robert Peel made him secretary to the Royal Fine Arts Commission, a position that put him in close contact with Prince Albert. In 1842 he became librarian to the Royal Academy and was its president from 1849 to 1853. He was Keeper of the National Gallery from 1843 to 1847, then Director from 1855 until his death. He traveled regularly on the Continent to find pictures that laid the foundations of that great collection.[35]

Eastlake certainly understood that art history is not altogether a matter of either/or. "It matters not how good or how bad the vehicle was which the old fellows used. The historian's duty is to get at it, as a mere fact, if he can."[36] Yet Eastlake's *Methods and Materials* is not evenhanded. Its subject is oil as traced from the van Eycks, and he puts down Cennini and other Italian old fellows who persisted with tempera as obstinate and unprogressive. After all, Pliny had known about drying oils used for varnishes. And treatises of the twelfth and thirteenth centuries represented "the state of the art [of painting] at the period when Cimabue adopted it from the Greeks: but the same general methods, inherited from Agnolo Gaddi by Cennini, [reappear in his *trattato*] but little altered, as regards oil painting; in the early part of the fifteenth century." Certainly early oil was unrefined and caused many problems, so that up to the year 1400 "tempera was not unreasonably preferred to it for works that require careful design, precision, and completeness."[37]

All that changed with the van Eycks. They had "overcome the stigma that attached to oil painting, as a process fit only for ordinary purposes and mechanical decorations. . . . they sought to raise the wonder of the beholder by surpassing the finish of tempera with the very material that had long been considered intractable. Mere finish was however, the least of the excellencies of these reformers." The "reformers" overcame "long established prejudices" by capitalizing upon "some of the best qualities which oil painting, as a means of imitating nature, can command."[38] The easier blending of colors in oil eliminated the necessity in fresco and tempera, so tedious and artificial, of hatching with the point of a fine brush as a means of joining one day's work to the next.

How was one to explain Cennini's obtuseness? wondered Eastlake. It was inexcusable, for Cennini knew that oil was being used in Germany, and a little more research would have brought him to the van Eycks. "Had Cennini been indebted, however indirectly, to Van Eyck, his treatise would have contained some notice of an improved system, instead of a repetition of the formulae which had been long received."[39] If oil *was* being used in Italy, why did Cennini deprive his students of this exciting information? When the Italians finally awoke to its advantages, they conceived a new appreciation for the younger van Eyck, who combined the new technique with "an extraordinary capacity for *seeing nature*, . . . which his predecessors had not attempted to represent. The same mind which was capable of receiving such impressions was also likely to devise suitable means to embody them, and to extend the language of imitation."[40]

"Reformers," "improved system," the summary dismissal of "long established prejudices," the innovative mind that thinks in terms of "suitable means" to an "improved" end—Eastlake recited the optimistic litany of Victorian faith in perfectibility. Everything seemed so logical and easy, so inevitable, and what seemed to belong irrevocably to the past was brought forward only if it could be shaped to a utilitarian approach to art instruction.

Ruskin had no faith in anything connected with the Westminster project, and that lack of faith seeped into his review of Eastlake's *Methods and Materials.* However much Ruskin tended to romanticize the Italian Renaissance, he knew that the spirit of the work in London was flawed. He was scornful of the artists' skills and of their motivations. In 1845, while they were hard at work, he spent six months studying frescoes in Italy, and from Venice, near the end of his stay, he wrote, scoffing at the painter Joseph Severn's enthusiasm for an English revival of fresco. Ruskin thought it "monstrously absurd in him to speak of inoculating England with the love of *Fresco* as if that were all she wanted, and men could be sublime on a wall who were idiots on canvas. Fresco does indeed afford glorious *room* for a man who wants it—it is a . . . sea for the strong swimmer . . . but you might as well throw a covey of chickens into the Atlantic as our R-A's [Royal Academicians] into fresco."[41]

Ruskin had long detested the architect Sir Charles Barry's designs for the Houses of Parliament, and his references to them burn with scorn for the "lacquered splendours" of that "absurdest and emptiest piece of filigree."[42] The sacred art of fresco demanded a purifying asceticism, and Ruskin abhorred the nationalist hubris that attended the frescoes project at the Palace of Westminster. Cennini's credo echoes in Ruskin's admonition to Severn that "it is the love of God and his creatures; it is humility, and charity, and self-denial, and fasting, and prayer; it is a total change of character. We want more faith and less reasoning; less strength and more trust." Giotto, Ghirlandaio, and Angelico were the true guides, "not a desire to be an R.A., and to dine with the Queen. . . ."[43]

Worst of all was the fact that while the artists in London were messing about with fresco, the real thing was being destroyed before Ruskin's eyes in Italy, and he alternated between rage and despair at Italian neglect and the mindless depredations masquerading as improvements. Six months of this put him in a fine flaring mood to review Eastlake's *Methods and Materials.* What, Ruskin asked, was the result of the current attitude toward art before the age of oil?

England's leading painters were adrift. Because they had lost the thread of historical continuity, they lacked the will to expend even so much effort as the German Nazarenes in Rome or the Pre-Raphaelites in England to get in touch with the spirit of the age that preceded the domination of oil.

> And of late, among our leading masters, the loss has been not merely of the system of the ancients, but of all system whatsoever; the greater number paint as if the virtue of oil pigment were its opacity, or as if its power depended on its polish; of the rest, no two agree in use or choice of materials; not many are consistent even in their own practice; and the most zealous and earnest, therefore the most discontented, reaching impatiently and desperately after better things, purchase the momentary satisfaction of their feelings by the sacrifice of security of surface and durability of hue.[44]

In Ruskin's opinion, Eastlake's views only encouraged this historical amnesia. Segregating pre-oil painters as "primitives" had done little to profit the present.

> The walls of our galleries are for the most part divided between pictures whose dead coating of consistent paint, laid on with a heavy hand and a cold heart, secures for them the stability of dulness and the safety of mediocrity; and pictures whose reckless and experimental brilliancy, unequal in its result as lawless in its means, is as evanescent as the dust of an insect's wing, and presents in its chief perfections so many subjects of future regret.[45]

It was true that in Ruskin's day visitors to the National Gallery could not get the best impression of the tempera painters. Time's ravages had detracted from effect and only reinforced the idea of the work as something undeveloped, inferior, to be left behind in the interests of progress. The viewer of the National Gallery's "primitives" who tried to determine "which picture represented with least disputable fidelity the first intention of its painter" had to try hard to peer through "hypothetical degrees of blackened shadow and yellowed light, of lost outline and buried detail, of chilled lustre, dimmed transparency, altered colour, and weakened force. . . ." To Ruskin, Jan van Eyck's portrait of the Arnolfini, Eastlake's first major acquisition of that school, purchased in 1842, came as a relief, not because of expression or treatment, but because time seemed to have had no power over it. Why do the Arnolfini seem to defy time? Not because oil was a sudden new discovery as a medium, but because oil, used in a new way to create a varnish that would dry in the shade, had preserved the picture's freshness.[46]

As Keeper of the National Gallery, Eastlake made a determined and courageous effort to acquire superior and better-preserved examples of the "primitives," although at the time historical completeness of the collection and opportunities for study were the principal rationales for such acquisitions. Ruskin applauded Eastlake's efforts and made the most of the opportunity for study. He decided that Carpaccio's *Venetian Ladies and Their Pets* was in tempera, not oil, "and I must note in passing that many of the qualities which I have been in the habit of praising in Tintoret and Carpaccio, as consummate achievements in oil-painting, are, as I have found lately, either in tempera altogether, or tempera with oil above. And I am disposed to think that ultimately tempera will be found the proper material for the greater number of most delightful subjects."[47]

When we recall Wilmot Herringham's description of Piccard's Rough as being full of Ruskin's influence, it becomes easy to imagine the effects of *Modern Painters* and essays like his review of Eastlake's book upon Christiana, who chose the nourishing continuity of history as the most fruitful use of revivalism. Cennini's *trattato* was *not* a "dying legacy." She assigned herself the tasks of reproducing as nearly as possible that lovely "bloomy quality" of quattrocento tempera and of opening the eyes of the public to its beauties. Deteriorated examples of tempera in the National Gallery and the failures in fresco at Westminster did not invalidate the right of "primitive" paintings to claim the beauties that are uniquely theirs. Yet the shibboleth of progress in art remained so entrenched that when she introduced the catalogue for the first exhibition of the four-year-old Society of Painters in Tempera in 1905, she felt obliged to justify "the reintroduction of an old and disused way of painting. . . . Why should we return to antiquated methods which have been succeeded by oil-painting? Can we even say that there exists sufficient knowledge of the earlier technique to permit the assertion that it really has been re-introduced?"[48]

In 1907 Christiana wrote the introduction to a collection of occasional papers read to the society. "It is somewhat remarkable," she observed, "that at the present time when the intimate and the personal are recognised and appreciated in art, as they have not at least been (consciously) recognised and appreciated before[,] there is so little record of individual practice in actual [tempera] craftsmanship."[49] Individual practice had indeed been rare; in 1905 Roger Fry wrote that the medium had dropped so completely out of use that when Ruskin one day had found Christiana copying in tempera in the National Gallery he "questioned her as to what she was about, and he was under the impression that Botticelli and all the Italian primitives painted in oils." There were still people who knew the difference between tempera and oil, but tempera had become "almost entirely a matter for the antiquarian and the forger."[50]

In 1909, when the society held its second exhibition, Christiana stated as its purpose "the study and practice of the methods and mediums of painting in universal use previous to the introduction of oil, methods which have justified themselves by the superior brilliancy and permanency of their results." The *Athenaeum*'s reviewer thought that the society had yet to prove its point but welcomed a revival "apart from the modest artistic achievement which is all it has as yet brought in its train." Here was still the theory that the pre-oil paintings, being "primitive" and therefore nonprogressive, had a certain usefulness as a gauge against which a modern painter might measure his own progress. Every painter, said this reviewer, should have a course in tempera, not for any superior qualities or satisfactions of the medium, but "on account of its difficulty" and a rapid experience "in the effect on a picture of successive paintings modifying, but not obliterating, one another." The early oil painters owed their "imaginative power to actual experience in the other mediums of quicker experiment." That discipline was "hardly recoverable without reversion to tempera painting." The reviewer hoped that modern experiments with tempera might counteract the influence of upstart impressionists, for they only made a smooth surface "coarser and coarser as more paint is put upon it," thus drawing too much attention to the material. On the other hand, tempera bred "weakness in another direction," for "its excessive delicacy" in blending tones weakened the pictorial structure.[51]

The Society of Painters in Tempera rejected absolutely the idea that tempera's delicacies were a source of weakness and that it was good only for academic exercise. They wished to make the point that this was a medium for any age, that a fine "primitive" is fine in and of itself and offers more than academic exercise and self-congratulation on progress in the era of oil. Cennini's *trattato* and the other old treatises had divulged the secrets of the old formulas. The society wished to discover the secret of using the secrets, and not as a mere exercise in precious antiquarianism. The last thing it wanted was exclusive possession of those secrets. Christiana wrote:

> We very much wish that this action of our Society might be followed by others, and that something like the priceless treasure of the old Guild "secrets" might again be within reach of those who care for such things.
>
> These secrets were very largely records of efforts to gain "quality"; sometimes of knowledge how to secure the subtle and elusive beauty of texture, we call by this name.[52]

There was no great rush to accept the society's kind invitation. In the official art world it was a fringe enterprise, quaint and quirky, even pointless, at a time when all painters of consequence preferred oil as a matter of course. Among authors in the society's first volume of occasional papers were a number of decorators and designers representative of other artists who felt so unrecognized *as artists* that they asserted themselves through separate organizations such as the Arts and Crafts Exhibition Society and C. R. Ashbee's Guild of Handicraft. There were no Royal Academicians among the tempera painters, but there were three members of the dissident New English Art Club, and among these the name of Roger Fry stands out.

This was not yet Roger Fry the evangelist for postimpressionism who in 1910 would so upset the orthodox with his exhibition of the new French painters—new, at least, to most of the English public. In the early 1900s Fry was absorbed in study of the Italian Renaissance masters. He exhibited his own paintings with the New English Art Club but was increasingly unhappy with oil as a medium. He agreed with Christiana that oil had been detrimental to painterly skills.[53] Fry became convinced that tempera could be truthful to nature in ways that oil could not. "There are in fact comparatively few effects of nature which lend themselves to quite literal rendering in oil paint in such a way as to bring out its characteristic and superlative beauties." Modern painters reproduced nature's effects "with great truth in oils, but only at the cost of the material beauty of their picture surfaces." Tempera possessed the secret, whose loss Ruskin bemoaned, of those luminous skies in early Renaissance pictures. Fry was convinced that an understanding and appreciation of tempera could serve as a corrective to the headlong painting habits of some of the English impressionists. If tempera was more difficult to use than oil, "it is yet far more difficult, almost impossible indeed, to produce with tempera those thoroughly ugly and uninviting surfaces which it requires profound science to avoid in the clayey mixtures of oil paint." Wrote Christiana, "Tempera can never forget its surface."[54]

Fry's was not an overnight conversion. In 1893 he had told his mother, "I'm getting so imbued with the older traditions of painting that I shouldn't be surprised if I were to copy an Old Master some day." In 1894 he wrote to his father, "The more I study the Old Masters, the more terrible does the chaos of modern art seem to me, and so far I see no way out of it except possibly the invention of coloured photography, which would put an end to most of it."[55] He wanted his artist friends to paint more like old masters and told the painter William Rothenstein, his fellow member of the New English Art Club, that the finish of his oil paintings left them looking unfinished. Rothenstein, for his part, thought that Fry was leaning perilously backward in an unnatural attempt to duplicate "the precious surface achieved by the earlier painters[.] 'If I could only have your pictures to work on after you have done with them!' [Fry] said."[56]

Fry was not to be dissuaded from the argument he had set out in his study of Giovanni Bellini, published in 1899, the same year as Christiana's Cennini translation. He was already in pursuit of a satisfactory definition of form. He found the Paduan artists seeking "always to distil from nature a statement of form," and the scientific side of his education persuaded him to dissect the "peculiar tempera technique, which their desire for decorative completeness and firmness of expression led them to elaborate, and which in turn dictated their outlook upon nature."

> Over a flat general tone circumscribed by firm outlines, which remained visible in the finished picture, they modelled with hatched strokes, whitish on one side of the figure, dark on the other, and finally, under pretext of a reflected light, they introduced a faint light edge within the outline on the dark side, in order to mark with yet one more contour their elaborately planned design. Although such a technique was incapable of rendering the more subtle beauties of natural objects, the softness of flesh or the bloom of a velvet, it was admirably suited to that patient hammering out of a definitive and unalterable form which the Paduans accomplished; and, in the hands of its best masters, the picture could by it be brought to an unyielding and lacquer-like firmness of surface, not without its charm when regarded rather as a beautiful substance itself than as symbolical of beautiful realities.[57]

The more Fry thought about old masters, the more he thought it possible that a revival of interest in tempera could help to revitalize English understanding of art. "It is not to be hoped that any change of medium, any technical recipes, could purify the mass of modern painting of its incurable vulgarity of sentiment, its bad *ethos,* but nothing would be more likely to have a more restraining and sobering influence on our art than the substitution of tempera for oils as the ordinary medium of artistic expression."[58]

Fry looked to the Society of Painters in Tempera for help in finding that new, nonacademic insight and making it a possible restraining influence on the excesses of popular art. "It was in Italian soil that Fry's aesthetics had its roots," Alistair Smart wrote in 1966. He liked "the discipline, the order and the sense of structure, of the great Italian masters, from Cimabue to Bellini and Fra Bartolommeo, that he found wanting in the French Impressionists and in their imitators at the New English Art Club." Smart traced Fry's line of descent from Signorelli to Rembrandt and thence straight to Cézanne. "Fry, indeed, was one of the pioneers of that fuller understanding of the techniques of the Old Masters which is so fundamental to art-historical scholarship today." If Fry's 1899 monograph on Bellini gives an impression of a young writer glancing warily over his shoulder at elders among the art historians, says Frances Spalding, it "must be recognised as a pioneering achievement. Bellini's debt to his predecessors was analysed for the first time," and 1460 was first marked for "the onset of Bellini's mature style."[59]

Fry's own paintings attracted only qualified praise. His study of past art, Spalding says, was a "more profitable use of his time, and this slight but definite shift of allegiance (he still continued to paint whenever possible) very quickly brought out his talents as critic." She thinks that "if Fry's career had ended in 1903, he would be remembered as a critic whose taste favoured the Old Masters and as a painter of mock seventeenth-century landscapes." But he worked endlessly at those pictures, always "investigating the various ways in which a beautiful surface could be achieved." That, and his passion for seeing into the structure of a picture, would have its logical development in the doctrine of a picture's essential interior shape, which Clive Bell would define in 1914 as "significant form."[60]

Christiana Herringham looked to Fry for guidance by argument. "To the end of his life he would never write a book or deliver a lecture without seeing the pictures themselves, . . ." wrote Virginia Woolf. "To have another pair of eyes to see with, another brain to argue with, was a very necessary process in making up his mind." Christiana, too, reached decisions by arguing. "I really couldn't count all the things you have told me, and taught me & made me see," she told Fry. "Don't think I dislike discussion. It does agitate me because I only argue if I am really arguing to convince or be convinced, and it is agitating for the time whatever happens. Still more so perhaps if the subject is only turned up rough & has to lie lumpy & fallow." This was one way for an inquisitive woman who had missed out on advanced education to fill in the blank spaces in her knowledge while at the same time increasing her intellectual self-confidence. Elizabeth

Gaskell, in almost the same words, had told Annie Shaen, another of her young friends, "I take the opposite side to the person I am talking with always in order to hear some convincing arguments to clear up my opinions."[61]

On one occasion, apparently, both Christiana and Fry had been too much in "fearful earnest" on some point, and Fry worried that he had offended her. One of the joys of art, she reassured him, was the endless latitude for differences of opinion.

> No doubt there is one domain of art that appeals to you more strongly and another to me—but I think we give rather different root explanations about expression—but the facts are always bigger than our grasp of them—and explanation will never be complete. It would be very uncomfortable to think we did exhaustively understand. At least so it occurs to me . . . I haven't *felt* treated badly. I hardly know what bad treatment you mean.[62]

Fry encouraged her in still another way. He believed in the value of copying. In early years he had disparaged it, viewing copying as a secondhand art stigmatized by the crowds of earnest amateurs planted before masterpieces in the National Gallery; but in the 1880s he came to believe that it could be much more than an empty exercise or a secondhand art. He continued to copy as a means of instruction and also as a process of reinvigoration. He realized, while copying Cimabue's St. Francis from his series of frescoes in the Upper Church of S. Francesco at Assisi, that he had never before seen it "with enlightened eyes." He found that "what I thought before were weaknesses of early incapacity are really the results of a sensibility one had never understood."[63]

Copies could be new translations, not mere replicas. Long after he was associated in the public mind with postimpressionism, Fry was encouraging his family and friends to work hard at copying the old pictures. In 1917 his Omega Workshops mounted the Exhibition of Omega Copies and Translations, which showed copies of old masters principally by Fry himself, his wife, his daughter, and his Bloomsbury Group friends Vanessa Bell and Duncan Grant, who later told William Rothenstein's son, Sir John Rothenstein: "I don't try to make exact copies but interpretations. . . . It isn't the painting that one does before another painting that teaches one. The real idea behind copying is to induce one to look at a picture for a long time." The Omega exhibition was not very successful with respect to sales, but Fry's preface to his catalogue stated in brief his motive for working at copies. "Each generation, almost each decade, has to remake its old Masters. If we did not go on continually revaluing and remaking them they would be not merely old but dead."[64]

Fry's enthusiasm for copying vindicated Christiana's choice of profession, and the emergence of the Society of Painters in Tempera in 1901 institutionalized her presence on the London art scene. Because the society was in effect a gathering of friends and had nothing to do with public policy, it went its way with little public comment other than the remarks of journalists who wrote about its infrequent exhibitions. In 1903, however, another of Christiana's friendly acts for the welfare of art projected her into the very center of national argument about public policy for administering the national collections. Private collectors, public officials, Parliament, and the general public were brought together—and frequently into collision—in an entirely new way, to find a way to prevent sale to foreign owners of masterworks from England's great private collections. The extent of the government's proper function in art patronage—an issue never thoroughly examined during the Westminster fresco enterprise—now became a question not only of government patronage but of the whole nation's participation in the preservation of its art heritage.

This story has been told before, but never from the viewpoint of the woman who seized the initiative and gave the money that made a new policy possible at a crucial moment in the history of British art collecting. Not one of the prominent recent writers on women in British art and art affairs—Nunn, Nochlin, Parker and Pollock, Chadwick, Cherry—has mentioned Christiana Herringham. Only Lisa Tickner, in her study of the graphic arts of the National Association of Women's Suffrage Societies, mentions her, and that only to say, "There is no information on Mrs. Herringham, who was credited with the needlework on several ASL [Artists' Suffrage League] banners."[65] Now much more is known, and this brings us to her part in the creation of Britain's National Art Collections Fund.

4

MAKING A PLACE FOR ART

When Christiana Herringham precipitated the movement to found the National Art Collections Fund, her motivation was the same as that for the revival of interest in tempera: something that could be done for art had not been done. William Rothenstein's feelings for art's welfare were similarly evangelical. He had studied at the Slade School in London and the Académie Julian, Paris, from which he returned to do a series of lithographs entitled *Oxford Characters* (1893–96); they established his reputation as a portrait artist. Friendships with his subjects—writers, artists, and public figures—created contacts that he put to generous use. He became known for his encouragement of younger artists and those he thought unfairly neglected. At Sheffield University, he was England's first professor of civic art from 1917 to 1926, a position from which he urged municipal employment of artists. He became principal of the Royal College of Art, a trustee of the Tate Gallery, and a member of the Royal Fine Art Commission. In 1931 he was knighted. Rothenstein came to know Christiana during the 1890s and would become increasingly involved in her campaigns. He described her as he remembered her in 1932.

> Mrs. Herringham had a dominating personality. Endowed with rare integrity of character, she expected much from her friends, both as artists, if they were artists, and as men and women facing the perplexing problems of life. There was something imperious in her nature, which at once commanded respect; and when she singled me out, insisting I had more to say in my work than other painters, I

> found it hard to maintain the standard she expected. Having gained a rare knowledge through copying—her copies were unique—she looked, in contemporary painting, for that combination of intense observation of particular form coupled with a worthy subject matter, which was the glory of Florentine artists.[1]

If she thought that his work sometimes fell short of that lofty standard, her criticisms were severe and uncompromising. She would say, "Why, that is only *genre* painting, which many artists can produce." Rothenstein's ideal was painting that avoided mere imitation, which was "*not* the sincerest flattery," and he tried to "wring all I could out of my subject, to aim at what was beyond me rather than achieve an easier and more attractive result. . . ." That aim sometimes exacted a penalty in discouragement. After seeing the Florentine frescoes for the first time, he came home with the feeling that he had experienced something new and immensely important, but his work "remained much as before." However, because he felt that she understood his aim, "Mrs Herringham's friendship was an asset to my life." Perhaps this unwillingness to countenance compromise was the characteristic that would complicate her relations with the committees of the National Art Collections Fund.[2]

Even before the formation of a provisional committee to consider the nature of the organization, there was an early, original, and smaller group of founders who came together to discuss ways and means of keeping for the nation at least some of the great works of art that private collectors were selling to foreign purchasers. The informal meeting was the result of a letter from Christiana in which she took up a suggestion from the painter, journalist, and art critic D. S. MacColl—a suggestion that for nearly three years had lain fallow and disregarded. In September 1900 MacColl had published in the *Saturday Review* three related reports on the great international exhibition at Paris, one of the many that succeeded the Crystal Palace Exhibition of 1851, and in December he added a fourth, concluding article, "Friends of the National Gallery."

The first report, "Art at the Paris Exhibition: I," begins, "I am not sorry to think that a growing distaste for the vulgarity of monster exhibitions has at least some share in the financial failure of the latest." That was the Brussels exhibition of 1897. According to *Times* reports, however, Britain's entry had covered its expenses by the end of July, and Britain's net balance (exclusive of the Fine Art Section) was £2,500 pounds. But there was no doubt about the vulgarity. Competitive numbers were the measure of quality, and there was dismay because Britain had failed to shine relative to Belgium and France in the "general industrial department, which is, of course, in the eyes of the organisers and the general public, the most important."[3]

However, those Britons who felt that they had been eclipsed in the industrial field at Brussels found some consolation in the final tally of gold and silver medals in the Fine Art Section. Nationality counted; the *Times* correspondent pointedly mentioned that "Mr Whistler is not here, but he is of uncertain nationality and of no school." Numbers counted; there were more than two hundred oil paintings by British artists, in addition to sculpture, engravings, and architecture. All this at least had shown that England was "no longer regarded by foreigners as it was regarded 50 years ago, as a barren and a stony land in which the arts cannot grow." Nevertheless, art had no place in the final accounting. Of a national Treasury grant of £5,500, £820 remained. The request was made that that balance be reserved, not for art, but "so as to insure the system of a ready and useful means of thus promoting British trade and of giving publicity to industrial enterprises."[4]

The Paris exhibition of 1900 was little different with respect to the fine arts, except that Whistler received a gold medal in the engravings division. The anxious competitiveness that MacColl had so disliked at Brussels prevailed also at Paris, for in a preemptive burst of chauvinism and on the basis of a rumor reported in *Figaro*, France had seized the initiative from Germany for this event intended as "a synthesis of the last century." According to the *Times*, many Germans believed the rumor was intentionally planted so as to foist off on France the risk of what must be an expensive failure. The exhibition's final balance sheet showed a deficit of two million francs, which the French government claimed was "satisfactory."[5]

MacColl hoped that the Paris exhibition would be "the last of the kind," for whatever the advantages to mechanical inventions, the fine arts would "have nothing to regret in losing these international outings." The inevitable competition was "cruel to all but the strongest" and destructive of the "concentration and singleness of mind that a work of art demands, so that a favouring mood may grow up about it, aiding and giving volume to its intention, is out of the question: all stand stripped and naked for a merely athletic contest, and, instead of being so many guides to reverie and emotion, look like candidates nervously estimating the marks they will win." English visitors, footsore and hungry, tended to go from room to room counting pictures by English painters and tallying medals "down to the small change of bronze." The whole experience was like a stopover at "some railway station, where savourless soup is served again directly dessert has been cleared away: only it is served to the same company."[6] The monumental catalogue, being only alphabetical, was not as helpful as it might have been.

The best that MacColl could suggest was a way for thoughtful visitors to get the most out of their time. "I purpose in this article to indicate how a visitor who has already a fairly wide acquaintance with French and modern art generally may best concentrate his energies." He quickly summarized the ground plan of the exhibition and warned that art in the Japanese, Spanish, and German pavilions could not be seen without written permission from the commissioners. He then drew out of the mass "the two great characteristic efforts of French art in this century," clues to the strengths of modern art: the painting and draftsmanship of Géricault, Delacroix, Daumier, and Millet. English visitors would learn more by appreciating "the real illumination that crowned them, than by worrying as to whether England has been well represented or properly marked"—if, that is, they could rid themselves of the prevailing spirit of chauvinistic competitiveness.[7]

MacColl's second and third articles continued his effort to make the English cast their sights across the Channel. In the second he discusses Manet, whose "open-air work" was instructive and satisfying because "the main positive point is always seized and not smothered by timid joinery." Manet's great secret was that he knew how to be selective; he carried "this abandon of pretence, this jettison of half the doubtful facts for the sake of certain precious salvage to an extreme point." The result was the "fresh daylight colour" that others failed to achieve. MacColl saw the Paris exhibition as the "last rally of the great generation of the *Refusés*," but even there they were cheated of their full effect, for works of Manet, Degas, Legros, Fantin-Latour, and Whistler were scattered in the crowd instead of having a gallery all their own.[8]

The third article discusses Rodin, whose work stood out from the mass of miscellaneous sculpture because he was "a fanatic of human form," "a real watcher, who knows the facts [of the human body] and can seize new patterns in them." This had nothing to do with the " 'well posed' statue, that soft vacant embarrassed porter of the luggage of his own limbs." English visitors should make an effort to see Rodin's drawings, which traced the steps by which he achieved such splendid effects.[9] The English must make an effort, do some homework, shed a lot of old ideas and make room for new ones.

MacColl's fourth article, "Friends of the National Gallery," contained the idea that he wanted to plant in the English public mind. This article begins, "Writing about the Paris Exhibition I urged English visitors, instead of frittering their attention, to fix it on two currents of genius," the great draftsmen of the first half of the nineteenth century and Rodin the contemporary, both currents French, each capable of illuminating the study of art of any period. Now MacColl brought the lesson home by urging readers to go and see three Daumier drawings at the Dutch Gallery in Brook Street and by laying blame for the general lack of perception where he thought it belonged: on the British art establishment.

> I suppose the directors of our national collections must shake an official head if one suggests that here are modern works of art worth scores of the pictures that appeal to the historical mind because they fill gaps—gaps in the second rate. In any case the committee system that rules the purchase of pictures makes such a departure past praying for. But the goodwill that has been shown in the recent Rodin subscription, (officials, free from official responsibilities and

> qualms, joining in as gladly as the rest,) makes one think that the want of courage and of money by which our national collection frequently suffers might be remediable by a little concentrated effort from without.[10]

Public spirit expressed through private subscriptions was not new; in that way the nation had recently acquired pictures by Madox Brown, Legros, and Burne-Jones. MacColl's article on Rodin had drawn a response from the sculptor John Tweed, who wrote to the *Saturday Review* to suggest that a bronze of one of Rodin's works be acquired for a London gallery. Louis-Antoine Barye's *Lion* was the only representative of modern French sculpture in any British public collection. The *Saturday Review*—MacColl, of course—endorsed the plan of private subscription at once as a way to redress "some of the stupidities of the past," and Ernest Beckett, M.P., wrote to say that anyone who had seen Rodin's *Le Baiser* in the sculpture gallery at Paris ought to have realized how different it was from "the monstrous regiment of white, gleaming, undraped females, that had confronted one on every side" at the Paris exhibition. An *ad hoc* committee of eight artists gathered, decided to request a bronze of Rodin's *St. John the Baptist Preaching,* and set out to raise the necessary £160.[11]

This was gratifying, but MacColl wanted more than ad hoc efforts by hastily constituted committees. More than one Rodin subscriber, MacColl said, had wondered why there could not be "a permanent body of subscribers" to "secure from time to time works of art that the officials and the Treasury cannot give us." The committee of Les Amis du Louvre considered it a duty "to mark down and stalk examples of painters who are badly wanted in the Louvre and quietly bag them when they come into the market." MacColl could have added that Wilhelm Bode, Director of the Kaiser Friedrich Museum in Berlin, who made it his business to know the contents of British private collections, had as his support the Kaiser Friedrich Museum Verein, "a body of wealthy and knowledgeable art lovers to whom he could turn as soon as any work of stature came onto the market."[12]

Bode was so well informed that in 1857 Prince Albert had brought him in as principal organizer of the British Art Treasures Exhibition in Manchester, "the first large exhibition for the public of works of art from private collections in England"—which was tantamount to setting the fox among the hens. Bode had only to refer to the writings of earlier German art explorers like Gustav Friedrich Waagen and Johann David Passavant, who had left systematic accounts of their visits to collections in Britain. In 1900 it was ironic that "far and away the most important work of its kind" was Waagen's *Works of Art and Artists in England,* published in German and in English in 1838, translated and expanded by Lady Eastlake in 1854 as *Treasures of Art in Great Britain.*[13]

In the 1880s the pace of the quiet bagging of works of stature from British private collections accelerated markedly, and American millionaires snatched up what France and Germany did not secure for themselves. Very aptly, this came to be called "the Great Exodus."[14] Reasons for it were principally three. First, the worldwide agricultural depression of the 1880s bore heavily on the owners of the great landed estates; agricultural output, land values, and rentals all fell; and in 1894 landowners were hard hit by an 8 percent levy in death duties on estates valued at more than a million pounds.

How did they cope? First, they sold off parcels of their ancestral lands. David Cannadine says:

> Psychologically and symbolically, as well as economically and financially, the sale of so much land so quickly by so many was the most significant evidence of the transformation and decline of what had once been the British landed establishment. . . . When agricultural acres were hard to sell (as they often were) and when sentiment dictated that they should be retained at all cost (as it sometimes did), many landowners preferred to realize alternative assets, which could find more ready buyers and also realize a much better price: collieries and minerals, docks and harbours, building estates and market halls, country houses and London mansions, works of art and family heirlooms. . . . the great accumulators had become the great dispensers.[15]

If the mansions went, there were fewer fine rooms in which to display great pictures and statues. When the Louvre, the Kaiser Friedrich Museum, and American millionaires all bid against one another for the works of art, prices rose and the money made it possible to retain the mansions and the land—for a time.

Another explanation for the foreigners' success was the Treasury's frequent failure to release funds that would save endangered works by putting them into the national collections. And sometimes the administrators of those collections let such works go, not only because of financial need but also because they lacked personal enthusiasm for specific works offered and therefore refused them. A number of great works were retained, but far too many got away, as was the case in 1885–1886 when the Duke of Marlborough sold masses of treasures from Blenheim Castle.

Ruskin advanced yet another explanation. He blamed the dissolution on democracy, by which he meant the consequences of the Third Reform Bill, which became law in 1884 and 1885; it doubled the electorate from three million to six million men and redrew constituency boundaries in ways that weakened the legislative influences of the landowners. True, said Ruskin, many masterpieces had been saved, some by prompt action from the Treasury, but there was, "be it to our humiliation remembered—small reason to congratulate ourselves on the enlargement of the collection now belonging to the public, by the sale of the former possessions of our nobles." Their estates, "once the pride, beauty, and political strength of England are doomed by the progress of democracy. . . ."[16] In the early days of the National Art Collections Fund, some of its members hesitated at first to embrace the broader, democratic approach wholeheartedly, but in due course it would enable the Fund to fill many gaps left by Treasury or art administrators or both.

In 1900 MacColl thought in terms of two committees and two funds: an elite committee of wealthy guarantors who would help to rescue the most expensive old masters, and another committee of "the comparatively poor and needy, artists and the like," who might see to the modern works that came more cheaply. With two such groups in action, "some of these losses of ancient art might be prevented, and some of the treasures of modern art secured before they reach a famine price." Two hundred members, he thought, paying an annual guinea each would "do the business." Any funds accumulated would be applied to the most urgent cases, and "there ought to be no rule of buying annually, the money being reserved until it is really wanted."[17]

Modern art, and the French school in particular, most concerned MacColl, but under the existing system modern English art, too, had fared badly. It was supposedly provided for under the provisions of the bequest from the sculptor Sir Francis Chantrey, which went to the National Gallery after the death of Lady Chantrey in 1875. It amounted to more than £100,000 for acquisitions, and it instructed its administrators to purchase "works of fine Art of the highest merit in painting and sculpture that can be obtained" by artists past, present, and future. The artists themselves need not be of British nationality, but the works must have been executed in the British Isles and must be exhibited for at least one month in the year following purchase in the annual exhibition of the Royal Academy or in some important public exhibition of fine art.[18]

Sir Francis had entrusted administration to the president and council of the Royal Academy "or of such other society or association" of sufficient prestige and good taste. Thus the president and council, whose members were often also trustees of the National Gallery, became the responsible body. However, they had got into the habit of assuming that the Royal Academy's was the *only* important public exhibition of fine art in Britain and looked no farther than their own exhibition rooms. Sir Francis had intended his bequest to encourage foreign artists to come and work in Britain, but the trustees resolutely ignored qualified expatriate painters such as Whistler, Sargent, Corot, Delacroix, Degas, Fantin-Latour, Pissarro, Sisley, and more—all of them artists whose work executed during residence in Britain could have relieved the Chantrey Collection's "accumulated dreariness." The collection was augmented by "other unwanted odds and ends from [the National Gallery's] own crowded rooms," and the whole was segregated in the gallery presented by the sugar magnate Samuel Tate.[19]

For some time MacColl and others had questioned the administration of the Chantrey Fund, but in 1900 he said only that it was "very badly administered, partly because of the defect in its provisions by which works are always bought raw from the exhibitions of the year, partly from its having been turned into a relief fund for academicians." MacColl admitted that his suggestion for a society of friends of the National Gallery was only "an indulgence in kite-flying," but he threw it out for "discussion by whom it concerns."[20]

Kites often come to grief or float away never to be seen again. Only two concerned persons responded. One suggested limited acquisitions from "the work of foreign living artists; foreign so that the association may not develop into a second Chantrey Fund." The other warned that a new society such as MacColl proposed should not hand over its purchases "immediately and unconditionally to the authorities in exchange for house room." It should lend, not give, them for a few years while opinion about them consolidated itself. Both correspondents suggested that interested persons give their contributions to John Tweed's Rodin Fund and that those subscribers might become the nucleus of a society of friends of the National Gallery.[21]

That was all. No further action was suggested. No response came from those whom the immediate crisis most affected, the Director and trustees of the National Gallery and the president and council of the Royal Academy in their role as Chantrey trustees. First with heavy irony, then in direct assault, MacColl concentrated on the Academy, whose position and influence gave it great powers for good, if it would but use them. "Poor Academy! Is everyone to turn against it?" he wrote in a review of its 1901 spring exhibition. A "lamblike press" had become captious. Even the recently crowned king, who turned out to have a mind of his own about art, "descends as the stern authoritative censor, re-hangs the exhibition, brings down despised merit to the line, packs off no end of masterpieces, substituting crepe for them, as something less extravagantly mournful." Even "that meek creature the Novel has revolted"—not the "dangerous observant moral novel, but the nice harmless sentimental" type beloved of Mudie's, the influential lending library.[22]

"The whole social machine, of which Academy and Novel are a part, is severely threatened," MacColl continued. A Royal Academician, not an expert painter or even an expert murderer, was the villain of W. J. Laidlay's novel *Lena Laird.* But, MacColl observed, Laidlay, who was already known as a stern critic of the Academy, if he intended an Academy-reforming novel, should have utilized his hero to explain "how you may go on pouring goodish men into the Academy to the end of time and they will never reform it." Let the villain be a young artist of middling skills who becomes discouraged when his avant-garde group falls into dissension. When invited to join the Royal Academy, "in he goes" and becomes progressively more insulated against the rest of society. "Of newcomers outside he is aware but vaguely; tends to think them rather a nuisance, and gradually takes on the determination of the office-holder to defend his privileges against the outside world." The preservation of averageness would be his crime.[23]

In April 1903 MacColl put aside the cloak of irony and charged the Chantrey trustees outright with maladministration of Sir Francis Chantrey's bequest, as intended for purchase of the best available works of art executed in Britain. MacColl challenged readers to go to the Tate Gallery with a copy of Sir Francis's will in hand and see whether those pictures were really outstanding. Sir Francis himself, could he now visit the Tate Gallery, must conclude that he had provided for work by *British* artists *only,* by *living* British artists *only,* and exhibited *only* in the year of purchase and *only* at the Royal Academy. With respect to quality, the verdict must be that the pictures represented "some passing dubious fashion" or "sensation of the year" that time had already discredited. Works of "promise" was the only charitable interpretation of the pictures—but Sir Francis's will mentioned no such category. It was impossible that the trustees might not know the terms of the will, for it was read at each of their meetings.[24]

MacColl suggested that the trustees begin to make compensation by buying for the nation a picture by Whistler. They may dislike Whistler's work or Whistler himself, but personal antipathy, "if it exists, should not interfere with a public duty." Chantrey money, he charged, was being used largely to benefit the Academy's own exhibitors. If there were no improvement, a Parliamentary inquiry was in order. The Chantrey Bequest had been assigned not to the

Academy but to the nation and was therefore public money. In May 1903, still emphasizing responsibility to the public, MacColl warned that the trustees "will find themselves no longer in sympathy with public opinion when they employ an official code less strict than the man of the world would expect in private affairs, and enforce in commercial."[25]

MacColl's articles stirred up a storm of letters, editorial articles, and responses (except from the Royal Academy) about shortcomings in the administration of the Chantrey Bequest, about the need for a Parliamentary inquiry, and about definitions of the arts—that is, were decorative arts distinct from fine arts and thus unwelcome at the Academy?

At the time of the Brussels exhibition, Charles Robert Ashbee, architect and crafts advocate, spoke for the craft designers and workers when he told the president of the Royal Academy that "so little appears to have been done for decorative art that I hardly feel justified in being called upon to [participate]." The Arts and Crafts Exhibition Society had hoped to submit work, but the Brussels exhibition was "treated so very much as a pictorial one" that they felt excluded. In March 1903 MacColl had joined the issue of the decorative arts to that of England's international standing when he charged that the Royal Academy had neglected still another duty. What, he asked, was being done about English art for the St. Louis exhibition of 1904? If monster exhibitions were to continue as a feature on the international scene, let England at least make preparations of which the nation might be proud.[26]

As early as 1900, MacColl noted, other countries had completed their arrangements and had reserved choice exhibition sites at St. Louis; the French and the Germans had snapped up the two main pavilions flanking the American pavilion. But "England, as in some other cases, seems to be content to occupy a small annexe to the German gallery." As usual, England had plenty of art but no organizing, whereas "Germany has first-rate organising, though very little art." No English committee even existed until 1903; all its members were Royal Academicians, and there was no indication that other artists would be included. Where were the New English Art Club, the Arts and Crafts Exhibition Society? "Is it to be expected that the art workers who are recognised neither in the exhibition nor the constitution of the Academy at home should take what is given them abroad without a word" with respect to space and arrangements? And painters "who have been driven by the unfriendliness of the Academy at home into forming their own societies, shall [they] entrust their interests abroad to this Committee with no guarantee of proper treatment?" The committee's policy "will certainly endanger the British Section at St. Louis." Once again, the Academy had shown itself "incapable of playing a national part."[27]

The Chantrey controversy, with all its ramifications, was now irretrievably in the open. Provisions of the Chantrey will were quoted, misquoted, explicated, contradicted, and also sidelined while partisans traded recriminations about personal tastes and political motivations. The Academy's defenders assumed that Academicians were English gentlemen and therefore incapable of dishonesty, a charge that MacColl had been careful not to make—yet. Still the Academy made no case for itself, which raised the question, why not?[28] However, all the arguments lost much of their point when placed against one salient fact: great works of art, if saved for the national collections, could inspire English artists, educate the public, and confer international standing. Their irrevocable dispersal abroad only increased British cultural parochialism. *National* began to be the key word, and repeatedly the point was made that art in the *national* collections belonged to the *nation;* a nation was made up of individuals, and nothing would change unless and until there was a larger body of concerned and well-informed public opinion.[29] That body was about to come into being.

In June 1903, very quietly, there occurred the first intimation that a wider public than ever before was soon to have an opportunity to share the responsibility for the nation's art heritage. On 10 June, Christiana Herringham wrote a letter to MacColl. Much later, he recalled her as a

> lady of remarkable artistic learning and public spirit. . . . She had borne in mind a project I had sketched in the *Saturday Review* of

> December 15, 1900, for the foundation of a "Friends of the National Gallery," and now revived it with the offer, "if I really meant it," of £200 for initial expenses. It is easy to make suggestions: Lady Herringham, by this act, became the real Founder of the Fund. The fiery cross was at once sent out: Mr. Roger Fry joined in recruiting; we secured the support of Sir Claude Phillips, who had written often and vigorously about the drain of masterpieces [from England]; of Sir Sidney Colvin, and of other elder critics and connoisseurs.[30]

Christiana Herringham, MacColl, Fry, and Phillips were the original four. A little later came Charles John Holmes, who brought practical experience from a family publishing firm. Indeed, all four of the men brought something from professions they had left behind. MacColl's father, the Reverend Dougald MacColl, was a well-known Glasgow preacher. The son, Dougald Sutherland MacColl, was educated in London and at Lincoln College, Oxford. He intended to follow his father into the ministry or to settle into the academic life but drifted instead into lecturing for the Oxford Extension Society. He had formal art training at the Westminster School of Art and, like Fry, educated his eyes by travel: three years of looking at pictures and sculpture in France, Italy, and other Continental countries. In 1889 he had moved into journalism by becoming art critic for the *Spectator.* In 1896 he began to write regularly for the *Saturday Review;* it became MacColl's pulpit from which to hurl jeremiads at artistic cant and administrative conservatism.[31]

Roger Fry had paid a severe price for his place in the brotherhood of artists, and he prized it. His Quaker father, Sir Edward Fry, had intended his son for science, projecting him toward a career that the father had been unable to follow. At Cambridge, Roger began in science, then declared for a career as a painter. Sir Edward's deep disapproval combined the disappointment of an ambitious parent and the Victorian reluctance to allow art equal ranking with the "useful" professions. He was a distinguished specialist in legal arbitration, but science received his spare-time curiosity. Had it been his profession, he would have followed it with the same passion that his son gave to art, but decisions to devote themselves to apparently opposing values drove a wedge between them. Roger's study of

Bellini, however, had given him standing among art critics; he began to write for the magazine *Pilot,* and in 1901 he became a writer for the *Athenaeum.* Thus he and MacColl between them reached readers of two of the most important contemporary journals interested in literature and the arts. "Criticism suited his abilities," Frances Spalding says of Fry, and "he quickly developed a conversational style and with his practical experience as a painter he revealed an insider's understanding of his subject."[32]

Claude Phillips, the son of a London court jeweler, had qualified as a solicitor and barrister but found the law uninspiring. In his late thirties he began to write on art for the *Portfolio,* whose editor was the liberally inclined Philip Hamerton, whose attitude of practical irreverence Phillips liked. Five scholarly monographs published by the *Portfolio* established Phillips as an art historian, and in 1903 he became Keeper of the Wallace Collection of paintings, only recently moved to Hertford House in Manchester Square. MacColl, writing on Phillips for *The Dictionary of National Biography,* said that his "approach to painting reflected a fervently emotional nature. If his sense of a painter's quality was not so strong, he was anxiously wide-minded, honourably and fiercely independent of personal influence or any taint of commerce."[33]

C. J. Holmes was another clergyman's son, from Preston, Lancashire. He made a muddled beginning, attending seven different and unsatisfactory schools. At Eton he was diligent but unsystematic. Ruskin's *Modern Painters* turned him toward landscape study and painting, and at Brasenose College, Oxford, he came under the influence of Walter Pater and his circle. From them he passed into the avant-garde art fellowship of Charles Ricketts and Charles Shannon at The Vale, London. He had worked in most departments of the family printing business, which made him a great asset to their Vale Press.[34]

Thus the new venture was to benefit from MacColl's sense of mission, from Fry's concern for historical and aesthetic continuities in art and from his scientific interest in the physical elements of a painting, from Phillips's honorable independence and his connections with the Wallace Collection, and from Holmes's practical experience. Christiana Herringham, bearing in mind her father's injunction to use her inheritance with "kindness and thoughtful liberality," contributed loyalty, ideas, and the money that brought the National Art Collections Fund into being and therefore made possible a redefinition of the national attitude toward Britain's art heritage. No doubt someone, sooner or later, would have made such a move. But at that time no one had, and in the meantime how many prized works would have left Britain for owners abroad!

The first *recorded* meeting of the Fund's original four organizers took place on 7 July 1903 at 40 Wimpole Street, which was now the Herringhams' home. An earlier meeting or meetings of the originators, equally or perhaps even more important, took place before that date. On 7 July, however, new recruits were present. Besides both Herringhams, Fry, and MacColl, there were John Postle Heseltine, Thomas Powell's business partner, now retired and devoting himself to art and art collecting; Charles Holroyd, Keeper of the Tate Gallery and thus of the Chantrey Collection; John Bowyer Buchanan Nichols, painter, poet, art critic, and an Oxford contemporary of MacColl's; and David Alexander Edward Lindsay, Lord Balcarres, Conservative M.P. and owner of a famous library and an important art collection. The ninth member of that group was Christiana's cousin by marriage, Robert Clermont Witt, solicitor, connoisseur. Holmes could not be present. Phillips was ill and had been ordered away to France for a rest cure from 4 July until 15 August.[35]

The invitation to Balcarres to join them as chairman came from the original four. On their behalf Phillips had written to Balcarres on 20 June 1903:

> We are very anxious to obtain your sympathy and cooperation in connection with the following matter. MacColl (Sat. Review) Roger Fry (Athenaeum) and I desire to form a "Society of Friends of the National Gallery" analogous in aim and also to a certain extent in constitution, to the "Société des Amis du Louvre" which has already done such good work in Paris. We propose to gather together a few of those most vitally interested in the plan, and to hold a first meeting—to settle the constitution &c—at 40 Wimpole Street, on Tuesday 7th July at 11:30 a.m.—this time [set as] being best for the occasion by

> Mrs Herringham, a lady greatly interested in the great cause. We are particularly anxious that you should, if possible, attend that meeting, and that you should consent to act as chairman or President of the Executive Committee.

They would reserve details of the plan until they met. Phillips closed with the hope "that you will see your way to actively promote a cause in which I know you are greatly interested."[36]

Balcarres was an eminently suitable choice. Born in 1871, he was young enough in 1903 to be interested and active in new movements, and he brought with him the prestige of an ancient name and a long and knowledgeable association with literature and the arts. John Vincent, editor of his journals, writes:

> The successive Earls of Crawford and Balcarres were the Medici of Britain. Many other landed families have had more wealth, and over a longer period. Some have applied their wealth for short periods, but with less skill, as at Mentmore. Many great collections founded in the eighteenth century ceased to grow in the nineteenth. . . . No family has sustained its interest over four generations so fruitfully, or combined collection, scholarship, and innovation with such impact upon the development of whole subjects. They showed what aristocracy might have meant, and what in nineteenth-century Britain it usually failed to mean.[37]

The Lindsay collections began with the book collecting of Alexander William Lindsay, the twenty-fifth Earl. He built up one of Britain's great libraries, and the twenty-sixth Earl, James Ludovic Lindsay, who wrote the influential *Sketches of the History of Christian Art*, continued to expand both library and historical collections.[38] "The great Lindsay collections," writes John Vincent, "were not built up, as is often the case, from capital, for no capital was ever realised. They were established by zeal, taste, discernment and originality, from income, and on a low market." The Lindsays' ascendance was made possible by ownership of Lancashire coalfields and by the Wigan engineering industry. In 1880 the twenty-sixth Earl had to pay £10,000 in estate duties upon succession to the title, and in 1913 Balcarres, by that time the twenty-seventh Earl, would have to pay £107,000 on his father's estate. "This was the point, therefore, at which the family collections ceased to expand significantly or to enter upon new fields."[39] In 1903, however, that later blow had not yet fallen.

Balcarres must have responded to Phillips with some ideas of his own, for Fry next wrote: "We can discuss your view about the extension of its scope on which at present I have a perfectly open mind, although it seems to me that the conditions are not quite the same in England as in France or Germany where all the various branches of art are collected into a single institution. However, that is just one of the suggestions with which our preliminary meeting should deal."[40]

At the meeting on 7 July more names were added to the list: Ernest William Beckett, Sir William Martin Conway, Sir Herbert Frederick Cook, Herbert Percy Horne, and Sidney Colvin. Another meeting was set for 14 July at 74 Brook Street, Balcarres's London residence. That evening he wrote in his journal: "Presided at the inaugural meeting of what is to be a great Museum League."[41]

Decisions about procedures came first. On 8 July, Christiana, who had assumed, or had been assigned, secretarial duties, wrote to Balcarres to ask who was to send out invitations to the meeting on 14 July. Christiana had not sent them because she was waiting for typewritten copies of the agenda. She told Balcarres that "it would be more influential if you could send them yourself." (Apparently, he did so, for most of the replies came to him.) Her letter also made it clear that it was she who had brought Heseltine into the group.

> It was most gratifying to me that Mr Heseltine came to our meeting and seemed so keenly interested in the foundation of the league. I had scarcely dare[d] to expect it. He is an old friend but I was afraid he might feel fettered by his official position. His personal weight, connoisseurship and experience and his position as trustee for many years of the National Gallery may do much to guide us through difficulties which have sometimes seemed to me almost insuperable, and might we not hope for gifts from his fine collection?
>
> If we could by any means persuade him to become chairman of the sub-committee for pictures, his rare combination of knowledge both of art & of business would be of the highest service.

She did not specify the "insuperable difficulties," but we may assume that she meant, at least, the deficiencies in Chantrey administration and the possibilities of further public criticism. She stated also her opinion that since MacColl, as well as several of the newer members, must miss the meeting on 14 July, it would be better to "confine our efforts *principally* to arranging for a more fully representative meeting in October. Don't you feel that it is very important for the British Museum to be represented before any final conclusions are reached?" And she added, "They say I threw the stone in so you must forgive my watching the eddy!"[42]

That last statement is the first suggestion of the protective diffidence that she was more and more to place between herself and her male colleagues on the committee. At the same time, she indicated her intention not to be the reticent female who sacrificed her due credit to them. The alternation suggested the kinds of uncertainties that could give even strong-minded women pause as they stepped into the public sphere.

A letter of 9 July from Witt to Balcarres indicated a second tiny fault line in the solidarity of what was to become the provisional committee of the National Art Collections Fund. Witt suggested a private meeting with Balcarres, and as time went on this would become an increasingly fissiparous pattern. Colvin, who was just married, could not attend the 14 July meeting, but he pointed out another cause of potential trouble. He was, he told Balcarres, "persuaded of the extreme importance of the initial steps. It is a matter I have long had in mind and hoped some day to lend a hand. . . . It strikes me that one of the greatest difficulties, only to be got round by much tact and management, will be to avoid absolute discouragement and hostility on the part of the National Gallery board itself as at present constituted."[43]

On 14 July (whether before or after the meeting is unclear) a letter from Christiana to Balcarres made her discomfort more specific. "It would not be possible for me to bring other ladies without the permission of the rest of the provisional committee—and I don't think I could remain alone when the Council is rightly constituted." She mentions four women of her acquaintance who would be admirable additions, one of them the Newnham College classical scholar Jane Harrison. In a postscript Christiana suggested Lady Wantage, Balcarres's great-aunt and herself owner of an important art collection, as one who might suggest other women. But, she noted, "There are of course no women holding exactly the official positions of the men of the committee."[44]

Of course. Society's attitude toward women as working members of public-policy-making bodies was even more difficult of solution than prejudices about divorce and votes for women. Those at least could be made the goals of specific campaigns. The Society for Promoting Reform in the Marriage and Divorce Laws of England, like the fledgling Fund another new straw in the winds of hoped-for change, was founded in 1903 and the Divorce Law Reform Association soon afterward. In 1906 they would merge as the Divorce Law Reform Union, but a Royal commission to consider actual reforms was not appointed until 1909. The excesses of the suffragettes, which overshadowed in the news the more orderly educational campaign of the suffragists who rallied to Millicent Fawcett's leadership, created an image of woman on the rampage and therefore betraying home, husband, children, and society. Women who aspired to a role in policy-making and administration could be suspected of similar delinquency; in any case, many women feared that they might be thus suspected. "The trouble with women during the Edwardian period was simply that their troubles could not be kept separate and distinct, but kept getting mixed up with each other and with other social issues. . . . Edwardian Englishmen, seeing women rioting, burning, destroying property, and even dying, drew back in alarm from a cause that threatened to loose that rage for chaos upon the world of men."[45]

Christiana Herringham was far from being a rioter; she admired Millicent Fawcett's emphasis on education and persuasion instead of violence, and she knew very well that the acceptance of women on boards and committees that made national policy depended upon changes in public opinion that were even slower and more subtle than those governing divorce and suffrage. "They" said that she "threw the stone in," and she *knew* that that first stone was hers, but it seemed safer under the circumstances not to lay first-person claim to it. She remained a spectator on the bank of the river, watching the aftereffects and begging for recognition of her presence from those who would probably sail away from her. They must forgive her for "watching the eddy!" The exclamation mark was her self-protective signal that they must not take her too seriously.

Christiana went out of her way not to flaunt the fact of her gift of two hundred pounds. On 19 July she asked Balcarres "when I should pay the part or whole of the sum (£200) I offered for initial expenses. Please do not mention it at the Committee but let me know privately." She added: "I hope I shall not give further trouble this time of writing. I shall just await an intimation from you."[46]

The expanded committee met on 14 July at Brook Street. Those added since the 7 July meeting were Lionel Henry Cust, Surveyor of the King's Pictures and Director of the National Portrait Gallery; and Sir John Maxwell Stirling-Maxwell, a trustee of the National Gallery of Scotland. As Christiana had noted, Phillips and MacColl could not attend. Those present decided to call the new organization "The National Art Collections League." Its object would be assistance to acquisitions for the national collections. Members would pay an annual guinea each, and donations would be welcome. Those who had attended both meetings now constituted themselves a provisional committee to carry on until the new league was formally established. One-third of an elected council would retire each year, and the committee would appoint an honorary buyer of pictures. Provisional officers were Balcarres, chairman; Ernest Beckett, treasurer; and Roger Fry and Robert Witt, joint honorary secretaries.[47]

Christiana's proposal for more women on the committee was settled in private on 16 July. From the correspondence it appears that Balcarres at first agreed, then changed his mind. Whether the question was referred to other men on the provisional committee and perhaps vetoed there remains unclear, but originally his decision was certainly favorable, for Christiana now wrote: "I bow to your decision! You see it was right not to take you immediately at your word and bring any ladies I liked." Again the protective exclamation mark adds a jokiness to take some of the sting out of the rejection.[48]

However, she kept her foot in the door. She would not bring other women in "immediately," but she continued to press her point of their usefulness. "Those I suggested are those of my acquaintance who have expert knowledge but there are other useful qualifications to be considered." That is, women could have both expert knowledge of art and organizational wisdom. She demonstrated her own wisdom by writing that "I should prefer 'Fund' to League. I think the less combative the name is the more good can be done—and the name emphasises the need of money which is the great need." She reminded Balcarres of her "original Hope"—original, since the relaunch of MacColl's grounded kite had indeed originated with her—"that this society might start a strong influence which would make England rather less of a market for the foreigner. It seems [a] terrible pity that the results of the long work of our aristocracy in collecting pictures and fostering art should all be cast to the wind." On the same day, Witt told Balcarres that he liked the name "Fund" but thought it rather impersonal, which might prove a future disadvantage.[49] However, "Fund" it became and remains.

Once money was in hand, how was it to be distributed? Fry was concerned that the Fund should in every case avoid making anyone feel pressured, either by being asked outright for money or by being "put under some kind of moral pressure to give more than they wished." Willing contribution should be the goal. Members should give "in proportion to their interests and means, and it will be on these sums that we shall rely for the bulk of our purchasing." Some might give on an appeal to "their special hobby, who would be slow to give on grounds of public spirit." In that case, purchasing from a general fund could cause difficulty. Fry suggested three divisions for money: one for ancient pictures and drawings, one for other ancient works, and one for modern art. "You will I fear think me tenacious on this point," he told Balcarres, "but it is from my knowledge of other people and not from a personal preference for any one branch of our society. For except for a slight disinclination to buy modern pictures I am quite impartial."[50] The all-important requirement was that the widow with her mite be made to feel as welcome as the millionaire.

However, as planning proceeded, the widow and her mite seemed in danger of disappearing amid efforts to enlist conspicuously influential persons. This greatly worried Fry. By law, the Chantrey money was the nation's money, but no law specified how the Fund should present itself to the nation. Was this new Fund to be truly *national* in the sense that every citizen who contributed, no matter how modestly, might share the feeling of proprietorship in and responsibility for the national collections? Fry argued for the broader interpretation and for expansion and reformulation of the older tradition of English private connoisseurship and patronage. For several centuries that tradition had been empowered by the aristocracy's money and leisure for travel and collecting abroad, which established its influence in the art world. At the 14 July meeting it had been suggested that "influential persons be invited to become Vice Presidents, & that the Council sh^{d} consist as far as possible of working members." Fry read this to mean that there would be working members and there would be ornamental members whose names on the Fund's letterhead would set an elitist tone and demonstrate prestigious backing—but would also suggest to the ordinary citizen an unfortunate exclusivity. At the 22 July meeting the provisional committee determined that a "large and representative council (to include Vice Presidents) should administer funds."[51]

As influential names for vice presidents accumulated, Fry became increasingly perturbed, and on 23 July he wrote to Balcarres:

> I think to some extent we have fallen between *stalwarts* & *influentials.* We have aimed at big names for the most part though I think they will nearly all give in sympathy. Still I would include in this a few more whose names need not necessarily appear in the next circular but whose adhesion would be advantageous. I have a number of friends both artists & patrons, in a small way, some of whom wld. be energetic & public spirited & when assistance even from the first would do no harm though they would not count as influential. Mr. A. M. Daniel for instance whom I proposed is a very influential person in Scarborough & would bring in a good many local people and would also help with money though perhaps not with large sums. Then I believe Mr. Rothenstein's name wld. carry weight with the younger artists. I only suggest that we should get the adhesion of

> such men even though it is not thought important to swell unduly our list of supporters by printing their names.

Such people, Fry thought, would willingly join sooner or later, "but it is not a bad thing to get people who are enthusiastic at once for fear they shd. feel they had been left out too long."[52]

His misgivings only deepened when Witt submitted twenty-six names of prospective vice presidents. Of those, thirteen were knighted or titled. At the time neither Daniel nor Rothenstein would have been on such a list. In 1930 Augustus Moore Daniel of Scarborough would become Sir Augustus; in 1931 Rothenstein would be Sir William, but in 1903 his membership in the New English Art Club connoted open opposition to Royal Academy taste and policies.[53] Two years later, however, in the Fund's first great crisis of acquisition, the committee would discover that "influentials" could let them down, whereas "stalwarts" did much toward saving the day.

And yet, it came naturally to many connoisseurs and collectors, themselves both knowledgeable and influential in the British art world, to think first of the "influentials." They knew who owned what, and they kept in touch with one another. A passage from the constitution of the Burlington Fine Arts Club, of which Balcarres was a member, accompanies his confidential notes of the 14 July meeting of the Fund's provisional committee. The club's stated purpose was to "bring together Amateurs, Collectors, and others interested in art; to afford ready means for consultation between persons of special knowledge and experience in matters relating to the Fine Arts; and to provide accommodation for showing and comparing rare works in the possession of the Members and their Friends."[54] It was an exclusive brotherhood that, by "showing and comparing," performed a very important service.

Gallery officials, too, kept in touch with one another. They lived with the need to supplement Treasury appropriations with gifts and bequests that might come to them when shifts occurred in the circumstances of the collectors' families. The gallery-going public also kept in touch with art affairs by attending showings and had become accustomed to leaving selection of pictures to collectors and to gallery directors and trustees, who were frequently one and the same. By

1903, however, the economics of depression and taxation had shaken this comfortable arrangement. What was to take its place? An entirely new and comprehensive constituency, said Fry, a democratic coalition of collectors, gallery administrators and trustees, artists, and any of the general public who cared or wished to learn about art.

Forging such a coalition would be difficult. Because there was no British precedent, different groups had different ideas about the nature and function of the new organization. As the Treasury pulled its purse strings tighter, the anxiety level rose in gallery offices. Would there be enough money for everyone? Would the new organization be collaborator or competitor? At the outset, Sidney Colvin had warned about the possibility of "discouragement and hostility" from the National Gallery. Sir Caspar Purdon Clarke, of the South Kensington Museum, told Balcarres that helping to acquire works of art was a fine purpose, but even more he wanted "an independent body of influential people whose opinions would have weight with the public and become in course of time a salutary controlling body guiding and protecting institutions which at present are too much dominated by self seeking officials whose only idea is to stand well with the Treasury. There is also the great question of the coordination of similar groups of institutions which at present are overlapping and interfering with each other's functions."[55] This, however, was never the purpose of the Fund. It hoped to become a salutary influence but not a controlling body. Independence should be its most valuable asset; its function would be to assist the national collections with acquisition of works that were otherwise beyond the means of national budgets.

Explanatory publicity was essential. One of the then-untitled individuals on Witt's list became the means for a wider public campaign. This was Isidore Spielmann, brother of Marion H. Spielmann, editor of the *Magazine of Art*. Isidore Spielmann, born in 1854, was the son of a Polish immigrant and grew up in an atmosphere sympathetic to reform and liberal movements. He married into the prominent Sebag-Montefiore family and began a company of civil engineers and contractors. He left engineering because his father-in-law thought it an unsuitable profession, and after a brief career as a stockbroker, he retired and turned his energies to art. As the Board of Trade's

Director for Art (Exhibitions Branch), he had been secretary for the British contribution to the Fine Art Sections at the Brussels and Paris exhibitions; to those he had added the Glasgow International Exhibition in 1901 and the exhibitions of early Flemish art at Bruges in 1902. Whatever one's opinion of monster exhibitions, he had the contacts and the expertise for a public campaign.[56]

When Balcarres approached him, Spielmann had already been asked to join; now he offered Balcarres his assistance. "It is high time that the Art loving patriots of this Country should launch their new ship, & my sympathy is such that I am prepared to work for it if my services are wanted." On the same day, his brother Marion wrote to Balcarres: "It *does* appeal to me, very much, & I'll join with pleasure. . . . The French Society works so well, that your scheme (though it hardly needs it) can point to a good precedent." Isidore Spielmann then promised to drop all other involvements and work to bring in new members. In fact, he did much more. He volunteered his services as an unpaid honorary secretary, soon replaced Fry alongside Witt in that office, and began to conduct the Fund's business affairs out of his own office at 47 Victoria Street.[57]

Another timely offer of cooperation came from the financier Max Rosenheim, a trustee of the British Museum who had been urging a friends organization there. Rosenheim was a well-known collector of engravings and of Italian and German Renaissance medals, which he gave to the British Museum. The connoisseur Charles Hercules Read, who had been Keeper of the British Museum's Department of British and Medieval Antiquities and Ethnography since 1896, wrote to say that Rosenheim "quite agrees to sink the Friends of the B.M. in the more comprehensive scheme—so you have our adhesion. He, moreover, will be a most useful man to urge his City friends to contribute." To seal the agreement, Rosenheim sent £10 and promised a future £105 per annum. He remained somewhat cautious, however, about conflicts of interest, and Fry reported that Rosenheim wanted "to safeguard against certain dangers which he foresees."[58]

In fact, some members of the public and some of its own early members examined this fine gift of a National Art Collections Fund with extraordinary amounts of anxiety and suspicion. Some museum and gallery officials, as well as some Fund members, still worried about a conflict of interest. Heseltine had no such misgivings, but Alfred Rothschild thought that as a trustee of the National Gallery he should not join; he would lend influence when the time came.[59] Charles Holroyd of the Tate Gallery would do all that he could, "subject to the continued approval of my Directors." Henry Hucks Gibbs, first Baron Aldenham, another trustee of the National Gallery, would later more than prove his generosity, but at the outset he gave only the annual guinea and awaited developments, even though he was "always boiling over with indignation at the parsimony of our Treasury" and thought that "we ought never to cease bombarding all Chancellors of the Exchequer, present and future, until they treat the Arts, and especially that branch represented by you and me and our Colleagues in St Martin's Place [the National Portrait Gallery] in a manner more worthy of England." Lord Carmichael, who was soon to become a trustee of the National Portrait Gallery and of the National Gallery, sent Balcarres the draft of a letter he had once intended to send to the *Times*, on the need for better support for art.[60]

Some responses to the idea of such a fund suggested how entrenched was the belief that only spectacular private gifts could aid effectively with acquisitions. C. H. Read wanted a prospectus with "a few influential names." The first public announcements of the Fund were studded with titles both hereditary and honorary, but the journalist and author Humphry Ward advised Balcarres to enlist "some well-disposed rich men," for with such a fund in existence "the Treasury might become stingier than ever, & leave the Society to find money which the Gov^{t} ought to find." The Fund needed a really strong committee that could "hold its own against the Treasury!" Others' replies only revealed the feebleness of their faith in anything the Fund might try to do. Lord Ronald Sutherland Gower thought it would probably succeed and sent his guinea but had little confidence in the art community's ability to act in concert. Lord Knutsford thought the Fund a good idea but doubted that it would ever be large enough to do much good.[61]

Lord Arthur Wellesley Peel's letter stands out in contrast to the counsels of discouragement. In the tradition of his great ancestor, Queen Victoria's prime minister, he grasped at once the Fund's wider purpose. He was a trustee of the National Gallery but saw no conflict of interest and no contradiction in dependence upon both the large contribution and the widow's mite. He told Balcarres:

> The thing to be aimed at is the numbers of subscribers—you should feel that by the very fact of their numbers they are protected from any liability to be experienced further to be called upon for the purchase of costly pictures.
>
> Rich men may come to the rescue in special cases, but the rank & file should feel that they have done enough in subscribing their small sum to swell the general aggregate of the Fund.[62]

Christiana Herringham still had her own problem of clarification. What would be her role on the provisional committee, of which she was still the only woman member? In August she wrote to Balcarres a letter that said as much about society's prejudices as about herself.

> It seems to me that the time has come for my solitary splendour to end. I should like best not to come to the next committee meeting. If the committee would *like* to have two or three ladies of their number—and I am invited to remain I will do my best to be of use—but my solitary name is likely to militate against usefulness of the society. It looks odd.[63]

So does that paragraph look odd to us now. Again there is the ironically joking inflation of her own position—"solitary splendour"—and a subjection to the will of the otherwise all-male committee. But the letter had a more solid subtext. She was not withdrawing altogether; she preferred not to attend only the *next* meeting. Thus she was giving the men their chance to settle the matter and spare her the embarrassment of being present when they made their decision.

At the same time, however reticent she sounded, she was putting pressure on them to commit themselves one way or the other, not only about her presence as the solitary woman member but about the inclusion of *two or three* other ladies. If they wanted her, she would do her best to be "of use"; with her money in their hands, they must not ignore the fact that she had already been signally useful and had done what not one of them had thought to do. She referred not only to these men but to society at large; the idea that one woman's "solitary splendour" could militate against the usefulness of the committee as a whole said all too plainly that she was worried about society's view of women as designers of public policy, as differentiated from their decorative function at bazaar stalls and charity balls. She wanted the men to appreciate her tact; consciously or unconsciously, she nodded to the old code in order to allow them to save face while deciding to let the ladies in—only two or three in addition to herself and thus not a threatening majority. She reminded them that they could not fault her devotion to the cause.

Having been the properly compliant lady, she resumed. "I think it is a thing on which women could be decidedly useful. Had you proposed a small oligarchical society it might have been well to have had only men but if it is to be a wide basis, I believe you will do well to include women—& a few well-known women on the committee."[64] Thus she reinserted Fry's constituency issue. *Was* the Fund to be truly national? Were younger artists, members of societies such as the New English Art Club, interested persons outside the London art establishment, citizens of northern counties, *and* women to be welcomed, or were they not?

She returned to the question of her own role in the Fund. "My position has been a little curious. Every one has been most courteous to me, but I can't—just because I had a little audacity and had a little spare money—stay where I may not be wanted, without offering to withdraw. I was so very glad that a good society has appeared, because no committee would be effective if the secretary were handsome[?] and a mere clerk."[65]

Why was it "audacity" to offer a suggestion that had so promising an outcome? Were constructive suggestions unwelcome if they came from a woman? She skirted these questions because she hesitated to bring them out directly. And why did she begin to feel that she "may not be wanted"? She had had no such feeling when with MacColl, Fry, and Phillips. Not only society's prejudices but some chemistry within the committee had made her wary.

Other correspondence revealed that her cousin Robert Witt, at least, found her presence unwelcome. A letter from Spielmann to Balcarres suggested that Witt and Spielmann had seen her letter, for Spielmann, who tended to see the situation through Witt's eyes, told Balcarres, "You are right to allow all the names to remain on the first list I think, but your energetic Lady friend—or Witt's should be asked to select carefully in the first instance."[66] Now her more general reference to inclusion of women—"I believe you will do well to include women"—in addition to those "few well-known women" she had originally proposed for the provisional committee, suggests that she had submitted an expanded list and that it was the one about which Balcarres had changed his mind.

She continued her letter, and the dominating side of her personality took the form of persistence. She returned to Fry's question about constituency and her own about women in an active role. "I am more of an artist than anything else—and I fear neither an organiser nor a society woman. Still I can do something no doubt to help and I think the supporters whose names I gave you will be likely to attract subscribers. That was the reason of my choosing them. We want to appeal to various sorts and sections of society."[67] A "society woman" would be more likely to know her place. Christiana was not a society woman, and if that was the men's view of the acceptable woman, she could have appeared to them as the undesirable opposite: the organizer. Indeed, six years later in India she would prove what an expert organizer she really was.

She added a postscript to say that she expected no answer from Balcarres until after the next meeting of the provisional committee. Bowing out, but still with her foot in the door, she asked whether she should send "any further names to you or one of the secretaries." In a post-postscript she wrote that she had still more ideas for the Fund. "I admit to having all sorts of similar wishes in the background of my mind & hope that the Society might become an important influence."[68] "Admit" is a revealing word, as if even to offer her ideas was culpable.

A month later Christiana wrote to Balcarres, rather disarmingly uncertain "whether you expected me to answer." Again she combined reticence and assertiveness, and there was a hint of resignation. She was also somewhat tactless. "I am sure you are doing what you consider best for this scheme which you evidently care about a good deal." She demonstrated her understanding of the rhetoric of public appeal by saying that she agreed with one of her correspondents who had objected to the idea that "the picture-buying should be done by a *sub*-committee—could we say *expert* committee." "Expert" became the accepted usage. She asked when a further installment of her money would be needed and reminded Balcarres that "I can't contribute more than the second hundred, as I said. I have only paid £100 so far."[69] In other words, she had helped the Fund over the stile.

In that summer of 1903 three of the Fund's early supporters—Fry, Holmes, and Horne—were trying to construct another firm foundation. The *Burlington Magazine,* founded in March, had declared itself an advocate of a reformed art and a changed attitude toward artists. "Geniuses are born to us, but we have not found how to cherish them. They fall on ungrateful soil, and after a few years of promise show too often but a weedy growth." The remnants of "what our forefathers called historical painting, by which they conveniently summarised definite imaginative creations dealing with elevated themes," allowed only the "faint echo of an echo," for "all emit the same odour of false sentiment; in all we find the same cheap substitutes for thought and feeling that the theatre has rendered current." More and more, serious artists took refuge in "some odd aspect of vision, which in default of creative imagination will yet make the rendering of familiar things not too painfully obvious"—a reminder of Ruskin's warning that artists without a tradition tend to go off in eccentric and unproductive directions.[70]

The *Burlington Magazine* was dissatisfied also with collectors, who could be "art's most valuable friend or its most insidious enemy." Too many pursued "mere collecting only for its own sake," which was "one of the crudest of instincts. . . ." Loveless, merely legal possession disturbed "that estimation of real values which our study proposes. The atmosphere becomes tainted, and the study itself acquires ill-repute by the presence of these knowing ones, these tipsters of the saleroom."[71]

Nor was that all. It was "another curious and shameful anomaly" that Britain, among "all cultured European countries," had no scholarly journal for "the serious and disinterested study of ancient art [as] its chief occupation." France had the *Gazette des Beaux-Arts,* founded in 1859; Germany had the *Zeitschrift für Bildende Kunst,* founded in 1873. They kept collectors in touch with the best that was currently known and thought about art and provided a harvest of tips about treasures in private collections. The *Burlington Magazine* intended to do the same.[72]

Founded on such premises, the *Burlington Magazine*'s success was to be of great importance to the Fund, but in September 1903 Fry told Holmes that the magazine was "*in extremis.* It is a really sound thing, I believe, but has been run on insufficient capital and with absolutely no business method. [Bernhard] Berenson and I are only just now aware of the true state of things. . . ." Fry saw Holmes's publishing experience as the saving grace; he would be joint editor with Robert M. Dell, the current editor, and would work half days for the first six months; if the magazine survived, his work load would be decreased and his pay increased.[73]

Fry told his mother that he, Berenson, Horne, and Holmes would not have lent their names if they had known how shaky the finances were, and "now that at the eleventh hour we are undeceived, we find or think that it will be a great blow to us if it fails, since people will never realize that it was only financial mismanagement and not want of influence in matters of art that brought it about. That is why we feel we must move heaven and earth to save the situation." If the magazine pulled through, it would be "a very powerful influence for the kind of serious and scholarly study of the subject which we have at heart, and which is beset with many enemies, among the chief of which is the unscrupulous falsifications of dealers."[74]

Fry and Holmes set out together on begging expeditions to every likely art lover (Christiana Herringham was among the first subscribers). Holmes remembered that even the *Burlington Magazine*'s creditors wished it well and "to that end encouraged Fry's efforts to raise new capital." At "the money-begging business I proved to be utterly useless," Holmes wrote. However, he proved his own worth by vetting accounts and "the plausible schemes which various interested parties laid before us. Fry on the other hand was simply magnificent. No rebuff could shake his determination to carry the matter through." According to Benedict Nicolson, the *Burlington Magazine*'s editor in 1953, Dell cast his lot with Fry and Holmes after he learned that, without telling him, William H. Spottiswoode, the publisher and printer for the magazine, had intended to turn the editorship over to MacColl, who had declined. Rigorous economies and new capitalization set the magazine on its feet. To this day it has never missed an issue.[75]

All at once, and all through the efforts of a small group of hard-working enthusiasts, Britain had a really scholarly art journal and a new fund as promising allies for the national collections. Both answered to the demise of the old pattern, when generous patronage and private collecting went hand in hand. The general public, however, had been left out of that equation. More than half a century earlier, Thomas Wyse, M.P., had called for a program of public education in the essentials of art, to make it a public resource.

> [Artists] must have co-operation on the part of the public. It is needless to hope for this cooperation, on a truly public or national scale, until the public be educated up, in essentials at least, to the general level of the artists. . . . If art be not widely supported, it is because it is yet considered a private luxury, not a public enjoyment. How can we expect the public should enjoy unless they appreciate, and how can they appreciate unless those preliminary studies, which lay the foundation of taste, and develope the sense and value of artistic excellence, form a portion, according to their respective means and position, of their early instruction?[76]

The National Art Collections Fund, therefore, must be public educator as well as money raiser if it wanted the kind of broad support that Wyse and Fry, more than half a century apart, advocated. And the private collectors, too, needed education on one point; they tended to think in terms of pedigree. "The desire of possessing a fine picture is doubtless much increased by such picture having a *pedigree*," wrote Thomas Winstanley in 1828. A glance at membership lists of the Burlington Fine Arts Club shows to what an extent collecting was the province of persons of ancestral pedigree, who formed the club in order to have "a common meeting-place to compare their treasures."[77]

With striking frequency, some leading collectors who gave the Fund important support still thought of art collection in terms of a quintessentially aristocratic sport: hunting. The banker Robert Henry Benson called pictures "the big game of collecting."[78] Sir William Martin Conway emphasized degrees of social prestige when he pointedly mentioned Henry Willett, a brewer who collected paintings with profits from a trade that was socially unprestigious. "He loved the fun of the hunt and the joy of acquisition . . . picture-collecting yielded a definite series of pleasures; first there was the hunt, then came the bargain . . . glory of attainment . . . delight in contemplation . . . amusement of hanging it . . . then . . . hardly noticed it any more." If he sold the work for more than he originally paid, he pocketed his profit "after the fun of another bargain." The brewer may have enjoyed the hunt, but the implication is that pictures and beer were all the same to him. Conway was less ready to trade pictures for profit, but he certainly loved the fun of the hunt. He begins *The Sport of Collecting* by saying that "the passion for 'collecting' must correspond with some deep-seated instinct in man." We have a compulsion not only to "acquire that kind of wealth which is strength, but to obtain possession of objects . . . by which our lives thenceforward are conditioned. . . ." The beauty of this servitude is that "we have enjoyed the passion of the hunt without killing and our trophies are not consumed."[79]

In 1948 Denys Sutton echoed Robert Witt's view when he introduced an exhibition of British drawings from Witt's collection and wrote that "collecting is a pursuit which suits our taste, combining a love of the arts with an element of chance and sport." In a lecture in 1950, "The Art of Collecting," Witt himself began by saying that "it is far more than an art, it is also a science and a sport. It is the chase, not the quarry that counts, the pursuit of the unattainable, the discovery of the unexpected, with all its vicissitudes of success and failure."[80]

Even as metaphor, the hunt, a rich man's sport, connotes the exclusivity of money. Hamerton had observed in 1872 that surplus money rules art talent. "The simple truth is, that capital is the nurse and governess of the arts, not always a wise or judicious nurse, but an exceedingly powerful one." The man with money will rule the artist unless the artist has enough of his own to enable him to resist and keep to his own highest standard, but "starving men are weak."[81] Surplus income would always be the strength of private collecting, whether for speculation or for lifetime enjoyment. The Fund, if it wanted a truly broad base, must persuade those who could give less that their modest contributions made a difference to the national collections.

Charles Robert Ashbee, architect and craftsman, was not starving, but he had no surplus income, and he made the case for artist stalwarts when he replied to Balcarres's letter about the new Fund.

> As to the artists remember that guineas usually frighten ~~them~~ us though ~~they~~ we peons[?] give proportionately more than men of *land* & *cash*, for we live from hand to mouth & our generosity is determined by how our work comes along.
>
> I find for my part that during the last 4 or 5 years 25% of my annual income has gone in public work for aesthetic purposes. What the "rich man" would reckon as "charitable margin" & set within the biblical tithe! So I should write a little note to the artists if I were you—saying you don't want their money as much as their name and help!

"Certainly," he continued, "I will do what I can," and he would help in ways other than money, for he was putting all of his money into the community of his Guild of Handicraft at Chipping Campden. Ashbee's letter contrasted pointedly with another from a coroneted "influential" who could not spare the subscription guinea because he was in the costly process of furnishing his Mayfair residence.[82]

The provisional committee met again on 11 October, a Monday, and presumably without Christiana Herringham. Witt had visited her on the preceding weekend at Guildford, where he had drawn up an agenda for the first General Meeting, now set for 11 November at the rooms of the Society of Antiquaries in Burlington House. He was eager to make the first public meeting a really notable occasion, for the Fund might not have another such chance until it could do something really spectacular. He suggested to Balcarres that when the provisional committee met next, on 28 October, it should settle on names that would appear to best effect on the list to be proposed for the first executive committee. Spielmann told Balcarres, "We are working off all the 'outstanding names' of important people whose membership it is desirable to have." He listed, among others, Lords Ribblesdale, Lytton, Devonshire, Halsbury, and Bedford.[83]

From the beginning, most of the daily and periodical press had commented promptly. The *Times*'s announcement, heavy with titled names, stated that "the bulk of purchases" would be made from donations other than membership guineas. The *Spectator* pointed out that the difference between the new Fund and charitable organizations such as the Hospital Fund was that "it will be difficult to convince the general public that a large capital sum is needed at once." The promoters of the National Art Collections Fund understood this, the *Spectator* continued, and therefore wisely decided to ask more people to give a guinea each. And why not give those contributors free passes to the national collections, thus encouraging them to "take their friends to look at the works of art which they had helped to buy for the nation"? This Fund should be "one of the most successful ventures of the kind ever inaugurated in the United Kingdom." The *Athenaeum* rejoiced that "we shall no longer be the merely helpless and irritated spectators of the depletion by foreigners of our treasuries of art. . . . It is therefore, perhaps, something of a slur upon us, who have long understood how to carry on works of public utility by private enterprise, that we have not already combined for so necessary and worthy an object."[84]

MacColl, in his *Saturday Review* article, took pains to allay suspicions that the Fund would be just another unwieldy organization. It would enable the "volunteer forces" who cared about art to be "a central body that will make it its business to watch for opportunities and that will be able to appeal to its constituents with the necessary authority." Could a committee avoid the delays that caused the national collections to lose so many opportunities to purchase? This committee's duty "will be to appoint in each case a highly qualified buyer and give him the maximum of discretion. These buyers will give their services gratuitously" so that there could be no suspicion of personal gain to individual members of the Fund.[85]

In the *Nineteenth Century,* Witt set forth the facts of national art finances. The national collections were in trouble not only because of high prices for art but also because of "the persistent refusal of Parliament to meet this by increased grants." The National Gallery was poverty stricken at home and "starved" when compared with galleries abroad. In the previous thirteen years, it had obtained just 112 pictures at an average cost of £1,248 per picture. The Treasury allowed only about £8,000 per annum; the really expensive acquisitions had been private gifts. But merely increasing the grant was not enough. Speed was essential, for when a fine picture came onto the market, there was no time to haggle and cast about for subscribers. The Berlin group snapped up treasures because it had elasticity in the use of its funds. If individuals gave more, would the Treasury shirk its duty and give less? No, because for the first time, a fund would "focus an influential and organised body of public opinion upon this very question."[86]

A few commentators were openly skeptical. "A. U.," writing in the *Star,* asked about conflicts of interest if directors and trustees of the national collections were on the list. Such an organization should be entirely independent. "But is it?" asked A. U. "Look over the list of men who have promised their support, and who are the most conspicuous? Why, the very officials" who "bring with them not only their obligations to the institutions they have in charge, but the prejudices and preferences they may already have shown in their administrative methods." Arthur Clutton-Brock, in the *Speaker,* got both name and idea wrong. He hoped that the "National Art Collectors' Fund" would have qualified experts and not merely "vague enthusiasm or self-advertising non-entities." *Free Lance* was sarcastic, noting that the Fund must intend to outbid American millionaires for modern works of art that they "will not take at any price." Frank V. P. Rutter, art critic for the *Sunday Times,* hoped that the National Art Collections Fund would have a competent buyer and would work in harmony with directors of the public collections that would receive the works acquired. However, he was annoyed in 1903 (and for years afterward) because he believed that the Fund would attract most of the available money. He was trying to obtain a Monet through his French Impressionist Fund, which had MacColl and Phillips on its committee. (Instead of a Monet they got Boudin's *The Harbour at Trouville,* which the National Gallery was more willing to accept because Boudin was safely dead.)[87] Most of the press, however, applauded the National Art Collection Fund's intentions and wished it well. The *Morning Post* observed that "those who have originated this fund are of the sort that are credited by artists with some understanding about painting, which, after all is a more or less necessary quality in a buyer of pictures."[88]

However, no one who had paid attention to the art news all through 1903 could be unaware that all was not well in the British art world. MacColl had lit the flame in April 1903 with his *Saturday Review* article on Chantrey "maladministration." In the *Athenaeum* in November, Fry stoked the fire by pointing out that a hospital or a charity would not tolerate missteps like the Chantrey violations. Even in the midst of its financial troubles, the *Burlington Magazine* quickly proved itself a new and liberal voice in art history and criticism. In July, Whistler died, which kept alive the reminder that the National Gallery had had fifteen years in which to purchase his portraits of Thomas Carlyle and Whistler's mother but had let Carlyle go to Scotland and Mrs. Whistler to France.[89] But most important by far was the fact that the Fund began to be a center where all concerned—private collectors, artists, administrators and trustees of national and provincial collections, and the general public—might rally to a concerted effort to solve problems of taste, finance, and the Great Exodus.

Success did not come easily. On the afternoon of 10 November, Balcarres opened the General Meeting with an explanation of the Fund's finances and purpose. The organizers intended the Fund to be "elastic and flexible," bound by the smallest possible number of rules. Formal incorporation would be only a measure for dealing correctly with legacies. There was no conflict with the national collections:

indeed, the opposite was the case; nor did those collections' directors and trustees intend to control the Fund. (At this, the audience cheered.) The Fund's independent expert buyers would have power to refuse as well as to acquire pictures. The immediate needs were subscribing members, gifts of money, publicity, and patience, since tastes in art were certain to differ. Balcarres concluded by asking that the public not judge the Fund's worth by the achievements of any single year and that it be regarded always as a *national* society with a national object that allowed for every shade of philosophy in art. As of November 1903 the Fund had 308 members and seven hundred pounds in the bank.[90]

What happened next was unexpected, not to say sensational. The names were read out for the proposed executive committee and the council. According to the *Times*, a gentleman who did not identify himself "was understood strongly to deprecate the nomination on the council of Royal Academicians." He then "hurriedly left the room." Fry then rose to move an amendment to the resolution that established the executive committee. Christiana Herringham seconded his amendment.[91]

Neither the *Times* nor the audience had any idea of the reason for so startling an interruption. Fry's motion and Christiana's amendment protested the omission of the four originators—MacColl, Herringham, Fry, and Phillips—as well as four others who had either attended the first two meetings of the provisional committee or had given valuable advice at that early stage—Nichols, Holroyd, Colvin, and Conway. Fry's amendment called for all eight to be included in the executive committee. Such a move was unexpected at an organization's first public meeting, and certainly not at one under so distinguished a chairman, or from persons who by the going definition were not "influentials," and one of them a woman.

Charles Ricketts described the event in his diary.

> . . . the meeting opened by Ld Balcarres advocating toleration and catholicity[?] for while there were some who advocated the immediate purchase of a Whistler, there were others who were all for Spinello Aretino for instance. Then an amazing person rose, removed a patch from his left eye and asked if it was necessary to admit any member of

> the R.A. to the formal Executive[;] this resulted in a panic, with which the chairman coped perfectly; several eminent nobodies then spoke advocating patience and moderation and poured soft sawder on the committee. An elderly lord read out the list of council honorary and otherwise, this was followed by the usual applause, when up rose a nervous woman, who apologised for speaking, who then pointed out that the originator of the scheme was Phillips, whose name had not been included on the list. She also demanded the inclusion of the original provisional committee, who had worked for the scheme, she brought this out with one or two snaps at the polite but entirely futile meeting. How like England in miniature, pompous nobodies nobbling everything.[92]

Unfortunately, Ricketts omitted Christiana's "snaps." Holmes, who had been unable to attend, received a further description from Ricketts.

> Ricketts gave me an account of the inaugural meeting. All the recognized authorities, including the recognized obstructionists, attended, and, regardless of the real promoters, the latter elected themselves as the Committee. So surprised was the meeting that the election came near to being approved by stupefied silence. Then from the body of the Hall a lady rose, and, speaking with reckless, breathless frankness, pointed out that none of those responsible for the meeting had been chosen, while most of the chosen were just the people who were not wanted. Thanks to this plucky action by Mrs. Herringham, a new election had to take place, and the Fund was correctly started.[93]

Christiana had so impressed Ricketts that he neglected to say that she was seconding Fry's amendment. Just who were the "recognised obstructionists" depended on one's point of view, but for Ricketts, who stood with Fry and his friends, they were the art establishment officials so conspicuous on the first lists submitted by the provisional committee. Some months later he observed to MacColl that the National Gallery, "after acquiring a small number of the masterpieces now in this country, might almost close down, not to hurt the great moderns by the inclusion of rare or obscure tosh." He prophesied, with accuracy, that "we shall live, perhaps, to see pictures rated at the price of dreadnoughts and useful in international business adjustments. . . . But, alas, what is to be done with these mandarins of ours in power who do not know, who will not learn, the perpetual value of art or the things for which they stand in trust."[94]

When the subsequent correspondence with Balcarres is read in sequence, it becomes clear that the provisional committee had met as scheduled on 28 October. Members were to bring suggestions of forty names for the council and ten for the executive committee. However, the final lists were not decided at that meeting, as Witt had expected, but at an *extra* meeting to be held on 9 November, the day before the General Meeting.

On the 11th Phillips wrote to Balcarres to say that he regretted missing both the provisional committee meeting on the 9th and the General Meeting the following day, "and was more so as things seem to have taken a quite unexpected turn." He now resigned from the subcommittee for purchasing pictures because he thought that he and the other three originators of the Fund had been shabbily treated. He objected not only to their exclusion but also to the inclusion on the council, even as honorary members, of the heads of the national collections.

> I assumed that as a matter of course I and my colleagues, as well as Mrs Herringham without whose practical support the matter could not have gone on, would have been placed on the Executive Committee, to which the Sub-Committee will in all essential respects be subject. Personally I have no intention of serving on any Sub-Committee under any other conditions. The Executive Committee, as I understand it to be at present constituted, contains certain names which no doubt carry weight, but which, on the other hand, represent just those official influences from which it is indispensable to keep away, if the independence of the Society is to be preserved. Moreover, it appears to me unnecessary and undesirable to add to the Executive Committee the names of the two honorary secretaries, when those of myself and the other founders of the Society are so pointedly omitted. In these circumstances I shall be obliged if you will omit my name from the list of the Sub-Committee upon which, as I understand, [I am to serve] until we have come to some understanding about the whole matter. I am sorry to be again too unwell to attend to-day.[95]

Balcarres wrote a careful reply, of which a draft survives. He had not received Phillips's letter until "this evening after I had finished addressing the meeting at the Antiquarians & while the resolutions about Council & Executive were being actively moved so there was very little time to reconsider the situation. I quite thought from our conversation that you preferred being on the Picture committee." However, the meeting had "readily acquiesced" in the suggestion for the executive committee. It was now "rather numerous [but] we shall be able to work things all right." He attributed the "misunderstanding" to "conversations being rather hurried, & from the fact that our recent [provisional] Committee meetings where these matters were settled were rather sparsely attended."[96]

Two days after the General Meeting Christiana wrote to Balcarres, and at last the events that had preceded the meeting were made clear. Fry, still convinced that the lists did not represent a fully national constituency, had intended to protest, not at the General Meeting, but at the provisional committee's extra meeting on 9 November. He and Phillips, just returned from his rest cure in France, were to have met beforehand with Christiana to clarify any last-minute questions about his statement, but that plan went awry. At the General Meeting on the 10th she had had no opportunity to explain all this to Fry before he moved his amendment. She herself had been ill on 28 October, and on 9 November, as a letter from Witt to Balcarres makes clear, she had invoked her self-imposed rule of reticence. She explained why Fry and Phillips were not at the provisional committee meeting on 9 November, and also why she had arrived late for that meeting.

> Yesterday I had to spend in my garden. I was so tired after my effort at peacemaking. I want to thank you for the friendly way in which you seemed to take my little speech—and to apologise for the late arrival of the Claude Phillips letters. It was not unpunctuality on his part or mine. It was arranged that Mr Fry should meet him at my house at 4 o'clock and act as a spokesman. Mr Fry was prevented from coming—detained at his wife's mother's funeral. Mr Phillips stayed till the last minute [then left feeling unwell] & then sent the

> letter [to Balcarres]. I could not explain matters properly to Mr Fry & felt compelled to hastily say something myself.[97]

To Christiana, too, Balcarres drafted a careful reply. He regretted only that

> delays shld have occurred, following upon what was understood to be accepted as the general policy of our Committee meeting—because it might well have resulted in giving to the public the impression of internal discord.
>
> This of course is what must be avoided, not merely in substance, but in appearance as well, the art world being somewhat sensitive in such matters. I am confident that we shall work together in a smooth & harmonious manner.

Another draft, essentially the same, adds that "our success is bound up in mutual confidence & forbearance."[98]

The issue was much more than an intramural squabble. It came at a point when, for the good of the hard-pressed national collections and indeed for Britain's reputation in the international art world, the nation must choose between an elitist and a comprehensive philosophy for the support of the arts. Fry, who felt that the Fund's independence was at stake, contended that the choice should be made clear at the outset. However, until the Fund had a common cause large enough to command everyone's ingenuity and energy, the consciousness of a rift remained. Spielmann thought that all had gone well at the General Meeting, but added, "We shall have to preach patience & moderation all round, or the jealousies we have so plainly seen will be our breakers ahead." He told Balcarres that he would resign from the executive committee if his being there *ex officio* "causes C. Phillips annoyance; I am willing to leave it for the good of the cause." He hoped that "your tact with CP. will induce him to calm down."[99]

Phillips had no personal animus against Spielmann; he wanted the honorary secretaries off the executive committee, but he would not have wanted to lose Spielmann's services, which were invaluable. Spielmann managed office affairs, engaged clerical assistance, saw that circulars went out on time, kept up contacts with the press. In the end, the honorary secretaries remained on the executive committee *ex officio,* and Phillips remained on the subcommittee for pictures. He still thought it a pity that they should have begun with a misunderstanding "and that the originators of the Society should be compelled to take steps on their own account for an assertion of their share in the Executive, which is surely theirs as a matter of right and justice." He agreed that the committee was now "too large for working purposes," but he objected to the presence of those who were "brought in at the last moment, and are very possibly not in absolute sympathy with its chief aim and object." Balcarres's draft survives on the verso of Phillips's letter. He assured him that the list "was not drawn up in any 'spirit of exclusion,'" that independence was indeed important, and he had made his "opinion on that point clear at the general meeting."[100]

Balcarres wrote about all this to Witt, whose reply was spiteful and anything but forbearing. He hoped that the newspapers would ignore the incident at the General Meeting and was relieved when the *Times* said only that Mrs. Herringham had seconded Roger Fry's amendment. The *Outlook,* however, thought it too bad that the unidentified man who "urged the impropriety of having any one on the committee who was a member of the scandalous R.A. made a strategic mistake in so precipitately retreating after he had delivered his bomb." Lord Balcarres, the *Outlook* remarked rather flippantly, had worn a striped shirt "to make the poor artists feel at home" and had "grappled with the Nihilist most pluckily. It is a melancholy fact that with the exception of Mr. Roger Fry, who is always clear and modest and to the point, the artists spoke worse than the Lords."[101]

Unfortunately, Christiana's uncertainties about her presence on the executive committee now made her begin to regret her temerity. She began another protective withdrawal. To Witt she wrote an apologetic letter, which he forwarded to Balcarres, and she also called on Witt at his home. He told Balcarres that he had advised her and her friends to keep their intrigues in the open. He added the gratuitous implication that Wilmot Herringham knew enough about the protocol of public life to know that he ought to keep his wife at home. Witt was still convinced that Christiana, Fry, Phillips, and MacColl wanted Spielmann out, which was not the case.[102]

Christiana then wrote again to Balcarres:

> I have the contrition of a Meddlesome Matty. I hope that the demon which suddenly took possession of me was a well-meaning demon.
>
> The Society had a kind of double origin, and I feel that I ought to have been a cleverer link, but will you forgive my asking you that if the suggestion is made to you that there should be a free discussion between yourself, Mr Witt, and if possible Mr Claude Phillips—and *not* me—you would, if possible agree. Mr. Fry & Mr. MacColl are most anxious for the success of the society, and want a free conversation—less formal than a committee—about forming plans for future work & getting money.
>
> I am going to Egypt soon . . . .

The reference to the "double origin" should be borne in mind; in 1906 she would explain it. Witt applauded her departure for an Egyptian holiday, then went to Guildford for the weekend.[103]

Balcarres's correspondence shows how much time and thought he gave to letter writing, press relations, careful consideration of the Fund's possibilities, and mediation, and all at a time when he had just become a Junior Lord of the Treasury, to represent H.M. Office of Works in the Commons. He had been the youngest M.P. and now became the youngest minister then in the House of Commons. However, Christiana's request that he meet with Fry, MacColl, and Phillips brought up an important point: policy discussions were becoming fragmented. Witt and Spielmann had had meetings with Balcarres at which pressing Fund business was considered. Fry, Phillips, and MacColl—but not Christiana—met with Balcarres on or about 20 November. Spielmann, very curious about the outcome, told Balcarres, "I rather pity you, but think you are quite equal to the task." He added, "Some of the papers are criticising our Movement as being likely to fall too much under the influence of the R.A., but if they only knew how much greater is the danger from the opposition, how much quieter they would be!"[104]

Even before the first public announcement of the Fund, suggestions for acquisitions began to come in. Most were well beyond its resources at the time. Purdon Clarke was hopeful about a Limoges cup to be sold at Cologne in November. Robert Gibb, the Director of the National Gallery of Scotland, had been on the lookout for a fine Millais, and the donor he had in mind would accept five thousand pounds.[105] Lionel Cust, although of the opinion that the nation would never get pictures of first-class importance because money was always the sticking point, had heard that a Vandyck, a Titian, and a Reynolds were available for eighty thousand pounds. What about a syndicate of rich men to buy these for the National Gallery? Also, his cousin, Lord Darnley, might part with another Reynolds and a Sargent. Heseltine tended toward caution. He thought Cust's suggestions too ambitious, for "all undertakings which endure begin in a modest way, failure in any large project at the beginning, would kill the Society at its start and make us ridiculous. . . ." He would be of this opinion, he said, even if times were more propitious.[106]

In fact, Heseltine had a picture in mind that was not—or not yet—on the market, which he thought would be a more modest beginning for the Fund. This was a work by Velázquez known as the Rokeby *Venus.* It belonged to James Morritt of Rokeby Hall in Yorkshire and had been exhibited at the Royal Academy in 1896. Ever since, Heseltine had hoped that "it would some day come to the National Gallery. The subject is one more suitable for a public gallery than for a private house. . . ." If the owner would sell, "the price ought not to be prohibitive." Heseltine guessed it at four thousand to five thousand pounds. Perhaps this was not an accurate estimate, he admitted, but "I am certain it would be an irresistible addition to any Public Gallery."[107] Indeed, as the Fund would discover when the Rokeby *Venus* was for sale only two years later, the price was by no means "modest." Charles Ricketts's gloomy prediction that art prices would begin to approach the cost of dreadnoughts was already too correct. The stated price of *Venus* would be forty thousand pounds, and the final price, after expenses, forty-five thousand. The Fund, barely over the stile but moving briskly forward, resolved that this masterpiece must go to the National Gallery in London, not to Paris or Berlin or an American millionaire. Internal disagreements laid aside, it set out to raise that stupendous sum.

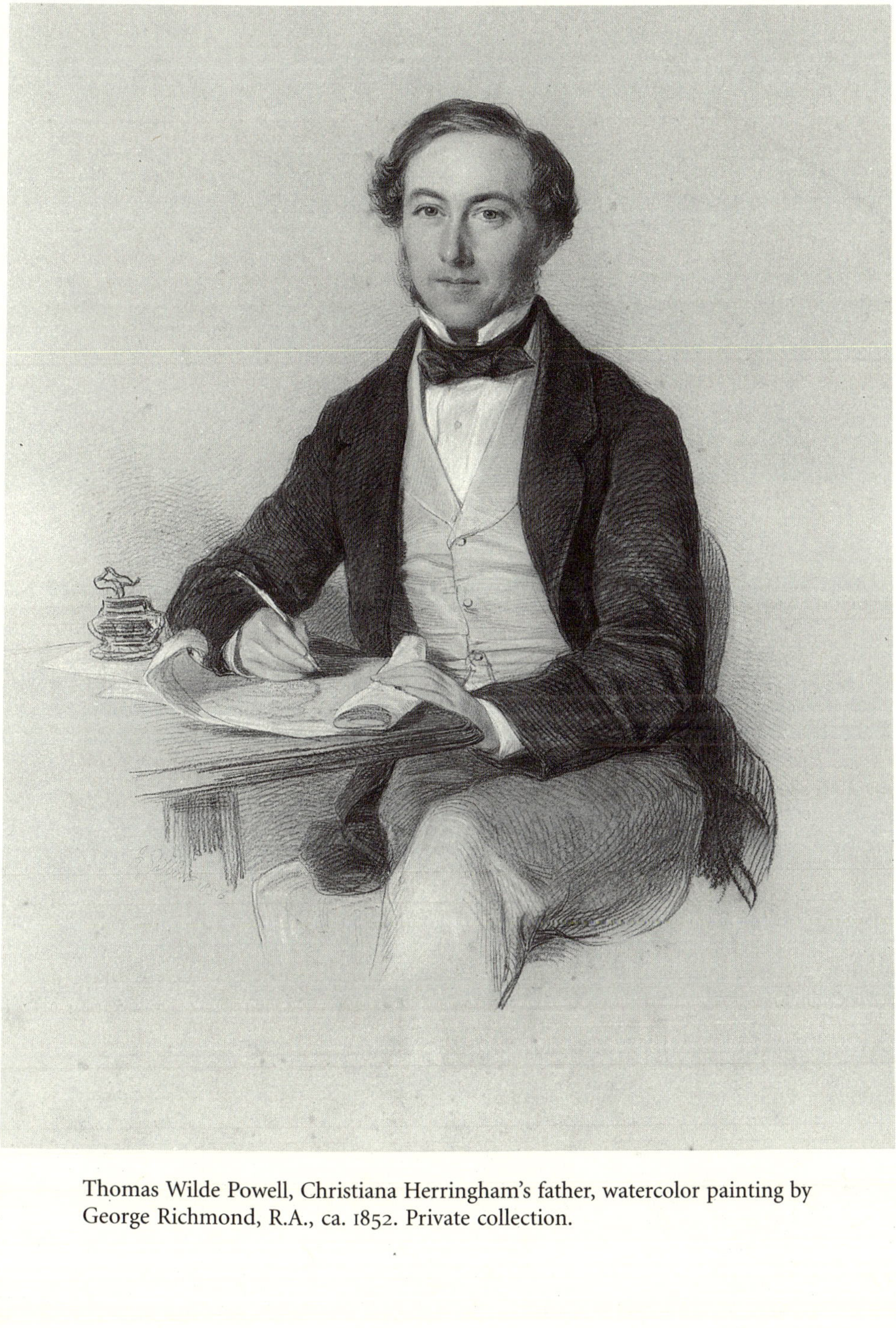

Thomas Wilde Powell, Christiana Herringham's father, watercolor painting by George Richmond, R.A., ca. 1852. Private collection.

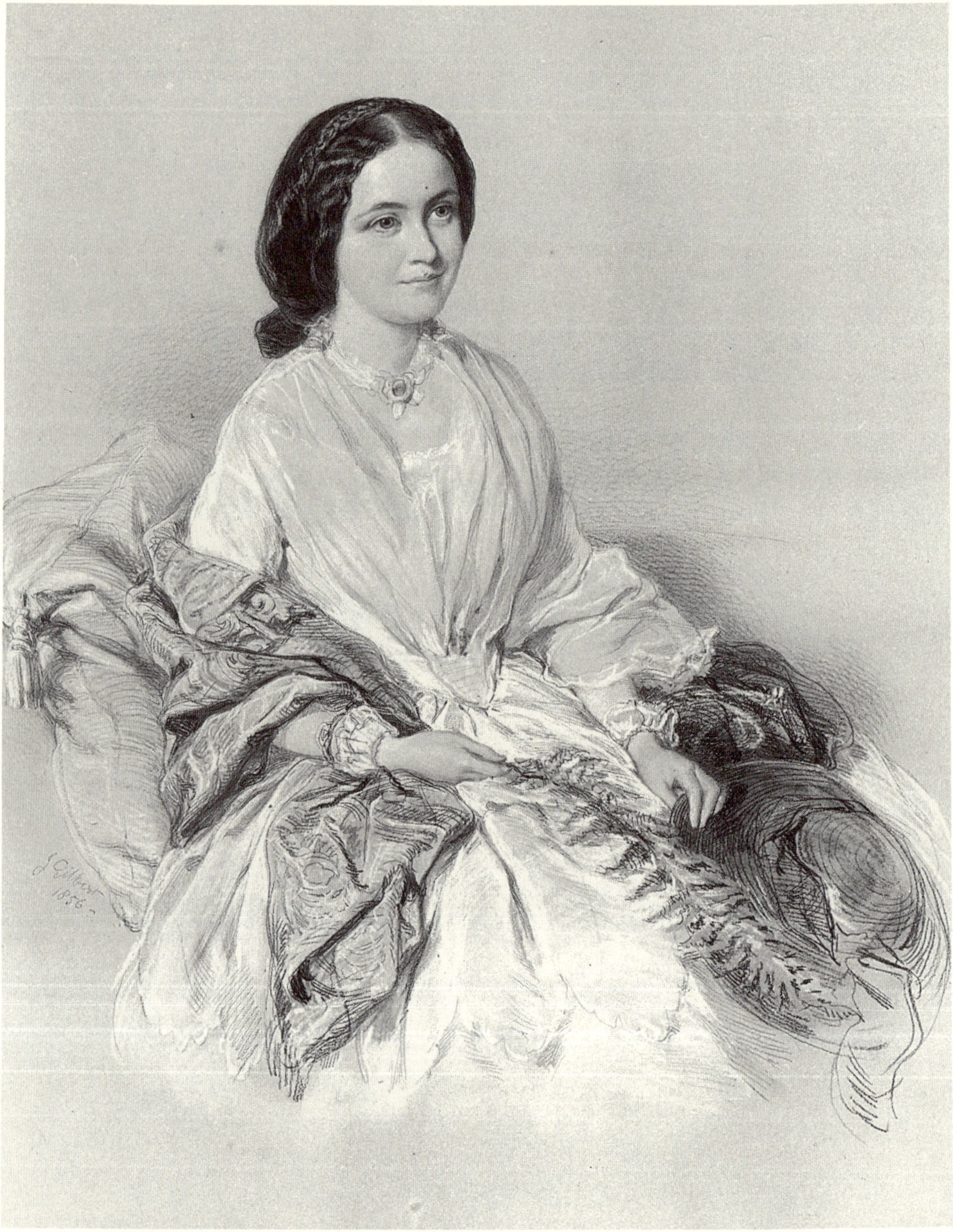

Mary Marten Powell, Christiana Herringham's mother, watercolor painting by George Richmond, R.A., ca. 1852. Private collection.

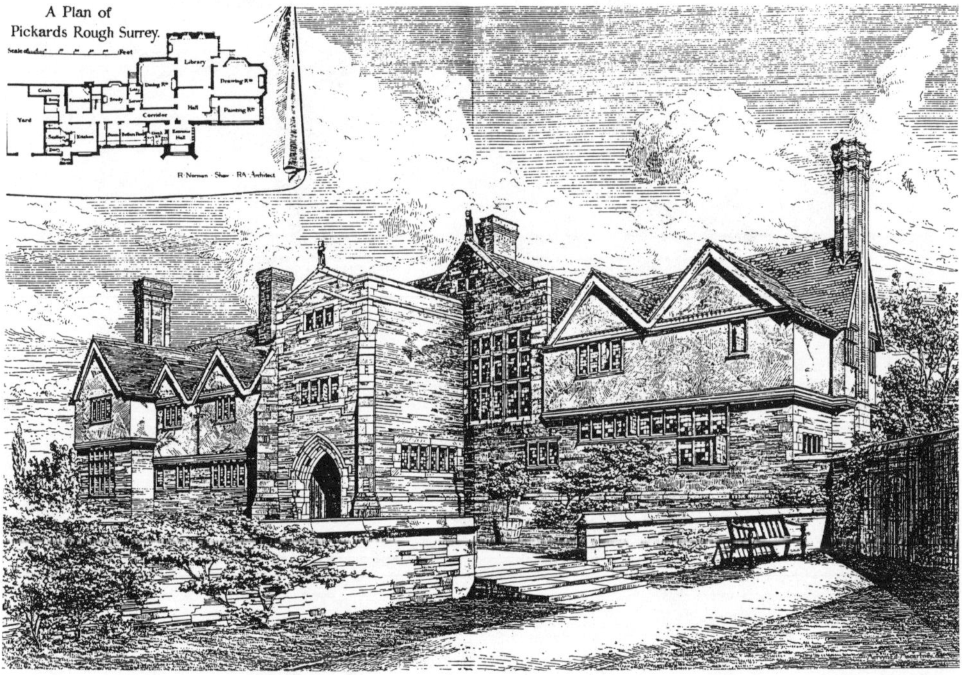

Piccard's Rough, Guildford, Surrey, designed for Thomas Wilde Powell by Richard Norman Shaw in 1887. Shown before demolition of central section in 1953. Reprinted from *Architect*, 11 February 1887, 82.

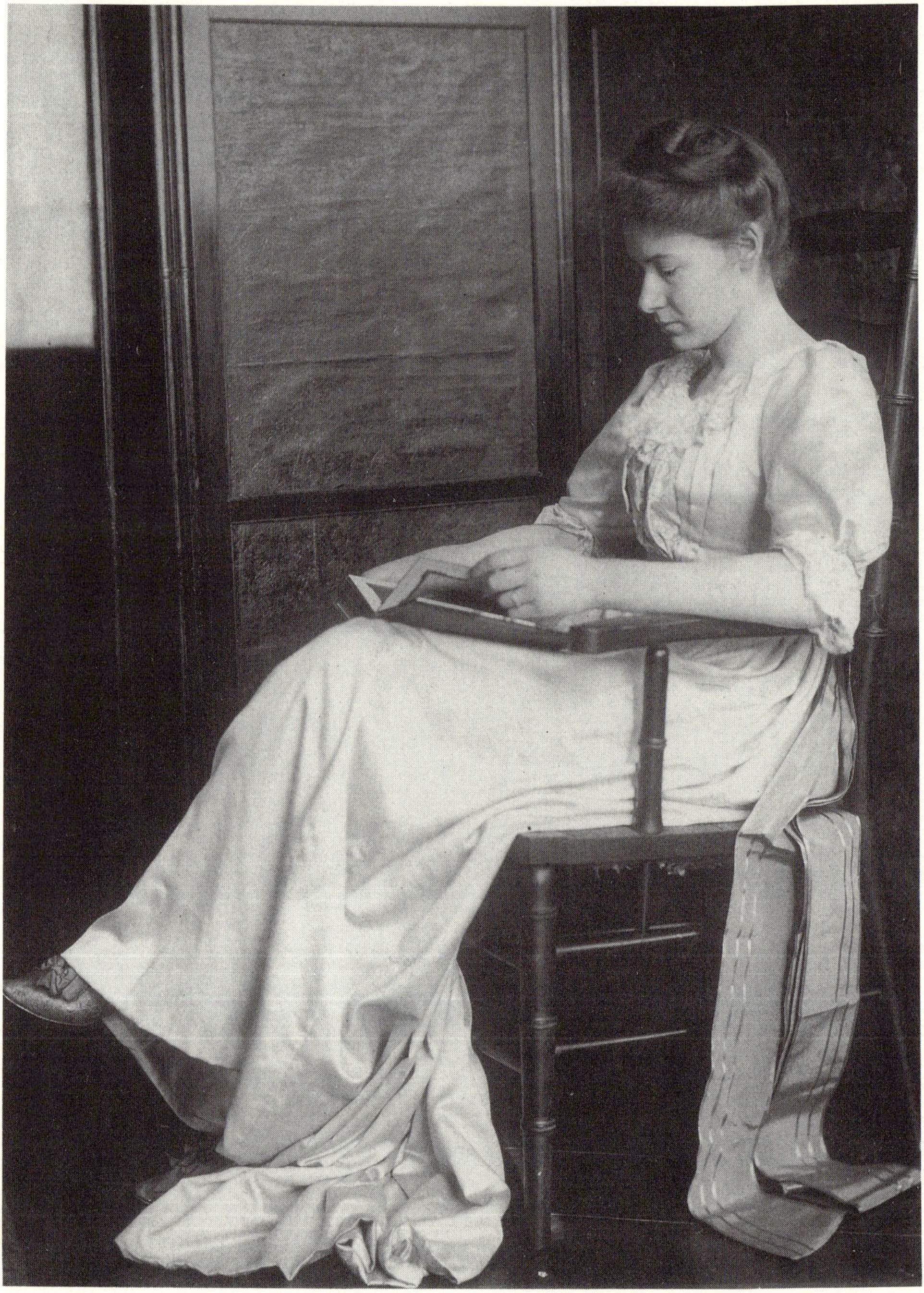

Christiana Jane Herringham, ca. 1880. Private collection.

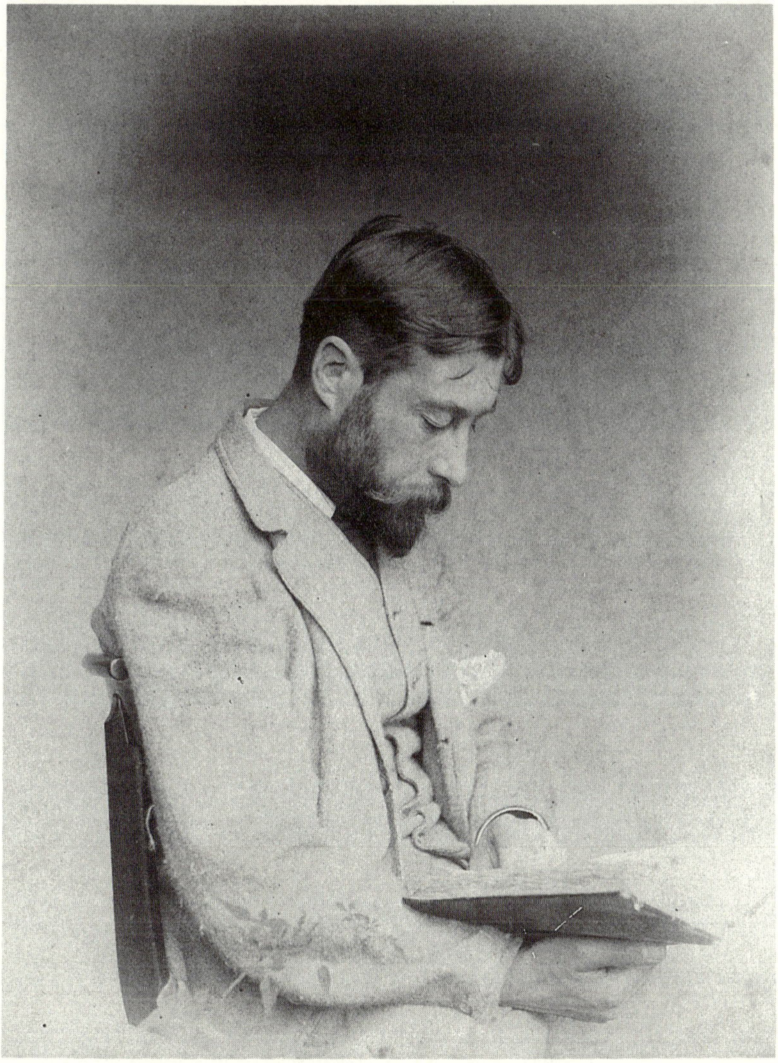

Wilmot Herringham, ca. 1880. Private collection.

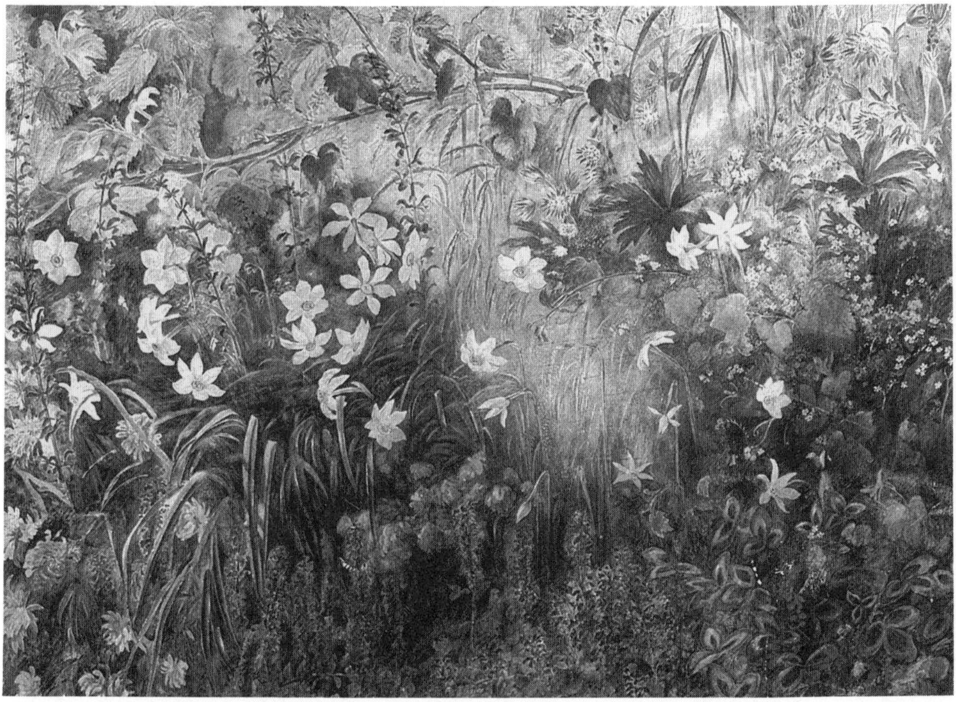

Floral tempera paintings by Christiana Herringham, dates unknown. *Above,* Courtesy Collection of Bedford College for Women; *right,* private collection.

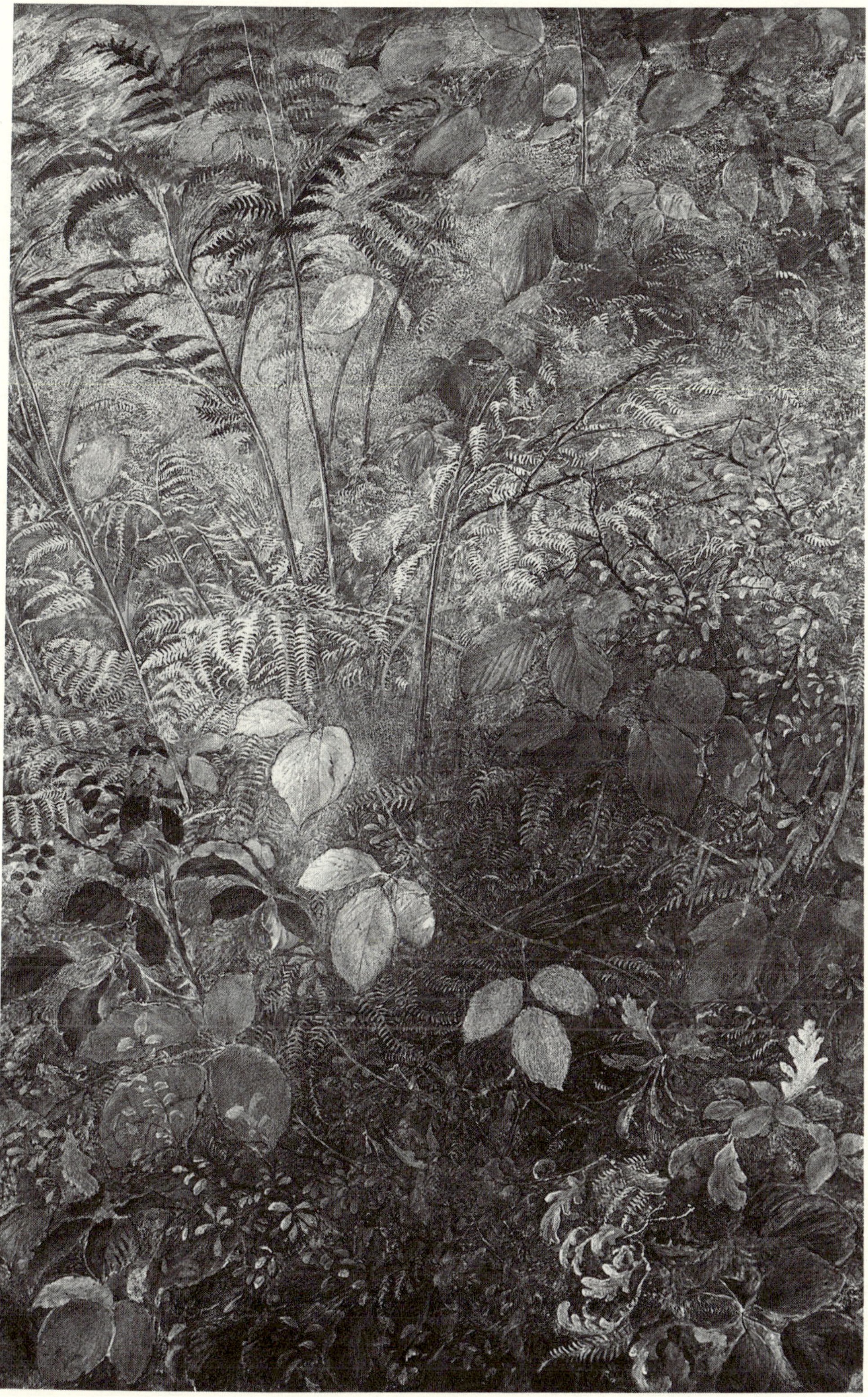

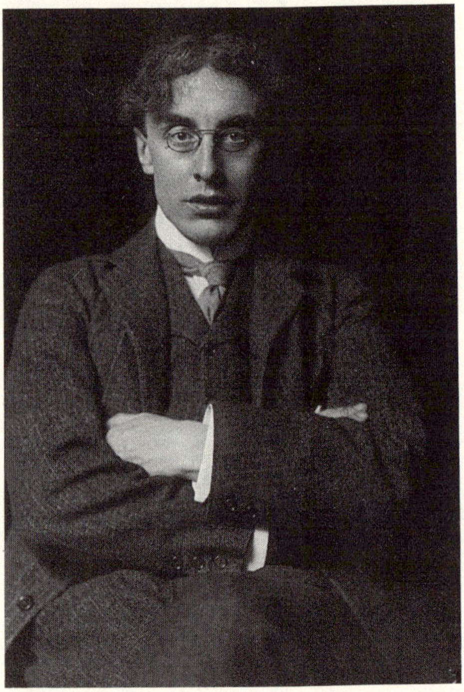

Roger Fry, ca. 1900. Private collection.

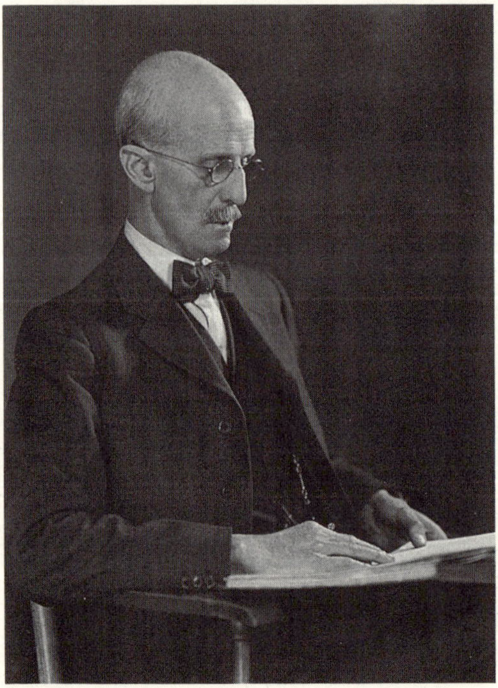

Dougald S. MacColl, ca. 1925.
Private collection.

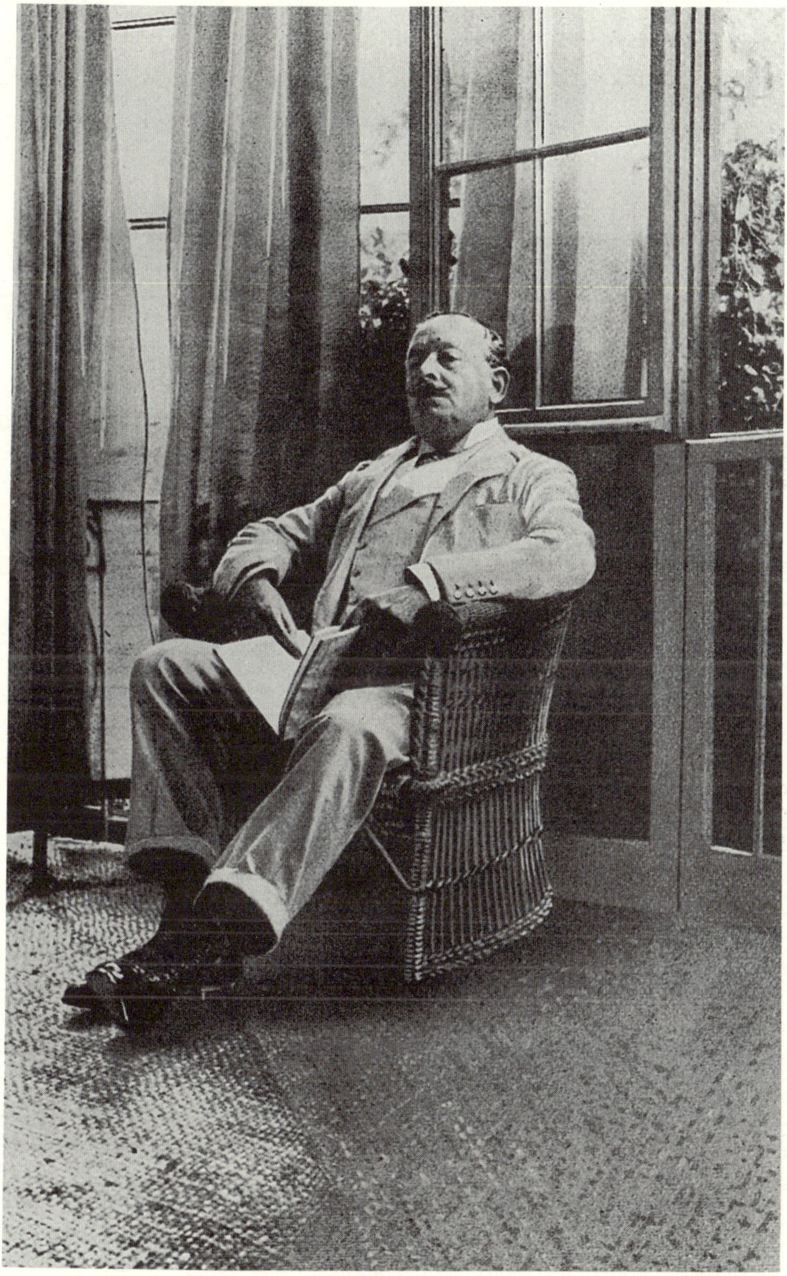

Claude Phillips, ca. 1905. Courtesy Wallace Collection, London.

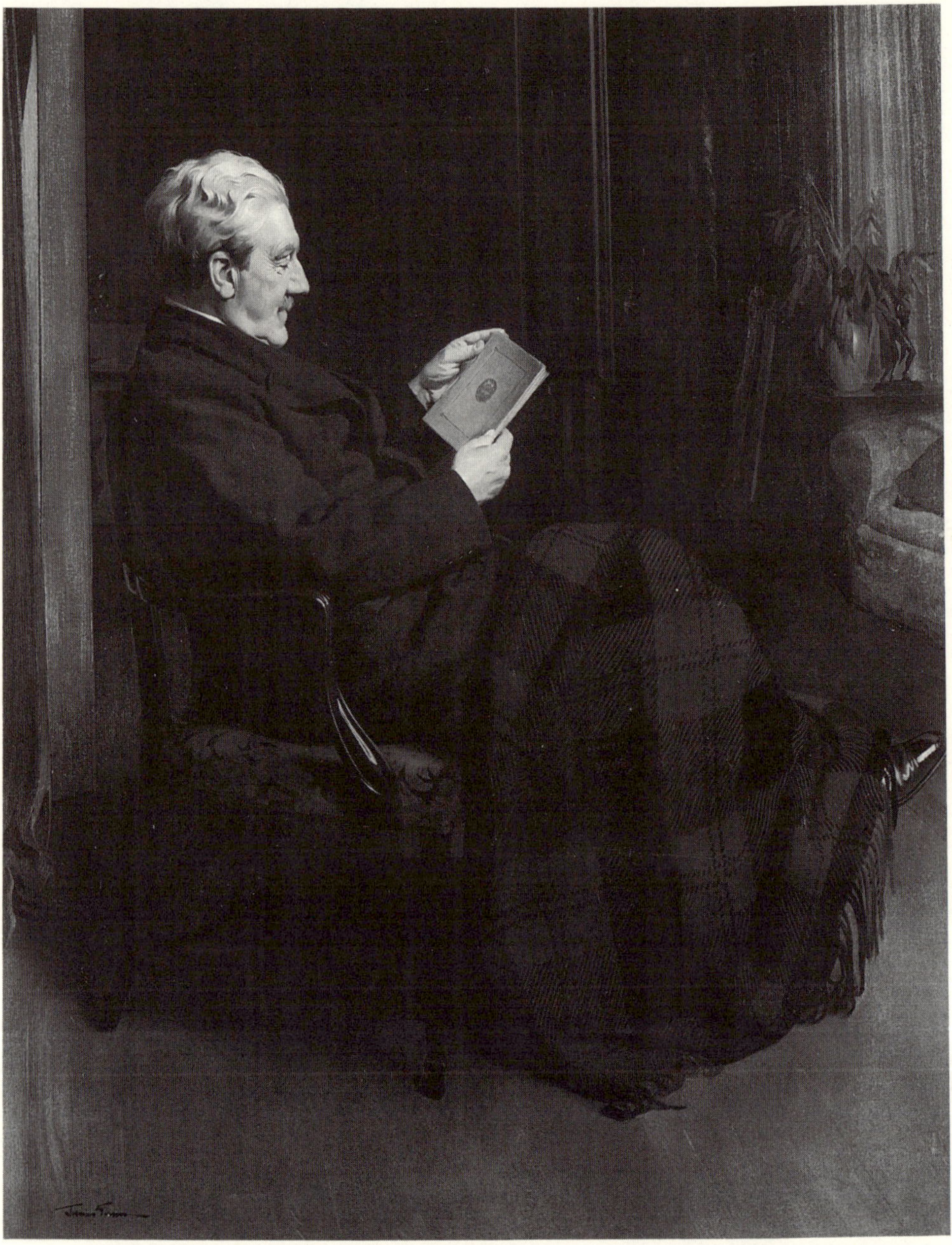

David Lindsay, twenty-seventh Earl of Crawford and tenth Earl of Balcarres, oil painting by Sir James Gunn, R.A., 1939. Courtesy National Portrait Gallery, London.

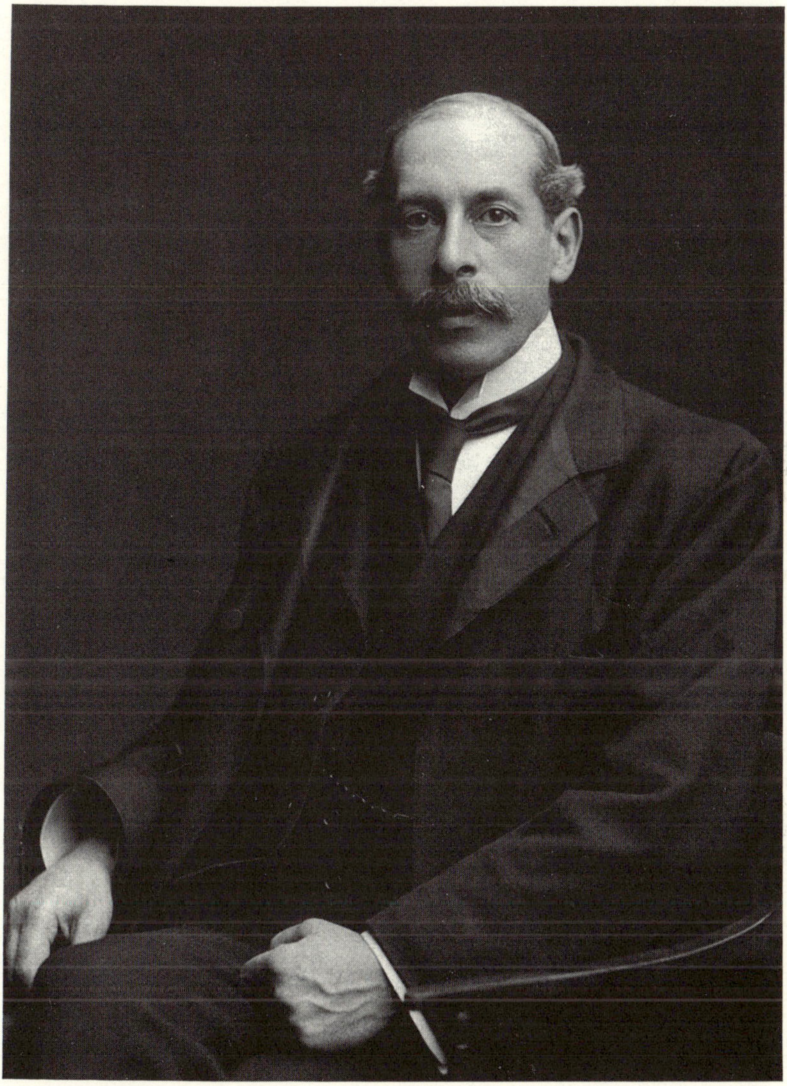

Isidore Spielmann, ca. 1905. Private collection.

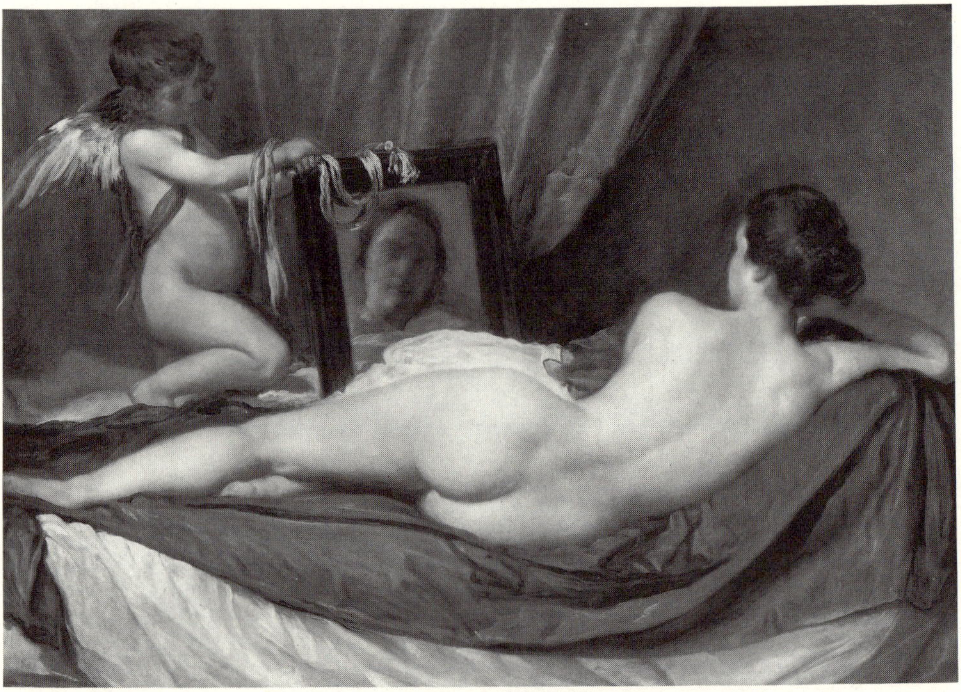

The Toilet of Venus, or the Rokeby *Venus,* oil painting by Diego Velázquez, ca. 1648. Courtesy National Gallery, London.

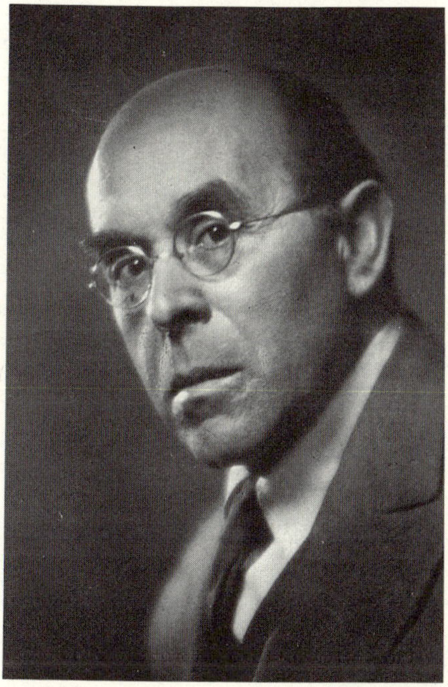

William Rothenstein, ca. 1910.
Private collection.

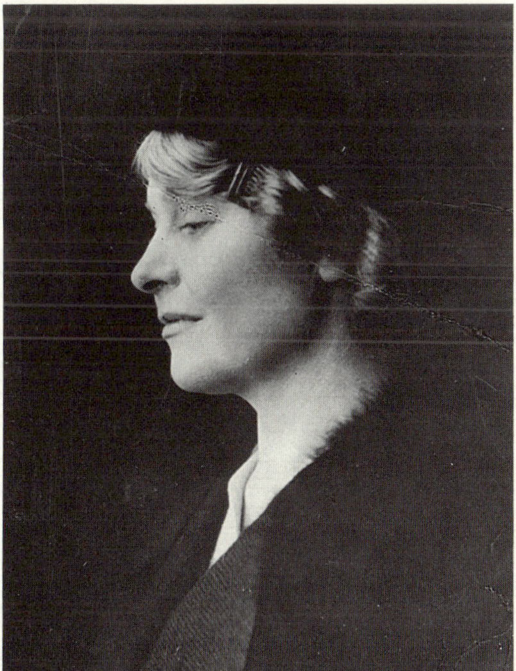

Alice Rothenstein, ca. 1910.
Private collection.

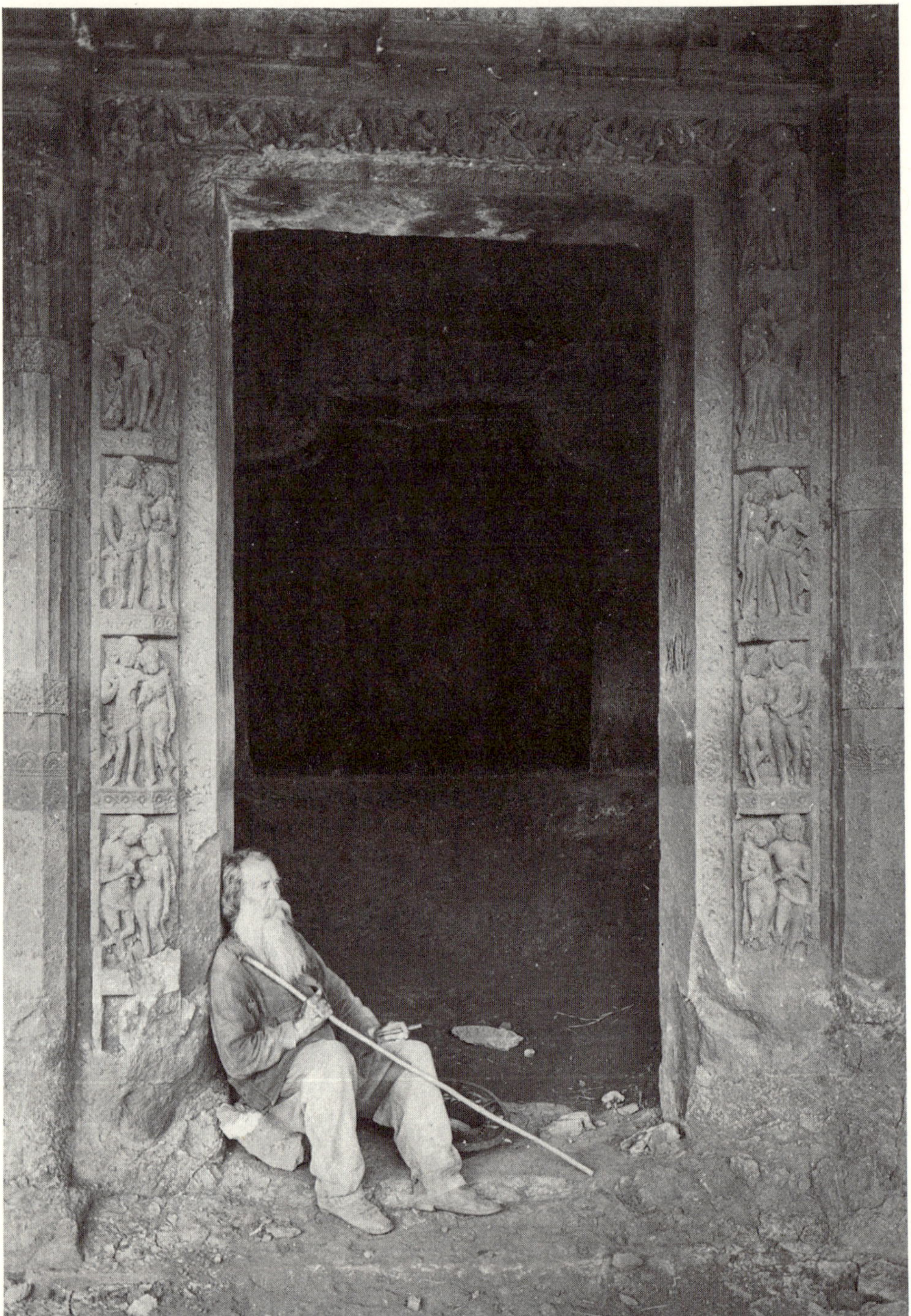

Major Robert Gill at entrance to Cave Twenty-four at Ajanta. Courtesy India Office Library (photo 125/1 [18]).

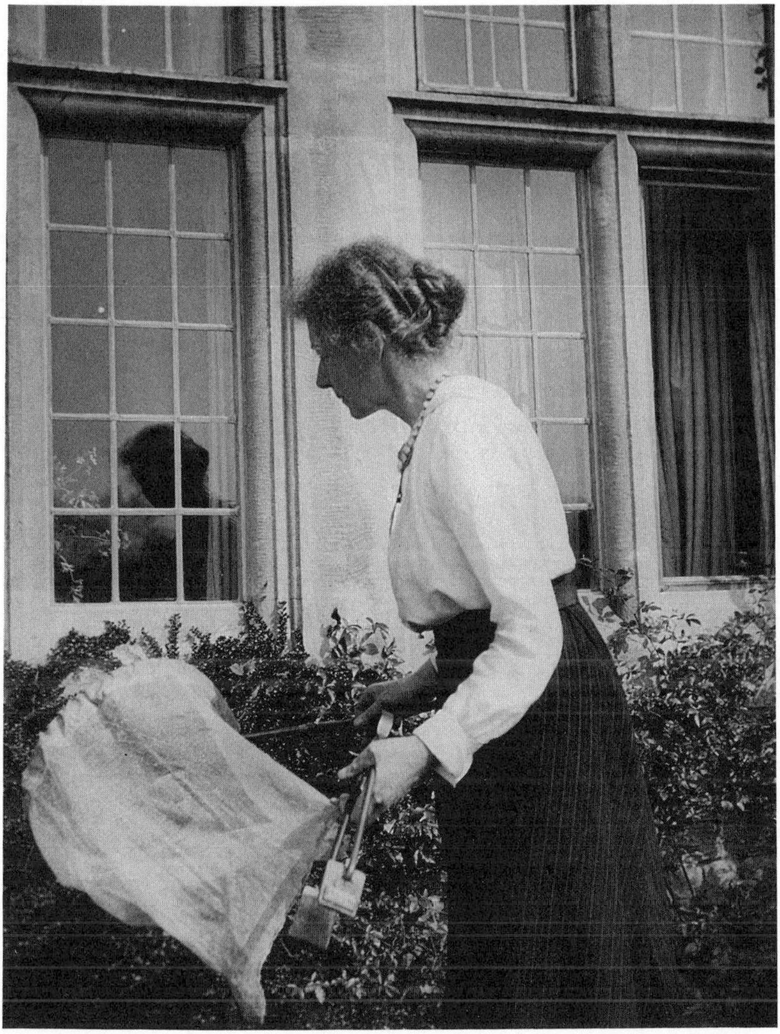

Christiana Jane Herringham at Piccard's Rough, ca. 1900. Private collection.

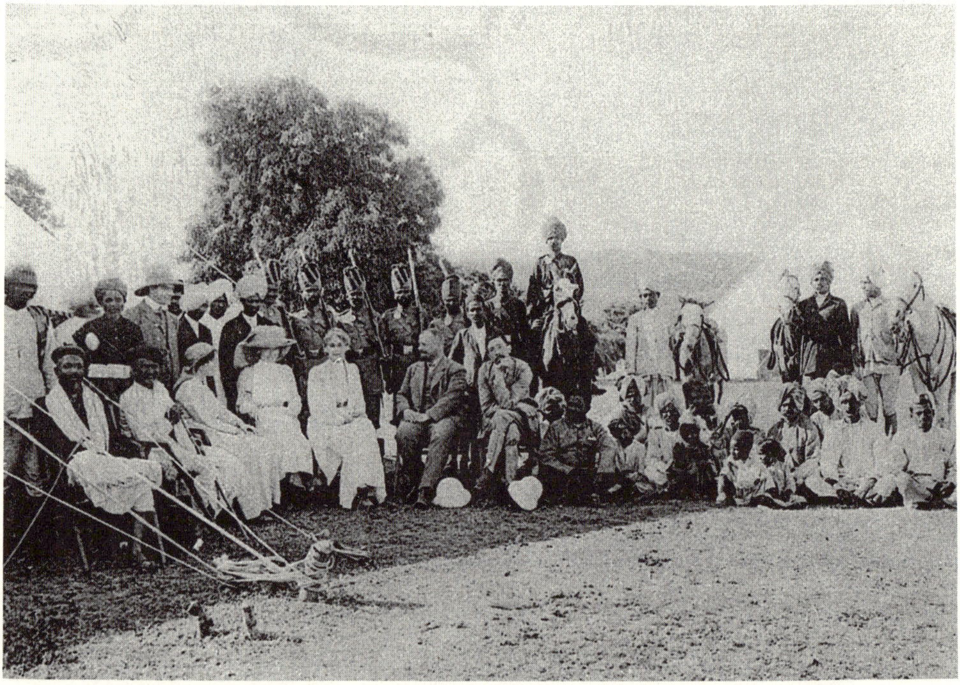

The only known photograph of the entire group of painters, camp personnel, and visitors at the Ajanta camp, November 1910–March 1911. It includes *front row, third from left,* Dorothy Larcher, then Sheila Casson Walker, Christiana Herringham, Victor Goloubew, and Charles Müller. Reprinted from Müller, *Cinq mois,* facing p. 114.

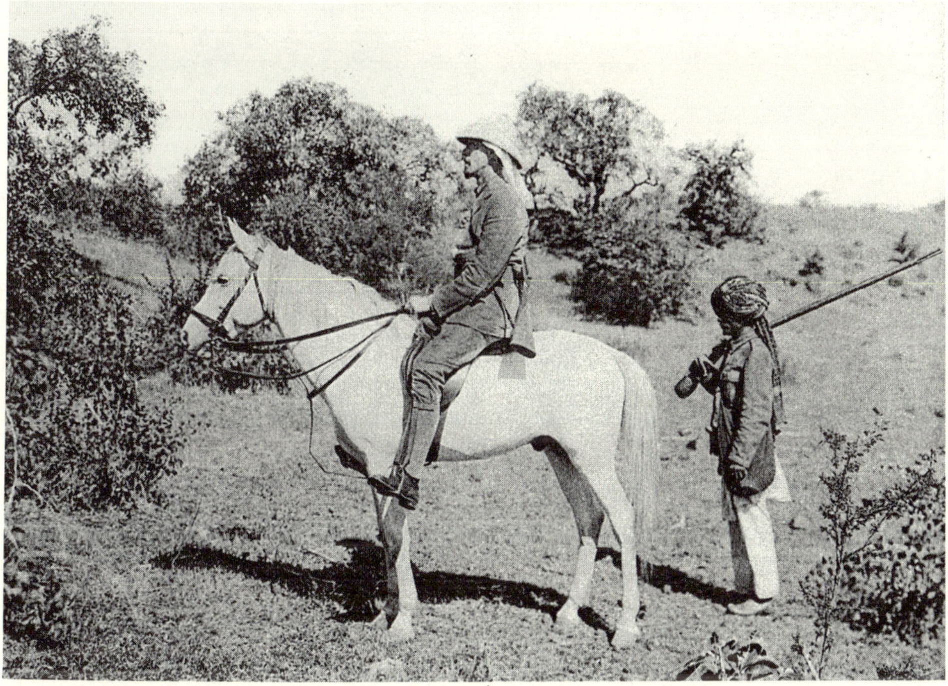

Charles Müller on horseback at Ajanta, late 1910. Reprinted from Müller, *Cinq mois,* facing p. 114.

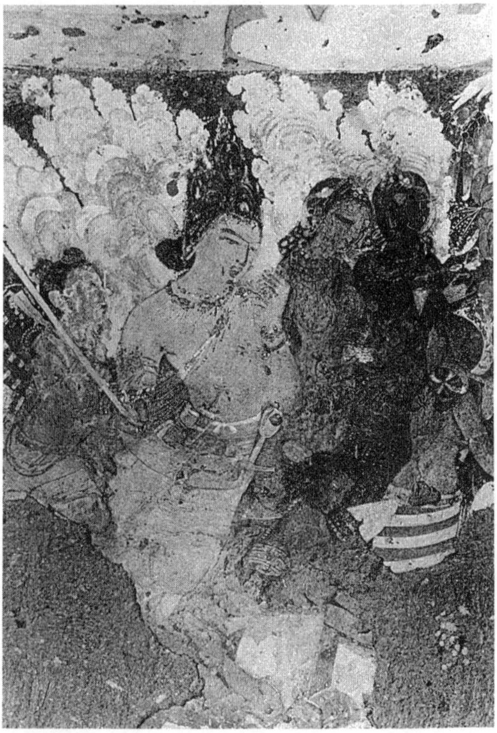

Wall painting in Cave Seventeen at Ajanta. Reprinted from Müller, *Cinq mois,* facing p. 82.

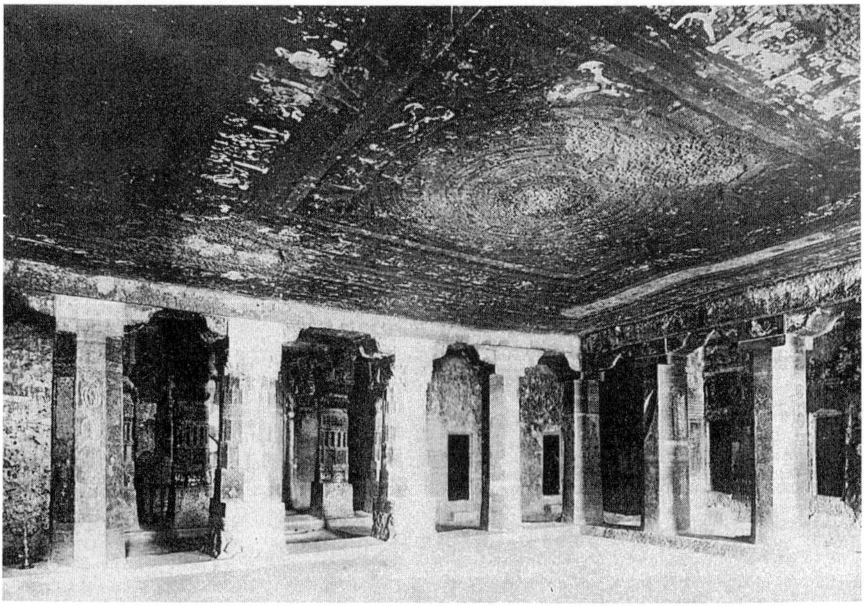

Interior of Cave Seventeen at Ajanta, with painted ceilings. Reprinted from Müller, *Cinq mois,* facing p. 128

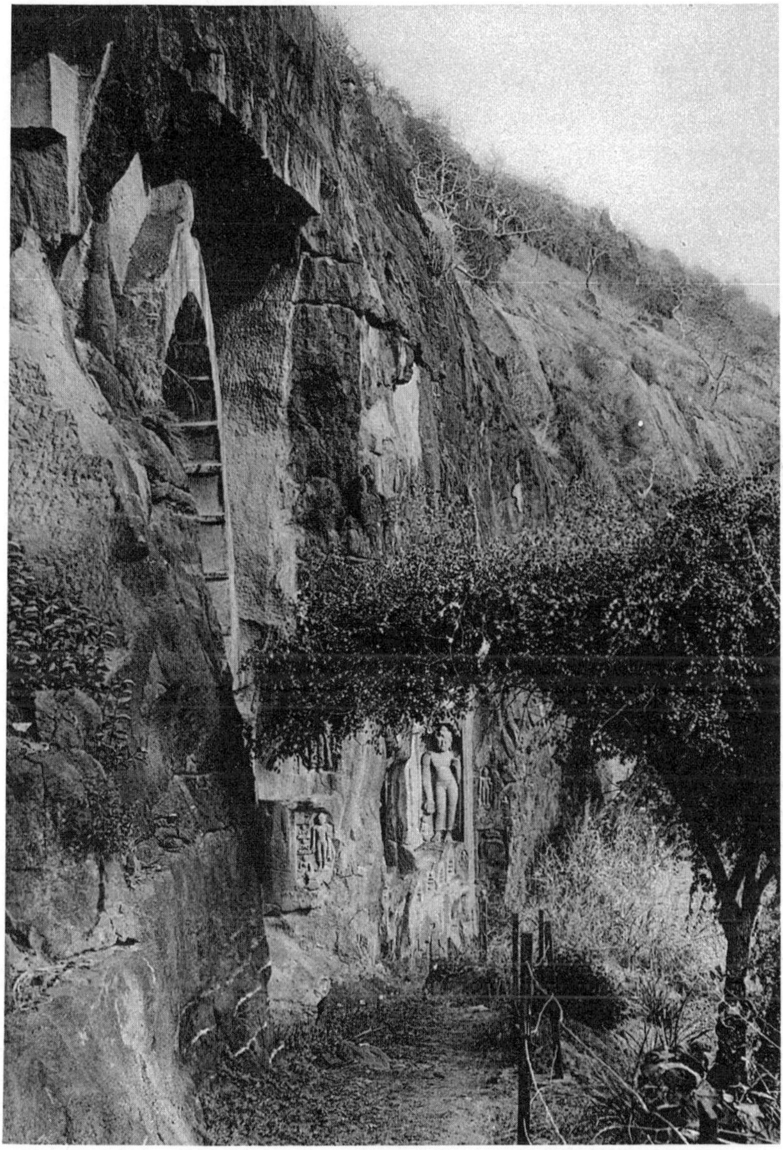

Great window of monastery, Cave Nineteen, Ajanta. Reprinted from Müller, *Cinq mois,* facing p. 50.

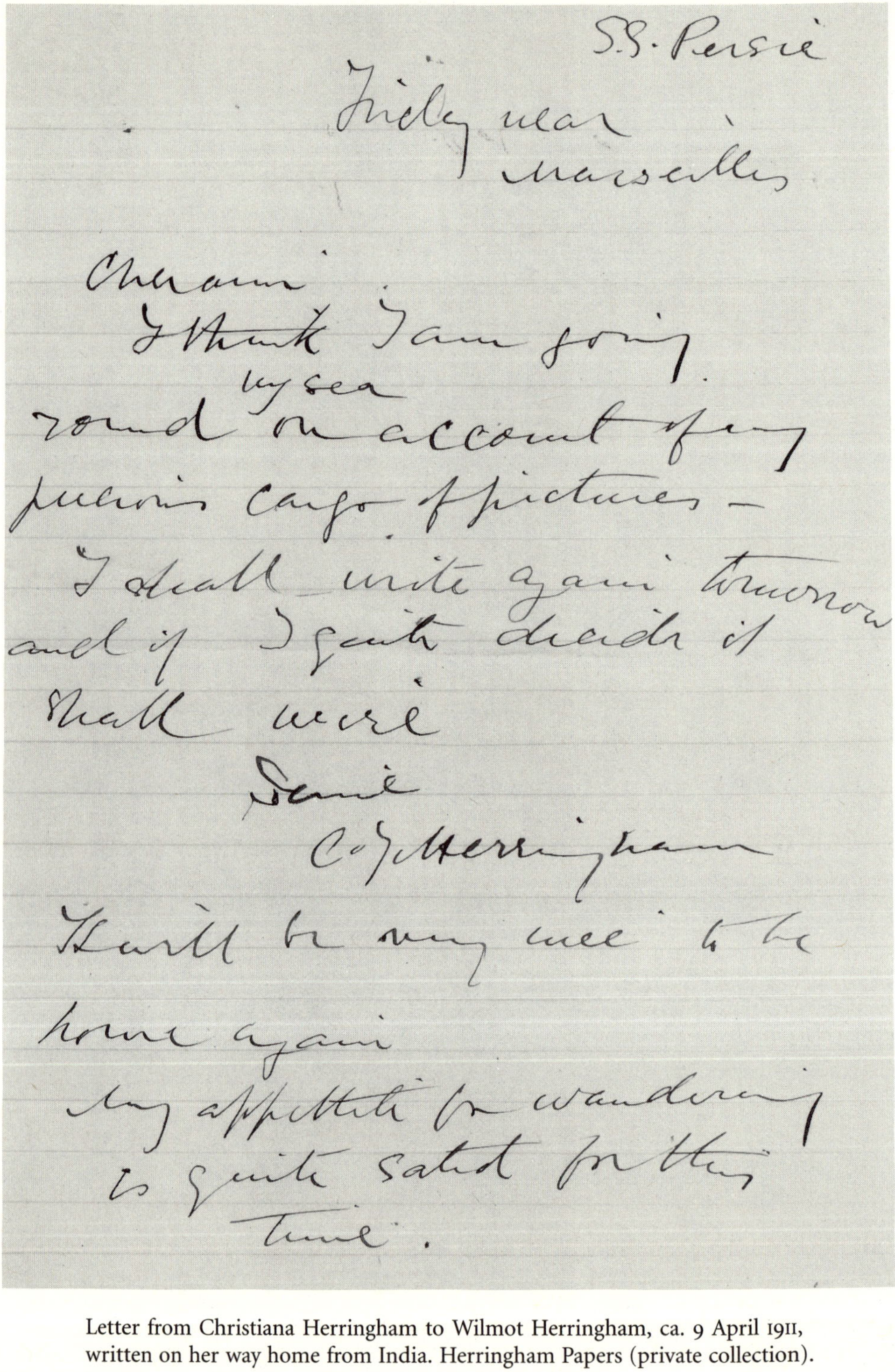
S.S. Persia

Friday near
Marseilles

Dearest
~~I think~~ I am going
by sea
round on account of my
precious cargo of pictures —
I shall write again tomorrow
and if I quite decide it
shall wire

Dearie
C J Herringham

It will be very nice to be
home again
My appetite for wandering
is quite sated for this
time.

Letter from Christiana Herringham to Wilmot Herringham, ca. 9 April 1911, written on her way home from India. Herringham Papers (private collection).

5

VENUS ASCENDING

DURING THIS, the Fund's first great campaign, Christiana Herringham appeared to stand aside, watching the surprising eddy that her first stone had set in motion. She was still constrained by her discomfort about her position as the only woman on the executive committee. Like the others who had had differences of opinion, she suppressed hers and joined the campaign to persuade general public, private collectors, and Treasury that Velázquez's lovely *Venus* should be in the National Gallery and that it was worth the forty-five thousand pounds finally needed to put it there. The united spirit in which the members went to work bears witness to the strength and timeliness of their appeal. If Balcarres had uncomplimentary opinions about any of his colleagues, he did not commit them to paper. If some animosities persisted, they no longer impeded the progress of the work. Robert Clermont Witt may have found Claude Phillips difficult, but they could not get on without Phillips, for, as C. J. Holmes wrote, "his long experience of European picture-galleries, his wonderful memory and repute as a critic, gave his pronouncements an authority which no one since his day (and perhaps before it) had exercised in this country. I am not forgetting Ruskin or Berenson." Witt began to bear differences more patiently. Everyone's nerves had been stretched, he told Balcarres, and it was no wonder that everyone was on edge.[1]

Roger Fry's nerves were clearly on the edge, and with good reason. Only two years after his marriage in 1896 to the artist Helen Coombe, she had had a baffling illness characterized by depression and disorientation. This recurred in 1903, and Fry had carried that burden along with his worries about the *Burlington Magazine,* the Fund, and the problem of finding someone to care for their two children. He told Holmes that he was "almost at my wits' end with anxiety and momentary hope and fear."[2] In such circumstances his earlier misgivings about Balcarres had increased. He told Mary Berenson, "Balcarres has by now got up a pretty strong hatred of me over this National Art-Collections Fund and [Herbert] Cook is almost the only staunch person."[3] In fact, Cook was not the "only staunch person," but all of Fry's frustrations had mounted under the increasing pressure of his family's troubles and the lack of money for coping with them. Nevertheless, he carried on.

In 1904 D. S. MacColl was largely occupied with the consequences of his 1903 article on Chantrey Fund administration. On 21 June 1904, the Earl of Lytton moved for a select committee of the House of Lords to inquire and recommend corrective measures. He justified this on three grounds: first, the "accumulation of evidence over a series of years"; second, the "growing tide of hostile criticism"; and third, the Royal Academy's continued refusal to "meet any of the charges which are brought against them or to give any explanation of their conduct, and their repeated assertions that they are responsible to no one, and that probably those who criticise them are actuated by motives either of wounded vanity or jealousy."[4]

On 1 July a committee was appointed; on 8 August it reported. "That report," says Samuel Hynes, "is an extremely interesting social document; few Edwardian records show so clearly the abyss of mutual distrust and misunderstanding that separated the conservative established order from the spokesmen of liberation." One has only to refer back to the hearings of the Royal Fine Arts Commission of 1856 to find that the charges are essentially the same.[5] In 1904 as in 1856, when the inquiry ended, the Academy was allowed to go its way undisturbed in any major respect, to MacColl's great disgust. In 1905 he looked back at the 1904 inquiry and

> the imaginary history, the desperately ingenious interpretations of a phrase or two in the will, the scruples that had beset the purchasers

> only when there was danger of purchase falling outside the Academy Exhibition, all this failed to impress the Committee. Its members politely allowed the Academy the plea of a mistaken interpretation, and fully confirmed the perfectly obvious reading of the Will insisted upon by the critics.

No fundamental change occurred in the Academy's procedure for purchases from the Chantrey money.[6]

Nevertheless, the fact that the Chantrey inquiry and the Fund's first efforts should have coincided was salutary. The message to everyone was that the welfare of the national collections must depend upon a cooperative spirit in administrators, Treasury, connoisseurs, and a concerned public—all four together. For the Fund, the disappointing outcome of the Chantrey inquiry suggested the difficulties ahead, for future success would depend upon a combination of resources from the old, elitist and the new, more democratic constituencies, and it had to decide upon the scope of its activities. William Rothenstein, who was always concerned for the welfare of living artists, hoped that the new Fund might help galleries to purchase their works more often and more liberally. Christiana had the same vision but felt overwhelmed by the need to save single great works from leaving the country. With her father's village hall at Guildford in mind, she had written:

> I don't think the Nat Art Collections Fund can do both jobs, old and new—the old one's hard enough, but the buying of the works of living men, does bristle with difficulties. I do so wish the movement to have local art galleries would grow.
>
> Every town, even quite small ones should have a Hall of the people full of pictures and statues and pleasantness—These things might sometimes move from one to another. This is Socialist—but socialist life, if not socialist production is the only hope for better things.[7]

If assistance to the national collections was to be its function, the Fund must decide also on its procedures for selecting—and helping to buy—the works that it would support. Robert Benson told Balcarres that he was "emphatically against appointing *anybody* even the angel Gabriel as our buyer of pictures etc—except the chairman i.e. yourself." The chairman should have power to act "wherever time or secrecy demand instant action, & to employ any agent he likes Phillips or Colvin or anybody else. No well managed Department, or Bank or House of business would dream of tying themselves up to one broker or agent." He had reservations about Phillips as buyer, not on grounds of incompetence but because Phillips was so fastidious about the quality of a work of art. Benson described him as an "excellent man & a friend of mine . . . , who shrinks from a bad piece of work like a flower before a rough wind but whom I seldom employ to drive a bargain." Like Christiana, who had preferred "expert" over "subcommittee" as the operative term, Benson preferred "expert" over "buyer," though he did not want "to see our association tied to any expert. While I am all in favour of an autocrat for head—(the exact constitution of the paralyzed body of Nat. Gallery Trustees) I want the autocrat to be the Chairman—i.e. yourself & not a professional."[8]

Buying pictures would be much more difficult than buying consols or securities, Benson continued. The chairman should decide what he wants, then get a reliable agent. "The best buyer is probably he who is least sensitive to the merits of the work you want." He trusted Agnew's. "They are always willing to buy & charge no commission to a public gallery & they know *how to buy well.* That is the point."[9] In a little more than a year, Agnew's was to be of crucial importance to the Fund.

Sidney Colvin thought that the duties of the pictures committee should be so defined "as to enable us to work together in all matters."[10] The eventual solution was a plan by which Phillips was general coordinator for paintings, and Colvin for prints and drawings.

Very soon, both collectors and members of the public began to send the Fund suggestions for national acquisition. The recurring motif was the disgrace to the nation if this or that masterpiece were allowed to leave Britain. Even useless suggestions indicated hope and confidence. More knowledgeable individuals reported art-market rumors. Phillips feared that Lord Pembroke might sell the incomparable Wilton Diptych, which was to be exhibited in Paris in the spring at the Musée des Arts Décoratifs. What if some foreign buyer were tempted to purchase it? Its sale would be "an irreparable loss to the country on account of its unique historical as well as artistic importance, and the fact that it was originally among the treasures of the Crown." Such a loss would be "a lasting disgrace both to the seller and the nation if such a picture" should go to a private French collection.[11]

A certain testiness toward some of the suggestions indicated that the Fund's very existence had stirred up a host of long-frustrated expectations. The *Evening News* pointed out that Whistler's famous—or infamous—Peacock Room, created for Frederick Leyland's London residence in 1876–1877, was about to go to the United States—and where was the National Art Collections Fund? Isidore Spielmann replied that the Fund must be the judge of what to buy, and of what it *could* buy, for financial competition with the Americans and the Germans was very difficult.[12]

There were expectations also that the Fund must stand as surrogate for the delinquent Chantrey trustees. Frank Rutter, in his regular column for the *Sunday Times,* needled the Fund about Whistler's *Symphony in Grey: Early Morning, Thames,* on sale at the New Gallery. If the Chantrey trustees would do nothing, what about the National Art Collections Fund, "of which we have heard so much? Now is its opportunity to prove its worth to the nation and to art," and to atone for the official carelessness that had allowed Whistler's portrait of his mother to get away to France. If the Fund did not bestir itself, "the blame and the shame of it will this time rest not only with the Chantrey trustees, but also with those self-constituted watchers of our treasure-houses who control the National Art Collections Fund." Three months later he carried his argument into MacColl's own territory with a letter to the *Saturday Review.* The Chantrey trustees, true to their deplorable form, had done nothing, but was the National Art Collections Fund, "of which we have heard so much, hoped so much, taking any steps in the matter" of the *Symphony in Grey*?[13]

In December the *Daily Mail* observed that

> experience has taught us not to expect wise discernment from the former [i.e. the Chantrey trustees], but the administrators of the

> National Art Collections Fund that was started with so much beating of drums for the express purpose of taking advantage of opportunity for acquiring notable works of art for the nation might be more on the alert. Their scheme was well received, and does not lack financial support, but so far we have not heard that anything has been done.[14]

Lord Curzon, when invited in August to join the Fund's council, had replied that he would be very glad to join, "though I do not clearly apprehend if they do anything." Indeed, the Fund had not been idle. By the end of 1904 it had 551 members, an increase for the year of 243. It had begun to help the national collections with acquisitions, of which there were seven in 1904; the first was an early Watteau, *Fête de Champêtre,* for the National Gallery in Dublin. In 1905 the Fund did not buy Whistler's *Symphony in Grey* because it was already raising two thousand pounds for his *Nocturne in Blue and Gold—Old Battersea Bridge* for the Tate Gallery. Rutter, when the painting was on display at the New Gallery, asked, "Can nothing of Whistler's be saved from the wreck of our national art administration?" He had launched another campaign, with Phillips and MacColl assisting, to place a Manet, a Monet, or a Whistler in one of the British national collections, but in May 1905 he suspended the appeals of his French Impressionist Fund with a promise to return to them as soon as the *Nocturne in Blue and Gold* had been rescued.[15]

By 8 July the Whistler painting was safe, and Rutter acknowledged that the Fund had expunged at least some of "the blame and the shame" of Chantrey failures. "Thanks to the generosity of individual subscribers, that admirable institution, the National Art Collections Fund, has been able to purchase one of Whistler's most beautiful and characteristic nocturnes." Of course, Chantrey trustees should have bought it, he declared, but "one cannot be too thankful that there exist in our midst generous and unselfish individuals willing and able to repair one of their most glaring omissions." However, he cautioned that Londoners should remember that there were still gaps to be filled, and not even a Whistler could make up for the lack of a Manet or a Monet.[16]

The *Nocturne in Blue and Gold* was one of twenty-one acquisitions in 1905. Christiana Herringham was as delighted as were any of its other supporters, but she had begun to worry that the Fund, if it were trying to impress with quantity, was spreading its efforts too thin. On 26 October she wrote to the executive committee and Balcarres:

> Will the other members of the Executive Committee forgive an expression of individual opinion on my part—
>
> If we are to influence public opinion we ought only to buy for the nation work that is of its kind first-class—A gift from the Nat. Art Coll^ns Fund should bear looking in the mouth. It should be worthy of a prominent place and we should be proud to have presented to the Nation work of intrinsically fine quality. I have not felt that this has been always sufficiently recognised as a guiding principle. I feel I am of very little use at the committee meetings, but I should like to come occasionally, and to receive special appeals.[17]

Less than a month later a work as fine and first-class as anyone could wish came onto the market. This was Velázquez's *Toilet of Venus,* called the Rokeby *Venus,* the painting that John Postle Heseltine so hoped might belong to the nation. The Fund's campaign to keep it in England was a landmark struggle over standards of taste and methods of acquisition, a David-and-Goliath contest between the Fund, only two years old, and blatant philistinism as represented by a deadweight of Treasury and art-establishment apathy and bias. It brought into the open some of the most unpleasant of lingering Victorian attitudes: provincialism and prudery; snobbishness about "trade" as represented by art dealers in particular; and, most distasteful of all, anti-Semitism. On the other hand, the campaign proved that there were enormous untapped reserves of generosity and goodwill among both "influentials" and "stalwarts" who were impatient with existing standards and welcomed an opportunity to help turn the balance.

The *Venus,* which was painted at some time in 1648, had been exhibited in England only twice since 1813, when art importer and entrepreneur William James Buchanan had brought it into England and J. B. S. Morritt of Rokeby Hall, Yorkshire, had purchased it for five hundred pounds on advice of Sir Thomas Lawrence. It had been included in the British Art Treasures Exhibition at Manchester in 1857, and it was shown at the Royal Academy in 1890, when

Heseltine had seen it. Since 1813 the owners had refused many offers, but in 1905 the pressures from competing foreign galleries and millionaires proved irresistible. The whole nature of the British art market had changed. "Wealth, indeed, there still was," Holmes wrote, "but English fortunes were usually weighted by social and territorial obligations which left little to spare for art patronage. . . . Those who had anything saleable rushed to take advantage of the golden harvest: the few who had bought cautiously till then were frightened out of the field."[18]

Therefore, *Venus* was on show and on sale at Agnew's for forty thousand pounds. Insurance and transportation were five thousand more, bringing the final price to forty-five thousand pounds. The escalation of Heseltine's 1903 estimate of four thousand to five thousand pounds was staggering. Spielmann was cautious at first. He thought that special appeals should be made only rarely and did not yet feel that this was one of them. He had spoken to a wealthy friend who had said "that all the money he could spare would be given to the fund for the unemployed ~~in the East End~~ and to the families of the massacred Jews in Russia long before he thought of pictures, 'Because,' he said, 'he preferred to buy bread for the starving rather than cake for the comfortable classes.' This is a view I think a great many will take at this moment." Probably only a few very rich would give to initiate so large an amount of money. But if the committee decided "to make a move as a matter of policy, and only tackle the wealthy few," he would of course stand ready to help.[19]

Witt, too, weighed the relative advantages of a public appeal against an approach to a few rich persons. In either case, he knew that the Fund would forever regret missing this chance to acquire such a picture. R. A. M. Stevenson, the leading British authority on Velázquez, called *Venus* the one work still missing from Spain's great museum, the Prado, that could enable that collection to give "a full understanding of the painter's art." The executive committee met on 16 November and decided to approach the National Gallery, the Treasury, and the Royal Academy, and at the same time to appeal to selected wealthy individuals.[20]

There were particular hopes of a contribution from William Waldorf Astor, but as of 21 November he had not been heard from. The trustees of the National Gallery held a special meeting, but nothing came of that, either. They would accept the picture and hang it if offered, but they could not contribute and did not want to approach the Treasury themselves. Robert Benson was indignant at "such a spectacle of weakness and uselessness when there was a national object to be gained." How could "such good men individually" be "collectively so weak and inefficient"? It was no excuse that the National Gallery was about to enter an interregnum, for the Director, Sir Edward Poynter, would retire in January 1906, and no successor had been selected.[21] Benson had heard that Poynter opposed the purchase—although he was "the man who missed it, or ignored it, when offered to the Trustees." The price at that time was rumored at twenty-five thousand pounds. Now foreigners besieged the picture from all sides. There were the usual reports of American millionaires ready to pounce. Benson had heard about a "rich Parisienne" who was interested, and Wilhelm Bode of Berlin's Kaiser Friedrich Museum stood ready with a check until Agnew "choked him off by asking £60,000 & he replied (A. read me his letter) that at that price his gallery could not afford it. The picture is now held for us."[22]

On 27 November, Benson told Balcarres that he had met Arthur James Balfour, the prime minister, at Agnew's, and that Balfour was "very keen" when Benson told him "the *whole* story." Balfour did not think, however, that a Treasury grant would be forthcoming, "but he does not see why the [National Gallery] Trustees should not help with money." This was the rather obtuse view also of Austen Chamberlain, Chancellor of the Exchequer. Balfour told Benson that he "wanted to see big important things secured for the nation instead of small things; this one is one of the biggest & most important chances." In view of the attitudes of both the Treasury and the National Gallery trustees, Balfour's view was unrealistic on all counts. Nor was there any sign of succor from the Royal Academy; five Academicians and associate members had responded, "all half-hearted or averse."[23]

By this time Benson was ready to put his faith in a public appeal. He drafted a letter that he asked Balcarres to send out as his own, asking for members and money for the Fund. It appeared in a fairly obscure corner of the *Times* over the names of Balcarres, Spielmann, and Witt. It stated that the National Gallery trustees had said "that they would accept the picture with the greatest pleasure and satisfaction." Two weeks later the trustees again expressed regret "that there are no funds at all at their disposal for any contribution towards the purchase of the Rokeby *Venus.* The trustees have no power to anticipate further income."[24] This, unfortunately, was true. They were chronically hampered by the Treasury's stubbornness and unpredictability with respect to supplementary funds, and by what often seemed its sheer lack of business acumen. Well within living memory was the sale of the art treasures from Blenheim Palace in 1884–1885, when the Treasury haggled endlessly over the few pictures it was willing to subsidize. As a letter writer to the *Times* had observed at the time, the Treasury seemed to "proceed as if this new grant were to be reckoned against future disbursements alone. It certainly seems hard upon the Trustees to subject them to so one-sided an arrangement." In 1905 Benson complained to Balcarres: "You remember the Trustees treated the Burne-Jones Committee in just the same way. (We had got over £5000 for [Burne-Jones's] King Cophetua & wanted £6500, & they did nothing.)"[25]

While the Treasury stood aloof, the Louvre wrote to Agnew's offering to submit a formal bid for the *Venus.* Benson had more faith in Agnew's than in the Treasury. He was still confident that the firm would give its services without a commission, for it "behaved very generously & *quite* unselfishly over the King Cophetua, & in many other cases I have heard of it giving their services for nothing where the nation is concerned."[26]

Even before the Fund's appeal appeared in the *Times,* conservative opinion declared itself. The Rt. Hon. Lord Ronald Sutherland Gower, a member of the Fund and a trustee of the National Gallery, objected to the "absurd and ridiculously high figure" being asked for the Rokeby *Venus.* His real objections were to the Fund's involvement with the Whistler purchase and to Venus's nudity. The Fund had

> recently wasted a couple of thousand pounds in the purchase of a painting, or rather a sketch for a picture, by that over-rated artist,

> James Whistler. I trust that the nation will not be hoodwinked by a small artistic (?) clique into the folly of subscribing such a stupendous sum as £40,000 (especially to be deprecated at the present day, when thousands of semi-starving people are wandering through the streets) in order to buy a painting suited for the sanctum of some multi-millionaire, but not for an English public art gallery

—for a gallery in some country less concerned with public morality, perhaps, but not for Britain. Unlike Spielmann's affluent friend, Sutherland Gower did not mention an alternate charitable use for his own money. And unlike Heseltine, who considered the *Venus* more suited to a public gallery than to a private home, Sutherland Gower had in mind for it some male hideaway off limits to the ladies.[27]

At least one member of the public refused to believe that the *Venus* presented an emergency. S. H. Whitehead submitted "a humble word of protest against the idea that there lies upon us any peculiarly patriotic obligation to acquire for the National Gallery the Velasquez 'Venus' at anything like the price which is generally mentioned in connection with it." He disputed the claim that if the picture were not purchased now, "the lady would turn her lovely back on us for ever. That is the old story over again. The nations are not going to be rushed into these Sybilline bargains either by fiscal reformers or by fine art dealers." In any case, *Venus* was not an important picture, and the National Gallery "is not a freak museum."[28]

A Fund member lost his or her nerve and confided to the *Times* doubts about whether it would be "expedient" to acquire "this highly realistic study of a nude Spanish dancer" if education is the purpose of an art gallery. This brought up the vexing question of whether a gallery exists for education, for moral improvement, or for aesthetic pleasure. This member had thought that the Fund prided itself "on the comparative absence of pictures of such like subjects on the walls of the Royal Academy, and I, together with many other lovers of art, feel that those who claim to direct and influence the public taste should be guided by higher considerations than of mere technical skill, however great."[29]

The education and morality issue had its best answer in a letter from "A Woman Member of the National Art Collections Fund," perhaps the classics scholar Jane Harrison. Would the *Times,* she asked, allow her to protest against

> the mischievous prurience which condemns the nude human form as something inherently impure? To convey this impression to the young is a crime of *lése-humanité* [*sic*]; to proclaim it to the thoughtful is to censure our admiration for Greek art; . . . to uphold it as an axiom of morality is to justify the absurdity of the "London Council for the Protection of Public Morality," which, confronted with the vast public vice of London, recently met to consider amongst other business, "the question of low-neck dresses," and will infallibly land us in the puerility of the Boston crusade against open-work stockings.[30]

Neither irony nor sarcasm could be the complete antidote to Sutherland Gower's next accusation. He had resigned his membership in the Fund, and in answer to a diplomatic letter from Balcarres, he asked, with a nastily anti-Semitic reference to Spielmann, how much Spielmann and Witt, as well as various unidentified (presumably Jewish) picture dealers, stood to make from the forty thousand pounds being asked for the picture. He wound up this diatribe with another blast at Whistler.[31]

Sutherland Gower's shabby supposition hung over the transaction to the very end, although he was the only one to be so brutally frank about it in print. Dealers were "in trade," were creatures of commerce. How could they not be profiting by escalating art prices and perhaps escalating them artificially? Even the prime minister wanted to know how much went to the facilitators of the purchase. Members of the Fund's committees were well aware of rumors that they, too, were profiting on the side. Christiana wrote to Rothenstein:

> If you care about the Velasquez coming to the nation, can you influence any rich man to help? We think people have been put off by the bigness of the sum and so have offered moderate or small donations. . . . There is a story about that my respectable and irreproachable colleagues are in Agnew's pay—I am, too, I suppose—it is very funny. I hope I shall be able to live it down.

Ten days later she told Rothenstein that there was no further news about "the last efforts for the Velasquez. I know now how it feels to be a political agent[,] to be cunning, and to be slanged."[32]

A complete contrast of spirit to Sutherland Gower's was that of the painter Sigismund Goetze. When the campaign for the *Venus* lagged because the wealthy failed at first to come forward in sufficient numbers, he publicly offered five hundred pounds toward the Fund. No one, he told the *Times*, could doubt either the value of the picture or the importance of acquiring it.

> But having waited in vain for the Tritons of art to lead the way, perhaps you will allow one of the smallest of the minnows to rise to the surface and make his Lilliputian ripple.
>
> Therefore, as something practical must be done, and done at once, the writer of these lines is prepared to offer £500 toward a fund to acquire this masterpiece for the nation.
>
> He is aware that this sum represents but a tiny drop in the ocean; nevertheless, as one whose personal wants are as slight as the wherewithal to gratify them, he humbly trusts that his example may be followed to some better purpose by others whose names represent all that is best in our national life.[33]

His generosity awed and delighted the officers of the Fund, although Witt was slightly dismayed, for he had hoped to begin with a publicity-worthy gift from William Waldorf Astor. Goetze had come out of nowhere to seize the initiative and set the example. Small gifts had come in but not rapidly enough to meet Agnew's deadline, after which the picture must be released to other bidders. No doubt publicized skepticism about the picture gave some people pause. Experts certified its authenticity, but some questions remained. *Was* it a Velázquez? Was it the best available example of his work? Was it true that there had been fire damage? Had two different models posed? Did Venus's face in the mirror devalue the work? It was a peasant's face, not a lady's.[34]

On 22 November the Fund had three thousand pounds in hand. On 27 November the executive committee planned a new public appeal. On 7 December a circular went out to announce the result. It stated that by that date fifteen thousand pounds had been promised; this included ten thousand from an anonymous subscriber, and two thousand from "a well-known art lover and collector."[35] By Christmas 1905, the total was twenty thousand pounds, and an anonymous donor promised the balance if the Fund could raise its total to thirty thousand.

To complicate matters still more, a political crisis was imminent, with Sir Henry Campbell-Bannerman about to replace Balfour as prime minister. The government formally refused to help the Fund. With the national finances in their present uncertain state, the Lords of the Treasury could not feel justified in approaching Parliament about a special appropriation. At that point, Agnew's came forward to help by extending the deadline to "Friday next," that is, 29 December. The executive committee of the Fund made last desperate efforts. "We are living in a very exciting time," Spielmann told Balcarres. He was "rushing about with an energetic friend to reach people (to *his* rich friends, for I have exhausted mine) . . . I think personally it is next to impossible to do it in so short a time"—even if all on the committees did their utmost.[36] Once again, Agnew's extended the deadline.

The eleventh hour was still upon them, and hope was fading. On 9 January, the executive committee sorrowfully confessed failure to raise the money. On 13 January the *Saturday Review* published an article by MacColl, "The Loss of the Velasquez," in which he wrote that although 120,000 persons had viewed the picture at Agnew's and the general feeling was that it must not be lost to the nation, the total of gifts fell short, and the government offered nothing.[37]

On that same day, Sigismund Goetze wrote again to the *Times*. The campaign had come so far and was it, he asked, to fail now?

> It is to be feared that the refusal of the Government to assist in the purchase of this masterpiece will not only make us the laughing-stock of artistic Europe but will create a precedent which bodes ill for future would-be benefactors. All that is wanted is £18,000 and the courage to face the possible loss of a score or so of votes at the approaching elections! But when the Government fail to do the right thing for fear of unpopularity among the unthinking and unwashed it becomes the duty of private citizens to make further sacrifices, and the writer of this letter begs therefore to double his original offer made in your columns.

If other donors would do the same, he pointed out, government help would not be needed.[38]

MacColl's article and Goetze's example seemed to inspire some of the stragglers, but the goal was still not met. The total of subscriptions was stalled at thirty-two thousand pounds when the king, who had seen the picture at Agnew's and had heard that it was slipping away, signified his approval of the acquisition. That royal word tipped the final balance. The catalyst was George Holford, Robert Benson's brother-in-law, who was in waiting at Buckingham Palace. Benson had sent him "a diplomatic letter" that Holford had shown to the king, who kept it. Holford then wrote "to ask what we needed to clinch things & [I] replied only £8,000." After Benson spent Saturday, 21 January 1906, at the palace, he was at last able to give the order to close for the picture at forty thousand pounds. He was only just in time. Another buyer had an appointment with Agnew's for 12 January, but "we were just in front of him." Lockett Agnew was willing to hold it just a little longer, but "there was much pressure from the younger partners, especially since *he* had subscribed £5,000." According to Benson's calculations, that five thousand seems to have been Agnew's margin of profit. On 24 January the committee could announce that *Venus* belonged to the nation, subject only to confirmation of a last three thousand pounds, "the balance of the purchase money," and Agnew's granted the additional time for this.[39]

It was a great victory, a splendid precedent. It transpired that Goetze had cashed in his savings in order to make his gifts, and Balcarres would have his check for one thousand pounds by the end of the week. He assured Balcarres that he was in no way trying "to pose as a martyr, but to acquit myself of any seeming discourtesy toward you and the secretaries who have so ungrudgingly given their services toward the end we all had in view." Balcarres, thanking him wholeheartedly, wrote that "your promised donation was announced at a moment when the fate of the picture was hanging in the balance & I feel convinced that your strong advocacy of purchase must largely have stimulated others to follow your most generous example."[40] Others, too, had made sacrifices, and those who could give only a few pounds had as much right to rejoice as those who had given thousands, for it had been a truly cooperative effort.

Benson exulted, as he had every right to do. "We may as well trim our sails to the fair gale, treble our subscribers & be a greater power henceforward; so that the Trustees may come to us when they want anything, & we shall say Yes or No!" Phillips wrote to Balcarres: "It is, indeed, as you say, one of the most noteworthy facts [feats?] of our time, and we are all, I think, entitled to our share of the credit due to the National Art Collections Fund for its victory over official obstinacy and intrigue. The example is a magnificent one, and we have reason to hope that it will be extensively followed." Colvin took little credit, saying that if he had done anything, it was to keep the proceedings in good temper, "a thing not always easy considering the amount of nonsense that has been talked and printed on the subject."[41]

One of the most egregious bits of nonsense came while the picture was on display at the New Gallery, for the "pleasure and satisfaction" of the public to whom it now belonged. The opposition fired a last unworthy shot, this time from poet and critic Edmund Gosse and Royal Academician Sir William Richmond. Gosse, with Richmond agreeing, charged that a "mystery" hung over the episode. "Everybody in London is privately aware that no transaction connected with the arts has for many years been wrapped in such a tissue of scandal and tittle tattle as this of the 'Venus' of Velasquez. The committee has but to be explicit and this fabric of malevolence falls to dust." Balcarres replied that there was no mystery and no scandal, as would be plain when the annual report then in preparation appeared a few weeks later. Gosse refused to give over; he rebuked Balcarres for "a little note of dryness" in his brief letter and protested that he suspected no one and that he spoke "on my own ignorance! But in common with hundreds of others, I feel intolerable the burden of being kept in the dark." He wanted to know exactly who had given how much. Richmond was equally explicit: were there "dealers or semi-dealers" on the committee? Was "commerce" involved in their transaction? His patience exhausted, Balcarres replied, "It would be impossible to convey a more direct and dishonouring charge of corruption." He listed all the members of the executive committee, against whom Richmond had brought "collective accusations . . . a cruel slur." Richmond retreated a little, saying that he had intended to invoke only "a broad principle, needful as a reminder in these days, that no dealer or semi-dealer should sit upon a committee of purchase; my remarks were general, not specific."[42]

It was not a bad thing that the lingering suspicions of the old guard should have been brought so prominently into the open. "All the ridiculous rumours about 'jobbery' and 'scandal,'" said the *Art Journal,* "died a sudden death the other day when the Report of the Fund was issued," which listed all the major subscribers to the purchase.[43] The integrity of the Fund was vindicated, established beyond all question.

The *Burlington Magazine* took the occasion to advise about future policy for art administration. In January it observed that the National Gallery should have an up-to-date want list and a consistent purchasing policy as protection in times of such fluctuating private fortunes, national budgets, and art prices. The government should have greater purchasing authority as well as more money. In March the magazine commented on the general disarray in art affairs, including the necessity for such a struggle to get the *Venus,* the vacant National Gallery directorship, a plea pending for a cabinet minister of fine arts, and the Chantrey affair, all of which "indicate that the artistic public had been dissatisfied with our haphazard way of managing our affairs long before Mr Balfour's resignation."[44]

The Fund's early trials at least helped to clarify fundamental issues such as purchasing policy. It would concentrate, as Christiana Herringham had urged, on significant acquisitions for which no other money was available. A network of affiliated provincial committees, to which Robert Witt gave much time and thought, was coming into being. The Fund had resolved its crucial constituency issue: it was to be truly *national.* "Henceforth," Holmes later wrote, "when any important work of art was in danger, there could be no doubt where to turn for help if help was possible."[45]

Christiana Herringham now began to distance herself from the Fund's activities. Whether her unease about being the only woman on the executive committee was still a factor she does not say; her name remained on that list until 1914. It is more likely that she acted in obedience to her father's principle of giving with thoughtful modesty then tactfully withdrawing when the recipient could go on alone. She had seen the Fund over the stile, and after a few more years her role consisted of paying the annual membership fee and contributing to special appeals.[46] First, however, in a letter to Balcarres, she made clear "how the very first beginning of the Fund came about (but not later)." She referred to a meeting or meetings of the Fund's four originators that took place even earlier than those documented in Lord Balcarres's correspondence. A meeting of the four at Hertford House, where Phillips was in charge of the Wallace Collection, preceded their meeting of 30 June 1903, at which they had decided to invite Balcarres to be chairman, after which Phillips had written to extend that invitation. It becomes clear as well that Christiana's letter to MacColl in June 1903 was not her first attempt to initiate a movement in aid of purchases for the national collections. MacColl's *Saturday Review* article of 1900, "Friends of the National Gallery," had convinced her that mere talking was not enough and that a combination of his journalism and her money might get something started. She explained as follows to Balcarres:

> For about a year and a half I had been trying to get various people I knew to start an Amis du Louvre in England. They all said it would be impossible in England because of cliques & jealousies. I scarcely knew Mr. MacColl at all and I heard somehow that he was favourable to the idea—and one day I talked to him about it. [H]e thought the time had come & got together the first little meeting of four people at Hertford House. Those four pledged themselves to bring each one more to the next committee[?]. I forget whether you came to that or the next.[47]

Those four were of course MacColl, Fry, Phillips, and Christiana. The fact that the very first meeting occurred at Hertford House may account for her mention of only Phillips when she made her nervous speech of protest at the General Meeting on 11 November 1903. Their "first little meeting" at Hertford House took place some time between 10 June 1903, when MacColl received Christiana's letter, and 30 June, when Phillips wrote to Balcarres. Also in that interim, there had been the meeting to which they had brought "each one more," with Christiana bringing two more: J. P. Heseltine and (probably) Robert Witt. Her phrase "but not later" suggests that, once the fully expanded provisional committee went to work, she refrained from mentioning the early Hertford House meeting so as not to confuse the public's impression of the Fund's origins as a concerted public movement. This was loyalty as well as tact.

Until 1921, when MacColl recognized her as the "real Founder of the Fund," there are no congratulations for Christiana in the published record. In 1928 Witt, in his introduction to *Twenty-Five Years of the National Art Collections Fund,* acknowledged MacColl's first suggestion and Christiana as "in a sense the Founder of this Society." But even there, a gender limitation crept in; it was "the practical common-sense of her sex"—not art as her vocation—that had motivated her gift of that all-important two hundred pounds.[48]

No doubt, if she had not come forward in 1903, sooner or later someone else would have made a move with money in hand. But in the meantime, how many treasures would have been lost to the nation! It was Christiana who *did* come forward at that crucial moment to fulfill her father's "pleasant anticipations" of the way in which she would use her inheritance. Those who go now to pay their respects to Velázquez's *Venus,* to Whistler's *Nocturne in Blue and Gold,* or to any of the thousands of other works that have been acquired with the help of the Fund, will do well to accord respect also to her and to her three co-originators of the National Art Collections Fund.

A POSTSCRIPT

The battle for *Venus* did not mark the end of the war, but in later years, even if there was not always enough money, the situation did slowly change with respect to the roles of both the National Gallery and the Treasury. In 1911 the National Gallery's trustees appointed a committee of their members, with Lord Curzon as chairman, to evaluate the situation. Robert Witt told them that "since you gentlemen became Trustees, the whole position has entirely changed. . . . about five or six years ago we did not get any sympathy or support, but now it is very different." And Fry added that "we had the utmost difficulty in, I will not say getting support, but even tolerance." When the chairman asked how Wilhelm Bode managed to get so much art out of England, Benson, Witt, and Lockett Agnew pointed out that Bode had had the Kaiser's support, plenty of money, and his own book on Rembrandt, in which English dealers had listed works all over England, "a vast machine" for the convenience of Bode and foreign dealers and collectors.[49]

Between 1903 and 1913 the Fund raised £120,730 for pictures for the National Gallery alone. Still, as the Curzon Committee had pointed out in 1911, those were primarily rescue efforts, "not conducive to buying cheaply," that is, no purchase that depended upon "the hue and cry of a public appeal" could get the most favorable terms. Export restrictions were suggested and rosters to be compiled of works of art in England. Benson, however, touched upon the heart of the matter when he said that "the object should be to put the Nation in the position of the ideal private collector with a long purse who can act swiftly" and with speedy access to expert advice if it was needed. The Curzon Committee concluded by emphasizing the fact that despite some changes in attitude the Great Exodus continued at an alarming rate.[50]

In 1950 the Treasury appointed a committee with Lord Waverley as chairman. Its members reviewed actions proposed and neglected since the Curzon Committee's report: a fruitless appeal to Parliament in 1917; an *ad valorem* stamp duty on art exports, proposed by a new National Gallery trustees' committee in 1919 and rejected by the Treasury; a private member's bill to prohibit export, proposed in Parliament in 1926 but never given a second reading. The only really useful measure was a wartime expedient: the Import, Export and Customs Powers (Defence) Act of 1939, whose restrictions could be applied to vetoes of art exports.

In 1951 the committee's membership was increased to allow for a greater number of independent views. It concluded that export controls were "best applied to a small number of objects of high importance," that there must be "a clear statement of policy and adequate safeguards," and that "even then, the fact that it operates at so late a stage is bound to cause frustration and disappointment." Like the Curzon Committee, the Waverley Committee warned that national treasures still left the country because of "the much greater enthusiasm which foreign buyers showed in seeking out what they wanted" and because they had more money. "The one could be offset by greater vigour on the part of the authorities here; the other could only be offset by more funds." It was the same old story: progress had been made, but there was no reason for the nation to relax its vigilance.

In its report, the Waverley Committee paid tribute to the National Art Collections Fund as the most instructive initiative for supplementary funds. "Fifty years ago the seriousness of this situation began to be recognised, and . . . [the Fund] is therefore associated with, and makes possible almost all major purchases." It was not, could not be, had never intended to be the whole answer. Treasury subsidies had increased, but so had the prices of great art. The art wars continued, but the battle for the Velázquez *Venus* had made one thing brilliantly clear: in all future efforts it could be assumed that the Fund was a welcome ally, a part of the solution.[51]

6

AJANTA I

IN 1932 CHRISTIANA HERRINGHAM'S friend Euterpe Ionides Craies, a daughter of the renowned London family of Greek merchants and art patrons, remembered that her son Constantine, when a little boy, "used to say, 'If Lady Herringham were Queen, how *well* Europe would be governed.'" Euterpe herself recalled that Christiana had been "one of the seven wonders of the world: she painted and wrote and organised dwellings for working-women and it would take me a very long time to tell all that she did."[1]

In 1906 she did something quite different from any earlier activity. She went to India, where she saw the sadly deteriorated condition of the Buddhist wall paintings in the caves at Ajanta and decided that she must make plans to copy them before they faded further. Once again, she would set to work to do something that could be done for art but had not been done.

Her closest colleagues in the Fund also found that their activities took new directions. Phillips was hard at work cataloguing the Wallace Collection. Holmes was simultaneously editor of the *Burlington Magazine* and Slade Professor of Fine Art at Oxford. In 1906 MacColl became Keeper of the Tate Gallery. "Behold me a rond-de-cuir!" he wrote to Rothenstein. "It's very odd at my years to be made a clerk because of a taste for pictures . . . even my rivals for the post write me the most generous and friendly letters."[2]

In January 1906 Fry, who had hoped to be asked to fill the vacant directorship of the National Gallery, accepted instead the post of Curator of Paintings at the Metropolitan Museum of Art in New York

City. He sent this news to his mother and added, "The race between them and the National Gallery was a very close one, but they won."[3] The appointment made him also art adviser at close quarters to J. P. Morgan, president of the Metropolitan. Fry understood perfectly the irony of his being thus tied to one of the most notorious raiders of foreign art collections, but Helen Fry's medical expenses were enormous, and he desperately needed the larger income. He knew that there were serious differences between his own and Morgan's views about art and collecting. Inevitably the gap would become unbridgeable. By January 1908 Fry would be back in England and fully involved in the promotion of postimpressionist painting.[4]

Fry's absence meant the loss of an important part of Christiana Herringham's patchwork education in art: the partnership in argument that supplemented her study of the old handbooks and the experiments with tempera. Now Rothenstein became the necessary person with whom to argue art. He, too, was a seeker after knowledge. Bored in Berlin in 1902, he had told his wife, Alice, "I feel the strain of being always in a family circle, no common friends to talk of, [the hosts] ignorant of German art and literature, and you know how dull I get when I have no human, moral or artistic subject in common with anyone."[5]

Very often Christiana's letters to William and Alice Rothenstein were the codas to evenings of discussion at their home in Church Walk, Hampstead, but Fry remained her point of reference. "I have been thinking about those Brueghels a lot," she wrote to Rothenstein after one such occasion. "They are very forceful—rampant, insistent. Mr Fry says why should the grotesque not be as high as anything else." She continued, working her way more insistently into both the picture and the principle.

> Caricature—burlesque [or] grotesque mustn't be a travesty of something—How in a picture you get the notion of the thing behind which is travestied I don't exactly know—but in some way you do I suppose—But that implication of a good thing behind is not the actual *statement* of a good thing, which is the object of classic art I suppose. Mr Fry said Breughel attained to the height of the finest comedy. The finest comedy can certainly represent noble characters

> the sport of circumstances. It is the action rather than the characters that makes comedy. It was not that I didn't think they had fine qualities—only the classification that I thought I disagreed with.[6]

After another such evening she wrote, "I have been thinking a good deal about things that yesterday evening suggested," and then went on to explain what she thought missing from the work of Puvis de Chavannes, whom Rothenstein as an art student in Paris had "worshipped from afar."[7] Christiana, always remembering Cennini's advice about the importance to both art and artist of joy in the work, thought Puvis lacked "delight in the telling, either delight in the scene he calls up or delight in the material means by which he renders it. . . . There is no *infinity delicate & subtle* in his work—the marvellous cachet of *all* really great work—inferring the infinity of the universe, expressed in the little, for at the other end of the scale there is less expression possible but only suggestion." She shared Rothenstein's great admiration for Augustus John's draftsmanship but not his esteem for Charles Conder's work, which she thought depicted "woman as man has made her. This is one way women come. It is quite as much a study for women as for men. Women also make themselves—and to this method I think we are returning. I trust so. Then we shall have queens & goddesses again—and many good things. Then the queens & goddesses can re-make men[,] a thing also much to be desired. The men who are as they should be have to hide their light under a bushel—and the others hold on to each other's coat tails and when the front one tumbles down they all tumble down together."[8]

She was soon to remake her career, if not, in every respect, herself. The Herringhams' surviving son, Geoffrey, was now in the army and soon to be posted to Egypt and India. In November 1906 Wilmot and Christiana set out as tourists to see India for themselves. At first, her interest in India was general and romantic. "You know it has been a dream of many years with me to see that middle of Asia, and all those old cities," she wrote to Rothenstein. "I should really like to be away a year—and see much more than is possible in one winter. It is sad to think what a perfunctory seeing it is when one knows no language but it is better than nothing and one will read more intelligently afterwards."[9] She did not suspect that the journey would involve her intimately with an art far older than that of the quattrocento tempera painters.

Soon she would become aware of the similarities between the European attitudes that had consigned tempera to the status of disciplinary exercises, and those of the British Raj that permitted neglect of the Ajanta paintings. Conservative ideas about art had infected alike the British art establishment and the Government of India, which simply transplanted British views to India. There, too, works considered deficient in perspective and simplistic in color were "primitive" and therefore insufficiently progressive.

The Ajanta paintings had still another handicap: a general assumption that although India excelled in handicrafts (which had commercial value), India had no indigenous arts that could be considered "fine." Indian students in the government's art schools were taught to imitate European art, and the message was that even inferior European art was a better model than anything that India could offer. The verdict of official and tourist alike was that indigenous Indian painting and sculpture were shockingly erotic, socially and morally unacceptable, a sight from which to shield the eyes of respectable ladies. The whole subject of European attitudes toward Indian fine art, says Partha Mitter, is

> a striking case study of the cultural reactions of a particular society to an alien one. And nowhere can this clash of the two essentially different, even antithetical, cultural and aesthetic values be better studied than in European interpretations of Hindu sculpture, painting, and architecture. Indo-Islamic architecture or Mogul painting did not present any serious problems of assimilation for the European, as they reflected a taste that could be understood in the West.[10]

It was simpler to deny the existence of anything else to qualify as Indian fine art. The inevitable result was the steady deterioration and eventual loss of irreplaceable works—and no art collections fund stood by to raise the alarm.

Christiana had every intention of trying to be the impartial observer. Apparently unaware that she was explaining her own contradictory pattern of involvement and withdrawal, she wrote to Rothenstein:

> Do you remember Dickens' short story of Marley's Ghost. He flitted across other people's lives unseen himself. That is the great fascination of travelling I think. You lose your own identity. You stop your own life, and get merged in the forms, at least, of other people's lives. All my life that little story has embodied my own feelings of wishing to observe other people's lives & doings rather than take part in the doing myself. One gets dragged in malgré soi and one has to struggle to a point of vantage to be able to get a glimpse of the other lives.[11]

Getting away from England, however, was not a simple matter. No matter how much she wished for detachment, Christiana's temperament was one of those in which momentum generates momentum. The more she found to do, the more she found to be done. The Wimpole Street house must be readied for tenants. "It is quite a heavy order to get off," Wilmot wrote to his sister, Mary Herringham. "Half the furniture appears to be stacked in my study, and the packing up of precious things has been endless. But besides this, and that by itself is enough to break most hearts in such a house as ours, Chrissie is of course in the thick of innumerable pieces of business, and has been writing about a dozen letters every night, and interviewing the same number by day." They had to see to their Guildford cottage as well. There Christiana discovered that the concrete bed ordered for a water tank had not been made, "so she set to work and found some cement, and then and there made it and laid it. Whether it will carry the tank remains to be seen." Their maids at Wimpole Street worked equally hard but seemed to think the whole thing "rather a joke than otherwise," and Christiana sent Mary Herringham instructions about "consideration [for them] in the event of our death, which cheers us all. What will happen in the event of our return I am by no means so sure."[12]

On 5 November, two days behind schedule, they departed for Paris, where they saw Geoffrey, en route to India with his unit. At Marseilles they collected an Indian Civil Service bride, whom they were to chaperone until they could deliver her safely to her fiancé in Bombay. Their itinerary was standard tourist—Bombay, Madras, Rangoon, Calcutta, Agra, Hyderabad—and the voyage out was standard P&O. There were "a few trippers like ourselves," but others were ICS officers, Burmah Oil officials, a tea planter from the Nilgiri Hills, a doctor working on typhoid prevention for the army. There was also a rich Parsi, "as clever as they are made" and frankly discontented with British rule. He irritated both Wilmot and a young English businessman from Bombay, who was "talkative, positive, but well informed and intelligent" and also angry when the Parsi lamented that "his own men marry such common English girls" instead of looking for girls of "education and position," in which case the Parsi community would find them less objectionable. Wilmot wrote that he and Christiana made few friends on board because "both Chrissie and I are very bad at striking up acquaintances." But Christiana made friends with the Parsi's wife.[13]

On 23 November they reached Bombay, delivered the Civil Service bride to her fiancé, disliked the new and fashionable Taj Mahal Hotel, and dutifully saw the tourist sites. Wilmot felt "rather a fool, not knowing a word of the language," and he discovered that he disliked himself for disliking Indians in the mass. "I am sorry to say I loathe the sight of them. I had no idea I should have anything like this feeling."[14] He reacted to this culture shock like the decent man he was, who had grown up accepting the empire as a legitimate extension of British geography and national psyche, always provided the administration was courteous, fair, and respectful. Now he caught himself being discourteous, unfair, and disrespectful. He did not analyze his description of the argumentative Parsi as one of "them," but he knew that he did not like this image of himself.

Christiana, too, encountered ideas of which she had never before had to take account. When she tried to analyze her own attitude toward Indians, she could only fall back upon the old stereotype of the charmingly simple primitive. "I often think how you would delight in the primitive life here with all its traditional expression," she wrote to Rothenstein. At once she realized that it was not all that simple. "These are the words that ran out of my pen, but 'traditional' and 'primitive' seems [*sic*] to have something conflicting in them. The self-conscious is a better word than primitive." When she tried to apply the distinction to East-West cultural relations, she again ran into difficulties of definition and took refuge in stereotypes of romantic simplicity.

> People are fond of saying that the West never can understand the East, but it seems to me that you go a long way towards understanding if you simply consider them many or fewer stages less removed from childhood—an essential of childhood is that you don't think how your actions appear to other people—only children would sin once and forget. They would not call evil good and systematize corruption as civilized European nations do.[15]

Wilmot Herringham's fundamental decency and good manners rapidly reasserted themselves. When their first Indian train journey began alongside a pilgrim train, he found that "these crowds are a wonderful sight. I could watch them for hours." He discovered, as they progressed from one official Anglo-Indian connection to the next, that he began to be more at ease with Indians than with some fellow British men and women of whom he became heartily ashamed. He was shocked and revolted when an Englishwoman arrived late at the Marwar station, found no space vacant on the train, waited until the last minute, then chucked out of the window all the luggage of the Indian whose place she appropriated, "obliging him to follow it in order to save his goods. He saved them, lost the train, and she had the carriage to herself."

> Then there are a certain number of strangers, globe trotting like ourselves. Some of them are of the fretful and overgrown aristocracy, very long ladies with eyeglasses and depressed mouths. Others are of that type of the upper classes which talks rather loud, and very distinctly, deprecates its surroundings, and has very bad table manners. It usually eats with its lips open. Others, like an old lady we know here [Agra], are witty and for the moment you think they may have human sympathies, but you shortly find that they are wondering what you are at home, and whether you are in Debrett. Others are of the frank Anglo Indian type, which I confess I do not like. The people we have stayed with have been all of them charming, but the

> average run of ladies seem to me neither refined nor educated. . . . They have nothing to do, but to talk of their servants, and to go to the Club, and they seem to have no other interests at all except their children. They get slangy and ill bred.[16]

Wilmot's letters to Geoffrey tended to turn into lectures based upon these unhappy revelations of the English in India. Geoffrey should select with care if he married an Anglo-Indian lady. He must pay attention to Englishmen who valued good manners, such as Sir Swinton Jacob, chief engineer of Jodhpur State. Wilmot found Sir Swinton full of scorn for an Anglo-Indian the Herringhams had met at Barsi, who had declared that "it was impossible for white and black to be friends, and he certainly acted in that spirit. Jacob was deploring it deeply. . . . the worst offenders are young fellows in the British Army and I don't want you to do likewise." It is a measure of the cultural separation between England and India that only when Wilmot met the Indian gentlemen who played tennis and had tea with Sir Swinton did it dawn upon him that they "can all trace their families to about Alfred the Great's time. . . . He looks upon a better behaviour on our part as of great political importance. I hope you will come out in that spirit. I should be very sorry if you behaved as I hear of some young fellows behaving here." Wilmot had heard that army men sometimes spoke to servants "in a way which no respectable servant would stand for a minute. I tell you all this, because I hate that sort of thing, and I hope you will too."[17]

Wilmot made conscientious efforts to become informed, and whenever he met officials, he pumped them for facts, "for one wants to pick up a little information." He began to realize how dependent the average English at home were upon the government's point of view, but he did not always recognize when he was getting only the official line. In Burma, Sir Harold Stuart, who in a few years was to become Home Secretary to the Government of India, assured him that India "was not getting poorer but richer," for land was selling for the highest prices in two years, houses were sturdier, the people were better clothed, and wages were rising despite the fixed rupee. But representative government, he said, was "an impossibility," an ideal for the future and not for the present. Wilmot was still too poorly informed to see that there were two sides to that question. He passed Sir Harold's opinions on to Geoffrey.[18]

However, both Herringhams began to understand some British deficiencies with respect to Indian culture. They discovered that the linguist Sten Konow, whom they had met on the ship and had assumed to be German, was really Norwegian. "It is extraordinary," Wilmot wrote to Geoffrey, "to find men collecting such curious out of the way learning. And it is rather remarkable that we who govern most of these places seem less interested in their languages than Germans and Norwegians who have nothing whatever to do with them." Thus Wilmot encouraged Geoffrey to continue the study of Arabic. "It will give you an insight into a new world. Your life is full of wonderful opportunities if you use them, and keep your eyes open. But it is perfectly easy to go through it without learning anything at all." Geoffrey must also learn Hindustani, "the key of the situation. . . . Half the mistakes are due to want of it, and the other half to English people not recognizing that there is such a thing as a native gentleman."[19]

Christiana was not greatly interested in the details of Indian politics, but her interest in the personal took her to the very center of the political problem. She wrote to the Rothensteins: "I feel as if we are like the old Romans in our position here—and people in England think as little of it as probably people in Rome thought about Gaul & Britain and Spain. You have no idea how queer it feels to walk about feeling that you have written on you 'Ruling Nation,' especially when it is also 'Woman of Ruling Nation.' "[20]

She was not a systematic tourist. Accompanying her had its hazards. On a train from Ajmeer she "got into an upper berth taking with her a candle-stick, two handbags filled with various, and three books. She did not use either candle or books, but in about an hour her berth broke loose and the candlestick, the handbags, and the books dropped one by one" onto Wilmot in the berth below. However, with a blend of spontaneity, intuition, and enthusiasm, Christiana got on famously in India, although she sometimes overdid it. At Chitor she caught a chill, became unwell, refused to rest, and insisted upon continuing. "I simply cannot, and do not, do as much as she does," Wilmot told Geoffrey. "Today she got done [up] while standing to watch the Viceroy's arrival, has had to go to bed, and is more amenable . . . and she will be a handful I know. I would rather attend any other person in the world." She followed where curiosity led, and crowds followed her. When she took photographs in the market, Wilmot "sat in the tonga," from which he "could generally tell where she was by observing a dense throng, and she used to reappear at intervals followed by a crowd of about 50, chiefly boys, to whom her proceedings were of the deepest interest."[21] No doubt many were beggars, but the typical Englishwoman touring India was not always so attractively enthusiastic. At Tanjore, Christiana convinced Wilmot that it would be "very silly to come away without seeing a nautch, so we had a nautch." Again India surprised him, and he was surprised at himself. Contrary to English reports of the ugly tunelessness of Indian singing, he discerned a pattern "and the tune was not a bad one." The rapport between dancer and musicians amazed him, and without understanding technicalities, he perceived how "the music changed to suit her, so that in some sudden actions the drum came down with a regular clatter in exact time with her. It was a wonderful study. . . . I was prepared to be greatly bored, for I had always heard nautch dancing was the dullest form of amusement ever produced. But I admired it very greatly, and honestly think it was the most beautiful dancing I ever saw."[22]

Christiana saw India as a panorama of pictures and continuities. Hindu ceremonies at Benares made her feel "as if I had been spirited back to a far-away antiquity into a quintessence of Pagan worship & beauty—& felt that the veil was lifted for a moment from the classic times of the Greeks as well as of the old Aryans. . . . it is not the dead past—but the living present." Britons who conceived of Hindu ceremonies as all mess and muddle would have had difficulty finding a parallel between the bathing festival at Benares and the hieratic classical rites described in their schoolbooks. Christiana longed for time to sit down and paint "a really splendid descriptive picture" before that living present was shouldered aside by Westernization and industrialism. "We are doing our best [to cause that change], and I suppose if we let it alone the Americans would step in and they would hurry on the climax of vulgarization much faster than we shall."[23]

The paintings that would be her abiding connection to India were the wall paintings in the thirty-one caves at Ajanta near Aurangabad in the Deccan. The caves also contained Ajanta Ras heroic sculptures of the Buddha and elaborate sculptural decoration, but the paintings spoke to Christiana's attraction to art in need of an advocate. Between the third century B.C. and the seventh century A.D., Buddhist monks had hewn monasteries (*caityas*) and halls of worship (*viharas*) from a spectacular semicircular rock escarpment and had decorated the interior walls with depictions of scenes and legends (*Jatakas*) from the life story of the Buddha. That they are prized as the most important surviving example of Indian painting is a relatively recent view. In the seventh century the work stopped because Buddhism lost its influence and place to the Moghul invaders of India. The monks abandoned the caves and disappeared, and their paintings were left to fall victim to damp and dark, the droppings of bats and other wild beasts, and the campfires of wandering Bhil tribesmen. Christiana Herringham would become the third copyist to record what remained of the paintings, and the only copyist to record what remained of them by 1911.

In 1821 William Erskine, in a paper read to the Bombay Literary Society, drew upon a brief report on Ajanta by a Captain Morgan of the Madras Army, who, while tiger hunting with several companions in 1819, stumbled upon the caves. The group expected Hindu antiquities but discovered "no traces of the Brahminical religion." They were ignorant of Buddhism and Buddhist iconography, for they were puzzled by the "sitting figures with curled wigs," monumental sculptures of the Buddha. They found "paintings in a decent state of preservation," but they could not have known how much damage had occurred during the centuries that had intervened. Erskine, trying to define characteristics of Hindu, Jain, and Buddhist temples for the Bombay Literary Society, included in his paper that one paragraph from Captain Morgan's report, which was, Erskine claimed, "the only information regarding them, which I possess." Morgan had described a "long inscription, apparently Shanskrit, engraven on a rock, which may throw some light on the excavations." Erskine concluded that "if the conjectures already hazarded are correct," the inscriptions were in the "Maghadhi or Prakrit tongue," a vernacular dialect that broke from classical Sanskrit; Gautama probably taught in the Magadhi Prakrit.[24]

In 1824 Lieutenant James Alexander of the Sixteenth Lancers set out to visit Ajanta. He expected trouble, for he got himself up "in my Muselmani costume." He, his servants, and a guide went "well armed with sabres, pistols, and hunting spears." They met some horsemen belonging to the Nizam of Hyderabad, whose officer prophesied that they would never return, "for if you escape the tigers, those stony-hearted robbers, the Bheels, will destroy you." Indeed, Alexander saw "many bushes covered with rags, pointing out the spot where unfortunate travellers had been destroyed by tigers." But suddenly they found themselves "at the top of the precipitous *ghat* or pass. The scene which now opened upon us was magnificent in the extreme." It was the amazing escarpment into the crest of which the Buddhists had hewn their caves. As if at a signal the Bhils appeared, "a most savage looking race, perfectly black, low in stature, and nearly naked," armed with bows and arrows. Firearms kept them at bay, and Alexander's party proceeded unmolested.

Alexander would not rank these cave temples above the Hindu caves at Ellora, but he conceded that "they evinced a far better and purer taste" in the excavators, and the situation was far more dramatic than "the low and barren ridge" of Ellora. He at least knew that Ajanta's antiquities were Buddhist and therefore much older than those in the caves at either Ellora or Elephanta. He described the wall paintings as "highly interesting and spirited delineations of hunting scenes, battles, &c." Elephants and horses were "particularly well drawn," and he noted depictions of cock and ram fights, odd knobby spears, three-stringed musical instruments, and an intriguing circular design "something like a zodiac." He emerged "highly delighted with my excursion." Of all the cave temples he had visited, he most wanted to return to Ajanta for "the paintings alone" because they gave a more gratifying impression of "the ancient inhabitants of Hindustan, than the grotesque, though beautifully sculptured deities of Ellora." He was undeterred by "the entire skeleton of a man" in one of the caves and by footprints of tigers, jackals, and bears. Unfortunately, he was not enough dismayed to raise an alarm about human footprints "impressed upon the dust, formed by the plaster of the fresco paintings which had fallen from the ceilings"—footprints of the Bhil tribesmen whose campfires had already done so much damage to the paintings.[25]

In 1829 came a Mr. Ralph, an East India Company employee from Bombay, with his wife. In 1836 he returned with a Captain Gresley of the Indian Army, who was not a wise choice as companion. They examined the caves for two days. Ralph's description, which combines his and Gresley's comments, came into the hands of James Prinsep, secretary of the Asiatic Society of Bengal. Prinsep included Ralph's report with one of his own on ancient inscriptions in the hope that Ralph's "most animated and scenic correspondence,—written as he clambered up the precipitous and crumbling entrance, and threaded his way through the recesses of the hollowed hill by the light of the brahman's torch" would "enliven the dry recapitulation of [philological] technicalities." This it does triumphantly.[26]

With apologies for an amateur's judgments, Ralph disavowed "knowledge of painting or design—only a perception of what is beautiful." He deferred too often to Gresley's judgment, but Ralph's own comments were indeed triumphant. He pleaded for special attention to the paintings. "There is nothing in India like them." He felt deep personal grief at the destruction caused by men, bats, beasts, seeping water, Bhil campfires, monsoon torrents that poured over the crest of the gorge, and hillside fires that sent smoke and debris rolling down to foul the air and clutter the entrances to the caves.

Ralph and Gresley dashed about like children opening gifts at Christmas. The Buddha figures' stylized coiffure intrigued Gresley, who assumed the role of docent.

> What a wonderful people these must have been! Remark the head dresses. Now, is this a wig or curly hair? All the statues, the carved figures of BUDDHA have them. How can I say? First wigs were made to represent hair, and then hair dressed to look like wigs. 'Tis the shape of your Welsh wig, and rows of curls all over. . . . These are chiefly

> domestic scenes—seraglio scenes. . . . No, certainly there is nothing monstrous except where we see some figure evidently designed for ornament . . . aye, every thing but the floor and larger statues and small figures—every thing has been painted. It is done while the plaister is wet—it is fresco painting. I have seen the operation while going about in Rome.

The paintings are not true fresco. Modern research has shown that the lime requisite for a ground was missing, nor were all of them done on a wet surface; when Christiana first saw Ajanta, the exact medium was a mystery. Gresley's surprise at finding "nothing monstrous" emphasizes the fact that they struck him as an exception to the West's received doctrine of Indian art as erotic and grotesque. James Alexander, too, had noted that he found the Ajanta figures more pleasing than the "grotesque, though beautifully sculptured" figures at Ellora. Indian art that seemed benign, that pleased the eye, came as a surprise.[27]

Gresley, however, who boasted expertise in art, committed an egregious act. In the deep gloom a particular painting was indistinct. "Now, RALPH, look here: can you see this figure. No. Bring the torch nearer. Give me the torch. You can see it better now—hardly! Let us light dry grass. Bring grass now: place it here." A portrait of a prince sprang to life, the draftsmanship admirable. "I can see it now; but throw water on it—now the colours are more vivid." Ralph, too much awed by Gresley's self-assurance, obeyed. Gresley rushed on.

> Here is a lovely face—a Madonna face. What eyes! She looks toward the man. Observe, these are all Hindu faces—nothing foreign. All the *sweet* faces are of one complexion. R., now remark. Here are evidently three beauties in this apartment—one an African, one copper-coloured, one of a *European* complexion. Yes; and how frequently we see these intermixed. . . . Observe; many love scenes, but little gross or grossly indecent: no nudities—nothing like the shocking sculptures on the outside of the temples in Telingana.

Then came more of the condescensions that were common to the comparative art commentary of the day: "Are these paintings as well done as Europeans could have executed? In the expression of the *countenances* certainly they are. The perspective is not good, and the pieces are crowded—yet here is a *small building*, the perspective of which is *quite* correct." European art was the point of reference for all great art; variety of skin coloring was a matter for special comment; Hindu temple sculptures were merely obscene; true perspective was an exception in Asian art.

Above a door, Ralph and Gresley found the "zodiac"—noted by Alexander—"very elaborate," but one-third seemed to be missing. (It is the Circle of the Five Buddhas.) Gresley speculated that the artist had "covered the top of the doorway with something in order to complete the circle." Ralph gently remarked, "You admire it so much: you are willing to suppose it must have been complete." But Gresley's attention was already elsewhere. "What a lovely female! Yes, the last one we discover seems always the sweetest." Conveniently forgetting that he himself had ordered up the burning grass and the water on the wall, he cried, "Shame to the villains who have destroyed these paintings!"

Ralph, the voice of reason, said "We *must* form theories—we cannot remain awake and not do so." Gresley, the tough old army man lording it over the civilian, interrupted by upbraiding him for sitting down and looking weary. "When you have 25 years added to your present age, and have completed 30 years in India, will *you* labour as well or have so much zeal? 'Tis five to one against my being alive.—But do get up and come hither. This man is going to ravish this woman;—he has a *sword*, too, in his hand. . . . See how the water brings out the colours."

A few days later Dr. James Bird, the Sattarah residency surgeon, who was full of erroneous theories, joined them. He quoted a favorite pundit who had claimed that the caves were of Jain origin. Bird horrified both Ralph and Gresley with his plans to "*carry away* some of the paintings by taking [them] from the wall" for the Royal Asiatic Society in London. Ralph warned that they could be taken away only "in *powder*," having "ascertained that they will not quit the walls in laminae, but crumble under the touch." Nevertheless Bird "contrived to peel off four painted figures from the zodiac or shield!"[28]

In 1838 a more likable, more thoughtful Englishman, a Lieutenant Blake, came to Ajanta. He had one day's leave but was "determined not to throw [it] away." It grieved him that the paintings' "many beauties" remained unknown, that "whilst many an insignificant watering-place in our own country is honoured with a guide[book] and full account of the ancient shops and milestones in the vicinity, these remarkable works of art remain neglected and unheeded." He, too, was intrigued by the Buddha's coiffure, which made him think of barristers' wigs and prompted a flight of linguistic fancy. "Query: were barristers' wigs derived from the Buddhists? Buddh, Budd, Badd, Barr—hist-iste-ister—why not?" He, too, noted that "Madonna fair—what eyes! (for disturbing the monks' contemplations). . . . Would that some of ye characters on the wall could speak!—many a strange tale could ye tell, much controversy terminate, and many conflicting doubts resolve." Had time, or "unchecked inroads of water," or "the vicious hand of some wretched despoiler" damaged the ceiling paintings? Blake found smoke stains from the campfires of the Bhils, "sad men! they do not appear to consider that the smoke injures the beautiful paintings."[29]

To whom must be added those other "sad men," Gresley and Bird. Blake saw less excuse for the English than for the Bhils, for "we who pride ourselves on our enlightened knowledge and tolerance, might make *some* effort to preserve these relics!—the remains of a faith no longer prevalent in our territories, and therefore destitute of any sanctity in the eyes of our subjects. Is it not a reproach to remain the passive destroyers of these antiquities?" The labor and expense of preserving the paintings would be "trifling," he believed, compared with the whole of the British investment in India. By studying Ajanta, scholars might answer some of their own questions about India's "three local religions," Buddhism, Jainism, and Hinduism. Blake implored "all ye lovers of antiquities and the fine arts, to rescue these caves from oblivion in which they have lain for so long a time, and the decay which they are daily suffering from lying choked in mud. Who can tell what beauties lie hidden below, until the soil, which probably imbeds them, is removed!"[30]

As Christiana discovered in 1906, rescue had been slow in coming, but in December 1843 James Fergusson marked a new stage of study with a paper at the Royal Asiatic Society in London. Fergusson was an Ayrshire entrepreneur who joined the family firm in Calcutta and then started his own indigo factory. When the family firm failed, he was secure enough to retire to London ten years later and devote himself to Indian archaeological studies. His paper, "On the Rock-Cut Temples of India," surveys the major temple complexes of the local religions. Except for Mexican antiquities, he wrote, he knew of no others so unexplained as India's cave temples. Scholars claimed to know the dates of every building in Greece and Rome and even Egypt, but "all in India is darkness and uncertainty, and there is scarcely a work on architecture published, or lecture read, which does not commence by a comparison between the styles of India and Egypt." Prinsep's enthusiasm for ancient Indian inscriptions had died with him, "and the subject of Indian antiquities relapsed into the former state of hopeless neglect." Bird had copied inscriptions in the Bombay area, but Fergusson found his conclusions secondhand and inadequate, whereas "mine have been arrived at almost entirely from a critical survey of the whole series [of cave-temples], and a careful comparison of one cave with another," and with "the different structural buildings in their neighborhood" whose dates were "at least approximately known."[31]

For Fergusson, chronology of the caves was primary, the paintings secondary. Toward the paintings he, too, was condescending. They "cannot of course bear comparison with European painting of the present day; but they are certainly superior to the style of Europe during the age in which they were executed." He could not decide whether they were true fresco "or merely water colours laid on a dry surface . . . but I do not think it could have been on the modern [*sic*] plan of painting each day all the plaster laid on each day."[32]

Fergusson's paper inspired the Royal Asiatic Society to draw the attention of the Honourable Court of Directors of the East India Company to "the present state of some very curious and important remains of ancient Hindu [*sic*] art" at Ajanta, "exhibiting, in a peculiar style of fresco painting, the characteristic forms and appearance of various races, at a period probably antecedent to the Christian era." The society earnestly requested "that some competent person" be found "to make accurate drawings" and thus "preserve faithful memorials of these highly curious remains of the graphic art among the natives of India." In May 1844 the directors agreed, not on grounds of artistic or archaeological value, but to save national face, for "it would be little creditable to an enlightened government to suffer them to perish without an effort to perpetuate their subjects by faithful and artistic delineation." Even so, it was to be only a spare-time operation, carried out by "occasional employment of some of our talented officers, when the calls of the public service permit it," or by other means if anything better occurred to anyone.[33]

The directors' order shows them less than knowledgeable about Buddhism. No one could explain the "zodiac." The word "Hindu" in the society's petition may have been a slip of the pen, but it suggests how automatically the British conceived of Indian culture as principally Hindu, although they found Islam, a minority religion and a faith of one God and one holy book, more comprehensible and sympathetic. No one suggested protection for the paintings by attending to conditions at the caves. This copying order was an emergency measure, a deathbed device, a last attempt to record the remains; anyone at hand with a bit of talent for drawing could fit it in among more pressing duties. And no one thought of the paintings as part of a worldwide tradition of living art. They were exotic curiosities, amazingly competent for their time, to be copied as a quaint addition to the utilitarian records of India's contents.

The directors were fortunate in their copyist. He was Captain (later Major) Robert Gill of the Madras Army, whose official duties seem to have been extraordinarily light. He made in all some thirty facsimile copies in oils. Except for a few interruptions, such as the Mutiny in 1857, Gill was at Ajanta from 1846 until the end of his life. In one amazing photograph he sits, a landlocked Robinson Crusoe, by a cave entrance. Not a trace remains of the trim army officer. His eyes and prominent cheekbones show deep contrasts of light and shadow. Hair and beard are long and white. He wears high boots, and against his right knee rests an implement of some kind—gun, hatchet, or spyglass. His gaze seems fixed on a distant point, as romantic a figure as any European conception of stout Cortez gazing at the broad

Pacific. Gill lived with an Indian mistress at the caves and in the village of Ajanta.[34]

A Dr. John Muir, who visited Gill in 1854, went to the caves, inspected the paintings, and found them "mostly effaced, but those which remain tolerably executed." He was reassured by the detachment of Madras sepoys assigned to guard the paintings—*not* the wall paintings, but Gill's copies. Muir, however, appreciated the sepoys principally because of rumors of tigers nearby. He was more gratified at nearby Jalgaon, once a thriving center of the cotton industry, where he found "an establishment for cleaning cotton, belonging to a Bombay house of business, which I regarded with pleasure, as a sign of European civilisation, occurring in a journey where few such objects met the eye." At Ajanta village he found Gill in "an old native building" that overhung a deep ravine. Muir described with great care that ravine and its seven-stage waterfall, but he preserved not one word of Gill's conversation.[35]

Gill's oil copies were shipped to London and installed in the East India Company's museum in Leadenhall Street. In 1851 they ornamented the Indian Court of the Crystal Palace. When the Palace was moved to Sydenham, Gill's copies went with it. In 1863 he was still sending additional installments. Then a jealous fire god laid hands upon them. On Sunday, 30 December 1867, when only one fire warden was on duty and fire-fighting equipment and skills were totally inadequate, a blaze broke out in a highly flammable storage space beside the boiler room. The entire south end of the structure was destroyed and with it the whole of the Indian Court and its contents.[36]

Oddly enough, although Gill was also a photographer, he never photographed his copies, and no one else thought to do so. Five not yet delivered to England filtered through official channels, a pitiful remnant, to arrive at the South Kensington Museum in 1879. There had been no appropriation for a duplicate set of copies as insurance against accident or loss. "Alas for official wisdom and forethought," lamented James Burgess, Director of the Archaeological Survey of India.[37]

At Ajanta, Gill reconnoitered and reported that some of the wall paintings had disappeared entirely during the past decade. Others had so deteriorated that tracings were the best to be hoped for, and perhaps finished copies of a few small portions, to give an idea of the original colors.

In 1872, at the urging of Fergusson and Burgess, the Government of India commissioned John Griffiths, principal of the Government School of Art at Bombay, to undertake with his students another set of copies. He received annual grants of five thousand rupees from 1875 (with some intervals) until 1885. He begged for funds for duplicate copies of this set, which was expressly for the South Kensington Museum, the duplicates to stay at the school in Bombay. The Government of India denied his request.[38] Again, alas for official wisdom and forethought! On 12 June 1885, 87 of Griffiths's 125 canvases were destroyed during an inventions exhibition at the South Kensington Museum. A flue overheated in the French restaurant adjacent to the old India Museum, which blazed away while visitors continued to enter and leave the exhibition. The fire brigade particularly exerted itself to save the statue of the Prince of Wales in the entrance hall, and the public was relieved to learn that most of the inventions were spared. The India Museum was left to burn itself out until it was roofless and "the interior greatly damaged by heat and water."[39] The charred remains of Griffiths's copies languish today in a storeroom at the Victoria and Albert Museum.

Still no one instituted preservation measures for Ajanta. In 1850 the Bombay branch of the Royal Asiatic Society had announced plans for a commission of orientalists to supervise preservation of evidences of the "history, literature, religion and art of ancient India." A committee met, but nothing came of it. In 1874 shutters were proposed for the openings of the Ajanta caves containing paintings, but by 1880 nothing had been done.[40] In any case, shutters would not have kept out bats and seeping water. In 1903 Sir George Watt omitted Ajanta from the catalogue for the Delhi Exhibition of Indian "art-wares," for the Ajanta style was "more decorative than pictorial so that it can hardly be classified among the Fine Arts, and is therefore omitted from a description of what is intended to be an account of painting in the pictorial sense only."[41] The Ajanta paintings, evicted from the history of the fine arts, continued to disintegrate in dampness and dark, alone with the bats and the wandering tribesmen. This was the state of affairs when the Herringhams went to India in 1906.

Wilmot and Christiana made a point of visiting Ajanta because Laurence Binyon, of the Department of Prints and Drawings at the British Museum, had asked her, if they should be near those caves, to try to make a few sketches. He was at work on his book, *Painting in the Far East,* and anything on Buddhist art was of the greatest interest to him. He would be grateful, she wrote, "if I could bring back some report of the quality and condition of the Ajanta frescoes."[42]

Ajanta was a manageable distance from Hyderabad City, and Hyderabad was on the Herringhams' itinerary because they were to visit Sir George Casson Walker there. Walker, a proficient linguist and financial expert, was assigned to Hyderabad in 1901. Hyderabad, at the east-west midpoint of the subcontinent, had been the most important of several semiautonomous states within the Moghul Empire. When Parliament took control of India from the East India Company after the Mutiny of 1857, Hyderabad State kept its semi-independent status and its hereditary ruler. Thus the Buddhist paintings were in the territory of a Muslim Nizam who ruled a predominantly Hindu population.

Hyderabad's relations with the British were anomalous.

> The English had always regarded the Nizams as their vassals and expected nothing less than unquestioning fealty from them. The vassals on their part always considered the English intrusive and meddlesome and struck defiant postures, whenever feasible[,] even though they paid them inadvertent homage by their unabashed imitation of the English ways. . . . The emphasis changed occasionally, depending on whether a particular Nizam was strong- or weak-willed, or whether a particular Resident or Viceroy was meek or imperious, and finally on whether the Nizam's ministers were inept or inefficient. The rest of the personae on either side were no more than mere embellishment.[43]

Casson Walker was the government civilian assigned to pull the Nizam's finances out of a muddle that had resulted from the government's having given the Nizam "too long a rope." The local minister of finance, a chronic procrastinator, "found himself pitted against an uncompromising Casson Walker. . . . It was not a happy situation."[44] Indirectly, it would benefit Christiana when she returned two years later to copy the Buddhist paintings. From the Nizam's point of view, assistance to a European's interest in indigenous art could have been a subtle assertion of his hereditary right to rule Hyderabad State. Nor could Casson Walker easily complain, since Christiana was his friend, if the Nizam spent money in aid of her project.

The Herringhams' first difficulty was simply to reach Ajanta. At Bombay, Wilmot spent an entire day trying to find someone who knew about the caves and could explain how to get there. At last someone in Cook's tour office suggested starting from Jalgaon on the Bombay-Calcutta rail line, thirty miles from Ajanta and another three from the caves. The 1892 edition of John Murray's *Handbook for Travellers in India, Burma and Ceylon* classified this trip as an "expedition" and advised travelers to prepare for the worst, with servant, interpreter, bedding, and all provisions. They must arrange well in advance with the local magistrate and must ask for one bullock cart per person, since "two persons in one cart will find it extremely uncomfortable." Access to the site involved a one-hour walk, four miles on a bridle path, and a narrow path to the caves. "The bed of the Wagora river [at the bottom of the ravine] is crossed and re-crossed many times. The ravine is wooded and lonely." Murray mentions the paintings only in passing.[45]

When the Herringhams reached India in December 1906, traveling to Ajanta had not become any easier. Wilmot telegraphed from Bombay for horse-drawn tongas but got bullock carts instead. They covered the thirty miles from Jalgaon to Ajanta at two-and-a-half miles an hour, but Wilmot and Christiana were not bored. "It is not particularly uncomfortable and you see all the life of the road," Wilmot wrote to his sister. "Women carrying their babies on their hip, and water pots, or more often baskets of cowdung on their heads, men with bullock carts, now and then a rather gaudy bullock cart with one or two fellows in white turbans, and now and again a closed cart with a woman's face peeping out of the curtain to see the Mem Sahib." They certainly attracted attention; sahibs and memsahibs did not usually travel in bullock carts. "You take the rough with the smooth when you are off beaten tracks in India," Christiana wrote, and "eat what you can get and when you can get it."[46]

About noon they reached the village of Ajanta. Wilmot's description of their climb helps to explain why information had been so sparse. Previous travelers, no doubt put off by Murray, had preferred comforts to caves.

> We got here about noon, had a bath and a meal [at the dak bungalow], then took a little cart, and put Chrissie and her drawing things in it, while I walked, to the caves. We went up into a line of hills, winding into a ravine with a stream nearly dry now, at the bottom. It took us two hours and it was as hot as we wanted. The little bullocks took the cart over the most impossible ground. Up and down steep rocks, across the bed of the stream, never the least put out, and never altering their pace. We left them at last, for even they could go no further, and finished the walk on foot.[47]

Stones slid about underfoot. The higher they climbed, the more merciless was the sun. Thick and tenacious underbrush caught at their clothes. At the caves the stench of animal droppings and old campfires met them at the entrances, and uncountable thousands of bats skimmed eerily about in the darkness. By candlelight, Christiana made watercolor sketches of "some very majestic figures—of one especially, called 'India' . . . a most majestic, god-like being [probably the Bodhisattva Padmapani in Cave One]."[48] There was more, much more, crying out, as it seemed to her, to be copied and recorded. Twenty centuries after the first of the thirty-one caves was hewn into the rock, twelve centuries after the unknown monk artists ceased to work there, even in their deteriorated state the paintings seemed to Christiana still part of the living present. Like the tempera paintings of the quattrocento, their precise medium was still a mystery. Like so much from the great age of Italian fresco, many Ajanta paintings were already beyond repair. To record all that was left, before more disappeared—what a calling for a copyist who cared about continuities with the past!

They stayed at the caves until five in the afternoon, when they returned to the bullock carts "and came slowly home [to Ajanta village] in the lovely evening—such evenings and such mornings as no English summer however fine can give." They had already been to the caves at Ellora, which Wilmot had found "an extraordinary sight to see."[49] In February 1907, almost at the end of their Indian travels, they went to see the Buddhist cave temples at Udayagiri, near Bhilsa in Gwalior State. In 1845 Fergusson had pronounced these "entirely Buddhist, and of a very early and pure type."[50] At the Udayagiri dak bungalow two incidents occurred, tiny but of interest to a future biographer. A formidable bee, "perfectly black, shiny, and about 3 inches long, frequents our verandah," Wilmot told Geoffrey. At the caves they followed a guide named Aparti Salai, "an elderly person clad in a loincloth and a battle axe. . . . He has an enormous laugh which strikes us with some terror." At the caves Aparti Salai

> motioned to mother to go into one small chamber. She crawled through the narrow doorway, and retreated backwards rather precipitately, for she found herself looking right into the face of a "yogi" or higher kind of fakir, who was sitting perfectly motionless on his leopard skin lost in contemplation. He did not move a muscle and when I went and looked at him I could not except that he blinked once or twice have told he was alive. . . . Aparti skeered your mother by mentioning the word Bagh which is being interpreted tiger. But I think it was only to induce her to return home and let him have his dinner.[51]

Christiana was not put off by momentary frights. Ever since the visit to Ajanta in mid-December she had been thinking ahead, conditionally but very precisely. She had told Rothenstein:

> You cannot think how I want to come again—but although in many ways we have been extremely fortunate in getting to know many interesting people I should like if I came again to travel sans cérémonie, and real[ly] able to paint & sketch, which this time I have practically not been able to do, and I should like to be able to talk a little to the people. I keep on saying I shall come again—but one can't tell. At present I feel a whirl of new sensations—and a ferment of ill-shaped desires & intentions.

For some things words seem more adequate than a paint brush.[52]

Words must satisfy her for the moment, but two years later she returned. It was through a "little audacity and a great deal of luck"—or "Kismet, shall we say"—that "it happened—the beginning of the happening."[53]

7

AJANTA II

THE HERRINGHAMS returned home in time for a fine English spring. However, it was the beginning of a period of unsettlement for Christiana and for several of her friends. The Frys' difficulties had multiplied. Roger applied all his expertise and his European connections to the task of filling gaps in the holdings of the Metropolitan Museum. In November 1906 he had pointed out to its committee that until he arrived, the museum had had "no Byzantine paintings, no Giotto, no Giottesque, no Mantegna, no Botticelli, no Raphael, no Michelangelo." Spalding writes, "He bought brilliantly, fifty-four paintings being acquired during his year as Curator."[1] But if there was a contradiction between Fry's connection with the National Art Collections Fund and his American work, there was an abyss between J. P. Morgan's connection with the Metropolitan and his own collecting. Fry's troubles with Morgan were art-circle gossip in London. "I don't think it is quite the right acct of Mr Fry," Christiana wrote to Alice Rothenstein. "If you heard his account of what happens it sounds a good deal different. He did find a picture lately, and some one betrayed him, and got it out of the dealer on false pretenses (I suppose) after Mr Fry had bought it for the Museum." This seems a fairly accurate account of an episode in May 1907, when Fry "found several other Italian pictures which I wanted for the Museum and on my calling Mr Morgan's attention to them he secured three for himself and expressed the pious hope that the Museum might be able to buy the rest."[2]

Christiana had doubts about Fry's abilities as a businessman; he was too great an idealist. She wrote the following to Alice Rothenstein after she had spent several days with Fry's sister Isabel, and she wondered about a connection between his lack of business acumen and an overdose of Quaker idealism.

> I have never known a quaker family intimately before. . . . I came to the conclusion, that no country with a large population of quakers would be able to hold its own against other countries, but that a small number to hold up good, though almost impossible ideals before us are a strength to a country. But all this quality in Mr Fry is being devoted to his wife—Lady Ottoline Morrell has been trying to make him see that it is hopeless and is simply wearing him out, but his reply is that he is able to make her more reasonable and less miserable and that if he leaves her to be forcibly controlled by nurses he feels like a murderer—Isn't the whole thing dreadful—and madness like this doesn't necessarily bring early death.

"I don't think he is at all a worldly wise man," Christiana told Alice, "and I can't see what is going to happen."[3]

Fry's great trouble was that he, too, could not see what was going to happen. Helen had had another serious setback. "Do you remember," Christiana asked William Rothenstein, "how you wrote to me about her being so radiantly happy—and that you hoped she would not do too much 'Society' and dinner parties."[4] During her setbacks, the doctors thought it wiser for Helen not to be with her children. Roger tried his best to look after them in between his travels or to have them cared for while he was away, but there was no real solution.

Certainly, Fry had less time for abstract argument about art. Christiana turned even more to Rothenstein, who had a dilemma of his own, far less threatening than Fry's but of crucial professional importance nonetheless. Three of his friends who were Academicians had submitted his name for Royal Academy Associate membership, but without his knowledge.

> I heard to my surprise from Frampton on Saturday that he and Sargent and Clausen had taken upon themselves to put my name down for the Academy without consulting me: Frampton was to

> write and tell me, and he didn't, and I met him by chance and he suddenly remembered. I could not be churlish or priggish enough to say—no, the name must be crossed out—it seemed only decent to acknowledge the compliment.

But principle raised its persistent head; he had been outspokenly critical of Academy policy and behavior, and "I believed my place to be with . . . the New English Art Club." He withdrew his name. His parents were horrified, and some of his friends, "Mrs Herringham especially," were much upset. "Kind things were said about my influence for good," he wrote, and so he was persuaded to ask that his name be reconsidered. But his conscience would not let him leave it at that, and "at the risk of being thought an absurd wobbler, which indeed I was," he took his name off the list again. Other friends, adamantly anti-Academy, could not forgive him for allowing his name even to be considered. It was impossible to satisfy everyone; having satisfied his conscience, he went his own way.[5]

The momentum of Christiana's Indian experience had not exhausted itself, and she went to Florence to copy in the galleries. She had barely arrived when she wrote to Wilmot, "You mustn't miss me *too much* because I shall have to go away from London [again] pretty soon it is so suffocating." Plainly, Wilmot was concerned about her, for she had written: "I can't have a proper lunch, as I can't possibly leave the gallery, but I am *not* doing myself any harm. . . . The picture is getting on."[6]

Being close to early Italian art again sharpened the memories of Ajanta. She had shown Binyon her sketches, and "he was interested notwithstanding the slightness, and my conviction of the fine quality of the pictures remained very strongly in my mind."[7] Every day that she worked on her panel in Florence, she saw in her mind's eye the progress of decay at Ajanta: more dirty water, more grime and damp destroying that heavenly madonna face, the noblemen and their elephants, the picture narratives from the Buddha's life and legends. All became part of her reassessments of her own work in relation to the Italian masters. Botticelli and Piero della Francesca had, she thought, "a similar 'inwardness' and wealth." Such inner resources explained some of tempera's "bloomy quality," and the artist who would revive it, or any other forgotten art, must learn to understand the methods of those earlier painters.

> They both seem to me so splendid in their self-trust—or rather their complete absence of self-distrust, and founded on the rock of ages of tradition they just went for their conceptions like a man at his red-hot metal—they must have had strong bodies and obedient hands in those days and clear-seeing eyes—I feel so much physical weakness in what is produced now—and I feel in myself if I had more strength and fewer wants I should do better.
>
> Certainly we pamper ourselves too much—these people went for hardness & splendour.[8]

She thought that present-day artists clung together too much. Was it because they felt embattled or because they believed, rightly or wrongly, that art's traditions were no longer a part of the social fabric? If society was unconcerned, if artists were groping for a tradition, was it not their duty to take themselves in hand? "But I am also sure that we ask each other's opinion too much, and that now there are no schools & no tradition[,] people must try hard to stick to their own instincts & cultivate quick precise vision rather than style." Christiana herself minded "less about epic art being in abeyance at the present time" because she thought that "greatness can be contained in seemingly little things." Artists could make a start toward finding a tradition by studying "seemliness & proportion & relations" in little things. For example, the absence of seemliness "ruins picture exhibitions. Frames & pictures have no connection with each other—& pictures hung indiscriminately look like a shop. Modern life is full of incongruity."[9]

She addressed herself to other modern incongruities for which corrections were within her power. In 1904 she had begun to aid the Mendelian geneticist William Bateson, whose sister, the Newnham College historian Mary Bateson, was Christiana's friend. Born in 1861, two years after publication of Charles Darwin's *Origin of the Species,* Bateson as a young biologist found himself "required by convention to suggest [an organism's] probable descent on the assumption that it had evolved from hypothetical ancestors, probably under the selective influence of its environment."[10] At the outset his career seemed destined to die for lack of funds. "Towards the end of 1903 we were strained to our utmost," his wife recalled. The work had expanded, but "confidence that help must come for work of such interest and importance was whittled away." He must whittle back the work itself or look for aid abroad, "but he could not bring himself to the point of really drastic action." Then Christiana offered one hundred pounds a year for three years. "If I died and left you a legacy for your scientific work you would be very pleased—with the legacy," she told Bateson. "If a person doesn't intend to leave legacies, may that person give gifts for similar sorts of purposes,—which means, could you allow your work to be helped in this way?" A paid assistant perhaps? An assistant was engaged. That was "not a solution," Beatrice Bateson wrote, "but it was a reprieve. We could not only ask for help with the work, but we could pay for it; in two years' time *something* might turn up. . . ." After three years Charles Darwin's son Francis turned up with money for a greenhouse.[11] Bateson went on to spend his life studying principles of heredity; support and honors came to his work, but Christiana's money had helped him over the stile.

She gave money also to the Artists' Suffrage League and, with Mary Lowndes, represented it on the organizing committee of the National Union of Women's Suffrage Societies, for its great London procession on 13 June 1908. She contributed some of her Indian silks for banners and helped to embroider one with the league's watchword, "Alliance not Defiance." (Another, with the words *Post Laborum Palma,* has not been found.)[12]

On 13 June women from all over England and from several foreign countries assembled on the outskirts of London for a march through the city to a great rally at the Albert Hall. The weather was bad, and the banners were heavy. Members of the Men's League for Women's Suffrage offered to help, but the women insisted on bearing their own burdens. Ragamuffins ran alongside shouting "Wher's yer 'usband?" Most of the adult male spectators were strangely apathetic. One man who walked beside the women from his family as a "steward" was most struck by the men's expressions of dumb surprise, of strained and puzzled wonder, as if they had "expected monsters." There was abundant comment in the press from both prosuffrage and antisuffrage quarters. Oswald Crawfurd, retired diplomat, reminded the women that by obstructing traffic they kept honest London merchants from Saturday afternoon profits. Christiana replied that London merchants and travel facilities had done very nicely indeed by selling fares, refreshments, and decorations. She skewered Crawfurd's argument by noting that he wrote from a Lausanne hotel and could have helped the merchants by spending his money at home instead of on a Continental holiday.[13]

Christiana gave money that helped to launch and support the *Englishwoman,* that excellent magazine of the Women's League of Suffrage Societies, published by Grant Richards and inaugurated in January 1909. It became a quarterly in 1911 and continued until 1921, when some Englishwomen at least and at last gained the vote. In the one letter that survives from Christiana's correspondence with Richards, she wrote: "The cheque for £50 from Messrs Heseltine & Powell Stockbrokers is my money & is a prepayment of the capital which will be shares . . . I am writing to say Miss Lowndes will be the responsible person on June 2. I am taking care of the cheques and some correspondence which I will hand over on that day—but if there is any further business Miss Lowndes had better be communicated with."[14] Richards's wife Elisina was editor until she left both Richards and the magazine in April 1909, at which point Mary Lowndes took over.

Being very busy did not abate the restlessness that Christiana had felt ever since her return from India. Pressures of gender were tangled up with logistics of painting. She found a room of her own. "I have taken a studio near our house," she wrote to Rothenstein, "and am hoping to do some work there. The room I have in this house [her home at 40 Wimpole Street] is too high up. The stairs are too tiring, as I am often fetched down. If I go out of the house to a 1st floor room it is not tiring & it is peaceful." Not stairs but interruptions most troubled her: why was women's creative work considered interruptible? "Could you write down," she asked Rothenstein, "what you said on Friday—shortish—especially about women having too much sympathy & too little faith, and their beginning with so much keenness and intelligence."[15]

She began to worry about her eyes. Was diminished vision only the normal need for glasses as one grew older? Should she take up miniature painting, since that was done with a magnifying lens? Mary Marshall, whose husband, William, had known Wilmot Herringham for many years, remembered Christiana's "eyes that blinked nervously" and manners that sometimes seemed "shy and awkward." When restlessness and worry set in, when outside demands pulled her too often away from her studio, her attentions became scattered, so that friends had to make allowances for a certain social absent-mindedness. That same friend recalled an occasion when, as one of two overnight guests after a party, she arrived in the afternoon to find the drawing room looking "more as if a business meeting were to take place in it, rather than a party for thirty. Pamphlets and papers and odds and ends were piled on tables and chairs, and I must say I admired the servants who tidied up the mess before the evening." The dinner guests arrived, but no hostess. Wilmot came in hurriedly, with apologies. Christiana "drifted into the room," and everyone went down to "an excellent dinner" with music to follow. In the morning the two overnight guests came down to find Wilmot "hurriedly finishing his breakfast before going to work. Mrs Herringham shortly appeared, with hat and coat on, and explained that she had to catch a train for Oxford." The guests had breakfast, "sat over the fire for a few minutes and then agreed that perhaps we had better go too—and so that party ended."[16] A revealing episode, and one that explains much that less-tolerant friends may have found unacceptable.

Christiana's indecision about living in London or in the country continued intermittently. They had now given up the cottage near Guildford for one at Chalfont in Buckinghamshire. "I don't think I shall live at Chalfont again," she told Rothenstein. "We shall perhaps some day go back to Surrey—But for a time I must give up two-house living. It is too disturbing & distracting. Wilmot will keep it for a time & I shall go sometimes but not to live. Next spring I think I shall stay some time at Burford & paint out of doors. It is a wonderful place."[17] The Burford idea apparently was dropped.

Neither Christiana nor Wilmot was ever without thoughts of the lost Christopher, and Geoffrey's being in the army was another cause of disquiet. When one of the Rothenstein children fell seriously ill, Wilmot sent a qualified nurse and wrote in angry despair: "What a damn nuisance the whole show is. If one was thoughtful enough I suppose one would pray the Gods that just such a thing as this should not happen. Perhaps if you had prayed it would not have. . . . Damn this fear." Christiana told Alice Rothenstein, "I did want more children, but as my big boy growing is so satisfactory that I am quite content—as long as we have him—one sometimes wishes he had another profession."[18] She found a small Buddha figure in a market and bought it. A talisman for Geoffrey? Certainly a reminder of Ajanta.

In August 1908 "Archaeology in India," a series of four articles by a special correspondent, appeared in the *Times*. In six months he had traveled ten thousand miles to inspect Buddhist, Hindu, Jain, and Muslim antiquities, and of Buddhist remains "almost the only things that exist intact [*sic*] are the rock-cut temples," of which there were in all more than a thousand. The Buddhist inscriptions, he wrote, were a precious historical record, but Buddhist monuments had suffered from the decline of that religion in India. Indian and English archaeologists were scathing about the carelessness of public works officials, who, "while engaged in the construction of roads, bridges, and railways, utterly effaced many valuable relics of antiquity." Muslim vandalism had done its share of damage because of the Islamic hatred of images. Even at Bodh Gaya, the very site of the Buddha's enlightenment, representations of him had been repainted as Hindu deities. Tourists had simply picked up many Graeco-Indian artworks, relics of Alexander's Asian expeditions, and had carried them away. Lord Curzon's Ancient Monuments Act of 1904 had halted the worst of the desecrations, and he had reorganized the Archaeological Department, but the government's archaeologists struck this correspondent as woefully unrealistic. They had only indirect control over the many monuments in the Native States—the Ajanta cave temples and a number of other sites in Hyderabad State, for example—but they seemed to think that in only a few years they could perform a comprehensive survey of all Indian antiquities. Even an untrained observer could see that that was impossible. Whether a survey would lead to the correction of conditions was still another question. Some conservation work was under way, but at Ajanta water stood several inches deep on the floors. Wire netting was carelessly strung across the entrances to the caves. The correspondent had heard that panthers and tigers still prowled the immediate environs. Whether Hyderabad State officials intended to do anything about all this, he did not know.[19]

On 21 August, Christiana wrote to the *Times* to corroborate the report on Ajanta, with reference to her visit two years earlier. She wished to "add to what has been said already, that unfortunately the copies of the best [paintings], which are very fine and important, must have been destroyed in the fire [at South Kensington Museum]." None of the surviving copies by John Griffiths and his students, she said, coincided with her sketch made in 1906.[20]

These communiqués from the archaeological front catalogued the very kinds of deficiencies that the National Art Collections Fund was seeking to correct in Britain, including an unwillingness to reexamine the standards by which to judge great art, and outmoded administrative machinery designed on eighteenth- and nineteenth-century principles and too ponderous to change direction in response to new needs. In India the machinery was set even more rigidly than that in Britain, for distance and the unwieldiness of bureaucratic communication made its operators nervous and defensive. Flexibility, they told one another again and again, officially and privately, could appear as weakness. If time-tested British principles were not retained and reinforced, the rising tide of Indian nationalism could sweep them away. Therefore, every subject, every issue, went through two fine-meshed official filters: first, political necessity and expediency; second, the social and economic principles according to which the administrators had been educated. Position, property, and education determined one's place in society, and the successful economy conducted its affairs by the rules of laissez-faire. Indian nationalists had built their platform of protest on the fact that, on all four of those scores, Indians' success was restricted and often nonexistent.

It was true that George Nathaniel Curzon, Baron Scarsdale, as Viceroy from 1899 to 1905, halted the worst of the abuses. He had obtained a qualified director for the Archaeological Department, had increased its annual budget from seven thousand to thirty-seven thousand pounds a year, and had taken characteristically meticulous personal interest in certain preservation projects. However, he was a man of his time, and even his most appreciative comments were framed in the contexts of imperialism. In 1899, in a speech to the Asiatic Society of Bengal, he said, "For nearly 3,000 years there had been a succession of kingdoms, dynasties, races and religions in India, all of them leaving relics of some sort, many of them relics of the highest value, which it was incumbent upon us to examine, to elucidate, and to conserve."[21] In 1900 he told that same body that the Government of India had "a duty to our forerunners, as well as to our contemporaries and to our descendants," who would not respect the great achievements of the present Raj if it neglected the works of the past. "Art and beauty, and the reverence that is owing to all that has evoked human genius, or has inspired human faith, are independent of creeds, and, in so far as they touch the sphere of religion are embraced by the common religion of all mankind."

> Viewed from this standpoint, the rock temple of the Brahmans stands on precisely the same footing as the Buddhist Vihara, and the Mahomedan Musjid as the Christian Cathedral. There is no principle of artistic discrimination between the mausoleum of the despot and the sepulchre of the saint. What is beautiful, what is historic, what tears the mask off the face of the past, and helps us to read its riddles, and to look it in the eyes—these, and not the dogmas of a combative theology, are the principal criteria to which we must look.[22]

"*Loud and continued applause*" rewarded this statement. Curzon had matched principle and practice by personally seeing to it that many precious sites had been preserved, but his choice of words revealed the limitations of his view. Indians figured in it not at all. The Indian arts that they created were at the service of British reputations. Conservation of antiquities was "a duty to our forefathers" (earlier generations of British rulers) and to "contemporaries and descendants" (British contemporaries in the India Service and descendants who would carry the burden of Indian rule into a supposedly infinite future). Images of violence implied the nature of the British relation with the Indian past. That past was deceptive, masked, and cunningly evasive; the mask must be "torn away." The Briton would confront it like a big-game hunter; he would "look it in the eyes" and prevail. "Combative theologies" must be rejected; conflating them as "the common religion of mankind" would do away with the necessity for understanding their separate geniuses. But Curzon's ordering of the categories was itself combative. On one side he placed Hinduism and Buddhism; on the other, Islam and Christianity. They have points of disagreement, but they have one God in common and stand together, apart from the pagan pair.

Another Curzon bias was plain when he turned to the care of antiquities. He readily admitted that, often in the name of progress, the British had caused some appalling damage and that past efforts at preservation were often inadequate. But he argued that the British were uniquely qualified to care for "the majority of Indian antiquities—of those at any rate that belong to the Mussalman epoch." Here the bond between British and Muslim Indians was that the British, like the Moghuls outsiders in India, were therefore more objective, better equipped to judge antiquities that were not products of "an indigenous genius or an Indian style." Moghul antiquities were "exotics, imported into this country in the train of conquerors, who had learnt their architectural lessons in Persia, in Central Asia, in Arabia, in Afghanistan." To these were added the Graeco-Bactrian influence in kingdoms "founded upon the remains of Alexander's conquest." Who better qualified than the British, with their classical education, to conserve and classify? "Indeed," said Curzon, "a race like our own, who are themselves foreigners, are in a sense better fitted to guard, with a dispassionate and impartial zeal, the relics of different ages, and of sometimes antagonistic beliefs, than might be the descendants of the warring races or the votaries of the rival creeds." The British were free of "religious fanaticism, of restless vanity, or of dynastic and personal pride" and would respect impartially "the treasures of all."[23]

This failed to explain why, even though Lord Curzon had visited Ajanta in 1902, its indigenous "relics of highest value" had slipped through duty's protective net and still decayed in damp and darkness.

They were still behind the "curtain of dark and romantic mystery [that] hangs over the earliest chapters" of Indian history, of which British archaeologists had as yet raised only a corner. Indian taxpayers were of course vitally interested in the whole subject, Curzon said, and were "in the last degree unlikely to resent a somewhat higher expenditure" for preservation, but, "after all, a few thousand rupees go a long way in archaeological work, and the outlay is exceedingly small—upon objects in which I believe them to be as keenly interested as we are ourselves."[24] Obviously, nothing would soon change at Ajanta. Perhaps there is an explanation in the fact that the British preferred buildings; buildings were *property* and thus were tangible reminders that India was now British, not Moghul, property. Reminders, to be effective, should be highly visible. Those hidden away in inaccessible caves and ravines were therefore less useful and less urgently in need of restoration.

In the summer of 1909 the Casson Walkers invited the Herringhams to visit again at Hyderabad. The "half-formed desires and intentions" that Christiana had brought from India, and all her questions about the Ajanta paintings, snapped into focus. Medical assignments kept Wilmot in England, and she traveled out alone to India to stay for six weeks. She had asked her host to "try to get me the means of copying a few selected portions [of the Ajanta paintings] to bring home to England." He had done more. He had enlisted three distinguished gentlemen to recommend her interests to the Nizam's government and to the Government of India: Ernest Binfield Havell, recently retired as principal of the Government School of Art in Calcutta; Sir Theodore Morison, retired principal of the Muslim Anglo-Oriental College at Aligarh, and influential on the India Council of the Secretary of State for India in London; and John H. Marshall, Director of the Archaeological Survey of India. The Nizam would be pleased to provide "a complete and satisfactory camp" at Fardapur, a village five miles from Ajanta, from which to travel back and forth to the caves, and all these "delightful arrangements" awaited her arrival in India. "I had only to fix my own date for beginning work, and, further, to carry on a correspondence according to advice given to me with a view to securing help from young Indians trained in the

Government Art Schools of Bombay and Calcutta."[25] These were five in all, Ahmad and Fazl ud Din, drawing masters trained at the Bombay school and on loan from the industrial arts school in Hyderabad; and three Bengali students of Abanindranath Tagore at the Government School of Art in Calcutta. All three—Nanda Lal Bose, Asit Kumar Haldar, and Samendranath Gupta—would later be prominent in the group that would become known as the Bengal school of painters, who gathered around Abanindranath Tagore and his artist brother Gaganendranath. The three Bengali students undoubtedly came with Havell's encouragement, and Abanindranath sent them at his own expense.

Christiana paid the expenses of a young English assistant, Dorothy Larcher, whom she had recruited at the Hornsey School of Art. Miss Larcher was already active in the arts and crafts movement, and she was to become a leader in a women's movement in original design, weaving, and block printing. Indian art would influence that work.[26]

On the political scene, Gilbert John Murray Kynynmond Elliott, Lord Minto, was now Viceroy. Not art preservation, but preservation of civil order was foremost among his concerns. Indian nationalists' agitation escalated at an alarming rate; bombings and assassinations monopolized official attention. British partisans of the Indian nationalists and conservative imperialists faced off in Parliament. On 15 December 1909, Minto wrote, unrealistically, to Joseph Chamberlain, the Secretary of State for India: "The outlook is full of difficulty. The worst of it is, as I have always told you, not any risk of rebellion, that is nonsense, but the effect on an hysterical population, such as that of Calcutta, and an unreasoning howl at home."[27]

Hyderabad by comparison was relatively peaceful. Also on 15 December 1909, Christiana arrived at the Fardapur camp and found the two Hyderabad assistants awaiting her. At the caves she found that indeed nothing had changed. Bats were still in possession, and damp and seeping water still did their worst. The camp's supply lines were complicated at best. Provisions came by rail from Bombay, to be collected at Jalgaon station and then transported by bullock cart the thirty miles to Fardapur. As in 1906, the last stage of the trek to the caves followed the river at the bottom of the ravine, at that time a series of pools but, during thunderstorms, a raging torrent, and the artists had to carry their heavy equipment on the final climb to the caves. For the camp the Nizam had thoughtfully provided "several servants huts—and our army of a police inspector Sahib, and some foot police soldiers as guards of the camp, and two or three mounted police who have swords and who look like cavalry who escort us to the caves (5 miles away) have other small tents."[28] Christiana was somewhat taken aback to find this detachment drawn up in military formation and saluting with a flourish as she and her party approached.

Difficulties of supply and transport were simple when compared with the conditions of sustained work inside the caves. Huge nests of wild bees hung between temple columns, and collision with them would be extremely dangerous. The uncountable numbers of bats slid and swooped in the gloom and gibbered in the darkest recesses. They crept along ledges and cornices, "unaware that the concentrated stench of their centuries of occupation is their most formidable defence against man's intrusion."[29] The gloom that made the bats secure became the artists' greatest problem. Only when a fugitive ray of sunlight penetrated a chink or an entrance or was reflected from walls or floor was it really possible to see the paintings clearly.

The Indian assistants were "very serious and keen in their work, and very discriminating . . . very pleasant to deal with and were by no means lacking in humour and fun—which always appeal to English people. . . . They were exceedingly nice to me, behaving with a simple delicacy which was very charming—and I was as courteous and considerate as I knew how." The Indians worked harmoniously at the caves, but camp life had to be carefully organized in view of the Hindu Bengalis' caste rules and the Muslims' regulations about food. A little cookhouse was separate. The Bengalis occupied one-half of the Fardapur dak bungalow. The two Muslims had a tent to themselves. Christiana had a very large tent, and Dorothy Larcher a smaller but still spacious one. The women ate in another, smaller tent unless meals were served out-of-doors. More tents housed the servants and the imposing police guard. The segregation eased relations within the group; after a strenuous day together in the caves the painters returned tired and in need of a little privacy. "Our daily contact was the easier," said Christiana, "because of the separation caused by their caste, and by the imperative necessity that, as a woman, I should keep up a sort of 'izat' or demand for respect."[30]

Still, there was some need for caution and convention. Christiana discovered that her own and her assistants' mutual acquaintance with a progressive Hindu lady who lived in Hyderabad "went a long way toward smoothing away any difficulties or prejudices." The lady was Sarojini Naidu, poet, social activist, and in later years the first woman president of the Indian National Congress, whom Christiana met through the Casson Walkers.[31] Preservation of *izzat*—personal prestige—was a commandment of Anglo-Indian, as well as Indian, behavior. Christiana knew that, to Anglo-Indians, at least, her company presented a variegated aspect: English and Indian; Muslim, Hindu, and Christian; and Urdu-, Bengali-, and English-speaking, with mutual communication possible only in English. Too, they were working together to copy Buddhist paintings in a largely Hindu state under a Muslim ruler, and all were under the direction of an unconventional Englishwoman. The villagers easily accepted her. What some of the Anglo-Indian visitors, curious about the activities at the caves, may have thought was another matter.

The Fardapur camp, Christiana told Alice Rothenstein, was "a great event here." For several days a crew belonging to the commissioner of roads camped on its outskirts and constituted themselves its suburb. A large party of Parsis from Bombay, "men & boys, came late in the evening in two bullock-carts and squeezed themselves into the spare half of the bungalow which is really only one room with two little dressingrooms." A German photographer stayed for four days, "a bounder and we are very much afraid his photographs may not be good." A "large Christmas party" came from Calcutta. Christiana tried to write "an amusing account" of the camp but had very little spare time. "There are such a lot of people around all the time. I am head-painter, head of the camp, and doctor." Many sick persons from the surrounding villages came to her for medicines. Sometimes, in the hope that the extraordinary memsahib had veterinary skills, they brought their ailing animals.[32]

At first the assistants were disappointed; there seemed so little left to copy. Christiana assigned particularly interesting bits to each one, and "they very soon became enthusiastic, finding one good fragment after another amidst what seems at first almost hopeless ruin." There was no alternative to lamps and candles, although they knew that those only added to the smudge already thick on the walls. A huge hanging lamp that burned brightly for two hours seemed to be a solution, but it came loose and crashed to the floor. Finally, Christiana made the forty-hour round-trip to Hyderabad for a lighter and brighter incandescent oil lamp, but "there was still much groping in half dark for some people and some subjects."[33] For much of their time in the caves the artists perched on wobbling ladders, stretching this way and that in order to catch any scraps of half-light. They had to keep their balance while holding large sheets of tracing paper firmly against a wall and leaning perilously backward for a clearer idea of the faded outlines underneath. Every chance glimmer of light was a precious increment. Casual visitors who went in with candles often came out saying that there was nothing to be seen inside.

For Christiana, a curious empathy with the painted people on the walls was liberal compensation for the exhaustion and discomfort. Little by little they seemed to step forward, cautiously at first and as if testing the faith of this visitor who brought with her the aura of another world. "The surfaces are decayed, chipped and dirty, and there is something eerie in the way the painted population seems to emerge from the dimness, as you might see a half-lighted tableau vivant through its gauze shrouding. This strange indeterminate populousness was oppressive to me at first. Gradually the subjects pieced themselves together, and became more articulate."[34]

Not only the subjects but the unknown painters became more real to her. They took on personalities, artistic trademarks, and convictions. They became individuals and cultural interpreters. They came of their own accord and "revealed themselves" to her.

> When daily association with the frescoes to some extent lifted the wall of obscurity, damage, and unfamiliarity they revealed themselves as [a] widely diverse grouping of the ideals and methods of many painters from districts far apart geographically. The difference is

> accentuated by great variety in the dresses and ornaments. . . . There is the feeling of a primitive art, with its wilful determination to say what it wants to say—and it wants to say so much. It is not the careless indifference of a decadent art which is Gandhara. There is an intense effort to characterize fine types, to express race, breeding, active gesture. There is a nervous strength in the hands with an intimate knowledge of their beauties and gestures and poses which the Greeks and Romans knew nothing about, and the impassiveness of the Greek face has given place to all kinds of expression. . . . Each visit was a surprise for me.[35]

She was in her element. She had no dark moods and no restlessness, only arduous, satisfying labor. She did not worry about the inscriptions or the chronology of the caves. She carried none of the ideological baggage of the professional orientalist. She was an artist at work, and she concentrated on recording what was left of the paintings. Her enthusiasm grew as the work progressed.

> My admiration was not nearly great enough. They are far finer and more interesting than I remembered. Though at first when you go in you think there are only a few battered, tattered darkened remnants, by degrees you get accustomed to the damage and you find a whole picture-gallery of all sorts of scenes & people and by a great many different hands. . . . I am staying till the end of January. We are trying to do what we do, really well, but there is an enormous amount. We cannot do it all.[36]

It was obvious that in six weeks they could make only a beginning. The more they copied, the more they found to copy. Therefore, her "intention to do some specimen copies developed into a strong wish to make a fairly complete record of this most interesting, but slowly perishing picture-gallery." Before she left at the end of January 1910, she asked Hyderabad's prime minister to thank the Nizam and his government for its generous assistance, reported on work thus far, and requested a renewal of camp facilities for the winter of 1910–1911. She explained that in her opinion "these pictures are far finer and more important than they have hitherto been thought to be and prove the existence of painters in the sixth century A.D. as good as the Persian painters of the sixteenth century." Griffiths had published some color reproductions and photographs, but those reproductions were of only "small and somewhat unimportant paintings, and his photographs are very indistinct." She pointed out that a copyist must be more than a competent replicator and must understand the fundamentals of good art; earlier copyists "were probably not good enough to understand very fine quality in a picture, and therefore their copies are bad and not like the original." She was convinced that the wall paintings were the "work of different schools,—perhaps of several different countries. No attempt has ever been made to show this in copies."[37]

She did not suggest that she agreed with the "racial romantics" in the West who, as Partha Mitter explains, wished art to be the expression of distinct racial groups. Those who concentrated on architecture, of whom Ernest Havell was one, tended to regard "the spiritual as a category" in "the evolution of Indian Art."[38] Christiana, herself so much an individual, thought of artists as individuals whose distinctive styles evolved from their responses to circumstances and from different geographical and cultural settings. Such artists were unique as interpreters with single, distinctive voices, not as racial spokesmen. She was a romantic, but her experience as a technician of forgotten media kept her from joining the ranks of the "racial romantics."

While Christiana was at Ajanta, obeying her own imperatives about Indian art and finishing as much copying as time would allow, a very important event in London opened a new stage of the West's progress toward appreciation of Indian art. This was a paper by Ernest Havell, "Art Administration in India," presented before the Royal Society of Arts on 13 January 1910. Partha Mitter calls "the year 1910 . . . the great watershed," for it marked the shift in the study of Indian art from archaeological and ethnographic emphasis toward the aesthetic.[39] Havell's paper criticized the entire rationale and apparatus of art education in India for its approach to design, which taught Indian students to look for success in the imitation of popular but inferior Western art, with the result that the inferior students came looking for an easy course and the best students avoided the government schools.

His paper had two crucial results. It impelled William Rothenstein, already inspired by Christiana's eloquent letters from Ajanta, to draft a letter to the *Times*. Twelve other English artists and critics who represented a variety of approaches to painting, sculpture, and the decorative arts signed it with him on 28 February 1910. Rothenstein further proposed that artists and anyone else interested should join forces to form a society, to be known as the India Society, that would educate the British public about the arts of India. Christiana returned home on 31 March to find Rothenstein's idea very much alive and a committee, of which she and Wilmot became members, already at work. Rothenstein already had an idea that, when she returned to India in November 1910, he might accompany her, to see Ajanta, to look for other examples of Indian art, to paint Indian subjects, and to try to meet Indian artists.

Havell's paper was one more contribution to the long argument between Western classicists and racial romantics about the correct standards of judgment for Indian art as determined by its more durable remains: architecture and its sculptural decorations. Partha Mitter explains how, for orientalists like James Fergusson and Henry D. Cole, Greek architecture and sculpture had set the universal and ineluctable standard of beauty. Early Indian art, they believed, excelled wherever Greek influence had come in to enhance it with principles of classical simplicity, proportion, and balance. Decline set in when the influx of foreign tribes and peoples diluted the purity of Aryan cultural hegemony. This hypothesis of cultural decline—a downward slide from a distant golden age—was useful to British imperialists; only with the help of a stronger, more enlightened power such as Britain could India begin to climb back up the slippery slope toward artistic purity. As a result, early Buddhist sculpture and architecture (but not painting), as exemplified in the buildings and carvings at Gandhara and at Sanchi, were exalted for their adherence to classical principles. The complexities and decorations of Hindu architecture seemed to be a senseless, and often obscene, clutter. Islamic art, with a classicism of its own, was, as Curzon had discovered, congenial to British classicists because it originated with a strong outside culture; this theory of the superiority of outside influence simplified the problem of classification within an Indian scheme of things.[40]

The "racial romantics," on the other hand, "had no such optimistic faith in the transforming power of Hellas. To them a style of art was determined from the start by the unique spirit of a race, whose special talents could not be imitated by people belonging to a different race without exposing themselves to grave dangers." Those dangers included the dilution of a race's "special talents" or, worse, loss of cultural identity. When the idea of racial romanticism was added to nationalist aspirations, as happened in Bengal in the late nineteenth and early twentieth centuries, the mixture could be potent and explosive. The Bengali painters who gathered around Havell's colleague Abanindranath Tagore at the Calcutta School of Art were neither political agitators nor bomb throwers, but their efforts to return to principles of traditional Indian design and subject matter carried subtle messages about the need to choose between indigenous cultural identity and an unstable self as constructed through imitation of half-comprehended Western ways. The unspoken message was the same as that from the Nizam of Hyderabad to Casson Walker and the Government of India when he provided the camp for Christiana Herringham and her party at Ajanta. Abanindranath Tagore conveyed the same message with his gift of the Bengali students' assistance at Ajanta. It was a logical progression from the principles that governed his teaching at the Calcutta School of Art.[41]

However, the Government of India, which followed British theory and practice, valued art education in India as a means of improved design of manufactured goods for export to the West. This utilitarian rationale had prevailed at least since the Crystal Palace Exhibition of 1851, and that exhibition's successors had revealed British shortcomings in industrial design. Art educators looked for models that would enable British manufacturers to compete more successfully with, in particular, French designers. Henry Cole urged his South Kensington Museum collections as one source of inspiration and improvement.[42] Spokesmen for the arts and crafts movement replied that what was needed was a comprehensive change in British attitudes—in Britain and in India—toward the arts of design. C. R. Ashbee feared the overorganization of art education. "It is in the nature of the Englishman to 'run' things; as the man of a type, he would be the strong man organising; but when he comes athwart something that will not be organised, he gets into trouble—and such a thing is Art." Ashbee proposed a synthesis of theory and practice. "The teaching function and the workshop function should be combined."[43]

The English poet and artist William Morris disagreed with Cole and said that it was useless for European designers to look to India for inspiration while Indian designers were being forced into abject imitation of bad Western models, for "Englishmen in India are, in their short-sightedness, actively destroying the very sources of that education [in art]—jewellery, metal-work, pottery, calico-printing, brocade-weaving, carpet-making—all the famous and historical arts of the great peninsula has [*sic*] been for so long treated as matters of no importance, to be thrust aside for the advantage of any paltry so called commerce."[44]

In 1901 Ernest Havell had complained that British methods of art education as applied in India followed "the traditions of the English Public School" by which "we have always regarded the schoolboy as an animal in which the imaginative faculties should be sternly repressed. . . . Cram the students with Shakespeare and Milton before they can express their own ideas in tolerable modern English—that is culture." If art had its rightful place, in Britain or in India, "we should never have placed any great reliance upon the artificial stimulants which the low vitality of our aesthetic constitutions renders necessary in Europe." In "the real India, which exists outside the semi-Europeanised society we have created, art belongs as much to the everyday-life of the people as it did in ancient Greece." Like Curzon, he deplored the state of contemporary Indian art because it reflected badly on British rule. Also like Curzon, he deplored the practices of the Public Works Department, which rampaged through sites of priceless antiquities to construct modern roads, bridges, railways, and nondescript public buildings. "The ordinary Public Works officer," he maintained, "ignores altogether the art of the country." Certainly it was important to keep India happy (and therefore controllable). "A people devoted to art are a happy and contented people." But under British rule "the old art of India has been almost killed; the taste of the people, formerly led into safe paths by the traditions of Indian handicraftsmen, has been changed and corrupted, while we have given nothing from our own national art to compensate India for what has been lost."[45]

This point of view tended toward golden-age romanticism, but Havell gave some compensation for what had been lost. Like Cole and Fergusson, he believed that "the history of the art of every country is contained in the history of its architecture, at least in countries where architecture has reached the dignity of an art," but he granted Indian design its aesthetic integrity apart from evidences of descent from external classical influences. Havell, with Ananda Kentish Coomaraswamy and others who rallied to them, "denied for the first time the unquestioned supremacy of classical art which [they] did not consider to be superior to the best of Indian art."[46]

There was little improvement in the years between 1901, when Havell's paper was first published, and January 1910, when he brought the same message to the Royal Society of Arts in London. In 1910, Mitter says, "Indian art could at last be said to have arrived."[47] Ananda Coomaraswamy, historian of Sinhalese and Indian art, and sixteen years Havell's junior, was a valuable ally, and not only because of his Sinhalese-English parentage. His father was Sir Mutu Coomaraswamy, barrister, legislator, and student of Tamil literature and Pali Buddhist texts. While in England from 1863 to 1866, he became the first Asian accredited to practice law in Great Britain. During a second visit he met and married Elizabeth Beeby, whose family was native to Kent. In 1876 the Coomaraswamys settled in Ceylon, where Ananda was born in 1877. Sir Mutu died in 1879, and Elizabeth raised her son in England, where he stayed until he was twenty-five. He became a geologist and from 1903 to 1906 was Director of the Mineral Survey of Ceylon. However, his interest in art studies drew him away from geology, back to England, and into C. R. Ashbee's crafts community. He visited India in 1906 and again in 1909 and had barely returned to England when Havell spoke at the Royal Society of Arts.[48]

For some time Coomaraswamy and Havell had been thinking along similar lines. In 1908 Coomaraswamy published *Mediaeval Sinhalese Art,* and Havell published *Indian Sculpture and Painting* and was planning another book, *The Ideals of Indian Art,* in which he would argue for spiritual values in the aesthetic approach.[49] Although Coomaraswamy thought that Havell had tipped the balance a little too far away from the classicist archaeologists, he prepared to support him at the Royal Society of Arts, for he expected, quite correctly, that Havell's views would encounter opposition. Therefore he recruited Rothenstein as reinforcement. "I shall be there to support," Coomaraswamy wrote. "I very much wish you could too."[50]

His first meeting with Rothenstein had occurred at Ashbee's crafts center at Chipping Campden, probably soon after Coomaraswamy returned from India in the summer of 1909. There he had shown Rothenstein some drawings by Abanindranath Tagore and his circle. However, Rothenstein was already interested in Indian drawings, and except for Charles Ricketts and Charles Shannon he knew few others in England who cared about them. "At Sotheby's they fetched insignificant prices," Rothenstein wrote, and he snapped up some drawings for three shillings each that the British Museum did not wish to buy and passed on to him. "I could never," he wrote, "understand the lack of interest in Indian art. I had heard vaguely of a man named Havell, who in India was preaching its significance; but here in London Mrs Herringham alone supported me in my estimate of Indian painting and sculpture."[51] Now, on 13 January 1910, he accompanied Coomaraswamy to Havell's lecture at the Royal Society of Arts, where they were joined by the designer and illustrator Walter Crane.

Presiding was Sir George C. M. Birdwood, retired from the Bombay Medical Service. His background and career were conventionally Anglo-Indian, and his parents represented two strong arms of imperial influence. His father was General Sir Christopher Birdwood of the Indian Army, his mother the daughter of a London Missionary Society agent. George Birdwood was sent to England at the age of seven for education, and he returned to India in 1854 a medical officer. In addition to medical duties and a variety of activities related to agriculture and Indian crafts, he reorganized the collection that became Bombay's Victoria and Albert Museum. When his health failed and he returned to England in 1868, he became exhibition planner for the India Office in London. For forty-two years, while representing the arts of India, he had not lived there. Birdwood, who was born in 1832, the year of the first Reform Bill, and Ernest Havell represented two generations during which momentous changes had caused problems still unresolved. If Coomaraswamy expected Birdwood's views to diverge from Havell's, he had guessed correctly.

In a Darwinian introduction, Birdwood paid tribute to artists among Havell's ancestors, particularly his artist uncle William Havell, who had traveled in India and China between 1816 and 1825. Thus "it happened most happily" that Ernest Havell benefited from heredity's "unearned increments (most fortunate factors in the evolution of humanity and civilisation, and of national individuality and greatness). . . ." Unfortunately, Birdwood thought that Havell was "something less than just towards the Government of India, both in this country and in India, [but] that would not disturb the truly well-earned Olympian serenity of either the Secretary of State for India in Council, or the Indian Viceroy and Presidency Governors." He could not agree with all that Havell was about to say "on the question of the existence of Fine Art in India," but he admitted that perhaps he did not quite understand Havell's point. In any case "the author's warmth of enthusiasm in his cause" would help to warm the audience on a day when freezing air rolled down "from Greenland's icy mountains."[52]

Havell began with his essential thesis, on the face of it not yet one to which Birdwood could take great exception.

> The dominating principle in art administration in India should naturally be based upon the all-important fact that, excluding the small fraction of the population which is mostly congregated in the great Anglo-Indian commercial cities, art still survives throughout the length and breadth of India as a part of a great traditional culture, intimately bound up with the religion and daily life of the great mass of the Indian people.

Next he listed the opposing forces: all Western, all introduced from England, all government supported and codified, and all detrimental to India's indigenous traditions of art. The Government Schools of Art that maintained this pattern were in the Anglo-Indian commercial cities—Bombay, Madras, Lahore, Calcutta—and thus were cut off from India's traditional culture. The schools had been established after 1835, when Thomas Macaulay's view prevailed in England, that "a single shelf of a good European library was worth the whole native literature of India and Arabia." Therefore, what applied to Indian literature must apply to Indian art. Havell gave Birdwood full credit for writings that had had a salutary effect on the quality of Indian handicrafts design over the past thirty years. Art school administrators in India now had instructions from London "not to force upon Indians European ideas of art, but to promote the development of Indian art and craft upon their traditional lines."[53]

But in practice, what happened? An art expert fresh from England with orders to "promote the revival of Indian art" soon found himself a very subordinate official in a department with no intention of changing its ways. He found that buildings had higher priority than paintings and sculptures that might have served students for models. They had no Indian role models. Principals were always Europeans, and students "naturally expect a European principal to teach European art." Indian parents eager to win official notice by anglicizing themselves and their offspring thought instruction in Indian art a "retrograde and inconsistent policy"—all right for small children. The older students, however, "must become painters and sculptors in the European style." A prize at the Simla Fine Arts Exhibition, "the Royal Academy of Anglo-India," was the pinnacle of success. The old-fashioned standards of the exhibition were those of England's Royal Academy. The assumption that "Indian art is only admirable when applied to industrial purposes, and barbaric, or undeveloped, in the higher flights of artistic expression" discouraged efforts to teach Indians about Indian fine art. "All art is one, and both in Europe and in Asia," Havell said, the same aesthetic philosophy applies to weaver, painter, and sculptor. "Indian art must stand or fall as a complete school of aesthetic philosophy: to maintain as an educational principle that the lower department of it has been successful and the higher a failure is to condemn all Indian art in the eyes of Indians who are capable of forming a considered and reasonable judgment for themselves."

When Havell went to Madras as principal of that School of Art in 1884, there was "not a single example of the best Indian painting or sculpture" in the school, and students scorned their own traditional handicrafts as desirable examples of design. The son of one of the city's best goldsmiths was "making shaded drawings from the antique in the most approved South Kensington fashion, and his great pride was, not that he was himself a good goldsmith, but that he had won prizes at the Madras Fine Arts Exhibition for still-life painting in oil." Havell introduced drawing classes and let the antique casts gather dust unless Europeans wished to copy them. Over the years, by capitalizing on the city's own crafts traditions, he had created a crafts school that excelled in design.

Even that was impossible when he went to Calcutta in 1896. Students were sons of clerks and shopkeepers whose dearest ambition for them was employment in government offices. None were from artisan castes; there was no design experience on which to build. The school had only a European collection "much inferior to that of many small provincial towns in England," but he could not expel it, for it had Viceregal origins. With difficulty, he introduced an Indian section, but when he tried to enlarge that by selling off the inferior European art, there was a student boycott and a public outcry about lowered standards. Behind it all was the fact that few Calcutta Bengalis had ever seen good specimens of indigenous art and were "taught to believe that Indian art was only a relic of a semi-barbarous age."

Havell's Indian collection survived, however, and it was a revelation to Abanindranath Tagore, said Havell, "as it was to myself, and has been to other European artists who have seen it." Abanindranath's "Bengal School is a school of idealists, for otherwise it would not be Indian"—but they were not the impractical idealists who "in our Indian administration [are] generally regarded with grave suspicion." Havell's condemnations extended to the utilitarian character of the whole of Indian rule.

> It certainly has been the practical men who are responsible for all the injury which we have done to Indian art and craft the last fifty years. It is the practical men who have vainly tried in India to detach the fine arts from the industrial arts, believing that we can impose upon India European ideals in the former without destroying all Indian traditions in the latter. It is the practical men who, in the name of scientific progress, have helped to ruin Indian handicrafts, and still continue to do so, in spite of the lessons they might learn from the industrial history of modern Europe.

At the heart of the problem, Havell declared, was the fact that the government was ignorant of the qualifications and training of art experts. For every step forward in art education, the government sent it two steps back. After Havell left Calcutta in 1906, the Bengal Education Department

> tore to pieces the Drawing Syllabus by which I had begun to co-ordinate the teaching of art in the School of Art with the teaching in the schools outside it, and, without consulting the School of Art, reverted to the old South Kensington methods, which are entirely opposed to the principle and practice of Indian art. . . . even when the right thing happens, as it were accidentally, there is no continuity of policy, and no official interest in art, except by accident.

Havell concluded by saying that "Indian art is not dead; it has been sleeping, but is now awakening; and to continue to ignore it in the future as we have done in the past is, I am convinced, the worst of all bad policies, and one which is fraught with evil consequences to our Empire." If Indian art was indeed awakening, the government was not the Prince Charming who had brought that about.

Birdwood, on the other hand, thought Indian art "wide awake, and as alive as are [*sic*] the social economy of the country that has endured for 3,000 years," but it was in need of being "inspired, purified, and elevated" from the outside, that is, through contacts with "the arts of other civilised countries" around the world, Muslim, Buddhist, and Christian. He apologized for "any apparent arbitrariness of language" regarding Havell's paper and attributed it to "having had to treat an interminable controversy very briefly, for, at heart, believe me, no one is readier than I am to acknowledge himself a fool."

Sir George Birdwood was by no means a fool, but he was a classicist of Fergusson's school, and he was also an organization man. He and Havell disagreed, he said, not about the value of handicrafts as such but about Indian fine arts as means of revitalizing them. Revival needed "strong men" such as Lockwood Kipling, who had been principal of the Bombay School of Art—and Havell, too. But "a strong man would never raise a quarrel with his superiors. To do so was to violate the cardinal obligation of 'holy obedience.'"[54] For Birdwood, Indian fine arts were not only irrelevant but nonexistent.

> Of this "fine art", the unfettered and impassioned realisation of the ideals kindled within us, by the things without us, I have up to the present, and through an experience of seventy-eight years, found no examples in India; and, judging from my experience, I should say that India had never prized art for art itself's sake alone. I never saw a Hindu painting, sculpture, bronze, wood carving, clay moulding, &c., that was not first, throughout, and last, and for all in all, in intention at least, either a sacrosanct article of utility . . . or a ritualised, and generally monstrous representation of the high gods, and epic heroes of the race of the Brahmanical Hindus. . . .

Here he turned to a photograph of the Buddha figure and damned it along with the French symbolists and all their works. "But few of us," he said, "have the faith of the new school of 'Symbolists' in a symbolism that outrages artistic sensibilities and proprieties by virtually regarding art as but a framework for its myths, and allegories, and strange semeiological devices." Algebraic symbols could as well be fine art, and aesthetic reverence for the Buddha figure was absurd. "This senseless similitude, in its immemorial fixed pose, is nothing more than an uninspired brazen image, vacuously squinting down its nose to its thumbs, and knees, and toes. A boiled suet pudding would serve equally well as a symbol of passionless purity and serenity of soul!"

It is unfortunate that Sir George Birdwood should be so often remembered for this remark, for he had performed great service by encouraging improvements in the quality of Indian handicrafts, handloom weaving in particular, which was hard-pressed by the products of the power loom. But he was loyal to the classicist idea that Indian fine art began to decline after the great period of pure Aryan culture, between 900 B.C. and A.D. 300, its genius having "exhausted itself in the production of the Ramayana and the Mahabharata." As industrialization advanced, Indian art forms survived only with the village craftsman, "a true artist, although he seldom rises above the tradition of his art," which originated with "archaic forms of the aboriginal negroid tribes" from the hills, "wild fantastic forms of the Indo-Chinese tribes," "monstrous forms of the Dravidian races," and "primitive beasts and flower forms imported by the Persianised conquerors of the Hindus." But Indian collections in British museums were "more and more overcrowded with mongrel forms," the result of European influences and education "and above all of the irresistible energy of the mechanical production of Birmingham and Manchester."[55]

Havell wanted the Government of India's Education Department to revitalize Indian handicrafts by recognizing the finest and most authentic from among those indigenous forms that Birdwood found repellent. Birdwood wanted his romanticized village craftsman to save both handicrafts and village life, both already shifting under pressures from foreign competition and *swadeshi,* the nationalists' campaign that encouraged boycotts of British goods and services.[56]

There is an explanation besides obedience to policy for the attitude not only of Birdwood but also of many others of his generation. A nagging sense of insecurity and a nostalgia for the old India (and, in many respects, an India that never was) pervade his writings. In a paper entitled "Indian Pottery at the Paris Exhibition," Birdwood had spoken with intense feeling about Balgaum, "that part of India known to me familiarly . . . from my birth, and dear to me as my native country, the 'great' basaltic 'kingdom' of Maha-rashtra." In a passage that is worth quoting at length for what it tells us about this wistful view of the old India, he described in lyrical terms rich with biblical echoes the land where for "leagues and leagues around the old Mahratta cities of Poona and Sattara" the fields are green and golden,

> like a green thread wrought in gold; and rich orchards, and high groves of mango mark the sites of the villages hidden in their shade. Glad with the dawn the men come forth to their work, and glad in their work they stand all through the noontide, singing at the well, or shouting as they reap and plough; and as the stillness and the dew of eve fall upon the land like the blessing and the peace of God, the merry-hearted men gather with their cattle in Indian file, in long winding lines, to their villages again; slowly, over all the wide champaign, the black lines disappear into the lengthening shadows of the mango trees, and the day is closed in night. Thus day follows day, and all the year is crowned with gladness. It is in the contemplation of such scenes as these that the Englishman in India drinks deep of the bliss of knowing others blest. Is not the existence of the Indian ryot under the "English peace," in fact, the ideal of the poet and political economist? . . . And are not these the conditions under which archaic art and song have everywhere sprung?—and which are everywhere found essential to the preservation of their pristine purity?[57]

In a letter written to the *Times* barely a week before Havell presented his paper, Birdwood scoffed at worries about the "so-called threat" of "unrest in India" as the work of certain classes of Indians made discontented by education on the English model, of some uneducated landlords, and of a few Bengali lawyers who were out of pocket as a "temporary consequence" of the agitation over Curzon's 1905 Partition of Bengal, where violent protests increased day by day. Thanks to British rule, India was sound at heart, and the so-called unrest *must* be only a passing reversion to the anarchy that had preceded "the revindication by Great Britain of Aryan supremacy in India." The Raj as heroic light-bringer would eventually restore the felicities of the golden age. Officials must be tactful but firm. At the same time, they must beware the sound of the "sacred sea-shell, or chaukya" in Maharashtra, the ancient signal for Hindu mothers to send a son to the bands who helped to repel alien invaders. "From the associations of my infancy the sound of that trumpet awakens echoes even within my heart of heart—my 'subliminal self.' "[58] This child of empire, deeply imprinted with the meaning of that ancient call to battle and rebellion, still feared changes to India as he had known it and to that idealized British Raj of childhood memory and adult imagination.

His quotation marks around "unrest" suggested how very much he wished to believe that unrest in India was only a so-called threat and that the Partition of Bengal was a temporary aberration—even though just one year later Bengali anger and protests would be one reason for removing the seat of government from Calcutta to a new city at Delhi.

When Havell had concluded his speech at the Royal Society of Arts, Walter Crane rose first to his defense. Speaking from the viewpoint of the arts and crafts movement, he said that Havell had done in India what some artists tried to do in England: "to raise the banner of the handicrafts," with the difference that at least "in India the handicrafts were in a living condition" while in England industrialism had made many crafts extinct, so that they had to be reinvented entirely. After his own "rapid visit" to India in the winter of 1906–1907, Crane agreed with Havell that there was a relation between "Hindu native sculpture" and "the higher imagination." South India's sculptures had reminded Crane of "the splendid vital sculpture of the French thirteenth century." Therefore it was "a great mistake to suppose that the higher imagination was not present in Indian (Hindu) art. Those buildings were animated throughout by that spirit which regarded the inner vision of its figurative symbolism rather than the realisation of the outward appearances of things upon which European artists had spent nearly all their force."[59]

During the discussion that followed Havell's paper, Coomaraswamy spoke up. In his opinion, Havell had said too little rather than too much about "the apathy of the British Government with regard to all matters connected with Indian art." The collection in the museum at South Kensington, which Henry Cole had recommended as the designers' model, was more "an emporium of industrial art, valuable as far as it went, than an effective record of India's creative imagination." One really important collection had "just been allowed to go to America because the Indian Government were indifferent to, and ignorant of, Indian art." How could English educators in India "be brought to realise their own colossal ignorance"? Many writers on Indian art were of little help, for they "merely pointed out the obvious, and demonstrated the divergence of their own from the Indian point of view; and the results could not be regarded as permanent contributions to the history of art." How could they interpret what they did not understand? Birdwood, said Coomaraswamy, seemed to think "that 'Fine Art' did not exist in Europe before the time of Raphael." He made the mistake, "common to all European art critics, of calling ideal art, 'merely decorative,' just because it was not 'realistic.'" In conclusion, Coomaraswamy asked Sir George to call on Rothenstein "to speak as a practising artist, on the significance of Indian art, in India and in Europe."[60]

Rothenstein was an interesting combination of practical organizer and mystic. The continuities of ancient cultures fascinated him, a tendency that Christiana Herringham's Indian experiences had directed even more ardently toward India. He said that Western art would have had "an entirely different character" if artists had realized sooner the value of Eastern art. Indeed, there was already a slight turn toward "the more abstract forms of reality" and an understanding that "reality and realism were not the same thing, and that the essence of art was reality. . . . It was only just and right that the character of Indian art should be fully recognised, and even exaggerated, if it were possible to exaggerate it, since it had been so neglected for whole centuries at least of learned archaeological civilisation." Artists owed "a very great debt of gratitude" to Havell for putting the case for Eastern art so forcefully.[61]

Rothenstein, with Christiana's Ajanta letters vividly in mind, was so offended by Birdwood's remarks about the figure of the Buddha that "there and then I proposed that we organize an India Society," and forthwith he drafted a letter to the *Times* cosigned by a group of artists who represented painting, sculpture, the decorative arts, and art education. This, too, is worth quoting at length, for it is the manifesto of their new order in cultural relations with India.

> We the undersigned artists, critics, and students of art . . . find in the best art of India a lofty and adequate expression of the religious emotion of the people and of their deepest thoughts on the subject of the divine. We recognise in the Buddha type of sacred figure one of the great artistic inspirations of the world. We hold that the existence of a distinct, a potent, and a living tradition of art is a possession

> of priceless value to the Indian people, and one which they, and all who admire and respect their achievements in this field, ought to regard with the utmost reverence and love. While opposed to the mechanical stereotyping of particular traditional forms, we consider that it is only in organic development from the national art of the past that the path of true progress is to be found. Confident that we here speak for a very large body of qualified European opinion, we wish to assure our brother craftsmen and students in India that the school of national art in that country, which is still showing its vitality and its capacity for the interpretation of Indian life and thought, will never fail to command our admiration and sympathy so long as it remains true to itself.[62]

Havell was not a signatory, but he warmly welcomed this plea for respect for Indian art. "I am very glad indeed to hear that you set up a united protest against Birdwood's extravagant utterances," he wrote to Rothenstein. "I think it is high time that artists began to counteract his influence, and Purdon Clarke's, at South Kensington, for as long as that lasts nothing of Indian art will be shown there, except what appeals to the early Victorian artistic understanding—and to archaeologists." He applauded the idea of the India Society and added, "Mrs. Herringham I am sure will help."[63]

She was more than willing. She returned from India in time for the second meeting of the provisional committee. Again she was the only woman member. She may have engaged in some cautious electioneering behind the scenes. "Of course an energetic secretary is highly desirable," she wrote to Rothenstein, "but it is extremely awkward when he is ignorant, and also does not understand the sacred laws of committees." Nevertheless she was enthusiastic and told Rothenstein, "I always think if once things are begun they can be gone on with in spite of hindrances & dulness—The sun-mood clings to its child."[64]

On 27 April 1910 the India Society was formally launched. It decided to prepare for its members an annual publication on some aspect of the arts of India. It issued publicity, and membership guineas began to come in. Again, as in 1903, a small private group with few resources beyond enthusiasm and energy set out to do what the government could not or would not do. Almost at once the society was a focus for those sympathizing with Indian cultural causes. Very quickly, in the nature of things imperial, cultural causes attracted political concern. Only three months after the founding of the society, Rothenstein would discover that he was a focus of the government's nervous attention.

Christiana Herringham spent the summer of 1910 principally in preparations for the return to Ajanta, but she found time to write an article for the *Burlington Magazine* in which she repeated substantially what she had written to the prime minister of Hyderabad State: her work thus far, begun in exploratory fashion with the intention of bringing back specimen copies to encourage a more fully organized expedition, had itself become that serious continuation. "Thus it seemed best to consider that we were ourselves at work on that record which I had only thought of as a later possibility." The *Burlington* followed this with an editorial reminder that the habit of regarding Indian art as novelty discredited Britain's "long and intimate connexion with India." It praised the India Society's "laudable object." In May it published a Coomaraswamy article on Indian bronzes and, in August and September, Roger Fry's two scholarly reports on the Exhibition of Mohammedan Art in Munich, a landmark event.[65] The architect Geoffrey Scott, Bernard Berenson's librarian at the time, was attending the Munich exhibition. He advised Rothenstein to "cut the countesses who have booked you to dinner, put away your own work, pawn your possessions and come. I kept thinking of you when I was there to-day, for I know nobody who loves these things as much as *you* do, and to me they were a revelation, the cumulative effect was so astonishing & the pleasure of seeing all the Persian things in succession without anything to clash."[66]

Rothenstein was painting at Vattetot when Scott's letter arrived, but he did not go to Munich. He was saving for a trip to India, which he had been thinking of ever since 1907, when he heard the Herringhams' reports of their first visit. "Tell Mr Rothenstein I wish I could spirit him to India for a couple of months and see his amazed admiration," Christiana had written to Alice Rothenstein. After her return in 1910 she wrote: "I wonder if your husband will really come to India. I think if he does he will want to come every winter. I expect to come again next winter to go on with this Ajanta[.]"[67] Two weeks later he decided to accompany her in October. He hoped to find subjects for pictures enough to justify the expense. Dorothy Larcher was to travel by an earlier ship. Wilmot, with Christiana's brother Herbert, planned to join them later in the winter. Geoffrey was no longer in India but was reassigned to Staff College in England.

Christiana worried that Rothenstein might dislike the comparatively small SS *Himalaya* because "he might want more opportunity of getting to know some of the upper rank of Anglo-Indian official people going out, who would not be on a second-class boat." However, he was not interested in Anglo-Indian officials. A visit to the India Office had made him wary. When he had discussed his plans informally with Sir Richmond and Lady Ritchie, the discussion suddenly became stiff and formal; Rothenstein and Sir Richmond, who was Permanent Under-Secretary of State for India, continued it at the India Office. Getting permission to travel and paint in India might prove difficult. Sir Richmond was "afraid that my sympathy for Indians and for things Indian would encourage the Nationalists, now beginning to be heard through Gokhale and Tilak; I must promise to keep in touch with the officials, and to this end he provided me with letters to Provincial Governors." Like a prisoner on parole, he must present them at each major stop.[68]

Actually, no two could have differed more about politics than did the educator G. K. Gokhale and the nationalist politician B. G. Tilak. Tilak, a Maharashtrian (and we recall Birdwood's subliminal memories of the ancient Maharashtrian call to battle), was so aggressively and vociferously nationalist that he condoned any measures, including assassination, that he defined as forwarding nationalist causes. As he had been imprisoned on sedition charges since 1907, he would seem not an immediate cause of concern, but he had won Bengali loyalty as champion of their protests against Curzon's Partition of Bengal. Rothenstein intended to visit Calcutta and meet Abanindranath Tagore. Abanindranath's uncle, the poet Rabindranath Tagore, was already in the bad books of the Bengal provincial government for conspicuous involvement in Partition protests. Gokhale, also a Maharashtrian, was a Native Member of the Imperial Legislative Council and founder of the Servants of India Society, which pressed for orderly reforms in cooperation with the British. Tilak and other extremists regarded him as a confused traitor to the cause, while the Government of India thought that he could be useful in marshaling Hindu support. But Gokhale had joined the India Society, whose membership was public information. The government was not yet certain what the society was really up to, but the India Office in London certainly knew about Gokhale's membership. Or, since the mail of such persons was usually under surveillance, did the India Office already know that Rothenstein was corresponding with Gokhale and that they planned to meet in Bombay?[69]

Rothenstein now began to understand how a deeply conservative, parochial-minded bureaucracy could fear the most innocent attempts at cultural exchange. The whole cumbersome mechanism had begun to feel the full effects of nationalism in India and of political upheavals at home. A general election in January 1910 had produced an unstable government, and another in December would do no better. In November 1910 the Indian guard changed: Lord Crewe replaced the ardent imperialist Joseph Chamberlain as Secretary of State for India, and Lord Hardinge of Penshurst replaced Lord Minto as Viceroy. This new administration had to prove itself at a time of exceptional uncertainties.

Was Christiana Herringham also under surveillance? No evidence of that has turned up. She did not return from India in time to sign Rothenstein's letter to the *Times*. Unlike him, she was inconspicuous in India Society leadership. She intended to stay in Hyderabad State for almost the whole of her visit. Perhaps the India Office worried less about a respectable lady daubing away in a dark cave.

If art was so low among educational priorities, why was one wandering artist a cause for worry? It was not Indian art that worried governments both in Britain and in India, but its revival as a subject with appeal to the nationalist sensibilities of educated Indians. If anything said at the Royal Society of Arts could have worried the Government of India, it would have been Havell's statement that he hoped, "for the sake of British Prestige[,] that Government will not wait [to remove the obstructions to appreciation of indigenous art] until the opinion of educated Indians in art matters is so fully formed as to create a popular agitation for their removal." Education was theoretically fundamental to the civilizing mission of the Raj, but there was a great distance between that theory and officials' fears that "educated India" was slipping beyond their control. Their correspondence of the period is replete with resentful and derogatory references to "the educated classes." In 1910 *Indian Unrest,* by Valentine Chirol, the *Times*'s conservative political correspondent, had wide influence with its thesis that the Indian educational system had produced "a semi-educated proletariat," "dangerous hybrids" susceptible to "the mischievous incitements of politicians."[70] Thus, to the orthodox official mind, the India Society's innocent intentions to educate both British and Indian publics about Indian art suggested possibilities of sedition.

When Rothenstein joined Christiana and the *Himalaya* at Marseilles, there was illness among the crew, and he had to board at his own risk. "I did not hesitate," he wrote. "Mrs Herringham was expecting me." The illness was plague, and five of the Indian crew died. At Port Said the ship was quarantined. Rothenstein and Christiana were not bored, for the sights and sounds of the port were endlessly fascinating, but the Anglo-Indians on board "were indignant; such a thing had never yet happened on a P&O boat, and no one could find out precisely how matters stood."[71]

On Thursday morning, 27 October, they docked at Bombay. That evening they met, for the second time, Victor Goloubew. A wealthy Russian emigré who had settled in Paris, and a collector and specialist in the art of Southeast Asia, he was well known in European art circles, and Rothenstein had recommended him as a desirable member of the India Society, which had entertained him at lunch at the Café Royale in June 1910. There he had proposed that he and Rothenstein work together in India, a "vrai pélérinage," a "confraternité artistique, de sympathie," a lasting memory for both. But it would be Christiana for whom Goloubew became a persistent memory in no way sympathetic.[72]

He traveled in style. He arrived in Bombay with a secretary, a photographer, several servants, and a large collection from the Pasteur Institute of antidotes for tropical diseases and snakebite. Before he went to Ajanta, he wanted to see the cave temples at Elephanta. When he and Rothenstein went to Cook's to hire a launch, they found, as Wilmot Herringham had discovered in 1906, that enthusiasm about such sites was faint indeed. "Cook's man told me confidentially," Rothenstein recalled, "that it was not worth while to hire a launch; there was nothing to see at Elephanta!"[73]

Goloubew's secretary was a minor French writer named Charles Müller. He kept a journal that provides our most direct impressions of Christiana and Rothenstein at this time. It is the first detailed description anywhere of the middle-aged Mrs. Herringham. When the journals were published as *Cinq mois aux Indes: de Bombay à Colombo,* Müller changed their names to "Mrs. Hoppkins" and "M. Blauenfeld," but there is not the slightest doubt of the identities, for "elle est peintresse; il est peintre." The journal's tone is caustic and condescending, and some references to Rothenstein are frankly and nastily anti-Semitic. Müller describes Christiana as pale, with a downy complexion and eyes "un peu troubles"—a reference to the tic that caused her to blink rapidly and frequently. She had pouches beneath her eyes, a pinched little nose, and a hat rather too youthful: "un chapeau trop jeune."[74]

Rothenstein he described as dominated by his black horn-rimmed spectacles that seemed larger than ever in the absence of a mustache. They went together to the Indian part of the city, and Rothenstein enjoyed wandering there, but when Müller suggested going to "le 'Japanese quarter,'" Rothenstein held back, "visiblement puritain." They continued their wanderings, "vertueux."[75]

Müller had the impression that by the time Christiana and Rothenstein reached India, they were on bad terms: "se détestent cordialement." If there was tension, it did not arise on shipboard and did not continue after Bombay. "It has made a great difference to me having a real friend on board," Christiana had written to Alice Rothenstein. "I don't want a lot of talking but I like the little to be of good quality." It is quite possible that at Bombay they were annoyed not with each other but with Goloubew and his entourage, and that they had not realized how fully he intended to take advantage of the camp that the Nizam again provided at Fardapur. Christiana's letters say nothing about her expecting to share the camp, and at Bombay she found that Goloubew's party already took a great deal for granted. On the day that she and Rothenstein arrived, Müller wrote that she had already made her own arrangements with British efficiency—"avec un vieil instinct d'Anglaise ménagère"—for staples such as potatoes, rice, and tea. Goloubew expected his party to be "en quelque sorte ses hôtes là-bas"—guests who anticipated pleasant days at Fardapur and Ajanta. That the news of these guests and an expanded camp was unexpected seems quite possible because, three days later, Christiana—"cette personne autoritaire"—asked Rothenstein to shop for more potatoes and mineral water, and he replied with some heat that his hotel room already resembled a groceries depot.[76]

Goloubew had negotiated separately with the Nizam for use of Christiana's camp, but his intrusion complicated more than the food supply. Christiana planned two books, one an informal account of her experiences at Ajanta, the other a scholarly volume on the history of the caves and the paintings. She mentioned the first to Alice Rothenstein. "I have been doing some reading & writing preparatory to a little book about Ajanta next spring—and I have been working a little at Hindustani." She and Rothenstein had discussed the scholarly report as the India Society's 1911 publication for members, and she mentioned that Goloubew had written to her to say "that if the India Society publishes a book on Ajanta his photographs there would be available for it. I think when you and he are there together we must try to settle what is going to be done." Was Goloubew already planning his own book on Ajanta? Müller indicates that he was, that Christiana's project was analogous to what Goloubew had in mind.[77] He planned no copying; he had M. Hollmann, his photographer. A book, therefore, must have been the analogous project.

Christiana and Rothenstein proceeded to Fardapur while Goloubew and Müller sampled Bombay's pleasures: the Yacht Club, the Bombay Club, a maharaja's audience, and an ingratiating call upon Sir George Clarke, Governor of the Bombay Presidency, and Lady

Clarke. They bought an additional two weeks' (later reduced to ten days') supplies and comforts for themselves, for camping "en pleine jungle." (Müller dramatized; the camp was not in a jungle but "by trees in the wide, gravelled expanse belonging to the dak bungalow of Fardapur.") Before leaving Bombay, they paid a round of visits to the Japanese quarter and, for purposes of comparison, to "une maison européenne."[78]

On 24 November the Bombay-Calcutta train deposited them at Jalgaon station in a bitterly cold dawn. The platform was crowded with Indian travelers huddled shivering in shawls. Müller used his favorite uncomplimentary simile: they looked like "singes fiévreux," feverish apes. He complained that station tap water for washing was colder than the preceding night had been, and throughout his stay at Ajanta he grumbled unceasingly about the cold at night and the heat by day. The congeniality of Christiana's work at Ajanta was already in jeopardy.

Goloubew's party were met by three horses, three "boys" (Müller's derogatory term for porters), two tongas, two bullock carts, and a special policeman whom the Nizam had assigned to them. Müller was scathing about tongas ("des pires inventions de l'imbécillité humaine") and rejected them in favor of a fiery stallion named Pera. He intended a dashing entrance at the camp and was not discouraged when Pera pitched him thigh-deep into the water at a ford. Müller's vanity was undamaged. As he rode along, he ascribed the *namastes* of the villagers to the Nizam's having trained his subjects in "des marques extérieures du respect," proper subservience apparently having gone by the board in British India. The Nizam, Müller says, had placed the camp at *their* disposal. What he found was much better than what he expected: a little city of some fifteen tents, each with more space than half the apartments in Paris, fully and comfortably furnished and with complete bathing facilities. He was thrilled when commands rang out as their column approached and the Nizam's soldiers presented arms. The newcomers filed before them, shedding *hauteur* and *noblesse*. Goloubew and Müller took one of the largest tents. Hollmann the photographer, with his laboratory, and the servants and their baggage, had two others. "Mistress Hoppkins" and her staff had the rest. Goloubew and Müller made the most of their privacy. They shot two wood pigeons and a quail, which they gleefully hid from Christiana for their secret delectation.[79]

Müller's book contains the only known photograph of the entire assemblage of visitors, soldiers, servants, mounted police, the "police inspector Sahib," and painting assistants: some forty persons in all. Seated in front are three English ladies in white. Müller, always ready with a cutting remark, says that Christiana had *two* Englishwomen as assistants who looked about twenty-five but were not really that old; they seemed prematurely to have reached spinsterhood. One of these is certainly Dorothy Larcher, dressed for work with a kerchief around her head. The middle lady, very Anglo-Indian in a large veiled hat, is not an assistant but is probably the Casson Walkers' daughter Sheila, about to be married and out from Hyderabad for a day's visit. The third lady, bareheaded, very slight, very erect, and alert, is Christiana. In this photograph, her hair is white; she is fifty-nine years old. At Christiana's left sit Goloubew and Müller. Goloubew, in suit and vest as if for the boulevard, with vandyke beard and a proprietary air, is a figure out of Chekhov. Müller sits with knees crossed, elbow on knee, and chin propped on his left hand. In every photograph, even on horseback, he lolls or lounges as if excessive boredom renders him unable to straighten his spine.[80]

Goloubew found the "frescoes" so impressive that he now began to plan his own commentary on them. They were a revelation and if not damaged would rank with those at Florence, would equal the most beautiful "primitifs" known to the world. Even Müller summoned up enough enthusiasm for the paintings to write a paragraph of grudging admiration for Christiana in which he said that her vocation as copyist of Italian old masters had won her the well-deserved reputation that had led her to Ajanta. He could not help feeling sorrowful admiration for "cette vielle femme"; perhaps, in some former life, she had played so much with puzzles that she was now condemned to this labor in expiation. Without hope of material reward she worked tirelessly in the fiery furnace of the days and the freezing night air, traveling three hours daily to the caves, where she perched on a ladder in the gloom and the stench of bat droppings, ruining her eyes and her health to piece together fragments of heads, hands, feet, animals. She would die before she could complete a task that Goloubew, with simple photographic equipment and an automobile lamp, would begin and finish in a few weeks. But such was her devotion, her "piété," that all this effort at reclamation was as nothing to her. When he thought of that, Müller conceded, he could not but disregard the small nose, the pinched lips, the blinking eyes of the "vielle copist"—old copyist.[81]

Christiana would never have settled for photographs as the only record. Vocation required the re-creator's hand as she transferred these pictures from her tracings to the canvas and then applied the paint, day by day and stroke by stroke. Her piety—Müller had hit upon the precise word—demanded that except for the brush no mechanism might come between the hand and the work. The hand was conduit for inspiration, which was of divine origin. With her own brush, from her own tracings and color codes, she would try to reproduce as nearly as possible the strokes of the unknown painters, which were a true outline of their history as artists. She felt, Wilmot wrote, "that she was face to face with the remains of a great civilization and a great art, of which little is left but tradition." And, Havell would have added, a tradition whose very existence was even then denied by those with responsibility for preserving it.[82]

Christiana's relation to the work was quite unlike that of the earlier copyists. A government directive had assigned Major Robert Gill to copy at Ajanta, and military necessity could call him away at any time. John Griffiths's project was in part an extracurricular exercise. Goloubew with his photographer, whom Christiana would not have called a copyist at all, was merely filling a space supplemental to his knowledge of Southeast Asian art. Brisk and blasé, in Müller's account at least, he never indicated the least emotional involvement with Ajanta. While she was there, Christiana invested all of her emotions, her strength, and at least two thousand pounds of her own money in the work. Defining the inspiration of Ajanta's anonymous artists was a way of defining herself. She was, literally, as nearly face-to-face with those unknown painters as it was possible to be, and Ajanta had no intrusive social code to say that a woman artist may do this, but a woman artist may not do that.

Coomaraswamy, who was in charge of a United Provinces Trades Fair at Allahabad, had been to Ajanta and understood the release and revelation in such labor. He had begun to think about devoting his life to the study of Indian art and its traditions. He told Rothenstein that in India he discovered more about himself and his Asian heritage, that he felt "the intense thinness of English life in contrast. There is such a deep emotional and philosophical background to this." He envisioned a lifetime's work ahead, to be spent collecting, pondering, writing, educating. He completely rejected Curzon's theory of "exotics imported . . . in the train of conquerors" as the formative influence on Indian art. He saw the Ajanta wall paintings as the progenitor of all Indian art. Each day he saw that continuity more clearly, and it contradicted all the received theories of Persian origins of the Indian tradition.

> I find the indigenous element in this even larger than I surmised, and the Persian element very much smaller. People have a mania for thinking that everything comes from somewhere else than where you find it. I am beginning to see that the best things are always *well* rooted in the soil. I have got hold of a magnificent lot of old Rajput cartoons and drawings of miniatures—I can't tell you how beautiful some of them are. Most are 18th century, and the best must have been earlier than that, even so, one can only think of Botticelli as giving an idea of one or two. This Hindu or Rajput art is the descendant of Ajanta[;] its rise and zenith and decline seem to cover at least 1500 years. The 200 years of Mughal art is but a breath beside it.[83]

Rothenstein was carried away by the glories of the paintings. Now he "understood better than hitherto [Mrs. Herringham's] zeal and devotion in coming to India a second time to make copies of these astonishing paintings. She had wanted my advice in selecting the subjects for future copies—but how to find my way through this jungle of masterpieces!" Reluctantly, he went on to Allahabad to join Coomaraswamy, and then to Calcutta, where he met Abanindranath Tagore's uncle, Rabindranath. It was a meeting whose outcome enlarged the activities of the India Society in unexpected ways, and Rothenstein's efforts on Tagore's behalf were to create the modern turning point in the history of literary exchange between India and the West.[84]

Meanwhile, Christiana had worries other than Goloubew's intrusion. In early December, Wilmot had emergency surgery for appendicitis; he recovered well, but he could not join her in India. Geoffrey was with him, and Christiana's brother Herbert Powell was coming out alone. She wrote to Rothenstein at Allahabad:

> The surgeon said the operation was absolutely necessary but now he will be as if there had never been any thing the matter at all.
>
> Mr. Hol[l]man[n] the photographer who is working here you know for Mr Goloubeff is to do some 50 photographs of the paintings or anything else I want, to be entirely my private property. He is getting near the end of his work and he will then go to Ellora and photograph a few things there. I have arranged to go too and meet my brother Bertie there. We shall start on Thursday. Bertie will come back with me here for a day or two.[85]

With Wilmot recovering and Goloubew's troupe now out of the way, Christiana settled again to her work. The two Hyderabad assistants had left, but two of the three Bengalis were still there. On 3 January 1911 she told Wilmot that she planned to leave Ajanta about 12 March,

> but it is difficult in this press of work to think about coming home—I have several large difficult things on hand and I have some of the others' work to finish. I have been going a good many consecutive days to the caves—it is not a fattening process. We shall have to start earlier and earlier as the sun is so hot. When we are there it is all right. Going out in the sun from cave to cave doesn't matter. Staying in camp the tents get very hot. Everything seems running more smoothly now. I hope it is not a calm before some unexpected storm. The last improvement will be the lamp and the lampman. He should be on his way now from Jalgaon. It will be great luxury if we even have two incandescent lamps regularly burning—and there may be three.

Even with relatively better light, the work was painfully slow. She had lost time at Christmas when Percy Brown, Havell's successor as principal at the Calcutta School of Art, brought his wife to Ajanta, and "they think me a very heroic person to go nearly every day in shaky bullock carts to the Caves—it certainly is rather severe."[86]

Then Coomaraswamy's domestic affairs intruded. In 1902 he had married Ethel Mary Partridge, and they lived at Ashbee's Chipping Campden crafts center. She had gone to India with him but by October 1911 had returned to England. Ethel's journal showed an "ominous pause" during September 1910 and then came a "sad letter from Allahabad" to Ashbee. She had been "clothing the break-up of her marriage in the disguise of Ananda wanting to live primarily in India" and carry on with a "big scheme" for a national museum. Alice Richardson, a designer and a former London flatmate of Dorothy Larcher's, joined him after Ethel's departure and carried on a distracting correspondence with Christiana.[87] Caught in this from several directions, Christiana mentioned it to Rothenstein and then had to ask Alice Rothenstein to be sure to tell him that "when I said I knew another girl" who had joined Coomaraswamy, it was *not* "the girl who had been with me this winter"—that is, not Dorothy Larcher.[88]

In February there was another crisis at the Fardapur camp. The widow who cooked for some of the Indians had a miscarriage. "She oughtn't of course to have been able to have a miscarriage," Christiana told Wilmot. "I was somewhat uneasy at the first, for I supposed an elderly person was coming [to cook], and she turned out to be young and pretty." The widow was quite ill, and the local midwife would not go near her. At last "some coolie women were found" to attend her. Christiana refused to allow an official investigation and "merely said [the Indian concerned] must be responsible for his servant." Then there was a report that the sergeant of the camp police demanded twenty-five rupees not to report the case to the local official. Christiana intervened, and he ordered her "to drive the woman away whether she was well or ill. I hoped they meant drive her away in a bullock cart—but I replied that an Englishwoman would not drive a woman away while she was ill." However, the woman seemed set to establish herself as the camp invalid. Christiana allowed her to stay until she became fit to travel. On the day of departure, she kept the cart waiting for six hours, until Christiana sent a message "that I should have the tent taken down at 4.p.m. This was effectual."[89]

Increasingly Christiana felt that time closed in on her. She gave up the idea of a visit to Coomaraswamy's exhibition at Allahabad.

The day she had set for herself and Larcher to finish their work was 21 February, which "seemed to be about as long as our own physical strength and the patience of the camp would respectively last. We two were left alone for the final wrestle with the task of the copying. After all the people and the going and coming, and the little festivities there was some feeling of relief and peace, but almost more of loneliness—and of a hard fight against time to get the work sufficiently finished." She had mapped out the last copying at the rate of so much a day. The heat increased, and she was now close to exhaustion. The incessant bumping of the bullock cart had always gotten on her nerves, but sometimes now she was so exhausted that even that did not register. "I don't find any benefit from a springless cart bumping over boulders—It's curious how entirely unconscious one can sometimes be of unpleasantness. There is a grating, crunching wide river bed that I particularly dislike, and noticed yesterday that we had crossed it without my having been aware for a moment that we were doing so—quite absorbed in thoughts about other things." The two women did not go altogether alone to the caves. "One of our police walks behind [the cart] or takes short cut occasionally. We part company at what we call the cart place and walk on over the boulders. . . ." Driver, cart, and bullocks waited all day until the women returned, usually between five and six. A kind and enterprising villager "who chooses to be really handy" brought their lunch basket, started tea, helped to steady their stepladders, and moved the frames for the large tracings.[90]

These last days were all much alike. Dorothy Larcher worked as much as possible by the available daylight, Christiana by lamps that were an endless nuisance. "You have to pour methylated spirits into a receiver below the mantles. Then you light the spirits, and going on putting more in till you judge the mantles are hot enough to vaporize the stream of under-pressure—combined—air and oil. The moment is one of keen anxiety. Sometimes the lamp won't light." The sheets of tracing paper were often as large as eight-by-ten feet, and she was increasingly exhausted with "standing on steps nearly all the time, balancing myself on account of the width of the copy & the difficulty of seeing the wall as I worked. . . . It was a matter of satisfaction that

I never did lose my balance and have a hasty jump to save myself—one might hurt one's feet rather." She ended her long 14 February letter to Wilmot, writing, "This is the last letter from here."[91]

There was, however, one pleasant interlude before they departed. The young Dutch Sanskritist Jean Philippe Vogel, then substituting for John Marshall as Director of the Archaeological Survey of India, came to see Ajanta. The women found him "a most satisfactory person." In view of his later eminence, Christiana's description is worth repeating at length.

> It was a pleasant easement of our solitary life to have Dr Vogel's visit. . . . He had written a very polite letter to ask if he would be in the way—if so he would borrow a tent from the Collector of Jalgaon. But our feelings were very much the opposite of finding him in the way—and I replied inviting him to mess [have meals] with us—which he did. He is a Sanskrit scholar and represents the literary side of the Archaeological Survey—but as I said before is at the present taking Mr Marshall's place of general superintendence. He is Dutch more like a Swede—rather tall & fair & very simple & modest. He was a little shy the first evening (he is quite young) but next day, seeing I think how keen we two women were, he became extremely friendly. His visit was of great importance to us for he knew the Jataka stories and made us two very important explanations, so that knowing the stories we traced in outline parts belonging to painted copies which would not have related their incidents properly without. We had also found a small unknown inscription which he translated for us and dated the character about A.D. 500 which is important.

Vogel was at the caves only one full day but did "an amazing lot of seeing in the time, and we helped him all we could. After that, it was like gaining the enemy's ground inch by inch. . . . Dr. Vogel's visit added work, and as really we were full up, we had to leave out some others that we wanted to do."[92] Still, they did not begrudge losing some of their precious time, for Vogel was such a pleasant contrast to Goloubew. His contributions in that one day suggest how much a really congenial resident scholar could have contributed to their understanding of the work.

There was at least another month's work, but Christiana now felt that she could stay no longer. "And I am sure all the camp people thought us half demented to work as we did." They were still painting on 21 February, the last day, while coolies and carts made "a final clearance of properties" at the Fardapur camp. The two women finally left the caves at twilight, carrying their copies and "leaving the carts with the heavy things to flounder in the dark over jungle stones & river beds. We met men & lanterns coming to meet us—not at all unwelcome."[93] Christiana was so exhausted that she had to go to bed after dinner, leaving until morning the complicated business of paying all the helpers.

In the morning everyone left for Jalgaon in a procession of six bullock carts. It was terribly hot, and a porter responsible for soda water had forgotten it. The head servant "began a furious scolding, but I stopped him for I was too tired & hot even to listen to another person being scolded." She had a filter and used it with brackish water from a local well, and "a crowd of people looking must have been much perplexed as to what was happening." Then there were protracted negotiations with a man who had two strong-looking bullocks, one of which Christiana's head man wanted to trade for one of theirs too tired to go on. "We were being escorted by two police," Christiana wrote, "and they were leading the argument rather noisily, . . . I couldn't have any oppression . . . so then I said we would pay the man 2 rupees. . . . The bullocks entirely disapproved. The first one would not go under the yoke at all, and the second made a great fuss."[94] She could only hope that the return exchange would be made on the way back, as arranged.

At eleven o'clock that night, the bone-shaking, nerve-shattering thirty miles to the Jalgaon rail station ended in a euphoria of exhaustion. In 1909 Christiana had complained that the station had no ladies' waiting room; it now had one, and she and Dorothy Larcher spent the night there. The stationmaster found two berths in a ladies' carriage in the Bombay train, and they tumbled into it the following morning. Christiana went to the Taj Mahal Hotel, Miss Larcher to a family with whom she was to stay as a paying guest. They packed and sealed some of the copies for shipment, a tedious business of rolling each tracing in tissue paper, of obtaining the specially made boxes and seeing to their being lined with tin and soldered shut, and of guaranteeing to Cook's that the Army and Navy Stores had packed the boxes according to regulations. Everything was done in a frantic rush that left no time for a meal. Christiana told Wilmot that she had an attack of some kind of skin rash—only from tiredness and something she had eaten, but she was plainly playing it down so as not to worry him. She confirmed her passage home for 25 March; Dorothy Larcher would leave on the 26th by another ship. Herbert Powell and Rothenstein, who had been touring India separately, had met in Bombay and then had sailed together on 25 February. Christiana returned to Hyderabad for a last visit to the Casson Walkers, who would soon retire to England.[95]

Goloubew now reentered the scene in the form of Christiana's anxious allusions. The fifty photographs promised to her had taken longer than expected, for Hollmann had stayed on to finish work at the Ellora caves as well as at Ajanta. She was now thinking more specifically about her two books on Ajanta: the popular account with those photographs as illustrations, and the scholarly report for the India Society to be illustrated with reproductions of her copies. In January she had written to Wilmot:

> On the voyage I want to get my book arranged. Could you send me my letters back again. . . .
>
> If you have any advice to give about the book please give it—I want it to be a popular account of the caves and the painting with something about Buddhism & the early Indian romances & court life & extracts from the Chinese travellers and then my own camp life—There will be lots of illustrations. Shall I keep the camp part in letter form. I should think not—This is quite separate from the big [India Society] library book. Don't think much about that.[96]

In January she had felt "as young and strong in this open air life as I ever have felt at all." But in February she felt neither young nor strong, and when Rothenstein met her at Bombay, he was alarmed. "She had overworked, as women will, and the long hours in the close bat-haunted Ajanta caves had done her grave harm." A very different, more ominous note now entered her letters. She feared that all of her professional, financial, and emotional investments in Ajanta were in danger. "Mr. de Goloubeff made proposals to me which were quite different from what he said to me when he came to the Camp," she wrote to Wilmot. "I have entirely refused to have anything to do with his publications or with Dr. Coomaraswamy's and I have sent a letter about my Ajanta work to the Indian press. Should Mr. de Goloubeff represent things differently please remember that my refusal to join with him is quite final." As Müller's journal indicates, the "projette Goloubew" was now to be specifically proposed as a joint venture. While she packed her copies in Bombay, she wrote to Rothenstein: "You said you would think about what to do with all the copies supposing I get them safe to England—I have got tiresomely nervous about their safety. I don't like taking a studio where they would be all right by their lovely selves—but I have got to work a good deal at the big ones, and have no big enough place except the billiard room."[97]

At the same time, she drew Coomaraswamy into the puzzle of her relations with Goloubew. In March he told Rothenstein that she seemed to think "I am responsible for Goloubew's change of plans. She has written me most extraordinary letters." The nature of the "change" remains quite unclear. Christiana's "irrelevant and incomprehensible letters" made Coomaraswamy feel both bewildered and hurt. He told Rothenstein that he greatly admired her and was "personally *grateful* for her work" and hoped that they might remain friends, and all the more because she had written kindly to Alice Richardson.[98] But Coomaraswamy had his own worries connected with Goloubew, to whom he had loaned two valuable pictures about which he had heard no more. This loan had been discussed and arranged while Rothenstein was at Ajanta in November.

Two days after Rothenstein sailed for England, Christiana wrote to him from Hyderabad, "It has been very fortunate for me that you are my witness and stand by me about the Coomaraswamy and Goloubew affair—otherwise I daresay there would have been difficulties for me." Her conception of the "big library book" expanded. She thought the India Society the logical publisher for it, "to some extent backed by the Calcutta [branch of the India] Society *and* Quarritch—Probably coming out in parts." She envisioned something on the order of the Japanese art publication *Kokka* but wanted this mentioned "to the Committee of the India Society only—& privately."

She expected to finish her more personal "small book" by the time she reached England.[99]

The days at Hyderabad were leisurely and interesting. The Casson Walkers' daughter Sheila was married. Christiana visited a girls' high school that was run by E. M. Forster's friend May Wyld. Sarojini Naidu took Christiana to a wealthy Muslim home where the ladies in purdah put all their jewels and a daughter's wedding clothes on display. Christiana was ambivalent, not because she did not care about jewels, but because purdah life seemed so bizarre. "I saw a phase of life which it is difficult to realize as actually existing, although I saw it and did not dream it."[100] She wrote a long and amusing account of the political tug-of-war over Casson Walker's successor, Sir Akbar Hydari, soon to be Forster's friend also.[101] About her own money spent for Ajanta, Christiana said only that the government had spent more than three thousand pounds for Griffiths's copies; her expenses had not yet reached that figure. At the same time, thoughts about returning to Ajanta another year became less specific. "I think you ought to come here some day," she wrote to Alice Rothenstein. "I had to wait a long time however—all my life I wanted to come and you can't wait to be as old as I was when my first visit happened. . . . I am still very busy gathering experiences in this city."[102] Her skin rash disappeared, and she conquered a sore throat.

Her Hyderabad letters to Wilmot were cheerful and witty—until she thought of Goloubew. Then the pitch of anxiety rose far above any normal uneasiness about precious belongings shipped by sea. The following disjointed statement is characteristic: "The Russian not playing up[,] I should if there is a book want a few photographs. Please be discreet about that. Speak if spoken to, but steer clear of libel. I have a very strong case if he were to try to be nasty to me and Mr Rothenstein [who have] independent knowledge of the facts and entirely on my side."[103] Was she referring to the proposal for joint publication, or to the photographs promised as her "private property," or to the pictures that Coomaraswamy had loaned to Goloubew?

Gill's and Griffiths's copies that were destroyed by fire became significant in a new context. In January 1910 the *Illustrated London News* featured photographs of Gandhara sculptures and commented, "It is a strange fact that an evil fate has followed previous importations of Gandhara art to this country." A fine Gandhara collection had burned with the Sydenham Crystal Palace in 1866, and another was lost at sea in 1885. Such a past history gave good reason to think of accidental fire damage, but Christiana went further. "But I have got horribly nervous about the pictures, feeling as if someone might try to rob me of them or get them destroyed under cover of the fire fatality which is supposed to haunt them—that is known about in India. I am considering how to insure their safety in England. Fire Fate does not exist really to me. Fire damage would be *wilful.*"[104] Was it England, not India, that threatened such damage?

Nevertheless she was very specific, even adamant, about wanting her copies to stay in England. She did not follow up a suggestion from Havell and Marshall that she negotiate a sale to the Government of India. She declined the proposals of their emissary, "a man who could probably have got it done." She told Wilmot, "Well I would rather they should be housed in England—I told him I did not see how I could see copies that were not yet made [from the tracings] (quite friendlily)—don't despair yet that they may get a fitting home!"[105] Several times she reminded Rothenstein that he had promised to advise her how to protect them once she got them to England.

Her imagination began to run wild; it would be so easy for arsonists to blame on someone's wish for vengeance the well-known "Fire Fate" that dogged art taken from India. Might not arson be the work of someone *not* Indian, who could then blame it upon English imagination about vengeful Indians or could employ an Indian for such an assignment and blame it on Indian superstition?

The "sun-mood" had deserted its child, and her old pattern of assertion and withdrawal reappeared. She begged Rothenstein to write at once to Goloubew and say that she was "extremely tired—that I have been talking things over with you, and that as I find from his letters that he is nervous about the use I might make of the photographic negatives—that I thought it at the time a very generous offer and now I think the best thing is to release him from his promise, which I think he made rashly." Rothenstein must get Goloubew to tell him candidly whether he would accept color negatives of "two or three of the students' copies—I have already suggested instead of mine." Or, "considering the funk I am in it would be better after all to send him some bits of my own. . . . I don't think you can appreciate the horrid feelings & half sentences that have bothered me so. Where could I send the copies to be safe?" She decided to offer Goloubew photographs of two copies by one of the Bengali assistants, "not conceding my own, because I had made difficulties to other people about doing that." She reserved copyright in her own work for her own publication, and Goloubew must state that the Bengalis' copies had been made expressly for her. He had replied, she said, "J'accept avec plaisir un des copies Bengalis comme frontispiece," and she added, "I have heard nothing more."[106] Did she imagine that the concession would ward off the threat of his using the same photographs for his Ajanta book before she could finish her own? She had both negatives and prints of photographs of the Bengalis' copies, but did Goloubew have prints as well?

She returned to England in early April. By the end of May, her letters to both of the Rothensteins were ever more elliptical and distraught. She feared that she had offended him by commenting too sharply on one of his own Indian drawings, then apologized by saying that she took his art very seriously. "It scarcely seems to me that *that* can be a cause of difficulty between us—but you may not quite understand this." However, something much worse was at work: she felt physically threatened. She told Alice Rothenstein, "I think that you have been so sweet to me lately—and I have seemed churlish sometimes." She was "going away on Friday—Please don't say anything about this where you could be overheard—I was very much frightened coming to you last Saturday. It suggested itself to me whether any one could hear the telephone at your end, and know I was coming. So don't telephone or talk to be overheard."[107] There was nothing sinister in her plan to leave London; she was going abroad for a fortnight with a sister and a friend, and having so recently returned after such a long absence, she did not want people to know that she had left England again. But that does not explain her forebodings.

On that same day she told Rothenstein that she was going away for two weeks, and in a headlong paragraph she begged him, if he should go to Paris, where Goloubew now was, to "try to get Goloubew to see that I do feel that I have done something which he minds or resents, and that I regret the accident very much and wish I knew what to do—I fancy he thinks I am embarked on a career of Indian expert connoisseurship and shall compete with him, which is not at all the case." She also told Rothenstein that she was "very definitely alarmed when I came to you on Saturday. Is it possible that you have a parlourmaid in your house who could report that I was coming if she heard the telephone?" Would he, without fail, return the photographs of the copies then with him? She had taken precautions about copyright, which she would give to the India Society, but she continued to worry about the negatives of the photographs. She told Rothenstein that she was determined not "to get into *art* [politics] or *Indian* politics. If I go to India again it would be for painting subjects, and perhaps to study one or two architectural points which interested me. But I am very doubtful about going again at all—I do dread getting drawn into politics and the difficulty of going for the winter is great, for I cannot stand London in the summer and I can't be away all the time."[108]

On 1 June, Frederick R. Martin, who had known the Herringhams for some time and who was an expert on Oriental carpets and one of the organizers of the Munich exhibition, called at Wimpole Street. Christiana was convinced that he came from Goloubew, "to clear the matter up—though he said but little about that, and we talked delightfully for an hour and a half about his own work." She told Rothenstein that Martin thought it a good idea for Christiana and Goloubew to collaborate, "instead of having two separate works. He said M. Goloubew always did what he (Dr. Martin) advised." Her copyright now belonged to the India Society, but Martin "thought it could be arranged. Don't say I guessed he was a sort of emissary. Please keep this letter very confidential." Saying, "I hate the name Imperial Festival," she resigned from the committee of the Festival of Empire to open at the Crystal Palace in Sydenham in

June, where the India Society planned to exhibit her completed copies.[109]

Then she was afraid again, this time that she had offended Alice Rothenstein.

> I am sorry I am so curt to you but honestly I thought that information to malicious people about my whereabouts might have been got through your parlourmaid and the telephone—
>
> You know I have been horribly frightened—and it goes on—you can do nothing at all for me—But I don't want the telephone used about *me* to your house at all. I shall forbid our servants to answer. If some one in communication with your parlourmaid wants to know if I am here or away it is so easy for her to find out.
>
> Be sorry for me—but not angry. . . . You must on no acct say this to your maid.[110]

Then, with total inconsistency, she wrote to the *Times* on 13 June to ask that any publicity attending exhibition of her Ajanta copies at the Crystal Palace be given to Laurence Binyon; to Havell, Marshall, Morison, and the Casson Walkers; to the Nizam of Hyderabad; and to Abanindranath Tagore.[111] It did not occur to her that a letter to the *Times* from 40 Wimpole Street was a public announcement of where she might be found.

Her copies were displayed at the Crystal Palace as planned. Just below them were "about a hundred fine photographs of the famous frescoes and the caves by M. Goloubew of Paris." Christiana did, however, supply a commentary with a summary of her conclusions about the medium and ground used at Ajanta. She now described the medium as a combination of tempera and true fresco, with the ground a mixture of clay, cow dung, and finely powdered traprock pressed firmly into the rock surface to a thickness of one-eighth to three-fourths of an inch. Over this went an "eggshell" coat of finer plaster on which to paint. As with fresco, the plaster was never allowed to dry until the picture was finished. Occasionally, she thought, the plaster had been applied directly to the rock wall. She also offered a justification for her having re-created the damaged parts of the paintings as accurately as possible in her copies. "I think we may fairly claim that this omission of damage has been done very cautiously, and the underfinished look of the copies is the consequence of our restoring so little. A copy of a damaged picture must necessarily look like the copying of a badly painted or unfinished one."[112]

Also by 13 June, she seems to have made a decision that indicated a new course of action. She wrote to Alice Rothenstein:

> Thank you very much for your letter and kind sympathy—something very curious happened last night—I do trust it meant that the worry is over but I can't tell yet—I do so badly want a talk with Mr Rothenstein. This letter is for him as well as you—I think it would very likely be better for me to go away rather far off, soon, for sometime, and leave things about the copies arranged. To carry out Dr. Martin's proposals & leave everything ready might mean a good deal for me to do before I can go. . . . [113]

Did she, after all, give up and intend to leave her Ajanta manuscript and photographs to be combined with Goloubew's publication as she thought Martin had proposed? On 31 May she had intended to be away for a fortnight from 2 June, but this letter to Alice, dated 10 June, suggests either a sudden change of travel plans or a screen for her intentions. There was no explanation of the "something very curious" that had happened the night before she wrote this letter. Subsequent events confirm that to her it was not only "curious" but threatening.

Wilmot Herringham's "Autobiographical Memoir" clarifies some of this. Unutterably distressed and alarmed, he had consulted an eminent medical colleague, Percy Bassett-Smith of the Royal Navy, a specialist in tropical diseases, which suggests Wilmot's suspicion that Christiana had contracted some exotic illness in India. It soon became plain that the problem was something more troublesome than contagion. On Bassett-Smith's advice Christiana "went to the home near Gloucester," Barnwood House Institution, a private retreat for the mentally ill. Only ten days elapsed between that letter to Alice Rothenstein and Christiana's first surviving letter to Wilmot from Gloucestershire. "She was glad to go," he wrote, "because she felt safe there."[114]

A Postscript

One thing more belongs at this point in the record of Christiana's life and work. It is more problematical, perhaps, than evidence from the National Art Collections Fund and from Ajanta, but it is substantial enough to justify a hypothesis. In 1972, when P. N. Furbank asked me to read the Indian chapters of his biography of E. M. Forster, I suggested that, even with my then incomplete information about Christiana Herringham, I saw some connections between her experience and that of Forster's Mrs. Moore in *A Passage to India*. Mr. Furbank included my tentative suggestion as a note.[115]

A few years later I located Wilmot Herringham's letters from India during the winter of 1906–1907 and Christiana's few surviving letters from Barnwood House Institution. Then the connection seemed even more possible, not only from Christiana to Mrs. Moore, but also another connection from the bride who had traveled to India with the Herringhams to Adela Quested, the "queer cautious girl" engaged to Mrs. Moore's son Ronny.[116] Forster, I feel quite certain, had seen those letters.

Forster's aunt, Laura Forster, was a friend of the Herringhams, and the young E. M. Forster knew Christopher Herringham, who was two years his junior, and he knew the precarious state of Christopher's health. In a letter to his aunt, written in 1890 from Kent House, his boarding school at Eastbourne, he asked, "Have you heard anything more about Christopher Herringham Is he any better?"[117] Unfortunately, any record of how or when Laura Forster met the Herringhams probably disappeared in the bonfires to which Forster consigned masses of family letters when he moved from West Hackhurst to King's College in 1946.

The Roger Frys were another link, a connection to the Herringhams and the Rothensteins and eventually to Forster. Fry and Rothenstein had known each other since 1890, when both studied at the Académie Julian in Paris, then became members of the New English Art Club. Forster, while still a Cambridge undergraduate, met Fry after a lecture in his series on the Venetian painters—this was the period of Fry's study of Bellini. Forster "remembered the lectures for the rest of his life," and acquaintance increased through Goldsworthy Lowes Dickinson, King's College mentor to both Forster and Fry.[118]

At this point Rothenstein enters the chain of connections. Forster probably met him before 1912, for they had other mutual friends besides the Frys. Forster was not enrolled as a member of the India Society, but he was well aware of its activities. In 1912 he was a dinner guest, with Rothenstein and Rabindranath Tagore, at the Herringham home. Tagore was not yet famous, but this was the summer when Rothenstein set in motion the publishing career that brought Tagore his Nobel Prize for Literature in 1913. In the summer of 1912 he was simply the impressive Indian gentleman whom Rothenstein had met in Calcutta early in 1911 and was now introducing to his wide acquaintance in literary and artistic London. Forster was at the dinner because he was going to India in October with Dickinson and the poet Robert Trevelyan. Forster had been preparing diligently, reading, having riding lessons, talking to members of old Anglo-Indian families and friends who had traveled there, including the Herringhams and Rothenstein. Wilmot's letters of 1906–1907 to his son Geoffrey and his sister Mary had been carefully transcribed and bound in leather. I find inescapable the thought that Forster read those letters at some time either before he went to India or when he began *A Passage to India,* after he returned to England later in 1913. Small but specific passages in Wilmot's letters, as passed through the novelist's mind, suggest specific connections.

The Herringhams, when they set out for India in the autumn of 1906, had had with them, Wilmot wrote, "a bride to take out to India to be married, a Miss T., rather a nice looking girl, and not at all bad, though I suspect her of talking about her food." She was the stepdaughter of a physician, presumably one of Wilmot's colleagues. Wilmot mentioned her again as their ship passed through the Red Sea. Their charge, he wrote, was "tall, not unpleasing but by no means pretty, and awfully weedy and delicate, and not particularly interesting. We have spent a good deal of time in trying to fathom the reasons that impelled her fiancé to propose. Perhaps they will be apparent when we see him. But she is quite a good girl and pleasant." At Bombay they met "the bride's new husband, Capt. H., an extremely nice man. She is very lucky."[119] The captain, too, is lucky if his bride is what Wilmot's description further suggests: a young woman who is sensible and sober, conscientious and fair minded, careful about plans and proprieties, courteous under pressure, and perhaps a little too modest, so that she underestimates her own strengths.

Miss T.'s qualities—if we accept this projected profile of her personality—are the very ones that cause Adela Quested's troubles in *A Passage to India.* She, too, is specifically not a beauty; she is "plain" and "angular," and Dr. Aziz thinks the freckles on her face "terrible defects." Adela is not only the "queer cautious girl," she is "the logical girl," "the reliable girl" with a "dry, honest way" about her. Adela "loved plans . . . plans had been a passion with her from girlhood." Like the Herringhams puzzling over Miss T., Forster's Anglo-Indian community "spent a good deal of time" wondering why Ronny Heaslop had proposed to Adela. She is quite candid about herself and says that "there's nothing special about me, nothing specially good or strong."[120] In the end, she proves to be better and stronger than she thinks she is. Practical, pleasant, and above all straightforward, both Adela and Miss T. have virtues to make them a credit to the empire. One hopes that Miss T.'s destination was less provincial, less constricted and constricting, than Forster's Chandrapore.

In Wilmot's description of Christiana's encounter with the *yoga,* her fright in the cave at Udayagiri was rather farcical. The caves at Ajanta, however, were for her a great satisfaction and fulfillment. The longer she was there, the closer became her feeling of empathy with the spirits of the unknown artists. Her real and lasting fright was the fear that credit for the copying work, and even the work itself, might be taken from her. She withdrew more and more into the unreality of those fears.

Mrs. Moore finds nothing spiritual about the Marabar caves, only an appalling emptiness of meaning and importance. Her first experience of India had been her best: "A sudden sense of unity, of kinship with the heavenly bodies" and with the Universal God, which she had carried with her into the mosque where she encountered Dr. Aziz. From that point onward, she finds it more and more difficult to summon up interest in the complications of other people's lives, and she "felt this with such force that it seemed itself a relationship, itself a person, who was trying to take hold of her hand." The dark oppressiveness of the one cave that she enters completes the process of detachment. She finds "no repose to her soul . . . she didn't want to communicate with anyone, not even with God." Indians understood what had happened; she had passed over from the life stage of *gri-hastha,* householder, to that of *sannyasi,* the saintly contemplative, a passage that is the right of every person who has faithfully discharged all domestic responsibilities. To the Indians, she is the only one of the Chandrapore English whose behavior has both dignity and logic: hence her canonization as "Esmiss Esmoor." She does not realize that she stands between the expectations of two cultures, that the Western ethos, unlike the Indian, does not absolve her from responsibility for Ronny's engagement, the futures of her other two children in England, the outcome of Aziz's trial for rape. Guilt overwhelms her, and she condemns herself without trial as a "bad old woman, bad, bad, detestable."[121] She carries that unnecessary guilt with her when she dies on the voyage to England and is buried at sea. Christiana Herringham was beset by the terrible and unnecessary fear that she had intruded in a sacred place and that retribution must destroy her.

In 1941 Forster and Rothenstein were among the speakers at a London observance of Rabindranath Tagore's death, a public meeting sponsored by the India Society. On that occasion Forster recalled the evening in 1912, on the eve of his own journey to India, when he, Rothenstein, and Tagore had been Wilmot's guests.

> Sir Wilmot was an eminent physician in his day. You may not know his name, but you should have heard the name of his wife, Lady Herringham. She was an artist and an enthusiast for the art of India which was then scarcely known over here. She went to Ajanta and her paintings of its Caves revealed to us marvels of which we were unaware. I knew her too, but she wasn't at this particular party.[122]

Forster knew that Christiana was not at the party because, as Mrs. Moore was to do, she had withdrawn from the world of demands and action, taking her fears with her.

This was the sad fulfillment of the note with which Wilmot had opened his "Autobiographical Memoir" at the time of his marriage in 1880.

> Feeling great happiness, & being desirous of recalling the same in future years when my life may be sadder, I intend to write something of the story of my life of late years, & from time to time add what may be deserving, that I may both know for certain that I have been most happy, and may remember in what spirit I lived, & intended for the future to continue, when this joy was given me.[123]

8

MARLEY'S GHOST

IN 1906, ON THE EVE of her first visit to India, Christiana Herringham had wished that as a traveler she might be like Marley's ghost in Dickens's fantasy *A Christmas Carol,* who "flitted across other people's lives unseen himself. . . . All my life that little story has embodied my own feelings of wishing to observe other people's lives & doings rather than take part in the doing myself. One gets dragged in malgré soi and one has to struggle to a point of vantage to be able to get a glimpse of the other lives."[1]

At Ajanta she achieved that point of vantage upon Indian lives both past and present. She had sole authority and a free hand to carry forward a project that took her completely out of herself. Instead of offering a committee courteous circumlocutions about her situation, as she had done in England, at Ajanta she attacked every problem with despatch and without apology. Even in the exhaustion of her last hours at Ajanta, she accepted the weariness and the physical discomforts: they went with the work. Like Marley's ghost when he reclaimed Scrooge to humanity, she had made it possible for a good thing to happen. Even so, Marley's ghost had to atone forever for his sins of omission committed while alive. Christiana carried with her an imagined and disabling guilt about her daring to invade the Ajanta caves. It was fueled by fantastic popular stereotypes (themselves not free of compensatory guilt) about Oriental riches, Western despoilers, and attempted retributions. Christiana knew that she had built a bridge between two worlds, and when E. M. Forster finally visited Ajanta in 1945, he, too, discovered that he had found "a connection between my own two worlds. . . . the Ajanta fusion convinces me, and the freshness there is part of the fusion."[2] But somehow, Christiana had lost her sense of the Ajanta fusion. Her two worlds had moved irretrievably apart.

Physical symptoms could be treated, but the physicians of that day had no treatment of promise for the fears that assailed her. On 19 June 1911 she arrived at Barnwood House Institution in Gloucestershire and was admitted on an emergency order. On 21 June she wrote Wilmot a long letter meant to carry reassurance, but it could only have distressed him the more. She began to draw away from the reality of his life and to come to terms with the unreality of her new situation. "Cher ami," she wrote, "Please don't bother about me more than as you care for me—what *I* want is that your life should not be spoiled by the trouble that has come into mine. I think in some ways I have enriched your life, though in some ways in some ways [*sic*] I have been a troublous element."[3]

Instead of an intriguing project awaiting completion, Ajanta had begun to seem the end of a road; the future could offer nothing to match the experience she had already had.

> I have had a very rich full life. This winter I often thought what could there be that could seem a large enough thing after all I had there in India. All that wonderful revelation of the old world—the old temples the old paintings & sculpture—and the surrounding life of the people going back to a hoary antiquity—Think of this place for me as a refuge at present. That is how I feel it. From the outside, and from my own disturbed state of mind.

Still, she was not quite ready to renounce the outside altogether; Barnwood House was a refuge "at present," but she still had "several things in my mind to do, and there is a good long space of time both morning and afternoon for doing as one likes." Would Wilmot send her, as soon as possible, more writing paper with the Wimpole Street heading?

Then again she drew back. "You know the feeling I have had for a long time that I was losing energy for life as it is for me now—It wouldn't much matter ~~to me~~ really if my life were not free to account for the future—I have done a good deal—perhaps as much as is wanted of me." What follows is a message of farewell:

> We have had one or two wonderful days together. Whatever happens think with a sacred feeling of sitting together in that train the other day—There was true love in that railway carriage, and I think perhaps it was a nobler love than if we just had the affection of superficially existing without even any rubs—I have a very great respect for you—you see also how I have leant upon you lately. Just now I feel to love you without rubs and alloy. If anything else happens keep that in your mind.

Then, as if she had said too much, she turned quickly to superficial matters. The Barnwood House grounds were beautiful. The weather was colder than in London. Attendants and doctors were kind. She had had several pleasant conversations with her physician, and he talked a good deal to all of his patients. He found her very anemic, and she weighed less than 115 pounds, her weight "before and after Christopher died." Until now, she had not mentioned, in any surviving letters, the division in her life that was marked by Christopher's death.

A friend had sent roses, and Wilmot intended to send more. "I wonder if your flowers will prove a bitter or a sweet reminder," she told him. "The rose or the thorn. If I find that they are a saddening reminder of what I have left, you must not have them sent." (He sent them, and she received them with pleasure.) She ended with a plea for understanding. "Please don't be hard on me or think me lacking in courage—Perhaps I am but I am trying to have a sort of courage here." This was certainly a response to an opinion of her brother Herbert, also a physician. "Bertie said I ought to have faced it and that would have been better."[4] Whether this was Wilmot's view as well there is no way of knowing; nevertheless, she felt the need to defend herself against it.

There had been extended consultations both within the family and with Bassett-Smith and other medical colleagues, but the best physicians of the day had little to offer beyond the Victorian premise that insanity was a bodily disease. In 1874 Henry Maudsley, a respected authority at the time, had described the condition as "an organic morbidity that was more severe when it attacked women because of the delicacy of their reproductive systems." Andrew Scull, in his research into the history of British attitudes toward madness and its treatment, finds that although the "propensity" of nineteenth-century men and women to go mad was "nearly equal," "Victorian alienists developed theories of a differential, gender-based etiology for mental disturbance. From neurological portraits of females as possessed of nervous systems of greater refinement and delicacy (and hence more susceptible to breakdown) to gynecological theorizing about peculiarly intimate ties between a woman's brain and her reproductive organs, medical men constructed images of creatures whose physiological equipment was of surpassing fragility, liable to give way at any moment under the strain of modern life. . . ."[5] When that "organic morbidity" prevailed, "the Ego or psychical person lost its power of self-determination and regressed to 'lower,' more automatic levels of psychological functioning, the mind becoming increasingly absorbed either by delusive constructions based on internal 'subjective' sensations (as in hysteria and hypochondriasis) or by externally suggested dominant ideas (as in hypnosis)."[6] That is, for reasons unknown the mind simply wandered away into realms of delusion based upon erroneous internal sensations. Only *physical* measures could restore the balance. Thus food, rest, and seclusion were the treatment for the "nervous disorders" bundled together under the heading "neurasthenia." "It is not our business," said Maudsley, "it is not in our power, to explain *psychologically* the origin and nature of any of [the] depraved instincts [manifested in typical cases of insanity]. . . . The explanation, when it comes, will come not from the mental, but from the physical side—from the study of the *neurosis,* not from the analysis of the *psychosis.*"[7]

John Hughlings Jackson, a friend and follower of Darwin and an originator of the science of neurology, made his life's work the development of a "psychology of mind." According to Michael J. Clark, Jackson seems "never really to have regarded abnormal psychological phenomena as worthwhile or even legitimate objects of medicoscientific inquiry *for their own sakes.*" Physical imbalances showed up as mental symptoms; therefore, he concentrated all his attention upon diagnosis. Everything resulted from "the same fundamental quality—that of deficiency or defect."[8] In this scheme of things, mental symptoms simply indicated that women, whose physiological makeup was more delicate and more delicately balanced than men's, were especially prone to the "diseased state"—that is, neurasthenia—that led to insanity and contributed ultimately to the breakdown of society. Thus the woman who overly strained body and mind was a threat to the stability of the nation. British and American psychiatrists reinforced one another's opinions that, "because of the limited amount of energy nature allotted women . . . this brain work combined with their other duties could leave them in nervous bankruptcy."[9]

Was Christiana, after all, guilty of an offense? In every respect she had flouted the nineteenth-century image of the delicate womanly woman. She had engaged in strenuous brainwork, had hankered after higher education, had inserted herself into public affairs and worked for financial return—all an overload of brain and body, by those early standards. Tom Lutz observes that in America also too many " 'overly active' women were isolated in bedrooms to be taken care of by nurses, while many men feminized by the disease were sent out west to become men again."[10] He takes the title of his study, *American Nervousness, 1903*, from a kind of epidemic of neurasthenia among prominent Americans in that year, with Theodore Roosevelt as the prescribed example of manliness. For neurasthenic Englishmen, India was a British equivalent of the Wild West, and British women in India were similarly isolated by the code of womanliness transplanted from Victorian Britain. Christiana had reversed the "normal" order, and it was no wonder that curious Indians, Anglo-Indians, and tourists came to the Fardapur camp to try to find out what she was doing.

S. Weir Mitchell, the American whose influential approach encapsulated the rationale for treatment of such women, deliberately set out "to infantilize his patients, since they needed to turn their wills over to him for him to effect a cure." His regimen of rest, quiet, and seclusion reinforced "notions of feminine decorum, the exclusion of women from public spheres, and obedience to paternal authority."[11] This was the regimen prescribed for Christiana.

The preliminary examination at Barnwood House indicated that she was in "poor bodily condition," that her appetite was "poor and capricious," and that "her diet for a very long time has evidently been a very restricted one." Her heart fluttered, its beat "very feeble and distant." She had "a stern but restless and somewhat pained expression of countenance," and the frequently spasmodic movements of the face and rapid blinking of the eyes, a long-established neuralgia, suggested a form of tic doloureux. She had had malaria but had never had "fits of any kind." The report described hers as a case of "Systematised Delusional Insanity associated with marked depression," and this was "the first attack of Insanity from which the patient has suffered." This examiner observed also that she was "a highly cultured artist & painter." She proved to the physician that she knew perfectly well who she was, where she was and with whom, that her memory for recent events was excellent, and that her judgments were quite correct "except in matters affected by her delusion." In that context, she contemplated suicide in order to forestall those who lay in wait for her.[12]

The delusion was the immediate cause for the emergency order of admission. On the way home from India she had "imagined on board ship that some men were looking at her very suspiciously & thought that they were spies, sent by the seditious Indians who had plotted to capture her for having painted for exhibition the sacred frescoes of the Temples."[13] Is the word "seditious" hers or that examiner's? The activities of Havell, Abanindranath Tagore, and Coomaraswamy had helped to make art an integral part of the Indian cultural renaissance. As Rothenstein discovered, official circles had begun to realize that indigenous art could be put to the service of Indian nationalism, and many English in England and in India considered anything nationalist as automatically or potentially seditious. Until her breakdown, Christiana had not worried about official suspicions or, on the other hand, about Indian resentment at her having invaded sacred spaces.

The idea of sacrilegious intrusion was firmly connected to popular imaginings about India. From the novels of Wilkie Collins, Arthur Conan Doyle, and Rudyard Kipling, to those of Grant Allen and to any number of popular film concoctions since their time, the device of vindictive Asians out for revenge against an intruder in a sacred place was a feature of imperial fiction.[14] Christiana's letters and the Barnwood House reports show that to her, now, it was no fiction. The doctors recorded that she had told them of being "laid in wait for by people who come and look at her in a furtive way . . . watch her movements and make signs to each other." She wrote to Wilmot: "I feel haunted here too. Little things that might mean something if the past means what it seemed. I can only try to screw up my courage." Any strange man on the Barnwood House grounds was someone sent to report to the mysterious ones or to seize her himself. "But I find that if I wandered a little in the grounds which is often possible I should very likely be seized—and then that even seems the best thing to do—but so far I can't—I am afraid I am a horrible coward." More than she feared being killed, she feared imprisonment, "perhaps as a caught spy or murderess—or merely to be taunted." She added, "Keep this kind of letter *in case*."[15]

For a time she made efforts to find her way back. She could not bring herself to write to friends just then, she said, but she began to write "my early reminiscences[;] it keeps my thoughts off other things better than anything else I have found. If anything happens to me let the family have them as far as they go. I am intending to write a little besides, if I can."[16] There is no mention of this in the physicians' reports. We cannot know whether they encouraged or discouraged her writing the reminiscences. She gave the notebooks to the wardrobe matron, to be forwarded to Wilmot, but they have not been found.

Wilmot, too, was understandably depressed, and not only by Christiana's plight. He knew that he was a good physician, but he knew also that he was too candid to be always popular. He refused to pamper hypochondriacs and was brusque with malingerers. Christiana wrote in great concern about him: "Supposing anything happens to me. [D]on't let it sadden your life. It's the happy people that are useful though they must always keep sympathy for those who are unhappy. This trouble of mine should be mine only or mainly." She reminded him of the "many people who need you, and I am certain your work is *much* more important than that of a fashionable doctor with many patients." But there was always the fact that neither his medicine nor anyone else's had been able to save Christopher, or Wilmot's sister Kathleen, or her husband, who died only a year later; and now it could not restore Christiana. A moment of insight brought out the thought that she had felt second in importance to Kathleen. "Saying this about Kitty, that this is your greatest trouble since her death tells me more than almost anything that you care for me. You know I used to want to be as much to you as she was—but I think all that sort of feeling has gone long ago."[17] At last, in this dire emergency, she could be candid about something that had been buried for years: the knowledge that Wilmot had confided in his sister during a passage of great unhappiness about their own relationship in the years after Christopher's death.

Now she tied up some loose ends of her former affairs: one hundred pounds promised to the *Englishwoman* and now due, and a final disposition of her Ajanta reproductions. She wrote to Rothenstein:

> You know my trouble. I am writing to say that I very much wish that any publication of Ajanta reproductions could be only in association with the Calcutta Society [branch of the India Society]—or in some way associated with India. I shall never I am sure do anything myself. It was the copies I cared about, and that as far as possible Mr [Abanindranath] Tagore and his pupils should have the advantage of them by duplicates. I am unable to stand up against the difficulties that have come upon me in this work. I doubt whether M. de Goloubew really cares about any kind of joint publication—though Dr Martin tried to arrange it. But I am surrounded by a mystery about all this work which I cannot unravel. I trust no one else will come to any harm over it.[18]

She realized that she was among the privileged ones who were able to pay for the best available private care instead of being in a public asylum. She thought a great deal about the condition of women patients in mental hospitals. She told Wilmot that her fellow patients had too little to occupy them, and "I can't help thinking that some have been sent by relations who found them troublesome."[19] This was indeed sometimes the case. Christiana's organizing mind went to work on this problem. She expanded on it at length in a letter that she asked Wilmot to send "to some woman who is working for lunacy reform," but she addressed it to the physician Louisa Garrett Anderson, daughter of Elizabeth Garrett Anderson, Britain's first fully qualified woman physician. The holograph letter remains with Wilmot's papers; if a transcription was sent to the addressee, it has not been found.

Christiana's letter is full of acute observations and wise recommendations, all still pertinent to patient care today. She speaks directly, eschewing the more genteel and obfuscating British term "retreat"; she calls Barnwood House an asylum. "We know as suffragists," she wrote, "that one of our demands is a share in the management of lunatic asylums, and in the making of lunacy laws. A very slight acquaintance with life in an asylum under very favourable conditions, shows some extremely serious difficulties and defects." For many, "the life is difficult enough to make them worse and not better"; there should be a monetary arrangement to persuade asylums to take patients "on trial"; those who improved sufficiently should be allowed to leave. Nor did doctors adequately understand how "preventable health causes" initiated and exacerbated mental troubles. Her heart went out to "a poor old lady here who I am sure should be with a kind servant in her own home. She is very unhappy, I fear there is no chance of release."

Christiana had discovered that not all of the attendants were trained nurses. Though all of them were usually kind, some were not entirely trustworthy; a night nurse sometimes left her patient for hours or turned her over to a substitute. Even for the best-intentioned nurses and doctors the job "is a terribly difficult one." It was also "extremely difficult to be a patient—imprisoned—with a good deal in the life to make a sane person suspicious & even insane." The administration had "enormous financial difficulties in maintaining its reputation," for "if an asylum emptied too much it would look bad—and how would it pay?" Still, an asylum that did not "pass its patients through rapidly" should lose its accreditation. New laws should be enacted. Perhaps a "visiting committee of ladies" could do more "to occupy and interest those patients who ought to be here." Qualified persons "other than the asylum doctors" should inspect more frequently, and there should be women inspectors as well as women doctors. Finally, "the asylum doctors should not be able to put aside the recommendations for release [submitted by] the visiting inspectors."[20]

By keeping her hold on these threads of connection to the women's causes that had been important to her for so long, she kept for a time some connection to the world of reality. She drafted another letter and asked Wilmot to send copies to "the societies for assisting poor people legally." She "subscribe[d] to one at Whitechapel" and Wilmot must arrange for payment by periodic banker's order. This time her concern was for the thousands of girls who worked in supposedly genteel shops where they were required to stand all day, even if no customers were present. Even where seats were available, all the girls must stand if a single customer entered. Even if Sir Charles Dilke's Shops Bill No. 2/1910 became law, "a strong society of ladies" should visit shops and check on enforcement, and "some inspectors would be wanted for what ladies cannot do." The law should be written so that "all servers, *men* and women, should sit when they are not serving. The young people are of the same class as many clerks & Clerks are not compelled to add extreme physical fatigue to their actual work." Modern society disapproved of a man who left a woman standing instead of offering her his seat, yet it went on "with this cruelty of keeping young women on their feet unnecessarily. Ladies who play at shopkeeping at bazaars know the fatigue which they allow to be inflicted on these helpless young people. . . . I have been watching the matter for some years." Shop assistants were fined for the smallest infraction of rules; "some inspecting authority" ought to have access to the scales of fines as well as to the girls' living quarters above the shops. "Any shop act will need watching, as the children's laws require the Society for the Protection of Children." She asked that a copy of her letter go especially to Gertrude Mary Tuckwell, a leader of the women's labor union movement and an adviser to the Ministry of Health.[21] Again, the letter seems to exist only among Wilmot's papers.

If these letters, sane, sensible, and sympathetic, were the whole evidence, Christiana would seem to be one of those patients to be "passed through rapidly." However, the dark side of the picture grew steadily darker. In a letter to accompany that about the shopgirls, she told Wilmot that "the same kind of dark hinting goes on, with knocks, and it seems to include you and Geoffrey. If only there were not me, you would be safe." She insisted that a signal, a "subtle scent but strong," like Indian jasmine, came in puffs through her window at night; the window was near the ground, but she did not feel inclined to ask for another room, a reluctance that might have been related to the thoughts of suicide mentioned in the doctors' reports. "This morning I smelt strongly of it," she wrote of the insidious fragrance, and washing could not purge it. She feared that she might be forced "to write falsehood & betray people—I wish I could think I was brave." For the first time, she became testy and asked Wilmot not to say again that "it is all false[;] you have not seen the things I have seen." Another version written on the following day is heavily scored through, twice. She believed that she "was observed on the boat maliciously." The observer had a name: it was "Tinnijan."

> What I am going to say now you will certainly think illusion. If Tinnijan comes, and I *was* observed on the boat maliciously he would be known to other people here. Mightn't it be the worse for you—I feel very despairing of getting out of this tangle. I don't want other people to suffer from it. I don't want even Tinnijan to suffer—say by losing his steamer berth & then perhaps losing ours. You will see how this thing has gone into me.

Is Tinnijan an Indian name clumsily transliterated? An Armenian name badly misspelled? There is no such name anywhere else in her Indian correspondence. Nor does it appear on the passenger list of the SS *Persia*. Was his "berth" a job as crewman or steward?[22] There is no list of the crew.

She made a few more efforts at connection, but they were all valedictories. More and more she seemed to have resigned herself to the fact that she was not in the asylum merely "for the present." In a last letter to Alice Rothenstein she expressed her concern that India's influence had wrought a change in William's painting, and in her opinion not altogether to the good. She wished that he would return to the subjects and the portrait drawings of earlier years. "I would *not* go to India I think. I would do what can be done here. He will find his life dreadfully broken up—if that spell comes on him. Ruskin says you never paint well except what you have known from your childhood." Wilmot, too, received her last words on India. "You have only been drawn to India through me—I think you had better hold aloof—both you and Geoffrey should behave to India in the spirit of that little article *I* sent. If we behaved better to them they might accept our protection till better times come—till nationality is respected and war dies out."[23]

She sent Wilmot another letter of instructions, this one about belongings that she wished given to friends—books, jewelry, beautiful objects collected during her travels—before the remainder was distributed among the family. Wilmot or Geoffrey must sell "three valuable rugs" and give the money to the suffrage movement through Mary Lowndes. "I have so many friends," she wrote, but "there would be something for all."[24]

There was no change in the tenor of her delusions. Her fears became concurrent themes in her letters and in the reports from Barnwood House: the belief that she was watched on the voyage from India; the fear that she might be made to lie or commit a betrayal against her will; fears for the safety of Wilmot and Geoffrey (even though Wilmot spent the summer of 1911 in Gloucestershire in order to be near her); her wish that she might perish in their place; the smell of Indian jasmine and the mysterious knockings; the conviction that she was trapped and that there was no escape. She imagined that all her money was gone and that she owed vast sums to the nurses. She was by turns restless, or morose and very quiet and withdrawn. Her physical health improved, but it was reported that "her affection for her husband & son appears to be in abeyance." On 30 April 1913 she was "Discharged not improved." Food, rest, and sedatives had been her only treatment. Wilmot had her admitted to The Priory, an excellent private asylum at Roehampton, where Helen Fry had stayed for two periods of treatment between 1907 and 1909.[25]

In 1912 Wilmot Herringham became vice-chancellor of the University of London. When war broke out in August 1914, Geoffrey was sent at once to France, and Wilmot was placed on leave to take up duties as consulting physician to the British forces in France. Already in uniform and ready to depart, he was presiding at the October meeting of the University Senate when news came of Geoffrey's death. Wilmot left the meeting and went straight to the embarkation port.

In France in 1915 he received one more letter from Christiana, erroneously dated 1914 but otherwise lucid and logical. However, it made no mention of Geoffrey. She wished to put "all my property at your disposal and I have not been able to understand how to do it." Would he please take appropriate legal steps? She had headed this letter 40 Wimpole Street, then crossed that out and substituted the address of The Priory. Wilmot noted, "I had not had any letter from her for a long time, & it for a time gave me hopes she would recover her senses. But it was only a flicker."[26] Threats of zeppelin raids over London made him uneasy about her safety. Roehampton was too close to the city, and he arranged for her to be transferred to St. George's Retreat, a home for the mentally ill in the charge of Belgian nuns at Burgess Hill, Sussex. Whenever Wilmot visited her, he would find her reading or doing needlework but quite uninterested in art or Ajanta or women's suffrage. She often seemed unaware that he was there, and he was certain that she had never comprehended the fact of Geoffrey's death. She died at Burgess Hill on 25 February 1929, aged seventy-eight.

In 1931 Wilmot resumed the "Autobiographical Memoir" that he had begun in 1880 at the time of his marriage to Christiana and had laid aside in 1898 when his sister Kathleen died. "I now begin again, when I am 76, to recall something of my past life."[27]

Even during the war, he had pondered choices of occupation. Colleagues at St. Bartholomew's Hospital wanted him to stay there and aim at future appointment as president of the Royal College of Physicians—an appointment he felt he probably would receive if he stayed. "They want the honour for the hospital. But I am so sick of all things, that even if I could afford it I do not think I could face that life alone." What he most wanted was to "go away and be quiet, above all things I long for the company of one person."[28]

In 1914 he was knighted. In 1915 he was made a Commander of the Bath. He returned from France a major general. In 1919, he was made a Knight Commander of the Order of St Michael and St George. Christiana never understood that she had become Lady Herringham. She had been ambitious for him, and he felt that "it was very sad that whatever success I have had came to me after Chrissie had left the world," for "she would have enjoyed the opportunities which my position gave. It always annoyed her that I had not made any position which brought me into notice." He knew, however, that he had not been a failure. "At the hospital I was known as a good teacher, & my scepticism stimulated men, as I meant it to do, to work for themselves."[29] As vice-chancellor he had presided, against opposition, over the acquisition of the indispensable Bloomsbury site for the University of London, which was desperately in need of space for expansion. He was medical member of the University Grants Committee from 1919, when it was founded, until 1932. In 1922 he became chairman of the General Nursing Council for England and Wales, only two years old and already in crisis; he made it an efficient working body, then insisted that a registered nurse, not a physician, should have his position. He traveled in the United States as a guest of the Rockefeller Institute, to collect information about methods of advanced medical education there.

There was no doubt, however, that his enthusiasm for a medical career waned along with the hope that Christiana might one day be restored to him. He turned his energies to areas that he knew would have interested her. He was a governor, then chair of the board, of Bedford College for Women from 1913 until his death in 1936. From 1922 to 1929 he was chairman of the Governors of the Old Vic Theatre and dealt also with its housing crisis, which involved much money raising. He was that rare creature, a chairman able to subordinate his personality. "This masterful man with strong opinions on almost everything," wrote a colleague, "appeared to have none as he sat there on the bench sifting the evidence. . . . he had the chairman's final gift—courage, for he was quite without fear. . . . What was unusual was that the man who possessed this gift was a scholar whose life was ruled by a passion for beauty." After retirement, he took up watercolor painting.[30]

He became more outspoken about politics. In *A Physician in France*, published in 1919, he criticized British lack of political foresight in such forthright terms that the government at first blocked the book's appearance. How, he asked, could so obvious a war have descended with so little warning upon a commonwealth like Great Britain? Insularity was the reason—insularity of a general public ignorant of other nations' languages, cultures, and politics, never dreaming that behavior and ideas that were a matter of course to themselves "may to other nations be a perpetual source of envy and of rage." Christiana's voice could be heard in his statement that real progress lay in education and the appreciation of beauty, on neither of which the British could yet congratulate themselves. Art is the saving grace, he wrote: "Art—plastic art, at least— is in part a perception of things, in part a reproduction of them, and in part appreciation of their loveliness." And Roger Fry's voice could be heard in his statement that one age discovers perspective, another realizes that the painter may paint not only what he sees, but "a better impression of what he does not see, the thing as it is."[31] Wilmot combined education and art, according to Christiana's and his own wishes, when he divided their art collection and many of her paintings and copies between Bedford College for Women and Newnham College.

He had decided to live on his own income and not rely on Christiana's money, even though this meant leaving Wimpole Street. He moved to Arkwright Road, Hampstead. "I don't want to ask to be allowed to live on her income & therefore should like to start clear," he told Christiana's sister Rosamond. "Poor dear! How she would hate it if she knew. She thought that I might be in money difficulties."[32]

In 1931, when he looked back at the war's aftereffects on so many veterans, he saw little hope of substantive progress in the treatment of manic-depressive psychoses.

> Physiological explanations seem to me meaningless. The brain is not the mind, but as Hughlings Jackson said "the way out from the mind".

> I never can pass from one to the other. It seems to me like walking through a looking-glass and pretending the mirror is not there. I believe the truer thing is to say that we do not understand what mind is, & yet that it is the only reality. What for instance happened to poor Chrissie? It would have been impossible to find any changes in her brain. There are none in such cases that we can recognise. And where or what was she all those 20 years?[33]

Understanding and treatment of mental illness did not improve substantially in Britain until later in the 1930s, but Wilmot did not live to see it. With its experience of dealing with war's traumas, the medical establishment had been ready to move to a new understanding, but the reality of postwar finance and a drastically straitened national budget in 1921 fell with devastating effect upon the brave new initiatives. For patients like Christiana, the treatment remained substantially unchanged. To Lilian Baylis of the Old Vic, Wilmot wrote: "My poor wife, who was always too full of work like you, used to think of Convent life as a haven of rest from the world. She is in one now, poor thing, but she is not herself, & it is to her only a prison. Of all the awful things in the world insanity is far the worst."[34]

After Christiana's Ajanta copies were shown at the Festival of Empire in 1911, Binyon and Rothenstein, on behalf of the India Society, offered them on loan to the Victoria and Albert Museum, which promised to exhibit them all together, copyright and right of reproduction to remain with the India Society. Again there was official nervousness about sympathizers with indigenous Indian art that might encourage the Indian nationalists. A museum memorandum reads as follows:

> Mr. Rothenstein was very pleased with the idea that there is a reasonable prospect of Mrs. Herringham's things being brought here. He says that Mrs. Herringham would be delighted herself to think that they were here. Apparently she has no animus against the museum.
>
> Mr. Rothenstein made it quite clear that he dissociated himself from any of the Nationalist business, which he described as being a trouble in the India Society; but of course he is anxious to see a general Oriental Museum in London.[35]

In 1914 Mary Richardson, a militant suffragette, slashed the Rokeby *Venus* as it hung in the National Gallery, as her protest against woman as sexual object.[36] Also in 1914, Hyderabad State, inspired by Christiana's enthusiasm and initiative, established the Department of Archaeology; the *Journal of the Hyderabad Archaeological Society* began publication in January 1916. After independence in 1947 the Ajanta caves became the responsibility of the Central Department of Archaeology of the Indian Government.

In 1915 the India Society published a volume with a selection of Christiana's reproductions and essays by her, Wilmot, Binyon, Rothenstein, and others. Her essay was substantially her *Burlington Magazine* article, "The Frescoes of Ajanta," written in 1911.[37] Christiana's "small book" about her experiences at Ajanta was never completed.

In 1919 Victor Goloubew, returned from the trenches and shorn of his wealth, used the Ajanta photographs to set up in business in Paris. In 1927 he published a large volume of photographs from Cave One at Ajanta. In 1930 the Hyderabad Department of Archaeology began publication of a four-volume series of Ajanta photographs. It was interrupted by World War II but completed in 1953.[38]

In 1931 the India Society allowed Christiana's Ajanta copies to go back to India. Thirty-three copies were to be packed up "in order to send them to the Nizam of Hyderabad," who, apparently through Sir Akbar Hydari, by then Sir George Casson Walker's successor, had requested their return to Hyderabad. The Victoria and Albert Museum had misgivings about the transaction; one of its officials, who seems to have been under the impression that a loan was being arranged, forwarded the India Society's letter to the museum's director. The letter, "which of course is quite out of order," requested "the necessary sanction for the release of the [copies of the] frescoes." The society appointed a small committee, none of whom had known Christiana, "to examine the paintings to ascertain whether anything should be done to them before being packed." No one in the society informed either Rothenstein or Wilmot Herringham that the copies would leave England. Wilmot wrote to Rothenstein, who was in poor health and no longer so active in the India Society: "I was not consulted about moving the pictures, but I took no part in the agreement with the Museum. The India Society carried it through. I was, I think, abroad at the time. I am sorry that the drawings have been sent away."[39] They are now in the Hyderabad State Collection, reportedly well cared for, but not, as Christiana had wished, in England.

In 1948 the India Society became the Royal Society for India, Pakistan and Ceylon. In 1967 it turned its back on its past history and destroyed its archives for 1910 to 1920, which had included letters from both of the Herringhams, Rothenstein, both Abanindranath and Rabindranath Tagore, Havell, Coomaraswamy, W. B. Yeats, and the many others who inaugurated that brave enterprise in 1910.[40]

In 1984 a Conservative Ministry of Education combined Bedford College with the Royal Holloway College. The Bedford College share of the Herringham collection went with it to Surrey. The Regent's Park campus of Bedford College, with Herringham Hall at its center, was sold to an American college.[41]

The record of Lady Herringham's life leaves room for many regrets, but it allows also for much gratitude. The wall paintings at Ajanta, conserved insofar as is possible, are now the particular charge of the Indian Government. And the Rokeby *Venus,* invisibly repaired after the suffragette's attack, still graces the National Gallery.[42]

In 1994, the National Art Collections Fund had thirty-eight thousand members (including individuals, corporate members, museums, and galleries). It had seventy-eight regional representatives throughout the United Kingdom. Its assets were worth 21.5 million pounds. And since the Fund was founded in 1903, it has "handed out almost 5,600 grants and bequests. Many of these grants and bequests comprised more than one object, and in some cases, whole collections. . . . the total number of objects now in public collections thanks to the assistance of the Fund easily exceeds 10,000."[43]

NOTES

Abbreviations

BM	*Burlington Magazine*
CP	Crawford Papers, Acc. 9769, National Library of Scotland, Edinburgh
HP	Herringham Papers (Private Collection)
RP:HL	Rothenstein Papers, Houghton Library, Harvard University. Catalogue numbers for individual letters refer to bMS Eng 1148. One number refers to bMS Eng 1148.3.
SR	*Saturday Review of Politics, Literature, Science and Art* (London)

Chapter 1. Introduction to an Artist

1. William James Buchanan (1777–1864), art importer and entrepreneur, recorded his efforts to introduce fine arts into Britain, in his *Memoirs of Painting, with a Chronological History of the Emportation of Pictures by the Great Masters into England since the French Revolution,* 2 vols. (London: R. Ackerman, 1824). Francis Haskell calls it "by far the frankest ever written by any dealer anywhere" (Haskell, *Rediscoveries in Art: Some Aspects of Taste, Fashion, and Collecting in England and France,* Wrightsman Lectures, New York University Institute of Fine Arts [Ithaca, N.Y.: Cornell University Press, 1976], 27). Buchanan's letters supplement his *Memoirs of Painting.* See Hugh Brigstocke, *William Buchanan and the Nineteenth-Century Art Trade: One Hundred Letters to His Agents in London and Italy* (Guildford, Surrey: privately published for the Paul Mellon Centre for Studies in British Art [London], 1982). See also Frank Herrmann, *The English as Collectors: A Documentary Chrestomathy* (New York: Norton, 1972), 127.

2. D. S. MacColl, *Confessions of a Keeper, or Culture Is Anarchy* (Glasgow: A. Maclehose, 1931), 7.

3. Press comment, *Colne and Nelson Times* (Lancashire), 23 March 1901, 15, quoted in Jill Liddington, *The Life and Times of a Respectable Rebel: Selina Cooper, 1864–1946* (London: Virago, 1984), 111.

4. Robert Alexander Lindsay to the author, 8 April 1991.

5. Florence Nightingale, "Cassandra," first published in Ray Strachey, *The Cause: A Short History of the Women's Movement in Great Britain* (London: Virago, 1978), 395, 409. In 1858 Nightingale planned to include this in "Suggestions for Thought to Searchers after Truth" (n.p.: privately printed, 1860; published as *Suggestions for Thought: Selections and Commentaries,* ed. Michael D. Calabria and Janet A. Macrae [Philadelphia: University of Pennsylvania Press, 1994]). Even the redoubtable Nightingale could be intimidated; in 1860 John Stuart Mill, Benjamin Jowett, and others advised her against including "Cassandra" (Strachey, *The Cause,* 395).

6. Pamela Gerrish Nunn, *Victorian Women Artists* (London: Women's Press, 1987), 6.

7. [P. G. Hamerton], "Lady-Artists' Exhibition," *Art-Journal* 9 (1857): 163, 215–16; Anne Sutherland Harris and Linda Nochlin, *Women Artists, 1550–1950* (New York: Los Angeles County Museum of Art, with Alfred Knopf, 1981), 55. On women's status in the art world, see Rozsika Parker and Griselda Pollock, *Old Mistresses: Women, Art, and Ideology* (New York: Pantheon, 1981).

8. Laura Anne Herford was twenty-nine when she submitted her drawing. No rule prohibited admission of women, but a limit was "imposed unofficially on the admission of the fair sex into the Academy Schools over the next few years." However, it was difficult to maintain the quota after another woman, Louisa Starr, won a silver medal in 1865 and the gold medal for painting in 1867 (Sidney C. Hutchinson, *The History of the Royal Academy, 1768–1968* [London: Chapman and Hall, 1968], 118–19). On women's disabilities with respect to drawing from the nude, see Linda Nochlin, "Why Have There Been No Great Women Artists?" *Art and Sexual Politics,* ed. Thomas B. Hess and Elizabeth C. Baker, Art News Series (New York: Collier Books, 1971), 1–39.

9. G. D. Leslie, *The Inner Life of the Royal Academy with an Account of Its Schools and Exhibitions Principally in the Reign of Queen Victoria* (London: John Murray, 1941), 48–49, 50.

10. "The Royal Academy," *Spectator* 48 (1875): 594–95; John Ruskin, "Academy Notes, 1875," *Works,* Library Edition, ed. E. T. Cook and Alexander Wedderburn, 39 vols. (London: George Allen, 1903–1912), 14:308. Elizabeth Thompson, later Lady Butler (1846–1933), sister of the poet and

essayist Alice Meynell, grew up mostly abroad. In 1866 she went to the South Kensington Schools of Art and in 1869 to Rome for private study. She first exhibited at the Royal Academy in 1873, and the Royal Army quickly appreciated her work for precision and accuracy of research. In 1877 she married Major (later Lieutenant-General) William Francis Butler.

11. Elizabeth [Thompson] Butler, *An Autobiography* (London: Constable, 1922), 20; Leslie, *Inner Life of the Royal Academy*, 222–25. The only two women members until the 1920s were Mary Moser (1744–1819), a fashionable flower painter, Swiss-born and the daughter of the Royal Academy's first Keeper; and Angelica Kauffmann (1742–1805), also Swiss-born, a popular history painter who had a flourishing career in London until she made an unfortunate marriage and returned to the Continent. See Wendy Wassyng Roworth, *Angelica Kauffmann: A Continental Artist in Georgian England* (London: Royal Pavilion Art Gallery and Museums, with Reaktion Books, 1992). Feminist writers today often cite Johann Zoffany's painting, *The Academicians of the Royal Academy* (1772), as a pictorial statement of discrimination taken for granted. In it the male Academicians discuss principles governing the painting of the nude, present in the form of a male model. Moser and Kauffmann are present only as portraits on the wall *behind* the model, and so sketchily reproduced that their projected view of his back would be decorously hazy. "It is about eighteenth-century notions of the nature of the artist and the manner in which art should be pursued and practised," say Parker and Pollock, *Old Mistresses*, 87–90.

12. Thomas Wilde Powell, "Autobiography," in *A Family Memoir: Being Some Account of T. W. Powell and His Wife M. E. Powell and of their Ancestors, Compiled by Two of Their Children* (London: privately printed, 1903), 192, 23.

13. Dante Gabriel Rossetti, *Letters to William Allingham, 1854–1870*, ed. George Birkbeck Hill (London: T. Fisher Unwin, 1897), 179–80. A. Margaret Burr copied artworks in Spain, Italy, and Portugal. She worked closely with Sir Austen Henry Layard, of Nineveh archaeological fame, when he later studied Italian Renaissance frescoes. Intrepid in sustained work from the tops of ladders, she made many copies for the Arundel Society's program of reproductions. She exhibited at least twice with the Society of Female Artists but eventually lapsed into amateur and charitable art (Ellen Clayton, *English Female Artists*, 2 vols. [London: Tinsley Brothers, 1876], 1:408–10).

14. Anne Higonnet, *Berthe Morisot's Images of Women* (Cambridge: Harvard University Press, 1992), 202. The situation was no different in

France: "[Morisot's] identity as a woman painter—according to what she was told it meant to be a painter—was corroded by its very constitution; no alloy could be forged from her professional and personal identities; no self could emerge whole to be portrayed" (204). For a more detailed account, see Higonnet, *Berthe Morisot* (New York: Harper & Row, 1990).

15. Higonnet, *Berthe Morisot's Images of Women,* 202–3. See Nathaniel Hawthorne, *The Marble Faun; or, The Romance of Monte Beni,* Centenary Edition (Athens: Ohio State University Press, 1968), 206, 334. On portrayals of women artists in novels written in England between 1850 and the end of the century, see Parker and Pollock, *Old Mistresses,* 83, 101.

16. T. W. Powell, "Autobiography," in *A Family Memoir,* 26–27, 4. Thomas Powell traced his ancestry to Christopher Powell of Bramham (died 1548 or 1549). His father was James Powell (1785–1867), chief clerk of the Leeds "Old Bank," who married Christiana Wilde (1777–1825). The names Christopher and Christiana appear repeatedly in the genealogies.

17. Ibid., 14–15, 13; Samuel Smiles, *Self-Help with Illustrations of Character, Conduct, and Perseverance,* Centenary Introduction by Asa Briggs (1859; reprint, London: John Murray, 1958), 289. *Self-Help* sold twenty thousand copies in its first year and a quarter of a million by the end of the century. Eventually translated into dozens of languages, it became the ambitious young man's handbook, still in use today.

18. T. W. Powell, "Autobiography," in *A Family Memoir,* 15–16.

19. Ibid., 16.

20. Quoted in P. G. Warren, *Heseltine, Powell and Co., 1851–1951: One Hundred Years of Stockbroking* (London: privately printed for Heseltine, Moss and Company, 1951), 6–7.

21. Ibid., 17.

22. Mary E. Powell, autobiographical fragment, in *A Family Memoir,* 44, 53.

23. Ibid., 61, 63.

24. Ibid.

25. Ibid., 73–74.

26. Ibid., 71, 75.

27. Ibid., 161–62.

28. Charles Marten, his account, in *A Family Memoir,* 119.

29. Ibid., 44.

30. Smiles, *Self-Help,* 298.

31. *A Family Memoir,* 197, 193.

32. T. W. Powell to his children, [1882], transcript, personal collection of the late Peter G. Warren, London.

CHAPTER 2. CHRISTIANA JANE HERRINGHAM

1. WPH, "Autobiographical Memoir," MS, HP, begun 31 October 1880, one month after marriage to Christiana Jane Powell, and continued until 21 February 1897; resumed November 1931, two years after her death.

2. Ibid.

3. WPH to William Walton Herringham, [ca. 1875], HP.

4. Ibid.

5. WPH, "Autobiographical Memoir," HP.

6. WPH to Mrs. W. Wright Smith, 4 October 1877, HP.

7. WPH to Mrs. W. Wright Smith, 12 September 1880, HP. I know little about the Smiths beyond the Herringhams' letters and a visit to the Smiths' former home at Lyndhurst. WPH refers to Smith's first serious legislative appearance, probably in local politics (WPH to W. Wright Smith, 19 August 1886). He is not listed in *Parliamentary Debates* for 1886.

8. WPH, "Autobiographical Memoir," HP.

9. Ibid.; T. W. Powell, "Autobiography," in *A Family Memoir*, 173, 184.

10. Richard Norman Shaw (1831–1912) was apprenticed at fifteen to a London architect and eventually worked with G. E. Street (1824–1887), the Gothic Revival architect with whom William Morris had been associated. In 1861 Shaw opened his own office. His work for several Royal Academicians led to his being elected an Associate in 1872 and Academician in 1887. On origins and development of the Queen Anne style, see Mark Girouard, *Sweetness and Light: The "Queen Anne" Movement, 1860–1900* (Oxford: Clarendon, 1977), 10–37. On Piccard's Rough, see Andrew Saint, *Richard Norman Shaw* (New York: Yale University Press, 1976), 418. The name has variations: Piccard's Rough, Piccards Rough, Pickards Rough.

11. WPH, "Autobiographical Memoir," HP.

12. Ibid.

13. Ibid.

14. Henry Newbolt, *My World as in My Time: Memoirs, 1862–1932* (London: Faber and Faber, 1932), 135, 137, 138. Newbolt (1862–1938) left Oxford in 1885 and in 1887 was called to the bar at Lincoln's Inn. He left the law for literature and published Napoleonic and naval histories and romantically patriotic poems. In 1915 he was knighted.

15. Ibid., 136.

16. Herrmann, *The English as Collectors,* 40.

17. Haskell, *Rediscoveries in Art,* 98.

18. WPH, "Autobiographical Memoir," HP.

19. Clayton, *English Female Artists,* 1:408–10; Margaret Oliphant, *Miss Marjoribanks* (1866; reprint, London: Virago, 1988), 395.

20. WPH, "Autobiographical Memoir," HP.

21. Ibid.; John Henry Newman, "Discourses Addressed to Mixed Congregations, No. 6," *Sermons and Discourses, 1839–57,* ed. C. F. Harrold (New York: Longmans, Green, 1949), 2:162.

22. WPH, "Autobiographical Memoir," HP.

23. Walter Houghton, *The Victorian Frame of Mind, 1830–1870* (New Haven: Yale University Press, 1963), 83 n. 100; WPH to Mrs. W. Wright Smith, 24 March, 22 May 1879, HP.

24. Marcia Pointon, *William Dyce, 1806–1864: A Critical Biography* (Oxford: Clarendon, 1979), 128. Frederick Oakeley (1802–1880) was the youngest son of a former Governor of Madras. He took his Oxford degree in 1824 and in 1830 became tutor and catechetical lecturer at Balliol. He published forty-two works, many in support of Roman Catholic doctrine and polity.

25. Ibid., 84–85, 132–33.

26. WPH, "Autobiographical Memoir," HP. Powell may have been more than merely surprised at the engagement. Later, CJH told a friend that he gave in to the engagement and marriage because her illness so frightened him (Mrs. William Marshall, journal owned by Mrs. Geoffrey Hermges, on deposit at Selwyn College Library, University of Cambridge).

CHAPTER 3. MAKING A PLACE FOR HERSELF

1. WPH, "Autobiographical Memoir," HP; CJH to Mrs. W. Wright Smith, 17 November 1882, HP.

2. Parker and Pollock, *Old Mistresses,* 9; Ruskin, "Sesame and Lilies," in *Works,* 18:121–22.

3. Nunn, *Victorian Women Artists,* 8; Linda Nochlin, "Art and Sexual Politics," *Art and Sexual Politics,* 6–7. Anna Brownell Jameson (1794–1860) was the daughter of an Irish painter of miniatures. After work as a governess and a failed marriage, she began serious writing on art in 1842, with her *Companion to the Public Picture Galleries of London: Sacred and Legendary Art* (1848), which established her as an authority in the field.

4. H [Hamerton?], quoted in "The Royal Academy" [letter], *Athenaeum,* 30 April 1859, 581–82; Deborah Cherry, *Painting Women: Victorian Women*

Artists (London: Routledge, 1993), 55; Whitney Chadwick, *Women, Art, and Society* (London: Thames and Hudson, 1990), 166.

5. WPH to Henry Babington Smith, 11 October 1898, Babington Smith Papers, Wren Library, Trinity College, University of Cambridge.

6. WPH, "Autobiographical Memoir," HP.

7. Ibid.; Elizabeth Gaskell, *Letters,* ed. J. A. V. Chapple and Arthur Pollard (Cambridge: Harvard University Press, 1967), 106. The theater was Eliza (Tottie) Fox's earlier ambition, but her father apparently got the actor William Macready to tell her that she was too small for the stage. So Eliza took up art, "rather an unusual and independent step for a girl to take, when I was young" (Fox, quoted in Jenny Uglow, *Elizabeth Gaskell: A Habit of Stories* [New York: Farrar Straus Giroux, 1993], 221).

8. WPH to Mrs. W. Wright Smith, 1 July 1892, HP.

9. WPH to W. W. Herringham, 16 May 1893, HP.

10. WPH to W. W. Herringham, 20 May 1892, HP.

11. In 1904, WPH, as consulting physician to the Wanstead Infant Orphan Asylum, and A. A. Bowlby, its surgeon, resigned from its board after a futile two-year protest against replacement of trained nurses with untrained women and refusal to properly isolate infectious cases (Herringham and Bowlby, "Wanstead Infant Orphan Asylum" [letter], *Times,* 6 June 1904, 10).

12. WPH, "Autobiographical Memoir," HP.

13. D'Andrea Cennino Cennini, *The Book of the Art of Cennino Cennini: A Contemporary Practical Treatise on Quattrocento Painting,* trans. Christiana Jane Herringham (London: George Allen & Unwin, 1899), v. The American edition of CJH's translation is *The Art of the Old Masters, as told by Cennino Cennini in 1437 [1397?]: How they ground and mixed their Colours, painted their Pictures and Miniatures, tinted their Papers, made their Varnishes, etc. etc. A Reference work for the Artist, Picture Collector and Others* (New York: Francis P. Harper, 1899). The translation by Mrs. [Mary Philadelphia] Merrifield is *A Treatise on Painting written by Cennino Cennini in the year 1437 [1397?]; and first published in Italian with an introduction and notes by Signor Tambroni . . .* (London: E. Lumley, 1844). Cennino Cennini (1370–1440) was born in Florence. *Il libro dell' arte o trattato della pittura* (1397) is his only surviving published work; the earliest extant manuscript, perhaps a copy, is dated 1437. CJH's correspondence with George Allen & Unwin, 1898–1900, is available on Chadwick-Healey microfilm, Secondary Series, reel 14, vol. 2.

14. D'Andrea Cennino Cennini, *The Craftsman's Handbook: The Italian*

"Il Libro dell' Arte," trans. Daniel V. Thompson, Jr. (New York: Dover Publications, 1933), x. CJH, in the preface (v) to her translation, noted inaccuracies in Mrs. Merrifield's text, "owing perhaps to a want of practical knowledge of the processes; but the style is pleasant, and I have kept as far as possible to the words I had grown accustomed to before I knew the original Italian." CJH may have contemplated a corrected edition and further writing on early painting. On 3 December [1899] she wrote to Richard Garnett, Keeper of Printed Books at the British Museum, about corrections and possible additions: "I want to get all the information I can about records of early painting in England and elsewhere. I wonder if the British Museum has any treasures that may have escaped the writers of the middle of the century. The suggestion has been little touched upon lately by English writers" (MS File, Garnett, R., Misc., Humanities Research Center, University of Texas, Austin).

15. Cennini, *The Craftsman's Handbook,* trans. Thompson, xi, xiii.

16. Cennini, *The Book of the Art,* trans. Herringham, 6–7, 22.

17. Ibid., 87–88, 34. On Taddeo Gaddi (ca. 1300–ca. 1366), see Andrew Ladis, *Taddeo Gaddi: Critical Reappraisal and Catalogue Raisonné* (Columbia: University of Missouri Press, 1982). On Agnolo Gaddi (active 1369–1396), see Bruce Cole, *Agnolo Gaddi,* Oxford Studies in the History of Art and Literature (Oxford: Clarendon, 1977).

18. Cennini, *The Book of the Art,* trans. Herringham, 124.

19. CJH, "Notes on Mediaeval Methods," ibid., 188.

20. CJH, introduction to *Papers of the Society of Painters in Tempera, 1901–1907,* ed. Christiana Herringham (London: privately printed by Women's Printing Society, 1907), [i–ii].

21. CJH, preface to *Catalogue of an Exhibition of Works by Members of the Society of Painters in Tempera* (London: Carfax Gallery, 1905), v–vi.

22. Ibid.; Ruskin, "Modern Painters," in *Works,* 3:351.

23. Friedrich Overbeck (1789–1869), Franz Pforr (1788–1812), and Peter von Cornelius (1783–1867) are the best known of the group. See Keith Andrews, *The Nazarenes: A Brotherhood of German Painters in Rome* (Oxford: Clarendon, 1964). On Dyce and the Nazarenes, see Pointon, *William Dyce,* 7, 9, 12–15, 32–33, 78.

24. David Robertson, *Sir Charles Eastlake and the Victorian Art World* (Princeton, N.J.: Princeton University Press, 1978), 59. On Prince Albert and decorations for the rebuilt Houses of Parliament, see 58–77. See also Pointon, *William Dyce,* 85, and Andrews, *The Nazarenes,* 84–85.

25. Houghton, *The Victorian Frame of Mind,* 45, 53.

26. See F[rederick] K[night] Hunt, *The Book of Art. Cartoons, Frescoes, Sculpture, and Decorative Art, as Applied to the New Houses of Parliament and to Buildings in General: with an Historical Notice of the Exhibitions in Westminster Hall, and Directions for Painting in Fresco. Illustrated by Engravings in Wood* (London: Jeremiah How, 1846). This compendium, lavishly illustrated, was designed to inform and impress the public and also to justify this expenditure of public funds.

27. Mrs. [Mary Philadelphia] Merrifield, *The Art of Fresco Painting, as Practised by the Old Italian and Spanish Masters, with a Preliminary Inquiry into the Nature of the Colours Used in Fresco Painting, with Observations and Notes* (London: published for the author by Charles Gilpin, 1846), iii.

28. Quoted in Pointon, *William Dyce,* 101.

29. C. W. Cope, quoted in Robertson, *Sir Charles Eastlake,* 199.

30. Quoted in Pointon, *William Dyce,* 85.

31. James Ludovic Lindsay, *Sketches of the History of Christian Art,* 3 vols. (London: John Murray, 1847), 3:290. Ruskin, in his review, thought that the book offered hope for "human care and thought and love" instead of "machine-work once tolerated" in an age "thoughtfully unproductive of all art—ambitious—industrious—investigative—reflective, and incapable." He thought that promise somewhat obscured by an excess of "metaphysical analogies" ("The History of Christian Art," in *Works,* 12:172–73, 169, 175).

32. J. L. Lindsay, *Sketches of the History of Christian Art,* 1:xi, xiv, xv.

33. Ibid., 2:306.

34. Ibid., 3:419–20.

35. Charles Lock Eastlake, *Methods and Materials of Painting of the Great Schools and Masters,* 2 vols. (1847; reprint, New York: Dover Publications, 1960), 1:v. Robertson says: "No Englishman of his time was better informed in art; no English artist or connoisseur could match his combination of experience, knowledge, judgment and *savoir faire.* Ruskin certainly could not. . . . In experience Eastlake was both painter and connoisseur; in outlook, not insular but European; in habits of study, not amateurish but disciplined and thorough" (*Sir Charles Eastlake,* 244).

36. Quoted in Robertson, *Sir Charles Eastlake,* 70.

37. Eastlake, *Methods and Materials,* 1:25. Nineteenth-century artists had access to a number of the older treatises: see Mary P[hiladelphia] Merrifield, *Original Treatises Dating from the XIIth to the XVIIIth Centuries on Arts of Painting in Oil, Miniature, Mosaic, and on Glass; of Gilding, Dyeing,*

and the Preparation of Colours and Artificial Gems; Preceded by a General Introduction; with Translations, Prefaces, and Notes, 2 vols. (1849; reprint, New York: Dover Publications, 1967).

38. Eastlake, *Methods and Materials,* 1:88, 89.

39. Ibid., 1:70. How this climate of opinion affected art education may be deduced from an 1849 lecture by C. R. Leslie (1794–1859), professor of painting at the Royal Academy Schools: "Lecture III: Professor Leslie's Lectures on Painting," *Athenaeum,* 3 March 1849, 230–33. He declared with condescension that advance in painting was only "tolerably regular" until "that proud epoch" of Leonardo, Michelangelo, Correggio, and Raphael—this last the supreme standard of true art. Natural sciences progressed because they added to the work of past generations and moved on. The fine arts must learn to do that, for it was a mistake "in one age to repeat exactly what has been done in another . . . a deception practiced by the artist on himself and on the world." Painters studied old masters in order to advance in perfectibility. Ruskin, "Academy Notes 1855," in *Works,* 14:38–39, 39 n. 1, thought Leslie an admirable painter who should not have attempted criticism, for his lectures perpetuated "fallacious art-maxims of the last century" that were useless to the young and "a perpetual warning" to older painters.

40. Eastlake, *Methods and Materials,* 1:267.

41. John Ruskin, *Ruskin in Italy: Letters to His Parents 1845,* ed. Harold I. Shapiro (Oxford: Clarendon, 1972), 217.

42. See, for example, Ruskin, "Modern Painters," in *Works,* 7:451, 4:307 n. 4.

43. Ruskin to Joseph Severn, 21 September 1845, in "Letters Illustrative of 'Modern Painters,' Vol. 2," in *Works,* 4:393–94.

44. Ruskin, *Ruskin in Italy,* 76; Ruskin, "Eastlake's History of Oil-Painting," in *Works,* 12:253.

45. Ruskin, "Eastlake's History of Oil-Painting," in *Works,* 12:253.

46. Ibid., 256, and on tempera and new uses of oil, see 257–73.

47. Ruskin, "St. Mark's Rest," in *Works,* 24:364.

48. CJH, preface to *Catalogue of an Exhibition* (1905), 3–8.

49. CJH, introduction to *Papers of the Society of Painters in Tempera: Volume 1, 1901–1907,* 2d ed., ed. M. Sargant-Florence (Brighton: Dolphin, 1928), [ii–iii]. By 1928 the society had merged with the Society of Mural Decorators.

50. Roger Fry, "Tempera Painting," *BM* 7 (1905): 175.

51. CJH, introduction to *Catalogue of an Exhibition of Works by Members of the Society of Painters in Tempera* (London: Baillie Gallery, 1909); unsigned review, "The Society of Painters in Tempera," *Athenaeum*, 13 November 1909, 96–97.

52. CJH, introduction to *Papers of the Society* (1907), [ii].

53. CJH, preface to *Catalogue of an Exhibition* (1905), v–vi.

54. Fry, "Tempera Painting," 176; CJH, preface to *Catalogue of an Exhibition* (1905), [iii–viii].

55. Fry to Lady Fry, 22 May 1893, quoted in Frances Spalding, *Roger Fry: Art and Life* (London: Granada, 1980), 51; Fry to Sir Edward Fry, 27 September 1894, in Roger Fry, *Letters of Roger Fry*, ed. Denys Sutton (London: Chatto and Windus, 1972), 1:159.

56. William Rothenstein, *Men and Memories: Recollections, 1900–1922* (London: Faber and Faber, 1932), 131.

57. Fry, *Giovanni Bellini* (London: Unicorn, 1899), 10–11.

58. Fry, "Tempera Painting," 176.

59. Alistair Smart, "Roger Fry and Early Italian Art," *Apollo* 83 (1966): 262–71; Spalding, *Roger Fry*, 63.

60. Spalding, *Roger Fry*, 62, 76; Clive Bell, *Art* (New York: Capricorn Books, 1958).

61. Virginia Woolf, *Roger Fry: A Biography* (1940; reprint, London: Hogarth, 1969), 121; CJH to Fry, 10 April [ca. 1904], Western Manuscripts Archive, King's College, University of Cambridge; Uglow, *Elizabeth Gaskell*, 166.

62. CJH to Fry, 10 April [ca. 1904], Western Manuscripts Archive.

63. Fry to Vanessa Bell, 6 April 1917, in Fry, *Letters*, 2:408. See also V. Bell, *Selected Letters of Vanessa Bell*, ed. Regina Marler (New York: Pantheon Books, 1993), 205.

64. Quoted in John Rothenstein, *Modern English Painters: Sickert to Moore* (London: Readers Union/Eyre and Spottiswoode, 1957), 302; quoted in Judith Collins, *The Omega Workshops* (Chicago: University of Chicago Press, 1984), 149.

65. Lisa Tickner, *The Spectacle of Women: Imagery of the Suffrage Campaign, 1907–1914* (Chicago: University of Chicago Press, 1988), 245.

CHAPTER 4. MAKING A PLACE FOR ART

1. W. Rothenstein, *Men and Memories: Recollections, 1900–1922*, 97. William Rothenstein (1872–1945) wrote three volumes of memoirs that

are an invaluable source on art and artists: *Men and Memories: Recollections, 1872–1900; Men and Memories: Recollections, 1900–1922; Since Fifty: Recollections, 1922–1938* (London: Faber and Faber, 1931, 1932, 1939, respectively). All three volumes were edited and abridged as one volume: William Rothenstein, *Men and Memories: Recollections, 1872–1938,* ed. Mary Lago (London: Chatto and Windus, 1978; Columbia: University of Missouri Press, 1978).

2. W. Rothenstein, *Men and Memories: Recollections, 1900–1922,* 97, 79.

3. D. S. MacColl, "Art at the Paris Exhibition: I," *SR* 90 (15 September 1900): 326–27; unsigned review, "British Art at the Brussels Exhibition," *Times,* 29 July 1897, 8.

4. Unsigned review, "British Art at the Brussels Exhibition," *Times,* 29 July 1897, 8; "The Brussels Exhibition," *Times,* 18 February 1898, 2.

5. "The Paris Exhibition," *Times,* 13 April 1900, 4, and 17 December 1900, 6.

6. MacColl, "Art at the Paris Exhibition: I," 326–27.

7. Ibid.

8. D. S. MacColl, "Art at the Paris Exhibition: II. Manet," *SR* 90 (22 September 1900): 358–59.

9. D. S. MacColl, "Art at the Paris Exhibition: III. Rodin," *SR* 90 (29 September 1900): 392–93.

10. D. S. MacColl, "Friends of the National Gallery," *SR* 90 (15 December 1900): 751–52.

11. John Tweed, "Auguste Rodin—A Suggestion" (letter), *SR* 90 (10 November 1900): 587; unsigned note, "Rodin in a London Gallery," *SR* 90 (17 November 1900): 611; Ernest Beckett, "Rodin in a London Gallery" (letter), *SR* 90 (24 November 1900): 647–48. John Tweed (1869–1933) was best known for military and imperial figures. Louis-Antoine Barye (1796–1875) specialized in heroic animal sculptures. The cast of Rodin's *St. John the Baptist Preaching,* bronze (1878–1880), was presented to the South Kensington Art Museum in 1902 and transferred to the Tate Gallery in 1937 (*Rodin,* Hayward Gallery exhibition catalogue, London, 1970, 27).

12. MacColl, "Friends of the National Gallery," 751–52; Herrmann, *The English as Collectors,* 388.

13. Herrmann, *The English as Collectors,* 42, 312–23. See also Johann David Passavant, *Tour of a German Artist in England. With notices of private galleries and remarks on the state of art,* 2 vols. (London: Saunders and Otley, 1836); Gustav Friedrich Waagen, *Treasures of Art in Great Britain,* trans. Lady Eastlake, 3 vols., and its supplement, *Galleries and Cabinets of*

Art in Great Britain (London: John Murray, 1854 and 1857, respectively); and C. G. Carus, *The King of Saxony's Journey through England and Scotland in the Year 1844*, trans. S. C. Davison (London: Chapman and Hall, 1846). All three thought British appreciation for the nation's art treasures insufficient. Passavant was surprised that in England, "where all is to be found that wealth can purchase, or luxury desire," there was no national gallery until 1824, and its growth was "proportionally slow" because without government support it must rely on "the uncertain accrements of gifts and bequests" (1:23). Waagen thought that if the new building in Trafalgar Square encouraged "a sense of the importance of such an institution, towards forming an elevated taste, the more efforts will be made by purchases and bequests" (1:264). Carus, after he had seen Lord Ashburton's collection, exclaimed: "If private persons possess galleries of this description, what ought a grand British national gallery to be!" (130).

14. See Herrmann, *The English as Collectors*, 373–76, with passages from Robert Clermont Witt, *The Nation and Its Treasures* (London: Cassell, 1911).

15. David Cannadine, *The Decline and Fall of the British Aristocracy* (New Haven: Yale University Press, 1990), 112.

16. Ruskin, "The National Gallery: A Preface," in *Works*, 34:451–54. By the turn of the century some prominent estate owners shared Ruskin's gloomy view. Percy Wyndham, of Clouds House in Wiltshire, thought it "better to live in Spain or Morocco than in the England of our day. The people themselves appear to be completely changed" (Caroline Dakers, *Clouds: The Biography of a Country House* [New Haven: Yale University Press, 1993], 121).

17. MacColl, "Friends of the National Gallery," 751–52.

18. Samuel Hynes, *The Edwardian Turn of Mind* (Princeton, N.J.: Princeton University Press, 1968), 314. Sir Francis Chantrey (1781–1841) was best known for portrait sculpture and memorial statuary. Hynes selects Chantrey Fund administration as a paradigm for the shortcomings of Edwardian provincialism in art administration.

19. Ibid., 317.

20. MacColl, "Friends of the National Gallery," 751–52.

21. J. H. Gibson and H. P. Hain Friswell, "Friends of the National Gallery" (letters), *SR* 90 (22 December 1900): 793–94.

22. D. S. MacColl, "The Academy: IV. 'Murder!,'" *SR* 91 (13 June 1901): 766–67. The *Times* thought Royal Academy painting "by common consent a good deal below the standard of last year." Of landscapes on view, "how few leave any permanent impression on the mind." Sculpture had "nothing

of supreme interest" ("The Royal Academy," *Times*, 24 May 1901, 13; 8 June, 1901, 5; and 24 June, 1901, 3).

23. MacColl, "The Academy: IV. 'Murder!,' " 766–67.

24. D. S. MacColl, "The Maladministration of the Chantrey Trust," *SR* 95 (25 April 1903): 516–17.

25. Ibid.; D. S. MacColl, "The Academy," *SR* 95 (9 May 1903): 585–87.

26. Ashbee to Sir Edward Poynter, 16 November 1897, Isidore Spielmann Papers, MS Eng. misc. d. 87, fol. 25r, Bodleian Library, Oxford University; D. S. MacColl, "Some Political Matters of Art," *SR* 95 (7 March 1903): 289–90.

27. MacColl, "Some Political Matters of Art," 289–90.

28. See, for example, the prolonged exchange between MacColl and Marion H. Spielmann, editor of the *Magazine of Art,* which began with MacColl's "The 'Magazine of Art' and the Chantrey Bequest," *SR* 96 (7 November 1903): 573–74. It drew a riposte from Spielmann in the 14 November issue (614) and continued, deteriorating in tone while other correspondents joined in, until the 5 December issue (703–4). MacColl particularly resented M. H. Spielmann's suggestion that the Royal Academy's inadequate recognition of New English Art Club artists motivated his Chantrey campaign.

See also W. J. Loftie, "The Maladministration of the Chantrey Bequest" (letter), *SR* 95 (23 May 1903): 651–52, in which he writes that ten years earlier he had criticized Chantrey Bequest administration and that he now rejoiced to find a really vigorous protest in progress. In an unsigned article probably written by MacColl, the *Saturday Review* called for an official investigation of the Academy. Conditions had changed; the Royal Academy could "no longer pretend to speak for the general body of artists in this country or to command their confidence and those of the cultivated public. . . . In our view the time is ripe for a new commission to consider the whole constitution of the Academy, as a body enjoying the gift of a public site and buildings on the understanding that it fulfils public duties" (*SR* 95 [6 June 1903]: 706–7). Another writer was skeptical; not even a Parliamentary inquiry would make a difference.

29. See, for example, Herbert Chorley, "Parliament and the Chantrey Bequest," *SR* 95 (7 July 1903): 48.

30. D. S. MacColl, "Twenty-One Years of the National Art Collections Fund," *BM* 44 (1924): 175–79. Sir Sidney Colvin (1845–1927), to whom P. G. Hamerton gave a start in art criticism, was Slade Professor of Fine Art,

Cambridge, from 1873 to 1885; Director of the Fitzwilliam Museum from 1876 to 1883; then Keeper of the Department of Prints and Drawings at the British Museum, where he brought in a number of valuable acquisitions as well as Japanese and Chinese collections.

31. Beginning in 1892, MacColl (1858–1948) exhibited as watercolorist with the New English Art Club, which he joined in 1896. For the Glasgow exhibition of 1900 he organized the first British exhibition of French impressionists; his *Nineteenth-Century Art* (1902) stated the case for their importance. In 1906 he became Keeper of the Tate Gallery and brought to light Turner works long left in storage. He was Keeper of the Wallace Collection from 1911 to 1924.

32. Spalding, *Roger Fry,* 73.

33. Sir Claude Phillips (1847–1924) was knighted in 1911 for his contributions as art critic and as Keeper of the Wallace Collection from 1897 to 1911. The five *Portfolio* monographs, written within four years, covered a wide range: *Frederick Walker and His Works* (1899), *Antoine Watteau* (1895), *The Picture Gallery of Charles I* (1896), *The Earlier Work of Titian* (1897), *The Later Work of Titian* (1898). The author of his *Times* obituary (11 August 1924, 12) observed that in his art criticism for the *Daily Telegraph,* Phillips never gave himself exalted airs and always remembered that it is "a difficult thing to paint a good picture."

34. Sir Charles John Holmes (1868–1936) was Slade Professor of Fine Art at Oxford from 1904 to 1910. In 1904 he was one of the first editors of the *Burlington Magazine,* and in 1909 left it to be Director of the National Portrait Gallery and then, in 1916, of the National Gallery. On his work with Ricketts and Shannon, see J. G. Paul Delaney, *Charles Ricketts: A Biography* (Oxford: Clarendon, 1990).

35. John Postle Heseltine (1843–1929) was, "one might say, the last of the old school of cognoscenti." He collected prints and drawings and was a devoted etcher. With the Earl of Carlisle, he was Acting Director of the National Gallery between the tenancies of C. J. Holmes and Charles Holroyd. He was remembered as "courtly and considerate," as from "a more leisured and possibly by-gone age" ("Mr J. P. Heseltine: A True Amateur of Art," *Times,* 4 March 1929, 11). John Bowyer Buchanan Nichols (1859–1939) was born into an atmosphere of classical scholarship and connoisseurship. Painting was his profession, but he preferred criticism and was art critic for the *Westminster Gazette* ("Mr. Bowyer Nichols: Artist and Man of Letters," *Times,* 3 June 1939, 17). Sir Charles Holroyd (1861–1917), painter and etcher,

evaded family expectations that he become a mining engineer and in 1880 went to the Slade School, where he won prizes and a two-year Italian traveling scholarship. His artistic output diminished after 1897, when he became first Keeper of the Tate Gallery and then, in 1906, Director of the National Gallery. There he, too, discovered a forgotten Turner collection, of unfinished drawings, which he transferred to the Tate. He resigned in 1916, his health undermined by troubles with trustees and worries about the gallery's safety in wartime. Sir Robert Clermont Witt (1872–1952) took an Oxford degree in 1894, served in the Matabele War in 1896, and was a war correspondent with Cecil Rhodes. He became senior partner in Stephenson, Harwood and Tatum, which he made into a major London firm. In 1899 he married into the Marten family and thus became connected to the Powells. He collected English drawings, and his extensive photographic library of works of all periods is now at the Courtauld Institute, in whose founding in 1932 he took an active part. He was honorary secretary of the National Art Collections Fund from 1903 to 1920, and chairman from 1920 to 1945. He was a trustee of the National Gallery during the years 1916–1923, 1924–1931, 1933–1940; of the Tate Gallery from 1916 to 1931; and of the Watts Gallery at Compton.

36. Phillips to Balcarres, 30 June 1903, fols. 1–2, CP. National Art Collections Fund correspondence, 1903–1914, is numbered in sequence by folio. Documents quoted here, from 1903 to 1906, are selected from volumes numbered 97/18–19 to 97/25. A separate Folio Series, identified here as FS I, comprises numbered volumes of reports, minutes, and additional correspondence. Permission of the Rt. Hon. the Lord Crawford is required for access.

37. John Vincent, introduction to David Alexander Edward Lindsay, *The Crawford Papers: The Journals of David Lindsay, Twenty-Seventh Earl of Crawford and Tenth Earl of Balcarres, 1871–1940, during the Years 1892 to 1940*, ed. John Vincent (Manchester: Manchester University Press, 1984), 3–4. David Alexander Edward Lindsay (1871–1940) inherited large estates in Scotland and industrial properties in England. He was educated at Eton and Magdalen College, Oxford, then was Conservative M.P. for the Chorley Division of Lancashire from 1895 to 1913, when he succeeded his father as Lord Crawford. He was Junior Lord of the Treasury from 1903 to 1905, and Conservative Party whip from 1903 to 1913. In 1916 he was recalled from military service to be president of the Board of Agriculture and Fisheries and held a series of offices until 1922, when Lloyd

George's government fell. Lord Crawford left active politics for cultural causes. In the 1920s he was a trustee of the National Portrait Gallery, the National Gallery, and the British Museum, and he was chairman of the Royal Fine Art Commission founded in 1924. He was president of the Society of Antiquaries from 1924 to 1929, chairman of the Council for the Preservation of Rural England, and a member, then chairman, of the Royal Commission on Historical Manuscripts. A signal contribution was chairmanship in 1935 of the committee to advise on the future of the British Broadcasting Corporation under a revised charter. He was author of *Donatello* (1903) and *The Evolution of Italian Sculpture* (1909). He summed up his philosophy in advice to his son, quoted by John Vincent in his introduction to Lindsay, *The Crawford Papers:* "We should share our artistic patrimony with all who can benefit from our possessions. Nor do I in the least think myself materialistic for paying close attention to business matters and to safeguarding our property, for it represents the skill, diligence, foresight, and self-sacrifice of our ancestors. On the contrary these are qualities of which we should be proud, so long as wealth is not the vehicle for ostentation or self-seeking. *Ne glorieris in divitis si adsunt*" (8–9).

38. See Nicholas Barker, *Bibliotheca Lindesiana: The Lives and Collections of Alexander William, 25th Earl of Crawford and 8th Earl of Balcarres, and James Ludovic, 26th Earl of Crawford and 9th Earl of Balcarres* (London: Bernard Quarritch, for the Roxburghe Club, 1977).

39. Vincent, introduction to Lindsay, *The Crawford Papers*, 5, 7.

40. Fry to Balcarres, 1 July 1903, fol. 3, CP; Balcarres's annotated copy, "Provisional Results of Discussion at Informal Meeting at 40, Wimpole Street, July 6th [7th] 1903," fols. 4–6, CP.

41. Minutes of 7 July meeting, fols. 4–6, CP; Lindsay, *The Crawford Papers*, 68. Ernest William Beckett (1856–1905), was a Conservative M.P. from 1885 until he succeeded his uncle by special remainder as second Baron Grimthorpe in 1905. Sir William Martin Conway, later first Baron Conway of Allington (1856–1937), was a Cambridge extension lecturer from 1882 to 1885; professor of art, University College, Liverpool, from 1885 to 1888; Slade Professor of Fine Art, Cambridge, from 1901 to 1904; and a trustee of the Wallace Collection from 1916 to 1924. An Alpine traveler, he was prominent in archaeological and antiquarian organizations. Sir Herbert Frederick Cook (1868–1939), barrister and connoisseur, was knighted in 1886 for services to art. He served on international exhibition committees, including that of the Brussels exhibition in 1897 and the Paris exhibition in 1900,

and was a National Gallery trustee from 1916 to 1930. Herbert Percy Horne (1864–1916), architect, writer, collector, and a leader of the 1890s typographical revival, edited the *Hobby Horse,* published from 1882 to 1893 by the Century Guild and dedicated to rehabilitation of the arts. James G. Nelson, in *The Early Nineties: A View from the Bodley Head* (Cambridge: Harvard University Press, 1971), 151, describes the guild's program as "mildly Pre-Raphaelite, Ruskin-Morrisian, arts-and-crafts-oriented." Horne designed the original initials and cover of the *Burlington Magazine,* unchanged until 1948. In 1892 he retired to Renaissance studies in Florence and bequeathed a fine collection of paintings and sculpture to the Italian state.

42. CJH to Balcarres, 8 July [1903], fol. 7, CP.

43. Witt to Balcarres, 9 July 1903, fol. 9, CP; Colvin to Balcarres, 10 July 1903, fol. 10, CP.

44. CJH to Balcarres, 14 July [1903], fol. 11, CP.

45. Hynes, *The Edwardian Turn of Mind,* 211.

46. CJH to Balcarres, 19 July 1903, fol. 29, CP.

47. Balcarres, "Confidential" notes on 14 July meeting, fols. 431–32, CP. Sir Lionel Henry Cust (1859–1929), art historian, worked first in the War Office, which he disliked, until Sidney Colvin got him transferred to the Department of Prints and Drawings at the British Museum. From 1895 to 1909 he was Director of the National Portrait Gallery, which he moved from temporary quarters in Bethnal Green to its present site in St. Martin's Place. In 1901 he became Surveyor of the King's Pictures. From 1909 to 1919 he and Roger Fry edited the *Burlington Magazine.* Sir John Maxwell Stirling-Maxwell, tenth Baronet (1866–1956), was M.P. for the College Division of Glasgow from 1895 to 1906. Arboriculture was his great interest, and he was chairman of the Forestry Commission from 1929 to 1932. He was chairman of the Royal Fine Art Commission for Scotland, trustee of Scots National Galleries, and chairman of the Ancient Monuments Board for Scotland. He was a Wallace Collection trustee, an administrator of that bequest, and chairman of its board for the last twenty-five years of his life.

48. CJH to Balcarres, 16 July [1903], fol. 23, CP.

49. Ibid.; Witt to Balcarres, 16 July 1903, fol. 26, CP.

50. Fry to Balcarres, 16 July 1903, fol. 24, CP. In another note for a draft letter to prospective supporters, Balcarres wrote: "The difficulties & delays caused thru' large committees having to examine & sanction the purchase of any single work of art—which of course may be offered for sale in some distant foreign town—have led the promoters of this scheme to settle that

the committees responsible for the various branches of art shall appoint honorary buyers, to whom the maximum of power shall be delegated" (fol. 12, CP).

51. Balcarres, "Confidential" notes on 14 July meeting, fols. 431–32, CP (mimeographed copy, fol. 433, CP); minutes, meeting of 22 July 1903, fols. 31–34, CP.

52. Fry to Balcarres, 23 July 1903, fol. 63, CP.

53. Witt, list of proposed vice presidents, 25 July 1903, fol. 64, CP. Sir Augustus Moore Daniel (1866–1950) was Assistant Director of the British School at Rome from 1906 to 1907, a trustee of the National Gallery from 1925 to 1929, and its Director from 1929 to 1933. In 1940 he delivered the Rede Lectures at Cambridge, published as *Some Approaches to a Judgment in Painting* (Cambridge, England: The University Press, 1940).

54. Burlington Fine Arts Club brochure, in fol. 429, CP.

55. Colvin to Balcarres, 10 July 1903, fol. 10, CP; Purdon Clarke to Balcarres, 15 July, 1903, fol. 16, CP. Sir Caspar Purdon Clarke (1846–1911), an architect, was himself a product of the Government Art Schools at South Kensington. He collected for the Victoria and Albert Museum in India and the Near East and became Keeper of its Indian Art Collections in 1892, Assistant Director of the museum in 1893, and Director in 1896. He was Director of the Metropolitan Museum from 1905 to 1910.

56. Ruth Sebag-Montefiore, Magnus Lecture to the Jewish Historical Society, London, 9 July 1992.

57. I. Spielmann to Balcarres, 25 July 1903, fol. 66, CP; M. H. Spielmann to Balcarres, 25 July 1903, fol. 65, CP; I. Spielmann to Balcarres, 28 July 1903, fol. 86, CP.

58. Read to Balcarres, 31 July 1903, fol. 101, CP; Fry to Balcarres, 3 August 1903, fol. 106, CP. After Rosenheim's death, "A Correspondent" chided the *Times:* "I think the columns of *The Times* should contain something more than the bare statement of the death of Mr. Max Rosenheim" (22 September 1911, 7). Edward Miller, in *That Noble Cabinet: A History of the British Museum* (Athens: Ohio University Press, 1974), 317, omits mention of Rosenheim and states that "Read established a group of 'Friends of the British Museum' by whose aid he was able to purchase much needed antiquities in a period of rapidly rising prices. Before long the 'Friends' were merged with the National Art Collections Fund, of which Read was eventually to be Vice-Chairman."

59. Sir Edward Sassoon to Balcarres, 26 September [1903], fol. 217, CP.

60. Holroyd to Balcarres, 16 September 1903, fol. 155, CP; Aldenham to Balcarres, 26 July 1903, fol. 70, CP; Carmichael to Balcarres, 28 July 1903, fol. 80, CP. Henry Hucks Gibbs, first Baron Aldenham (1819–1907), was head of Anthony Gibbs and Sons, merchants and foreign bankers, London. He was a Director of the Bank of England from 1853 to 1901 and its Governor from 1875 to 1877. He was Conservative M.P. for the City of London from 1891 to 1892, and in 1890 became a trustee of the National Portrait Gallery. Sir Thomas David Gibson-Carmichael, eleventh Baronet (1859–1926), became keenly interested in art during an Italian tour in 1881 and 1882. He was a trustee of the Wallace Collection during the years 1904–1908 and 1918–1926 and of the National Gallery during the years 1906–1908 and 1923–1926. He, too, mentioned Rosenheim as an enthusiastic supporter. He mentioned also having heard a suggestion that Rosenheim's name might be a liability on the list—an early intimation of the anti-Semitism that would become an issue in 1905.

61. Read to Balcarres, 28 July 1903, fol. 78, CP; Ward to Balcarres, 26 July 1903, fol. 74, CP; Sutherland Gower to Balcarres, 29 July 1903, fol. 89, CP; Knutsford to Balcarres, 30 July 1903, fol. 93, CP. The Rt. Hon. Lord Ronald Sutherland Gower (1845–1916), younger son of the second Duke and twentieth Earl of Sutherland, was a trustee of the National Gallery and author of many books on art and artists.

62. Peel to Balcarres, 30 July 1903, fol. 97, CP. Arthur Wellesley Peel (1829–1913), first Viscount, was the youngest of the five sons of the great Sir Robert Peel (1788–1850), who began about 1820 to collect paintings by Dutch, Flemish, and English masters, and he acquired Sir Thomas Lawrence's collection of drawings by Rubens and Van Dyck. Sir Robert encouraged Prince Albert in projects to increase public awareness of the national art heritage, most significantly, the Crystal Palace Exhibition of 1851 and the Manchester British Art Treasures Exhibition of 1857. As Speaker of the House from 1884 to 1895, his son Arthur dealt with a series of disrupting issues such as the Irish Home Rule Bills of 1886 and 1893. He was a trustee of the British Museum from 1898 to 1907, and chairman of the trustees of the National Portrait Gallery.

63. CJH to Balcarres, 20 August 1903, fols. 114–15, CP.

64. Ibid. Cf. Kathleen McCarthy, "Museums and Marginalization," in her *Women's Culture: American Philanthropy and Art, 1830–1930* (Chicago: University of Chicago Press, 1991), in which she finds much that was parallel to CJH's situation in England. In the 1890s American women philanthropists became actively interested in museum affairs. "Yet within

museums even the wealthiest, most generous female patrons generally remained isolated from substantive policy-making processes, and strikingly passive in rendering of their gifts" (112). Louisine Havemeyer's patronage of Mary Cassatt enriched the history of women in art, and her munificence enriched the Metropolitan Museum. "But it also helped to strengthen an institution—and an artistic canon—that paid scant homage to women's contributions, whether as artists, as curators, or as potential trustees" (111–12). They remained " 'on the borders,' neither 'fully at home in male houses of power, though seeking to live there,' nor fully in command. . . . women's munificence reinforced the cultural authority of cadres of male professionals and elites" (115–16). McCarthy finds only one woman—Mrs. J. Crosby Brown—who "aggressively sought to claim a more meaningful role at the Metropolitan through her donations during these years" (122–23). In the National Art Collections Fund, CJH was the only woman on record who "aggressively sought" a "more meaningful role."

65. CJH to Balcarres, 20 August 1903, fols. 114–15, CP.

66. I. Spielmann to Balcarres, 6 September 1903, fols. 140–41, CP.

67. CJH to Balcarres, 20 August 1903, fols. 114–15, CP.

68. Ibid.

69. CJH to Balcarres, 23 September [1903], fol. 196, CP.

70. Editorial article, "The Burlington Magazine," *BM* 1 (1903): 3–5. For Ruskin on erratic painters, see "Eastlake's History of Painting," *Works*, 12:253.

71. Editorial article, "The Burlington Magazine," 3–5.

72. Ibid.

73. Fry to Holmes, 7 September 1903, in Fry, *Letters*, 1:212.

74. Fry to Lady Fry, 20 September 1903, ibid., 212–13.

75. C. J. Holmes, *Self and Partners (Mostly Self): The Reminiscences of C. J. Holmes* (London: Macmillan, 1936), 214–15; Benedict Nicolson, "Fifty Years of the Burlington Magazine," *BM* 95 (1953): 63–65. Savile Publishing Company was the original publisher. Robert M. Dell was first editor and then joint editor with Holmes from January 1904 to 1906. Holmes carried on alone until he became Director of the National Portrait Gallery in 1909. Fry and Cust then became joint editors, and More Adey joined them in 1913. Of early Fund supporters, Balcarres, Conway, Colvin, Cook, and Phillips served on its board, and

> most distinguished of all—Roger Fry, who did more than any one man to help the Magazine over its most difficult hurdles, and Bernard Berenson, who contributed to the first number an article

of fundamental importance on "Alunno di Domenico" [1:6–20] and was still writing for the Magazine in 1950. . . . Even in the years of most abject poverty, the Magazine has never betrayed the ideals to which it owed its existence. Its aims and policy were set out in the editorials for the first few issues, and from these basic principles it has never had reason to depart.

76. T[homas] Wyse, 17 December 1842, quoted in John Pye, *Patronage of British Art. An Historical Sketch: An Account of the Rise and Progress of Art and Artists in London, from the beginning of the Reign of George the Second; together with A History of the Society for the Management and Distribution of the Artists' Fund, from its Establishment in 1810, to its Incorporation in 1827* (London: Longman, Brown, Green, and Longmans, 1845), 176 n. 8. Sir Thomas Wyse (1791–1862), was an Irish politician and diplomat. A long visit to Paris encouraged his interest in art and, eventually, art education. He advocated school inspection and state control of the educational system. He was a lord of the Treasury from 1839 to 1841, was secretary for the Board of Control (India) in 1846, and in 1849 became British minister to Athens, where he died.

77. Thomas Winstanley, quoted in Herrmann, *The English as Collectors,* 199; Robert H. Benson, ed. *The Holford Collection* (London: privately printed for Sir George Holford and members of the Burlington Fine Arts Club who subscribed at the Winter Exhibition, 1921–22, by Oxford University Press, 1924), 19–22.

78. Herrmann, *The English as Collectors,* 23. Robert Henry Benson (1850–1929), banker and art collector, after several years in America became a junior partner in the firm of John Cross, who was the husband of George Eliot. When Benson became senior partner, the firm became Robert Benson and Company, with wide American connections. He became a trustee of the National Gallery in 1912 and one of its representatives on the boards of the Tate Gallery and the Victoria and Albert Museum. He owned famous collections of Chinese porcelain and old masters. His wife was a daughter of R. S. Holford, owner of the great collection at Westonbirt, Gloucestershire. He thus had connections to Balcarres and the Lindsay family.

79. Martin Conway, *Episodes in a Variable Life* (London: Country Life, 1932), 36; Conway, *The Sport of Collecting* (London: T. Fisher Unwin, 1914), 7–8, 147.

80. Denys Sutton, *Some British Drawings from the Collection of Sir Robert Witt* (London: Arts Council, 1948), quoted in Herrmann, *The English*

as *Collectors*, 22; Robert Clermont Witt, *The Art of Collecting* (London: privately printed for the National Art Collections Fund by Shenval Press, 1950), 1.

81. P. G. Hamerton, *Thoughts about Art* (London: Macmillan, 1873), 125.

82. Ashbee to Balcarres, 3 October 1903, fol. 253, CP; Ivor Guest to Balcarres, 9 October [1903], fol. 282, CP. Charles Robert Ashbee (1863–1942), architect, designer, craftsman, and town planner, was articled to the architect G. F. Bodley, who specialized in church restoration. Ashbee began early to work for the revival of artistic design in handicrafts, and in 1888 he organized his Guild of Handicraft. In 1902 his community of Ashbee-trained crafts workers—150 men, women, and children—moved to Chipping Campden, Gloucestershire. Financial difficulties ended it in 1907. After World War I and until 1922 Ashbee devoted himself to the development and civic refurbishment of Jerusalem. On his career, see Alan Crawford, *C. R. Ashbee: Architect, Designer, and Romantic Socialist* (New Haven: Yale University Press, 1985). Of the Chipping Campden project, Crawford says: "Ashbee was actually less interested in making designers out of individual Guildsmen than in making design a collaborative affair between himself and the Guildsmen, and so developing a common Guild style. He wanted to make room for his Guildsmen to exercise their Ruskinian freedom" (217–18). On the guild at Chipping Campden, see also Fiona MacCarthy, *The Simple Life: C. R. Ashbee in the Cotswolds* (London: Lund Humphries, 1981).

83. Witt to Balcarres, 10 October 1903, fol. 284, and 20 October 1903, fol. 303, CP; I. Spielmann to Balcarres, 21 October 1903, fols. 305, 306, CP.

84. "The National Art Collections Fund," *Times*, 21 September 1903, 4; "A National Art Collections Fund," *Spectator* 91 (1903): 452–53; [Roger Fry], "The National Art Collections Fund," *Athenaeum*, 26 September 1903, 420–21.

85. [D. S. MacColl], "A National Art Collections Fund," *SR* 96 (26 September 1903): 393–94.

86. Robert Clermont Witt, "A Movement in Aid of Our National Art Collections," *Nineteenth Century and After* 54 (1903): 651–59.

87. A. U., "Art and Artists," *Star*, 29 September 1903, 1; Arthur Clutton-Brock, "The Friends of the National Gallery," *Speaker*, n.s., 9 (1903): 12–13; "An Art Project," *Free Lance*, 3 October 1903, 3. Frank V. P. Rutter (1876–1937) was educated at the Merchant Taylors' School and Queens' College, Cambridge. He edited *To-Day* from 1902 to 1904, became *Sunday Times* art

critic in 1903, and founded *Art News* and edited it from 1909 to 1912. He was Curator of the Leeds Art Gallery from 1912 to 1917 and editor of *Art and Letters* from 1917 to 1920. In 1933 he still blamed the National Art Collections Fund for "a short-sighted policy . . . inertia and snobbish ineptitude" that had prevented its helping to secure the Boudin (Rutter, *Art in My Time* [London: Rich and Canvas, 1933], 117–20). The Boudin was "presented by the French Impressionist Fund through the National Art-Collections Fund to the National Gallery" (see no. 23 in "List of Acquisitions," D. S MacColl, ed., *Twenty-Five Years of the National Art Collections Fund* [Glasgow: Robert Maclehose with the Glasgow University Press, 1928], 26).

88. "National Art and Voluntary Aid," *Morning Post,* 25 September 1903, 11.

89. [Roger Fry], "The Chantrey Bequest," *Athenaeum,* 7 November 1903, 621. On these paintings, see John Walker, *James McNeill Whistler* (New York: Harry N. Abrams, with the Smithsonian Institution, 1987). *Arrangement in Gray and Black, No. 2: Portrait of Thomas Carlyle* (1872–1873) is in the Glasgow Art Gallery and Museum (65 pl. 1), and *Arrangement in Gray and Black: Portrait of the Painter's Mother* (1871), purchased for the Luxembourg Museum, is now in the Louvre (58 pl.). Both left England in 1891. A proposal that the National Portrait Gallery purchase *Carlyle* got "the laughter of the director at the thought of buying it," and Whistler's "theories and his art" prevented purchase by the National Gallery in Edinburgh (96).

90. Balcarres, notes for his opening remarks at the General Meeting, 10 November 1903, fol. 323, CP.

91. "The National Art-Collections Fund," *Times,* 12 November 1903, 6.

92. Ricketts diary, 11 November 1903, Transcripts, Correspondence and Journal Entries, Ricketts Papers, Add. MSS. 61714, II, 1903–96, British Library. CJH's mention of only Phillips was perhaps the effect of her nervousness, or Ricketts got the reference wrong.

93. Holmes, *Self and Partners,* 221.

94. Ricketts to MacColl, [autumn 1906?], MacColl Papers, Glasgow University Library, Scotland.

95. Phillips to Balcarres, 11 November 1903, fol. 322, CP.

96. Balcarres to Phillips, draft, 11 November 1903, fol. 323, CP.

97. CJH to Balcarres, 13 November [1903], fol. 350, CP.

98. Balcarres to CJH, [13 or 14 November 1903], fol. 341, and draft, fol. 350, CP.

99. I. Spielmann to Balcarres, 11 November 1994, fol. 325, CP.

100. Phillips to Balcarres, 14 November 1903; Balcarres to Phillips, draft, 15 November 1903, fols. 350, 350a, CP.

101. Witt to Balcarres, 12 November 1903, fol. 332, CP; "Notes," *Outlook* 12 (1903): 417.

102. Witt to Balcarres, 16 November 1903, fol. 365, CP.

103. CJH to Balcarres, 16 November [1903], fol. 358, CP; Witt to Balcarres, 16 November 1903, fol. 365, and 18 November 1903, fol. 363, CP.

104. Lindsay, *The Crawford Papers,* 68; I. Spielmann to Balcarres, 20 November [1903], fol. 418, CP. "Opposition" was apparently the four originators and their friends.

105. Purdon Clarke to Balcarres, 21 October 1903, fol. 310, CP; Gibb to Balcarres, 17 July 1903, fol. 27, CP. Robert Gibb (1845–1932) was also a painter best known for scenes from British military history.

106. Cust to Balcarres, 10 September 1903, fol. 145, CP; Heseltine to Balcarres, 15 September 1903, fols. 149–50, CP.

107. Heseltine to Balcarres, 15 September 1903, fols. 149–50, CP.

CHAPTER 5. *VENUS* ASCENDING

1. Holmes, *Self and Partners,* 227; Witt to Balcarres, 9 January 1904, fol. 440, CP.

2. Roger Fry, quoted in Holmes, *Self and Partners,* 215; Spalding, *Roger Fry,* 60, 66, 77.

3. Fry, *Letters,* 1:217.

4. *Parliamentary Debates,* Commons, 4th ser., 136 (21 June 1904): cols. 624–43.

5. Hynes, *The Edwardian Turn of Mind,* 320. See also "Report from the Select Committee of the House of Lords on the Chantrey Trust," *Reports from Committees* (London: H.M. Stationery Office, 1904). Cf. *Report of the Commissioners appointed to inquire into the Present Position of the Royal Academy in Relation to the Fine Arts; together with the Minutes of Evidence,* Reports from Commissioners, vol. 16, 5 February–28 July 1863, in vol. 27 (1966), Readex Microprints, New Canaan, Conn.

6. D. S. MacColl, "The Royal Academy and National Art," *National Review* 45 (May 1905): 505–14.

7. CJH to William Rothenstein, 25 October [1903], 694 (46), RP:HL. In later years Charles Rothenstein (later Rutherston; 1866–1928), William Rothenstein's elder brother, applied this principle in Yorkshire. With William's advice, he gathered an outstanding collection of contemporary

art, to be circulated from the Manchester City Art Gallery among schools and smaller galleries.

8. Benson to Balcarres, 7 January 1904, fols. 437–39, CP.

9. Ibid.

10. Colvin to Balcarres, 10 January 1904, fol. 441, CP.

11. Phillips to Balcarres, 5 February 1904, fols. 451–53, CP. The Wilton Diptych (ca. 1400), painter unknown, is the most important example of early English painting. In brilliant blue and gold, it depicts St. John the Baptist, St. Edmund the Confessor, and St. Edmund commending King Richard II to the Christ child (E. H. Gombrich, *The Story of Art*, 15th ed. [Englewood Cliffs, N.J.: Prentice-Hall, 1989], 162–63). It was not sold in France in 1904; the National Gallery bought it in 1929 for ninety thousand pounds, toward which the National Art Collections Fund contributed five thousand pounds.

12. "Art Treasures," *Evening News*, 14 June 1904, 2. The Peacock Room went to the Smithsonian Institution, Freer Gallery of Art, Washington, D.C. See Andrew McLaren Young et al., *The Paintings of James McNeill Whistler*, 2 vols. (New Haven: Yale University Press, 1980), 2:pls. 16–20.

13. Frank Rutter, "Round the Galleries," *Sunday Times and Sunday Special*, 31 January 1904, 6; Rutter, "Mr. Whistler and the National Art Collections Fund," *SR* 97 (2 April 1904): 427–28. Whistler's *Symphony in Grey: Early Morning, Thames* (1871) is now at the Freer Gallery of Art, Washington, D.C. See Young et al., *The Paintings of James McNeill Whistler*, pl. 45.

14. Unsigned article, "The 'Slump' in Modern Art: Where Are the Trustees of the Chantrey Bequest?" *Daily Mail*, 13 December 1904, 3.

15. Curzon to I. Spielmann, copy, 24 August 1904, fol. 503, CP; Frank Rutter, "Round the Galleries," *Sunday Times and Sunday Special*, 26 February 1905, 2. See *Nocturne: Blue and Gold—Old Battersea Bridge* (1872–1873) in Young et al., *The Paintings of James McNeill Whistler*, pl. 109.

16. Frank Rutter, "Round the Galleries," *Sunday Times and Sunday Special*, 9 July 1905, 2.

17. CJH to Executive Committee and Balcarres, 26 October 1905, fol. 713, CP.

18. C. J. Holmes, "Paintings—Old Masters," in MacColl, ed., *Twenty-Five Years of the National Art Collections Fund*, 85–86. On this painting, variously referred to as *The Toilet of Venus* and *Venus and Cupid*, see José López-Rey, *Velázquez: A Catalogue Raisonné of His Oeuvre* (London: Faber and Faber, 1963), 143–44 and pls. 124–25. López-Rey dates the painting 1648,

some time before November. The Duke of Alba commissioned *Venus* as a companion to Titian's *Sleeping Nymph.* George Augustus Wallis, William James Buchanan's agent, acquired it in Spain during the art dislocations that accompanied the French occupation of 1808 to 1814; he brought it to England in October 1813. J. B. S. Morritt of Rokeby Hall promptly purchased it (Buchanan, *Memoirs of Painting,* 2:201–5, 243–44).

19. I. Spielmann to Balcarres, 15 November 1905, FS I, fol. 9, CP. Later, Spielmann wrote to Balcarres, "I have gone down on my knees to Sir Ernest Cassel to save us & the Venus, but do not know the result yet" (3 December 1905, fol. 828, CP).

20. Witt to Balcarres, 15 November 1905, fol. 738, CP; R. A. M. Stevenson, *The Art of Velasquez* (London: George Bell, 1895), 14–15; Witt to Balcarres, 16 November 1905, FS I, fol. 10, CP.

21. Benson to Balcarres, 26 November 1905, fols. 788–89, CP. One citizen thought the delay in choosing a director a miserly attempt to save the director's annual salary of one thousand pounds; when the trustees found no qualified candidate, the Treasury "eagerly seized upon" the excuse for economy ("Efficiency" [letter] and "The Rokeby Velasquez," *Times,* 11 November 1905, 6).

22. Benson to Balcarres, postcard, n.d. and no postmark, fol. 776, CP.

23. Ibid., 26 November 1905, fols. 788–89, and 27 November 1905, fol. 792, CP.

24. "The Rokeby Velasquez," *Times,* 29 November 1905, 12; Hawes Turner, secretary to the National Gallery, to Balcarres, copy, 7 December 1905, fol. 848, CP.

25. W, "The Grant for the Blenheim Pictures" (letter), *Times,* 14 March 1885, 6. In 1844 Anna Jameson had written in her *Companion to the Most Celebrated Private Galleries of Art in London:* "The great Duke of Marlborough filled Blenheim with pictures—the fruit of his campaigns—the gifts of cities and princes . . . to this day one of the finest in England" (quoted in Herrmann, *The English as Collectors,* 69). Only forty years later the *Times*'s editorial writer found rumors of a Blenheim sale "difficult any longer to disbelieve," and, if true, "Blenheim will remain a monument of the cruel kindness of a nation which voted a reward to a hero that was to prove a greater burden than his descendants could bear. . . . the nation has every right to ask whether some part at least of the treasures cannot and must not come into the national keeping" (*Times,* 14 February 1884, 9). Italy, a poor country, kept its art treasures at home, whereas the British

government dithered about works acquired by "the taste and knowledge of the upper classes of the past and preceding centuries" ("The National Gallery and English Collections," *Times,* 1 March 1884, 5). The stream of articles and letters continued into 1886. One commentator who saw some of the pictures at Christie's observed that if people knew how the Treasury had behaved, "the country would not approve of this disastrous parsimony, and that in future years we shall look back with unavailing regrets" (H, "The Blenheim Pictures" [letter], *Times,* 23 July 1886, 10). Burne-Jones's *King Cophetua and the Beggar Maid* went to the Tate Gallery in 1884 after efforts by another *ad hoc* committee (Benson to Balcarres, 26 November 1905, fols, 788–89, CP).

26. B. Michaels[?] to Balcarres, 6 December [1905], fol. 838, CP; Benson to Balcarres, 26 November 1905, fols. 788–89, CP.

27. Ronald Sutherland Gower, "The Rokeby Velasquez" (letter), *Times,* 23 November 1905, 6; Sutherland Gower to Balcarres, 29 November 1905, fol. 714, CP. From Brantwood, Ruskin's friend Arthur Severn took up Sutherland Gower's cue to perpetuate the old Ruskin-Whistler feud, with a sideswipe at Irish taste. Severn was "perfectly astonished" that the Fund, of which he was a member, "had given £2,000 for the Battersea-bridge study! And only the other day I heard that people in Ireland are being asked to subscribe over £30,000 for some modern French pictures—amongst them the Strolling Magicians, by Manet; though this last, in its blackness, daring, and over-eccentricity might certainly appeal to the Irish sense of humour. It seems to me that these artistic cliques who go about persuading towns or countries to buy certain pictures get almost hysterical in their enthusiasm, and often pitch upon what is not only eccentric, but very ugly" (Severn, "The Rokeby Velasquez" [letter], *Times,* 5 December 1905, 11). Balcarres drafted a meticulous reply to explain that the £2,000 for the Whistler had been "a good deal less than a private buyer was anxious to give." Of this, £1,700 was from subscribers' earmarked contributions. Only £250, or one-eighth, came from the "corporate funds of the Society" (6 December 1905, fol. 840, CP).

28. S. H. Whitehead, "The Rokeby Venus," *Times,* 30 December 1905, 3.

29. "A Member of the National Art Collections Fund" (letter) and "The Rokeby Velasquez," *Times,* 25 November 1905, 12.

30. "A Woman Member [Jane Harrison?] of the National Art-Collections Fund" and "The Rokeby Velasquez," *Times,* 29 November 1905, 12.

31. Sutherland Gower to Balcarres, 29 November, 7 December 1905, fols.

714, 849, CP. Balcarres replied with regret for the disagreement (4 December 1905, fol. 831, CP).

32. Witt to Balcarres, 19 December 1905, fol. 895, CP; CJH to William Rothenstein, 25 December 1905, 694 (3), and 3 January 1906, 694 (4), RP:HL.

33. Sigismund Goetze, "The Rokeby Velasquez," *Times*, 18 November 1905, 8. Sigismund Christian Hubert Goetze (1866–1939) painted portraits and genre pictures, principally religious and historical subjects; in later years he turned to landscape. He was a Londoner educated at University College School and the University of London, the Slade School, and the Royal Academy Schools, which he entered in 1885. An obituary stressed his benevolences (but without mention of the Rokeby *Venus)*: one thousand pounds to the Academy's Artists' General Benevolent Fund, new gates for Regent's Park, and thirty-six hundred pounds for its new main south entrance. The Royal Society of British Sculptors gave him its gold medal for "distinguished services to sculpture" ("Mr. Sigismund Goetze: Painting and Charitable Work," *Times*, 25 October 1939, 10).

34. Witt to Balcarres, 19 November 1905, fol. 760, CP. On discussions about authenticity of the picture, see the letters to the *Times*, all with title "The Rokeby Velasquez," excerpts from which follow: Sir John Murray Scott wonders if there is fire damage to the picture, and if the upper part is "not all that could be desired?" (24 November 1905, 7). Thomas Agnew and Sons "write immediately to state that the picture is in the most perfect original condition, as all the world may see," and there is no fire damage (25 November 1905, 12). C. J. Holmes writes that the picture is *not* fire-damaged, and it would be "difficult to find a work of the same age in a more perfect state of preservation; it is nowhere disfigured by patching or repainting, and the touch of the master can everywhere be followed as clearly as when the picture was first executed" (1 December 1905, 4). Edward Speyer believes that Scott has "strangely misread the author he quotes [Velázquez scholar Carl Justi, of Bonn]," who stated that the picture disappeared after a fire at the Alcazar in 1734 but reappeared "about the middle of the century" in the Alba Palace—"disappeared" not meaning "damaged" (14 December 1905, 7). Andrew K. Hitchens feels that it is not a masterpiece and that "about no picture is there so great a divergence of view." He agrees with Scott about a suspicious difference between upper and lower portions (14 December 1905, 7). MacColl, Fry, and Bowyer Nichols hold that such statements may have confused the public; as in other

Velázquez works, the canvas was enlarged and a strip added, probably at the top, to make room for Cupid and the mirror, and the paint was retouched at the joining. Except in a small portion of Cupid's forehead, "this repair is of no importance." A crack and an abrasion were mended almost invisibly, and the writers affirm "the perfect soundness of the picture as a whole" (23 December 1905, 9). Five years later, Phillips, Cook, Cust, Fry, Holmes, Witt, MacColl, and Colvin examine the picture and answer charges about a suspicious "monogram," of which they find no evidence (8 April 1910, 13).

35. I. Spielmann to Balcarres (and enclosure), 27 November 1905, FS I, fol. 11, CP.

36. I. Spielmann and Witt to Balcarres, with letter from G. H. Murray, for H.M. Treasury, copy, 22 December 1905, FS I, fols. 16, 16a, CP; I. Spielmann to Balcarres, 30 December 1905, fol. 914, CP.

37. David Alexander Edward Lindsay [Balcarres], Isidore Spielmann, Robert Clermont Witt, "The Rokeby Velasquez" (letter), *Times,* 9 January 1906, 8; D. S. MacColl, "The Loss of the Velasquez," *SR* 101 (13 January 1906): 43–44.

38. Sigismund Goetze, "The 'Venus' of Velasquez," *Times,* 13 January 1906, 4.

39. Benson to Balcarres, 26 January 1906, fols. 991–93, CP; Balcarres, Spielmann, Witt, "The Rokeby Velasquez" (letter), *Times,* 24 January 1906, 8.

40. Goetze to Balcarres, 14 February 1906, fol. 1048, CP; Balcarres to Goetze (draft), 13 February 1906, fol. 1045, and (another draft) 14 February 1906, fol. 1047, CP.

41. Benson to Balcarres, 26 January 1906, fols. 991–93, CP; Phillips to Balcarres, 26 January 1906, fol. 990, CP; Colvin to Balcarres, [26 January (?) 1906], fol. 1002, CP.

42. Edmund Gosse, "The Rokeby Velasquez," *Times,* 15 March 1906, 11; Balcarres, "The Rokeby Velasquez," *Times,* 16 March 1906, 5; Gosse, "The Rokeby Velasquez," *Times,* 17 March 1906, 14; Richmond, "The Rokeby Velasquez," *Times,* 20 March 1906, 8; Balcarres, "The Rokeby Velasquez," *Times,* 21 March 1906, 10; Richmond, "The Rokeby Velasquez," *Times,* 22 March 1906, 10.

43. "Notes," *Art-Journal* (1906): 172.

44. "The Lesson of the Rokeby Velasquez," *BM* 8 (1906): 225–28; "The Future Administration of the Fine Arts in England," *BM* 8 (1906): 375–78.

45. Holmes, "Paintings—Old Masters," in MacColl, ed., *Twenty-Five*

Years of the National Art Collections Fund, 86. For another account of the Fund's early years, see editorial, *BM* 135 (1993): 179; and Mary Lago, "Christiana Herringham and the National Art Collections Fund," *BM* 135 (March 1993): 202–11.

46. The only pertinent items in the Fund's office archives are a peremptory reminder that she had not paid her guinea for 1906, and her reply that this was henceforth to be paid by banker's order (25 April 1906, 24 January 1907, NACF Letter-book No. 3).

47. CJH to Balcarres, 15 June [1906], fol. 1539, CP.

48. Witt, introduction to MacColl, ed., *Twenty-Five Years of the National Art Collections Fund,* 3–4. She is not mentioned in *Art Treasures for the Nation: Fifty Years of the National Art-Collections Fund,* dedicated to the memory of Sir Robert Witt and with an introduction by the Earl of Crawford and Balcarres (London: Thames and Hudson, 1953), or in Benedict Nicolson and Francis Sitwell, eds., *Saved for the Nation: The Achievement of the National Art-Collections Fund, 1903–1973* (London: Victoria and Albert Museum, 1973).

49. [Curzon Committee], *Report of the Committee of Trustees of the National Gallery Appointed by the Trustees to Enquire into the Retention of Important Pictures in This Country and Other Matters Connected with the National Art Collections, with Appendices* (London: H.M. Stationery Office, 1915), 48, 54–55.

50. Ibid., 14, 78.

51. [Waverley Committee], H.M. Treasury, *The Export of Works of Art, etc.: Report of a Committee Appointed by the Chancellor of the Exchequer* (London: H.M. Stationery Office, 1952), 2, 5–6, 23.

CHAPTER 6. AJANTA I

1. Euterpe Ionides Craies, "Memoir," MS, 1932, private collection. Craies (1861–1955) described CJH as "one of my oldest and best friends." Her son Constantine was a contemporary of the Herringhams' son Christopher. I am indebted to Julia Ionides for access to this memoir and for permission to quote from it.

2. MacColl to William Rothenstein, 20 June 1906, 925 (37), RP:HL.

3. Fry, *Letters,* 1:248–49.

4. Spalding, *Roger Fry,* 81–107.

5. William Rothenstein to Alice Rothenstein, 29 March 1902, private collection.

6. CJH to William Rothenstein, [1905?], 694 (26), RP:HL. The context for these Brueghels is unspecified.

7. W. Rothenstein, *Men and Memories,* ed. Lago, 43.

8. CJH to William Rothenstein, 13 April [1908], 694 (47), and [February or March 1909], 694 (38), RP:HL. Charles Conder (1868–1909) lived in Paris from 1890 to 1895, and divided his time thereafter between France and England. He painted landscapes and portraits in oil but is best known for his watercolors on silk panels and fans, painted in *fin de siècle* style.

9. CJH to William and Alice Rothenstein, 8 November [1906], 694 (30), RP:HL.

10. Partha Mitter, *Much Maligned Monsters: History of European Reactions to Indian Art* (Oxford: Clarendon, 1977), vii.

11. CJH to William and Alice Rothenstein, 8 November [1906], 694 (30), RP:HL.

12. WPH to Mary Herringham, 5 November and 7 November 1906, HP.

13. Ibid., and 18 November 1906, HP.

14. Ibid., 22 November and 25 November 1906, HP.

15. CJH to William Rothenstein, 10 January [1907], 694 (7), RP:HL.

16. WPH to Mary Herringham, 30 November 1906, and to Geoffrey Herringham, 21 December 1906 and 12 January 1907, HP. *Anglo-Indian,* in the older usage, meant English who lived in India during British rule.

17. WPH to Geoffrey Herringham, 1 January 1907, HP.

18. Ibid., 31 January 1907, HP.

19. Ibid., 8 February, 12 January, and 1 January 1907, HP.

20. CJH to William and Alice Rothenstein, 10 January [1907], 694 (7), RP:HL.

21. WPH to Geoffrey Herringham, 26 December 1906, 8 January and 17 January 1907, HP.

22. WPH to Mary Herringham, 21 February 1907, HP.

23. CJH to William Rothenstein, [late December 1906], and to William and Alice Rothenstein, [10 January 1907], 694 (11), (7), RP:HL.

24. William Erskine, "Observations on the Remains of the Bouddhists in India," *Transactions of the Bombay Literary Society* 3 (1823): 494–536; on Ajanta, see 520.

25. James Edward Alexander, "Notice of a Visit to the Cavern Temples of Adjunta in the East-Indies," *Transactions of the Royal Asiatic Society of Great Britain and Ireland* 2 (1829): 362–70. See also John B. Seely, *The Wonders of Ellora; or, the Narrative of a Journey to the Temples and Dwellings Excavated*

Out of a Mountain of Granite . . . with Some General Observations on the People and Country (1824; reprint, Delhi: B.K. Publishing, 1975), 22–24. Seely, a captain in the Bombay Native Infantry, found that at Ellora, too, bad drainage had flooded the floors. However, Ajanta's difficulty of access spared it one kind of indignity. At Ellora, Europeans had been not only "sufficiently vicious to try to injure the figures and ornaments, but were actually so depraved as to indecently disfigure the deities with a variety of disgusting ornaments and appendages, so that a respectable female could not, without having her feelings outraged, visit these wonderful caverns." Mitter thinks that Seely, in an excess of romanticism, drowned his descriptions "in a rhetorical torrent of hyperbole and expletives," so that "subsequent writers felt obliged to come to the defence of other major monuments such as Elephanta and Ajanta" (*Much Maligned Monsters*, 137).

26. The following passages from Ralph's report are quoted in James Prinsep, "Facsimiles of Ancient Inscriptions, lithographed by James Prinsep," *Journal of the Asiatic Society of Bengal* 5 (September 1836): 554–61. James Prinsep (1799–1840) studied architecture under Augustus Charles Pugin, but weakened eyesight forced him into other work as an assay master at the Calcutta mint. Failed health forced him back to England, but he left various improved architectural and engineering installations in addition to research into his studies of Indian architectural antiquities, inscriptions, and coins.

27. Mitter says:

> What makes the travel reports fascinating reading is that, while the iconography of Indian art was uncomprehendingly received as the repository of esoteric wisdom or the outcome of demonic religion, early travellers did not hesitate to reflect on the architectural grandeur of Hindu temples and the delicate craftsmanship of the surface sculptures on them. . . . It may be argued that architecture, lacking the emotional and cultural connotations of figure sculpture, is generally far easier to come to terms with. (*Much Maligned Monsters*, 31)

Mitter refers here especially to Renaissance visitors to India, but, as in Ralph's report, their attitude lingered on into the nineteenth century.

28. James Bird was vice president and secretary of the Asiatic Society of Bombay. See his *Historical Researches on the Origin and Principles of the Buddha and Jain Religions: . . . with translations of the Inscriptions from those of Kanari, Karli, Ajanta, Ellora, Nasik, etc. . . .* (Bombay: American Mission Press, 1847).

29. A Subaltern [Lieutenant Blake], *A Description of the Ruined City of Mandu, The Ancient Capital of Malwa . . . Also, An Account of the Buddhist Cave Temples of Ajanta, in Khandes. With Ground-Plan Illustrations* (Bombay: Bombay Times' Press, 1844); on Ajanta, see 105–25, 139–[41], an account first published in the *Bombay Courier*, 9, 20, 23, 27, 30 April, and 21 May 1839.

30. Ibid.

31. James Fergusson, "On the Rock-Cut Temples of India," *Journal of the Royal Asiatic Society of Great Britain and Ireland* 8, no. 15, pt. 1 (1844–1846): 30–92. Fergusson (1808–1886) settled in England in 1845, but his Indian travels between 1835 and 1842 laid foundations for his subsequent scholarship. Later, he concentrated on architectural styles. Mitter points out that Fergusson wanted

> to bring the study of Indian architecture within the domain of science. . . . He was rightly critical of the limitations of a purely positivistic approach followed by archaeologists. He none the less inherited from them the eighteenth-century evolutionary doctrine of progress from the simple to the complex. It is true that Buddhist art appealed to him more than the Hindu, a feeling he shared with other Indian specialists of the age. It is not difficult to see that Buddhist art expressed a certain "classical" simplicity which was easier for Europeans to appreciate than the complex and rich imagery of Hindu art and architecture. (*Much Maligned Monsters*, 263)

32. James Fergusson and James Burgess, in *The Cave Temples of India* (1880; reprint, Delhi: Oriental Books Reprint, 1969), offered this explanation of the ground or gesso—but not of the medium itself:

> To receive these paintings the walls were left somewhat rough on the surface, and were then covered with a thin coating of plaster composed of fine dust, in some instances at least, of pounded bricks, mixed with fibres and the husks of rice. This was smoothed and covered with a coating of some ground colour, on which the designs were drawn and then painted. The pillars being smoothed with the chisel seem to have received only a heavy ground coating to prepare them to receive the scenes of figures to be drawn on them. (284)

On chronology of the caves, there is now a considerable literature. See, for example, Walter Spink, "Ajanta's Chronology: The Problem of Cave

Eleven," *Ars Orientalis* 7 (1968): 155–68; Vidya Dehejia, *Early Buddhist Rock Temples: A Chronology* (Ithaca, N.Y.: Cornell University Press, 1972); Sheila Weiner, *Ajanta: Its Place in Buddhist Art* (Berkeley and Los Angeles: University of California Press, 1877). Dehejia's study considers the early, formative (Hinayana) phase of cave building, 120 B.C. to A.D. 200, when the Buddha was not yet deified or represented in human likeness. Spink is primarily concerned to establish chronology from ground plans and internal sculptural and architectural forms. Weiner uses Buddhist contexts from coins, inscriptions, and stylistic evidence.

33. "Proceedings" for 11 May 1844, in "Annual Report," *Journal of the Royal Asiatic Society of Great Britain and Ireland* 8, no. 15, pt. 1 (1844): vi; East India Company Court of Directors, Despatch of 29 May 1844, India Office Records, London.

34. Clark Worswick, *The Last Empire: Photography in British India* (Millerton, N.Y.: Aperture, 1976), 3–4. The Madras government supplied Gill's camera equipment, and he was regularly in touch with the Photographic Society of Bombay. Fergusson, too, was a pioneer in the use of photography as archaeological tool. His *One Hundred Stereoscopic Illustrations of Architecture and Natural History in Western India* (London: Cundall, Downes, 1864) combines his text and Gill's photographs (now in the George Eastman Collection, Rochester, New York). See also Fergusson and Gill, *The Rock-Cut Temples of India Illustrated by Seventy-Four Photographs Taken on the Spot by Major Gill* (London: John Murray, 1864). Both volumes are available in *History of Photography Monographs,* Reel 69, Nos. 739 and 740, Research Publications, Woodbridge, Conn.

35. John Muir, *Notes of a Trip to Kedarnath . . . in the Autumn of 1853. With some account of a journey from Agra to Bombay by way of Ajunta, Ellora and Carlee in 1854* (Edinburgh: T. Constable, 1855), 48, 52–53.

36. "The Fire at the Crystal Palace," *Times,* 1 January 1868, 7. The lack of fire-fighting equipment was common knowledge at Sydenham. There were fire extinguishers, but no one knew how to operate them, nor were they charged and ready ("Destructive Fire at the Crystal Palace," *Times,* 31 December 1867, 7).

37. James Burgess, *Notes on the Bauddha Rock-Temples of Ajanta, Their Paintings and Sculptures, and on the Paintings of the Bagh Caves, Modern Bauddha Mythology &c* (Bombay: Government Central, 1879), 2.

38. "Ajanta Frescoes," in "Notes and Miscellanea," *Indian Antiquary* (1

November 1872): 354, reported that art lovers everywhere were "growing keenly alive to the importance of preserving accurate and careful records of the old works while it is yet time, before each tinge has wholly escaped the plaster." Fortunately, some 345 photographs of Griffiths's copies survive in the India Office Library, London.

39. "Fire at the India Museum, South Kensington," *Times*, 13 June 1885, 9. Among items lost were Buddhist sculptures too heavy to be moved. For more than a decade successive governments did nothing about the hazards at the South Kensington Museum. At last, a select committee of Parliament investigated in 1897. It found old buildings with wood and with lath and plaster sometimes covered with tarred felt, and temporary constructions of wood, beside the permanent buildings; eighty-one open fireplaces in private residences of the Art School staff; wood floors and stairs; partial party walls; walls boarded and canvased with space behind them—all evidence of lackadaisical attitudes toward the welfare of the national collections ("Protection of South Kensington Museum from Fire," *Times*, 27 May 1897, 8). The only benefit of the 1885 disaster was that, after years of ignoring artists' concern about the flammable quarters of the National Portrait Gallery, then next door to the India Museum, the government was sufficiently alarmed to move that gallery to its present location in St. Martin's Place.

40. John Wilson, "Memoir on the Cave-Temples and Monasteries and Other Ancient Buddhist, Brahmanical, and Jaina Remains of Western India," *Journal of the Bombay Branch of the Royal Asiatic Society of Great Britain and Ireland* 3, pt. 2 (1850): 36–107; *District Gazetteer for Jalgaon* (Calcutta: Government Printing Office, 1880), 187–88.

41. Sir George Watt, *Indian Art at Delhi, 1903, Being the Official Catalogue of the Delhi Exhibition, 1902–1903* (Calcutta: Government Printing Office, [1904]).

42. CJH, "Ajanta," TS, HP. In 1895 Sidney Colvin brought Laurence Binyon (1869–1943), poet and art historian, into the Department of Prints and Drawings at the British Museum; he was Deputy Keeper, Oriental Prints and Drawings, from 1913 to 1932. In *Painting in the Far East: An Introduction to the History of Pictorial Art in Asia, Especially China and Japan* (London: Edward Arnold, 1908), 35–36, Binyon observes that the Ajanta paintings have the "strong outline" of the early Asiatic style, with color apparently "heavy and hot" and animated figures with "force and individuality in them, a strong sense of life." However, he, too, considered

them at the "primitive stage." They had "all the feeling for life in individual figures," but "as yet little of that instinct which an art develops—the instinct towards unity, towards the conception of a subject as a synthetic whole."

43. Rajendra Prasad, *The Asif Jahs of Hyderabad: Their Rise and Decline* (New Delhi: Vikra Publishing House, 1984), 117–18.

44. Ibid., 132–33. WPH wrote to Mary Herringham (5 December 1906, HP): "Walker was at first only made a Secretary. He was forced on the Nizam by the Government [of India] and was viewed with great jealousy and dislike. He says he had a miserable time at first. But he gradually came through, and though there is just as much jealousy, yet he is thoroughly trusted by the Nizam and has made his position." In Casson Walker's opinion, WPH wrote, "no native has an idea of administration, still less of accounts, and the idea of honour in such matters is about what it was with us in Charles 2nd reign."

45. *Handbook for Travellers in India, Burma and Ceylon* (London: John Murray, 1892), 3.

46. WPH to Mary Herringham, 11 December 1906, HP; CJH, "The Caves of Ajanta," *Englishwoman* 9 (1911): 64–71.

47. WPH to Mary Herringham, 11 December 1906, HP.

48. CJH, "The Caves of Ajanta," 65.

49. WPH to Mary Herringham, 11 December and 8 December 1906, HP.

50. Fergusson, "On the Rock-Cut Temples of India," 53. The *Imperial Gazetteer for Central India, 1908* (Calcutta: Government Printing Office, 1908), 187–88, describes them as "rock-cut temples excavated in an isolated sandstone hill, with numerous buddhist remains in the neighbourhood."

51. WPH to Geoffrey Herringham, 12 February 1907, HP. CJH may have encountered the fakir in Cave Number 4, which the *Imperial Gazetteer for Central India, 1908,* 187–88, calls "remarkable for a colossal representation of the Vahara Avatar, the third incarnation of Vishnu, in which he is, as usually, represented raising the earth out of the engulfing waters."

52. CJH to William Rothenstein, [early 1907], 694 (11), RP:HL.

53. CJH, "Ajanta," TS, HP.

CHAPTER 7. AJANTA II

1. Fry, "Ideals of a Picture Gallery" (address to the museum committee), *Metropolitan Museum of Art Bulletin* 1 (March 1907): 59, quoted in Spalding, *Roger Fry,* 90.

2. CJH to Alice Rothenstein, 29 August [1907], 694 (25), RP:HL; Spalding, *Roger Fry,* 90.

3. CJH to Alice Rothenstein, 29 August [1907], 694 (25), RP:HL. See also Spalding, *Roger Fry,* x. Lady Ottoline Morrell (1873–1938), half-sister to the sixth Duke of Portland, was the wife of Philip Morrell (1870–1943), M.P. She knew the Frys at least by 1906 and, like CJH, gave his family what assistance she could. A flamboyant but vulnerable personality, she was a generous (and often underappreciated and underacknowledged) patron of Bloomsbury writers and artists.

4. CJH to William Rothenstein, 11 April [1907], 694 (27), RP:HL.

5. W. Rothenstein, *Men and Memories,* ed. Lago, 156, 157. George James Frampton (1860–1928) was a sculptor, creator of the Peter Pan statue in Kensington Gardens, the lions at the British Museum's north entrance, and the Edith Cavell monument in St. Martin's Place. Sir George Clausen (1852–1944), landscape and figure painter, was professor of painting at the Royal Academy Schools. John Singer Sargent (1856–1925), Boston-born painter, settled in London in 1884 and became internationally famous for portraits of the socially prominent.

6. CJH to WPH, 22 March [1908] and [late March 1908], HP.

7. CJH, "The Caves of Ajanta," 65.

8. CJH to William Rothenstein, 1 November [1908], 694 (5), RP:HL.

9. Ibid.; CJH to William Rothenstein, 13 April [1908], 694 (47), RP:HL.

10. J[oseph] H[ubert] Priestley, "William Bateson, 1861–1926," in *The Post Victorians* (London: Ivor Nicholson & Watson, 1933), 39–55.

11. Beatrice Bateson, comp., *William Bateson, F.R.S., Naturalist: His Essays and Addresses, together with A Short Account of His Life* (Cambridge, England: The University Press, 1928), 84–85. Bateson (1861–1926) was Silliman Lecturer at Yale University in 1907 and professor of biology, Cambridge University, in 1908 and 1909. In 1910 he became Director of the John Innes Horticultural Institution at Merton Park, Surrey. He was Fullerian Professor of Physiology at the Royal Institution of Great Britain from 1912 to 1914 and received many foreign honors as well.

12. On this procession, see Tickner, *The Spectacle of Women,* 80–91, 245 n. 3. Mary Lowndes (1857–1927) was a pioneer woman stained-glass designer. In the 1880s she studied at the Slade School and privately with the crafts designer Henry Holiday. In 1897 she founded the glass design and manufacturing firm of Lowndes and Drury and in 1906 moved to The Glass House, a purpose-built studio and workshop in Fulham. She was

on the executive committee of the National Union of Women's Suffrage Societies and chairman of the Artists' Suffrage League. She designed most of the banners for the women's procession on 13 June 1908, and Christiana embroidered at least that for the Women Writers' Suffrage League. Mary Lowndes contributed to and was editor of the *Englishwoman*. During World War I she helped to organize the Women Welders Union. See Peter Cormack, *Women Stained Glass Artists* (Walthamstow: William Morris Gallery, 1985).

13. "A Provincial Man," "In the Women's Ranks" (letter), *Nation*, 3 (20 June 1908): 417–18; Oswald Crawfurd, "Woman Suffrage Procession" (letter), *Times*, 14 May 1908, 12; CJH's reply, "The Suffrage Procession" (letter), *Times*, 18 May 1908, 14. See also Millicent Fawcett, "The Woman Suffrage Procession" (letter), *Times*, 13 June 1908, 9; and Fawcett, *The Women's Victory—and After: Personal Reminiscences, 1911–1918* (London: Sidgwick and Jackson, [1920]).

14. CJH to Richards, 26 May 1909, reel 60, 1909, Chadwyck-Healey Film, Richards Archive, University of Illinois. The *Englishwoman* aimed, as stated on its masthead, "to reach the cultural public and bring before it, in a convenient and moderate form, the case for the Enfranchisement of Women" and to inform women about literature, art, and politics. It published Parliamentary reports and commentary; articles on science and the trades; and short fiction, poetry, plays, and criticism. French contributions appeared in French, Italian in translation. John Drinkwater, G. S. Street, John Masefield, Constance Garnett, and Charlotte Mew were among its contributors. Grant Richards (1872–1948), novelist and journalist, established his firm in 1897. He accepted James Joyce's *Dubliners* in 1906, but the printer's fears of prosecution under the obscenity laws delayed publication until 1914.

15. CJH to William Rothenstein, [February or March 1909], 694 (38), and 30 November [1908], 694 (44), RP:HL.

16. Mrs. William Marshall, memoir, MS, on deposit at Selwyn College, Cambridge University.

17. CJH to William Rothenstein, [February or March 1909], 694 (38), RP:HL.

18. WPH to William Rothenstein, 9 April 1909, 695 (2), and CJH to Alice Rothenstein, 16 June [1907], bMs Eng 1148.3 (36), RP:HL.

19. A Special Correspondent, four articles, *Times*, 1908, 8: "Archaeology in India: Its Importance and Character," 10 August; "The Survey Department,"

11 August; "Conservation Work Now Going On," 12 August; "Exploration and Research," 14 August.

20. CJH, "Archaeology in India" (letter), *Times*, 21 August 1908, 4.

21. George Nathaniel Curzon, "[Reply to] Address from the Zemindari Panchayat," in *Speeches by Lord Curzon of Kedleston, Viceroy and Governor of India, 1898–1901* (Calcutta: Thacker, Spink, 1901), 69–70. While at Eton, Curzon (1859–1925) became interested in the East. From 1887 to 1894 he traveled widely in the Near and Far East, Russia, and India and became especially well informed about India's North-West Frontier country and tribes. As Viceroy, he halted much British and Indian damage to antiquities, but consequences of his imperious personality sometimes overshadowed his achievements.

22. Curzon, "Ancient Monuments in India," ibid., 189–91.

23. Ibid., 192–93, 195.

24. Ibid.. 193, 202.

25. CJH, "The Caves of Ajanta," 66. Ernest Binfield Havell (1861–1934) studied at the Royal College of Art and in Paris and Italy. He was superintendent of the Madras School of Art from 1884 to 1892; reporter to the government on arts and industries as related to indigenous handicrafts; then principal of the Calcutta School of Art and Keeper of the Government Art Gallery from 1896 to 1906. He served at the British Legation in Copenhagen from 1916 to 1933.

26. The crafts circle that Dorothy Larcher (1884–1952) belonged to included Phyllis Barron, Ethel Mairet (formerly Mrs. Ananda Coomaraswamy), and Enid Marx, who later recalled Larcher's accounts of the voyage, her unflattering opinions of Anglo-Indian first-class passengers, and work by candlelight in the Ajanta caves (Enid Marx to the author, 20 January 1980, 20 June 1987). See also Isabelle Anscombe, *A Woman's Touch: Women in Design from 1860 to the Present* [New York: Elizabeth Sefton/Viking, 1984], 148). Some of the work of this circle is at the Bath Crafts Centre. See its *Crafts* (September/October 1984): 39 for a photograph of Dorothy Larcher. The Cheltenham Art Gallery & Museums, which exhibited her work in 1954, states that she went to India with CJH in 1914, and Isabelle Anscombe writes that when the war caught Larcher in India she taught in Calcutta, where she lived with an Indian family and learned Indian techniques of dyeing and printing cloth (Isabelle Anscombe to the author, 7 February 1988). Larcher may have returned later to India, but she could not have accompanied CJH in 1914, for CJH was never in India after March 1911.

27. Mary, Countess of Minto, comp., *India, Minto, and Morley, 1905–10: Compiled from the Correspondence between the Viceroy and the Secretary of State* (London: Macmillan: 1934), 361. Gilbert John Murray Kynynmond Elliott, fourth Earl of Minto (1845–1914), was Governor General of Canada from 1898 to 1904 and Viceroy of India from 1905 to 1910. He inherited major political problems, which included Bengali protests against Curzon's 1905 partition of Bengal.

28. CJH to Alice Rothenstein, 4 January 1910, 694 (6), RP:HL.

29. WPH, "The Expedition," in CJH et al., *Ajanta Frescoes: Being Reproductions in Colour and Monochrome of Frescoes in Some of the Caves at Ajanta after Copies Taken in the Years 1909–1911 by Lady Herringham and Her Assistants, with Introductory Essays by Various Members of the India Society* (London: Humphrey Milford, 1915), 16.

30. CJH, "The Caves of Ajanta," 71.

31. Sarojini Naidu (1879–1949), daughter of a Bengali Brahmin educationalist, married the principal medical officer of the Nizam's Service. She was educated in Hyderabad; at King's College, London; and at Girton College. Three volumes of her poems in English, with romantic appeal for many readers in the West, were translated into major Indian vernaculars. After returning to India, she became involved in welfare programs for women and students. When CJH met her in Hyderabad, Mrs. Naidu was working to ameliorate Muslim women's purdah restrictions.

32. CJH to Alice Rothenstein, 4 January 1910, 694 (6), RP:HL.

33. CJH, "The Caves of Ajanta," 69. Another article, less personal and more technical, is "The Frescoes of Ajanta," *BM* 17 (June 1910): 136–39.

34. CJH, "Ajanta Frescoes," MS, [1911?], HP.

35. Ibid.

36. CJH to Alice Rothenstein, 4 January 1910, 694 (6), RP:HL.

37. CJH, "Ajanta Frescoes," MS, [1911?], HP; CJH to Sir Kishan Pershad Bahadur, prime minister of Hyderabad State, [February? 1911], Hyderabad State Archives.

38. Mitter, *Much Maligned Monsters*, 274–75.

39. Ibid., 270.

40. Ibid., 256–67. Henry D. Cole (1808–1882) was a Senior Assistant Keeper of the Public Record Office, where he became interested in medieval antiquities and assisted at the exhibitions of the Royal Fine Arts Society that led to the Crystal Palace Exhibition in 1851. He improved a state school of design with surplus Exhibition funds and increased the number of

subordinate schools from thirty-six to ninety-one; all emphasized "practical arts." Exhibition money also purchased the South Kensington estate upon which he began the South Kensington Museum, after 1899 the Victoria and Albert Museum.

41. Ibid., 268. On Abanindranath Tagore's Bengali art movement, see Tapati Guha-Thakurta, *The Making of a New "Indian Art": Artists, Aesthetics, and Nationalism in Bengal, 1850–1920* (Cambridge, England: The University Press, 1992).

42. On Cole's South Kensington Museum catalogue, see Mitter, *Much Maligned Monsters,* 256–58.

43. C. R. Ashbee, *A Few Chapters in Workshop Reconstruction and Citizenship* (London: Guild and School of Handicraft, 1894), 27.

44. William Morris, quoted in Mitter, *Much Maligned Monsters,* 250.

45. Ernest B. Havell, "Art and Education in India," in *Essays on Indian Art, Industry, and Education* (Madras: G. Nateson, [1910]), 92, 98–99, 115, 133, 137, 113. For an unimproved example of the Public Works attitude, see Mary Lago, *E. M. Forster: A Literary Life* (Basingstoke: Macmillan, 1995; New York: St. Martin's Press, 1995), 107–8.

46. Ibid., 121; Mitter, *Much Maligned Monsters,* 256. Ernest B. Havell, in "Art Administration in India," *Journal of the Royal Society of Arts* 58 (February 1909–1910): 273–98, replies to a paper by Cecil Burns, "The Future of Schools of Art in India," ibid., 57 (1908–1909): 629–41. Burns (1863–1929) considered the fine arts "but the development and higher expression of kindred crafts," and he deplored their separation in art education. He was principal of the Camberwell School of Arts and Crafts in 1897, principal of the Bombay School of Art, and Curator at the Victoria and Albert Museum in Bombay from 1902 to 1918.

47. Mitter, *Much Maligned Monsters,* 270.

48. Roger Lipsey, *Coomaraswamy: His Life and Work,* Bollingen Series 89 (Princeton, N.J.: Princeton University Press, 1977). Lipsey errs when he says that Coomaraswamy originated the India Society and wrote the letter to the *Times* (53). Rothenstein did both. In 1917 Coomaraswamy (1877–1947) achieved a Western appointment in Indian studies, as Fellow for Research in Indian, Persian, and Muhammadan Art, Museum of Fine Arts, Boston.

49. See Ananda Kentish Coomaraswamy, *Mediaeval Sinhalese Art: Being a Monograph of Mediaeval Sinhalese Arts and Crafts, Mainly as Surviving in the Eighteenth Century, with an Account of the Structure of Society and the Status of the Craftsmen* (Broad Campden, Gloucestershire: Essex House, 1908);

2d ed., with author's corrections (New York: Pantheon Books, 1956). See also Ernest B. Havell, *Indian Sculpture and Painting, Illustrated by Typical Masterpieces with an Explanation of Their Motives and Ideals* (London: John Murray, 1908), and *The Ideals of Indian Art* (London: John Murray, 1911).

50. Coomaraswamy to William Rothenstein, 22 December 1909, 320 (2), RP:HL.

51. In *Men and Memories: Recollections, 1900–1922*, 230–31, Rothenstein seems to place this purchase before Havell's lecture in 1910, but Campbell Dodgson, of the British Museum's Department of Prints and Drawings, made the offer on 21 December 1912 (412 [7], RP:HL), after Rothenstein himself had been to India. However, he already collected Indian drawings and considered those from Dodgson "among the finest in my collection."

52. George C. M. Birdwood, in "Proceedings," *Journal of the Royal Society of Arts* 58 (February 1909–1910): 273–74.

53. These and the following passages from the speech are in Havell, "Art Administration in India," ibid., 274–85. He responds to a paper by Cecil Burns, his successor as Principal of the School of Art at Calcutta (Havell, "The Functions of Schools of Art in India," *Journal of the Royal Society of Arts* 57 [June 1908–1909]: 628–41).

54. These and the following passages are from Birdwood, in "Proceedings," ibid., 285–88.

55. George C. M. Birdwood, *The Industrial Arts of India*, South Kensington Art Handbooks (London: Chapman and Hall, for Committee of the Council on Education, [1880]), 132.

56. Bengal was a hotbed of *swadeshi* activity. See J. H. Broomfield, *Elite Conflict in a Plural Society* (Berkeley and Los Angeles: University of California Press, 1968), 208–12.

57. George C. M. Birdwood, "Indian Pottery at the Paris Exhibition," *Journal of the Royal Society of Arts* 27–28 (February 1879): 305–13. This idyllic India theme characterized his writings on Indian crafts, although he knew that industrialization threatened the craftsman.

58. George C. M. Birdwood, "Pan-Hinduism" (letter), *Times*, 7 January 1910, 8. Two months later, in his "Gentes Aperimus Eoas" (letter), *Times*, 4 March 1910, 5, he expanded on this theme in connection with the restrictive Press Act for India. He blamed Hindu agitation on "the liberality of prophesying we permit to touring 'Americans' and English demagogues in India, and the free circulation of English newspapers of the most outrageous truculence of language, whether published in this country or in India." This

came of the "uncalculating and wholly worthless English education given in Government schools and colleges throughout India," where the Bible was "rigorously excluded" while students read subversive works such as Byron's "The Curse of Minerva." See also S. M. Mitra, *Hindupore: A Peep behind the Indian Unrest: An Anglo-Indian Romance* (London: Luzac, 1909), vii–viii, which validates its thesis with a Birdwood statement that unrest in India was "this momentary crisis in the affairs of India, for only the imbecilities inherent in our system of Government by party are artificially protracting a situation that to the ignorant alone seems so sinistrous."

59. Walter Crane, in "Proceedings," *Journal of the Royal Society of Arts* 58 (February 1909–1910): 188–89. See his *India Impressions, with Some Notes of Ceylon during a Winter Tour, 1906–7* (London: Methuen, 1907), 188–89. At Allahabad he saw much Manchester cloth, but "it was pleasant to see that native methods were in existence and were still in demand" (57–58). At Delhi, however, handicrafts seemed "now a craft as distinct from an art" (153). English cloth was plentiful, but Indian homespun linen and silks were scarce. Crane (1845–1915) painted portraits, figure subjects, and landscapes but is most often remembered for illustrations of children's books and for textiles, wallpapers, and other designs. He was greatly influenced by Sir Edward Coley Burne-Jones and the Pre-Raphaelites and by William Morris's work for the Socialist League.

60. Ananda Kentish Coomaraswamy, in "Proceedings," *Journal of the Royal Society of the Arts* 58 (February 1909–1910): 289–90.

61. William Rothenstein, ibid., 291. In W. Rothenstein, *Men and Memories*, ed. Lago, 162, he stated that Havell's paper was Birdwood's. Havell corrected him, and he replied:

> I am sorry for the inaccuracy. I met Coomaraswamy before I met you. He then knew little abt Indian painting. I had a Hindu painting (17th cent^{y}) & 2 or 3 Mogul ones, & I pointed out what I felt then (without any knowledge, such as you had, of Indian art) as a clear difference. At the time he only knew abt the new 'Calcutta School' & had a few of their drawings. I am sorry abt the lecture—I remember now that it was you who lectured. (Havell to William Rothenstein, [1933], MSS, Eur. D736/1, India Office Library)

62. W. Rothenstein, *Men and Memories*, ed. Lago, 162; William Rothenstein et al., "Fine Art in India" (letter), *Times*, 28 February 1910, 6. Rothenstein's cosignatories, which included Crane and G. J. Frampton, as well

as the following, brought impressive experience. Frederick Brown (1851–1941), a painter trained at South Kensington and in Paris, was a founder of the New English Art Club, head of the Westminster School of Art from 1877 to 1893, and Slade Professor of Fine Art, University of London, from 1892 to 1893. Laurence Housman (1865–1959), younger brother of A. E. Housman, was an artist, novelist, and playwright; from 1895 he was art critic for the *Manchester Guardian.* The sculptor Edward Lanteri (d. 1917), born in Burgundy and a naturalized Englishman, was professor of sculpture at the Royal College of Art from 1880. William Richard Lethaby (1857–1931), architect and writer on design, was first principal of the London County Council School of Arts and Crafts in 1894, Surveyor to Dean and Chapter of Westminster Abbey from 1906 to 1928, and a leader of the Society for the Protection of Ancient Buildings. Major works of Halsey Ricardo (1854–1928), architect, include the Terminal Railway Station, Howrah, Calcutta. Thomas William Rolleston (1857–1920) was the India Society's first treasurer and the Government's organizer of the Irish crafts revival. George William Russell, "AE," (1867–1935), Irish poet, artist, mystic, and nationalist, edited the *Irish Statesman* from 1923 to 1930. Sir William Reynolds-Stephens (1862–1943), sculptor, was president of the Royal Society of British Sculptors from 1921 to 1933. Sir Charles Waldstein (later Walston) (1856–1927) was Cambridge Lecturer in Classical Archaeology from 1880 to 1883, Director of the Fitzwilliam Museum from 1883 to 1889, reader in classical archaeology from 1883 to 1907, Slade Professor of Fine Art from 1895 to 1901 and from 1904 to 1911, and Director of the American Archaeological School at Athens from 1889 to 1993. Emery Walker (1851–1933), designer and typographer, was an organizer of the Arts and Crafts Exhibition Society and helped William Morris to start the Kelmscott Press. An editorial response (*Times,* 1 March 1910, 11) to their letter pointedly omitted "Fine" from its title: "Art in India." The gist was that Eastern peoples expect only an ideal, not representation, in art, and "the merely imitative work of art must always be inferior to the reality." The "modern Oriental" will settle for symbolism and "does not demand much effort of expression in the artist."

63. Havell to William Rothenstein, 15 February 1910, 680 (2), RP:HL.

64. CJH to William Rothenstein, [early summer 1910] and 22 July 1910, 694 (34), (1), RP:HL.

65. CJH, "The Frescoes of Ajanta" (June 1910): 136–39; CJH, "Oriental Art" (editorial) (April 1910): 3–4; Ananda Kentish Coomaraswamy, "Oriental Bronzes" (May 1910): 86–94; Roger Fry, "The Munich Exhibition of

Mohammedan Art" (August and September 1910): 283–90, 327–33—all in *BM* 17.

66. Geoffrey Scott, 6 September 1910 (RP:HL), quoted in W. Rothenstein, *Men and Memories: Recollections, 1900–1922,* 229.

67. CJH to Alice Rothenstein, 29 August [1907], 694 (25), and 15 March [1910] (incomplete), 694 (23), RP:HL.

68. Ibid., 24 June [1910], 694 (33), RP:HL; W. Rothenstein, *Men and Memories,* ed. Lago, 162. Rothenstein got less stringent advice from Thomas Arnold (1864–1930), India Office adviser to Indian students in England and Director of the Cromwell Road Centre, a social center for them but a headache for officials who suspected it as a hotbed of sedition.

69. Rothenstein's papers include five letters from Gokhale, 1910–1912, 584 (1–5), RP:HL. They *did* meet in Bombay. On the political situation, see Stanley A. Wolpert, *Tilak and Gokhale: Revolution and Reform in the Making of India* (Berkeley and Los Angeles: University of California Press, 1962).

70. Havell, "Art Administration in India," 284; Valentine Chirol, *Indian Unrest* (London: Macmillan, 1910).

71. W. Rothenstein, *Men and Memories,* ed. Lago, 162.

72. Goloubew to William Rothenstein, 19 June 1910, 586 (1), RP:HL. Victor Goloubew (1879–1945) was assistant and photographer to the head of archaeology at the Ecole Française d'Extrême-Orient in Pnompenh when André and Clara Malraux arrived there in 1923 to raid the then-abandoned and uncatalogued Vishnu temple at Banteai-Serai for sculptures to sell abroad. According to Axel Madsen, they thought him the "one clever European in Pnompenh. Only slightly older than they, Victor was a rather delicate intellectual with nervous dark eyes who (as he said) 'wore two if not three hats' as teacher, archaeologist, and journalist" (Axel Madsen, *Silk Roads* [New York: Pharos Books, 1989], 65). Goloubew's 1910 Ajanta visit was strategically timed; his domestic situation was in disarray. In 1908 Natalie Goloubew left him to be one of Gabriele D'Annunzio's mistresses. He in turn left her for the American expatriate artist Romaine Brooks (*The Letters of Bernard Berenson and Isabella Stewart Gardner, 1887–1924, with Correspondence by Mary Berenson,* ed. Rollin Van N. Hadley [Boston: Northeastern University Press, 1987], 475 n. 1).

73. W. Rothenstein, *Men and Memories,* ed. Lago, 163.

74. Charles Müller, *Cinq mois aux Indes: de Bombay à Colombo* (Paris: E. Floury, 1924), 58–59. Charles Müller (1877–1915) is remembered principally for collaborations with Paul Reboux on *à la manière de . . .*, a series of literary pastiches. He died on the western front. Victor Goloubew, *Charles*

Müller, Par ses Amis (Paris: E. Flammarion, 1918), 209–10, wrote: "J'avais choisi Charles pour compagnon à cause de son caractère et réfléchi et de sa constante bonne humeur, un peu aussi à cause de son tempérament sportif. Je n'ai jamais connu de nature mieux organisée que la sienne."

75. On Müller and Rothenstein in Bombay, see Müller, *Cinq mois,* 60–62.

76. CJH to Alice Rothenstein, 25 October [1910], 694 (9), RP:HL; Müller, *Cinq mois,* 59, 63.

77. CJH to Alice Rothenstein, 25 October 1910, 694 (9), and CJH to William Rothenstein, 9 August 1910, 694 (2), RP:HL; Müller, *Cinq mois,* 59.

78. Müller, *Cinq mois,* 77; CJH, "The Caves of Ajanta," 30; Müller, *Cinq mois,* 80.

79. Müller, *Cinq mois,* 112, 113, 114, 115, 119–24.

80. Müller said that CJH had "deux Anglaises" as assistants (*Cinq mois,* 115). She had only Dorothy Larcher; he mistook the visiting Sheila Casson Walker for a copyist.

81. Ibid., 115, 118–19.

82. WPH, "The Expedition," in CJH et al., *Ajanta Frescoes,* 16.

83. Coomaraswamy to William Rothenstein, 18 September 1910, 320 (6), and 10 October 1910, 320 (7), RP:HL.

84. W. Rothenstein, *Men and Memories: Recollections, 1900–1922,* 236.

85. CJH to William Rothenstein, 8 December 1910, 694 (22), RP:HL.

86. CJH to WPH, 3 January 1911, HP; CJH to William Rothenstein, 29 December 1910, 694 (10), RP:HL.

87. Ethel Coomaraswamy married the designer Philip Mairet, also in Ashbee's circle, in 1918 (Margot Coates, *A Weaver's Life: Ethel Mairet, 1872–1952* [Bath: Crafts Centre, with the Crafts Council, 1983], 335–36). Coomaraswamy told Rothenstein that Ethel returned to England for family business and for economy's sake (10 October 1910, 320 [7], RP:HL).

88. CJH to Alice Rothenstein, 14 March 1911, 694 (29), RP:HL.

89. CJH to WPH, 14 February [1911], HP.

90. Ibid., 26 February [1911], and 14 February [1911], HP.

91. Ibid., 14 February [1911], HP.

92. CJH to WPH, 26 February [1911], HP. Jean Philippe Vogel (1871–1951) was Superintendent of the Archaeological Survey of India at Lahore from 1901 to 1914, and substituted for John Marshall as director from 1910 to 1911. In 1914 he joined the faculty of the University of Leiden and became a Sanskritist of worldwide reputation. The university honored the fiftieth anniversary of his doctorate with a collection of essays, *India Antiqua: A Volume of Oriental Studies* (1947).

93. CJH to WPH, 26 February 1911, HP.

94. Ibid.

95. Ibid., and 24 February 1911, HP.

96. CJH to WPH, 31 January 1911, HP.

97. Ibid.; W. Rothenstein, *Men and Memories: Recollections, 1900–1922,* 254; CJH to WPH, 24 February [1911], HP; CJH to William Rothenstein, 2 March 1911, 694 (14), RP:HL.

98. Coomaraswamy to William Rothenstein, 29 March 1911, 320 (11), and 3 July 1911, 320 (12), RP:HL. The "change" was perhaps in the idea of collaboration with Goloubew.

99. CJH to William Rothenstein, 27 February [1911], 694 (13), RP:HL. The Quarritch firm has no record of such an approach.

100. CJH to WPH, [between 27 February and 5 March (1911)], HP. Her view of purdah life was already negative. From Tunisia in 1907 she had written to Helen Fry: "Didn't you feel it very curious going about in a masculine world (gay in dress to please one another) & the women hidden away. One feels that the whole of life including religion is arranged for men here. With us[,] women count for a good deal and don't in all respects get the worst of it" ("Monday the 18th" [December 1907], Fry Papers, Modern Archive Centre, King's College, Cambridge).

101. CJH to WPH, 5 March [1911], HP. Akbar Hydari (1869–1942) was Casson Walker's secretary and assumed that he would follow as Hyderabad's financial officer. Casson Walker, CJH wrote, "does not consider Mr Hydari quite stiff enough for the job though absolutely honourable—but another strong reason is that his birth is not considered good enough here. His race [*sic*] is the same as that of the Aga Khan but it doesn't satisfy the Hyderabad nobles, and the feeling is very strong." On E. M. Forster and the Hydaris, see Forster, *Selected Letters of E. M. Forster,* ed. Mary Lago and P. N. Furbank, 2 vols. (London: Collins, 1983, 1985; Cambridge: Harvard University Press, 1983, 1985), 2:14 n. 4; and Forster, *The Hill of Devi and Other Indian Writings,* Abinger Edition, ed. Elizabeth Heine (London: Edward Arnold, 1983), 218–19 and, on Forster's friend F. M. (May) Wyld and her purdah high school, 216–19.

102. CJH to Alice Rothenstein, 14 March [1911], 694 (29), RP:HL.

103. CJH to WPH, [ca. 28 February 1911], HP.

104. "The Gandhara Sculptures," *Illustrated London News* 136 (January 1910): 44, 49; CJH to WPH, [ca. 28 February 1911], HP.

105. CJH to WPH, 16 March 1911, HP.

106. CJH to William Rothenstein, Good Friday [14 April 1911], 694 (40), and 26 May 1911, 694 (15), RP:HL.

107. Ibid., 13 May [1911], 694 (49), and CJH to Alice Rothenstein, 31 May 1911, 694 (17), RP:HL.

108. CJH to William Rothenstein, 31 May 1911, 694 (16), RP:HL. She made the transfer to the India Society of her copyright in the Ajanta copies, which the society placed in the Victoria and Albert Museum, formerly the South Kensington Museum (MSS Eur. F 147/65A, India Office Library).

109. CJH to William Rothenstein, 1 June 1911, 694 (19), RP:HL. Rothenstein, too, resigned. This Festival of Empire was adjunct to the June festivities for the coronation of King George V. The *Journal of Indian Art and Industries* devoted its vol. 15, pt. 3 (1912) to the Indian section, of which CJH's copies and Goloubew's photographs were a major part. CJH contributed a lengthy account of her work (57–60). Vincent Arthur Smith (1848–1920) of the Indian Civil Service, who had not visited Ajanta, contributed a critical assessment to the effect that the Ajanta paintings were "of the Indian kind," not to be judged by "the canons of Asiatic, nor of modern European art, which has other methods and aims at more complex effects" (56).

110. CJH to Alice Rothenstein, [early June 1911], 694 (35), RP:HL.

111. CJH, "The Copies of the Ajanta Frescoes at the Festival of Empire" (letter), *Times,* 14 June 1911, 9. The letter is dated 13 June. See also "Festival of Empire and Imperial Exhibition," *Journal of Indian Art and Industries* 15 (1913): 117, 119–21.

112. "Festival of Empire and Imperial Exhibition," 56–57. A. Ghosh, editor of *Ajanta Murals: An Album of Eighty-Five Reproductions in Colour* (New Delhi: Archaeological Survey of India, 1967), 3 n, quotes H. Goetz on the problems of copying at Ajanta: "Unfortunately the very damaged condition of many Ajanta paintings often made copying rather a task of reconstruction which could not avoid introducing an element of subjective interpretation, and the first [*sic*] set of copies executed under the superintendence of J. Griffiths had not been free from a certain prettiness then cultivated by the Bombay School of Arts." Griffiths had varnished the paintings, still another barrier between original and copyist.

113. CJH to Alice Rothenstein, 10 June 1911, 694 (20), RP:HL.

114. WPH, "Autobiographical Memoir," HP.

115. P. N. Furbank, *E. M. Forster: A Biography,* 2 vols. (London: Secker and Warburg, 1977, 1978), 1:216 n. 1. Elizabeth Heine, ed., in Forster, *The Hill of Devi,* Abinger Edition, xii, repeats my suggestion of 1972.

116. E. M. Forster, *A Passage to India,* Abinger Edition, ed. Oliver Stallybrass (London: Edward Arnold, 1978), 19.

117. Forster, *Selected Letters,* 1:5.

118. Furbank, *E. M. Forster,* 1:56.

119. WPH to Mary Herringham, 5 November 1906, 17 November 1906, and 25 November 1906, HP.

120. Forster, *A Passage to India,* 19, 61, 26, 126, 128, 137.

121. Ibid., 24, 127, 141, 195.

122. "In Memory of Tagore," *Times,* 1 October 1941, 7. On the Herringhams, see Forster, *The Hill of Devi,* Abinger Edition, ed. Heine, xii–xiii, and on his visits to Ajanta, "Indian Journal," ibid., 268.

A few more links between WPH's letters and *A Passage to India* are worth a thought. At Udayagiri the bee, "perfectly black, shiny, and about 3 inches long, frequents our verandah" (WPH to Geoffrey Herringham, 12 February 1907), HP. Mrs. Moore (*A Passage to India,* 29) finds a wasp that has made itself at home on a clothing-peg; it had "long yellow legs which hung down behind when [it] flew." Forster first described the wasp as "small," more nearly like a bee, then as "large yellow" (*The Manuscripts of "A Passage to India,"* Abinger Edition, ed. Oliver Stallybrass [London: Edward Arnold, 1978], 42). The bee/wasp impressed both WPH and Mrs. Moore as India's particular creature, so indigenous and so self-assured that it was at home and at ease anywhere in that setting. "Pretty dear," Mrs. Moore says to the wasp." Forster says, "Perhaps he mistook the peg for a branch—no Indian animal has any sense of an interior" (*A Passage to India,* 29).

There is also Miss Derek, English secretary or companion to the maharaja of a Native State; she romps irresponsibly through *A Passage to India* and turns up in his motorcar, which she has taken without leave: "He doesn't want the car, silly fool!" (83). The Nizam of Hyderabad had thirty motorcars and an English secretary named Miss Cooper.

Finally, there is Dr. Callendar, the government's senior physician at Forster's Chandrapore: one of CJH's physicians at Barnwood House Institution was a Dr. Callendar.

123. WPH, "Autobiographical Memoir," HP.

CHAPTER 8. MARLEY'S GHOST

1. CJH to Alice Rothenstein, 8 November [1906], 694 (30), RP:HL.

2. Forster, diary entry for 23 November 1945 (after spending 22 November at Ajanta), in *The Hill of Devi,* Abinger Edition, ed. Heine, 268.

3. Quotes in this and the three following paragraphs are from CJH to WPH, 21 June 1911, HP.

4. Ibid., 30 June [1911], HP. Herbert Powell's Oxford University M.D. thesis was published as *The Surgical Aspects of Traumatic Insanity* (Oxford: Clarendon, 1893).

5. Andrew Scull, *The Most Solitary of Afflictions: Madness and Society in Britain, 1700–1900* (New Haven: Yale University Press, 1993), 160 n. 150. See also Elaine Showalter, *The Female Malady: Women, Madness, and English Culture, 1830–1988* (New York: Pantheon Books, 1985). Scull accepts the feminist position that madness in the nineteenth century became known as the "female malady," but he differs from Showalter's conclusion that it acquired this label because more women than men were committed to asylums (1871 census), for figures were almost equal, although women were confined for longer periods. He blames the misdiagnosis of women's problems on Victorian alienists' cumulative theorizing about women and insanity and calls Henry Maudsley's "Sex in Mind and in Education," *Fortnightly Review*, n.s., 21 (1874): 466–83, "a particularly egregious but by no means unrepresentative example of the genre." Maudsley (1835–1989) had wide influence because of his many positions and publications.

6. Michael J. Clark, "The Rejection of Psychological Approaches to Mental Disorder in Late Nineteenth-Century British Psychiatry," in *Madhouses, Mad-doctors, and Madmen: The Social History of Psychiatry in the Victorian Era*, ed. Andrew Scull (Philadelphia: University of Pennsylvania Press, 1981), 274.

7. Henry Maudsley, quoted in Clark, "The Rejection of Psychological Approaches," in *Madhouses, Mad-doctors, and Madmen*, 271.

8. John Hughlings Jackson, quoted ibid., 283–84. Jackson (1835–1911) was consulting physician to the London Hospital and the Hospital for Epilepsy and Paralysis. He concentrated on speech defects associated with mental disease, on epilepsy, and on the hierarchy of the nervous system.

9. Tom Lutz, "Sick Women and the Civilized Man," in *American Nervousness, 1903: An Anecdotal History* (Ithaca, N.Y.: Cornell University Press, 1990), 31.

10. Ibid.

11. S. Weir Mitchell, quoted ibid., 32.

12. On CJH, 20 June 1911–30 April 1913, Barnwood House Institution Medical Records, Gloucestershire County Archive.

13. Ibid.

14. See, for example, Wilkie Collins, *The Moonstone* (1868), which involves an Englishman's theft of a fabulous yellow diamond from the forehead of an image of the man-god, and mysterious Indians in vengeful pursuit. The superstition survived in connection with Ajanta at least into the 1950s. Alan Moorehead, who visited the caves soon after Indian independence in 1947, wrote: "There is supposed to be a curse upon Ajanta. It is said that anyone who tries to deface the paintings in any way, or even to reproduce them, will be overtaken by misfortune. As curses go, the Ajanta curse has not proved very violent (it claims only one case of suicide and one of madness), but it has proved remarkably persistent" ("Lovers on the Walls," *New Yorker,* 1 May 1954, 48). Was CJH's delusion that "madness"?

15. Barnwood House Institution Medical Records; CJH to WPH, 24 June [1911], HP.

16. CJH to WPH, 24 June [1911], HP. She described them as a "thick MS ruled book with an old oiled cloth cover and a red back" and a "thin black sketch book about the same size in which I might write. It is very difficult to read. Writing is easier to attend to."

17. Ibid., 26 June 1911, HP.

18. CJH to William Rothenstein, 27 June 1911, 694 (28), RP:HL.

19. CJH to WPH, 26 June 1911, HP.

20. CJH to Louisa Garrett Anderson, (draft), June 1911, HP. Anderson (1873–1943), who was the niece of Millicent Fawcett, carried on both private practice and hospital work.

21. CJH to WPH, 29 June 1911, HP. On this Shops Bill, see *Parliamentary Debates,* Commons, 5th ser., 22, 6 March 1911, col. 838; 32, 8 December 1911, cols. 1774–1874. On dangers of the "living-in" system, see the *Englishwoman* 7 (1910): 343–44. Gertrude Mary Tuckwell (1861–1951) was honorary secretary to the Women's Trade Union League from 1892 to 1904, member of an advisory committee to the Ministry of Health from 1905 to 1923, member of a committee on Women for Justices of the Peace, and member of the Royal Commission on National Health Insurance from 1924 to 1926.

22. CJH to WPH, "Saturday" 29 June 1911, 30 June 1911, and [late June 1911], HP; P&O Passenger List, SS *Persia,* arriving 11 April 1911, Board of Trade Records, BT 26, Public Record Office, Kew.

23. CJH to Alice Rothenstein, 7 July 1911, 694 (21), RP:HL; CJH to WPH, 10 July 1911, HP. WPH may have sent her one of the many euphoric articles about the coronation of King George V in June and plans for the November durbar at Delhi.

24. CJH to WPH, 5 July [1911], HP.

25. Barnwood House Institution Medical Records; Spalding, *Roger Fry,* 104. A loving and well-intentioned letter from Roger to Helen Fry in 1909 (*Letters,* 1:323–24) tells how distant was the understanding of mental illness. He pleads with her to submit to the doctors' orders, to "learn humility of mind, learn that your instincts and intuitions are fallible, believe that you may be wrong and others who are wiser and more experienced may be right. Oh Nell, if you can do this for my sake, all happiness and full freedom is ours."

26. CJH to WPH, "April 1914" [1915], and WPH, note, n.d., attached to 1911 letters from CJH, HP.

27. WPH, "Autobiographical Memoir," HP.

28. WPH to Rosamond Powell Wills, 2 May 1916, HP.

29. WPH, "Autobiographical Memoir," HP.

30. Richard Findlater, *Lilian Baylis: The Lady of the Old Vic* (London: Allen Lane, 1975), 181; Dr. C. M. Wilson, in obituary, "Sir Wilmot Herringham," *Lancet,* 2 May 1936, 1031–32. Findlater says that Miss Baylis "was particularly fortunate in her Chairmen, Everard Morrish, Sir Wilmot Herringham, and Lord Lytton, who were not only distinguished figureheads but hardworking, loyal allies" (181).

31. WPH, *A Physician in France* (London: Edward Arnold, 1919), 2, 28–29.

32. WPH to Rosamond Powell Wills, 11 June 1916, HP.

33. WPH, "Autobiographical Memoir," HP.

34. WPH to Lilian Baylis, 20 June 1922, Old Vic Archives, Bristol University Theatre Collection.

35. Minute Paper, "unofficial," 25 September 1911, Victoria and Albert Museum Records.

36. Tickner, *The Spectacle of Women,* 134.

37. CJH et al., *Ajanta Frescoes.* WPH partially subsidized this.

38. Goloubew to Havell, 3 December 1919, MSS Eur. D736/1, Havell Papers, India Office Library. See Victor Goloubew, *Documents pour servir á l'étude d'Ajanta: Les peintures de la première Grotte,* Ars Asiatica 10 (Paris: Librairie Nationale d'Art et d'Historie, 1927), and Ghulam Yazdani, *Ajanta: The Colour and Monochrome Reproductions of the Ajanta Frescoes Based on Photography, with an Explanatory Text by G. Yazdani and an Introduction by Laurence Binyon* 4 vols. (London: Oxford University Press, 1930–1953).

39. John de la Valette, for the India Society, to A. D. Campbell, Victoria and Albert Museum, 30 January 1931; Campbell to Museum Director, 2

March 1931, Victoria and Albert Museum Records, 1931, 50; WPH to William Rothenstein, 28 June 1930, 695 (8), RP:HL.

40. In 1967 I began to edit the thirty-year correspondence of Rothenstein and Rabindranath Tagore (*Imperfect Encounter*) and notified the India Society of my day of arrival. I was assured that everything I wanted would be available, but archives for 1910 to 1920 were already destroyed, and first editions of early India Society publications had gone to a secondhand dealer. I was told to take whatever interested me from the remainder. The lone survivor from that first decade of India Society history was one Minute Book. I arranged for transfer of this, with surviving papers of the East India Society, to the India Office Library. In 1978 the India Society was disbanded. Its membership, principally retired Anglo-Indians, had diminished, and greatly increased cultural exchange with India had produced other, more active societies.

41. The Herringhams' executor and I arrived at Bedford College just as its staff was packing for the move to Surrey. We saw the Herringham items not yet crated for removal.

42. On damage to the *Venus* painting, see Michael Kimmelman, "Getting to the Heart of an Image's Power," *Sunday Times* (New York), 5 November 1898, 37.

43. David Barrie, Director, National Art Collections Fund, to the author, 10 November 1994.

SELECT BIBLIOGRAPHY

Andrews, Keith. *The Nazarenes: A Brotherhood of German Painters in Rome.* Oxford: Clarendon, 1964.

Ashbee, C. R. *A Few Chapters in Workshop Reconstruction and Citizenship.* London: Guild and School of Handicraft, 1894.

Barker, Nicholas. *Bibliotheca Lindesiana: The Lives and Collections of Alexander William, 25th Earl of Crawford and 8th Earl of Balcarres, and James Ludovic, 26th Earl of Crawford and 9th Earl of Balcarres.* London: Bernard Quarritch, for the Roxburghe Club, 1977.

Bateson, Beatrice, comp. *William Bateson, F.R.S., Naturalist: His Essays and Addresses, together with a Short Account of His Life.* Cambridge, England: The University Press, 1928.

Benson, Robert H., ed. *The Holford Collection.* London: privately printed for Sir George Holford and members of the Burlington Fine Arts Club who subscribed at the Winter Exhibition, 1921–22, by Oxford University Press, 1924.

Binyon, Laurence. *Painting in the Far East: An Introduction to the History of Pictorial Art in Asia, Especially China and Japan.* London: Edward Arnold, 1908.

Birdwood, George C. M. "Gentes Aperimus Eoas" (letter), *Times,* 4 March 1910, 5.

———. "Indian Pottery at the Paris Exhibition," *Journal of the Royal Society of Arts* 27–28 (February 1879): 503–13.

———. *The Industrial Arts of India.* South Kensington Art Handbooks. London: Chapman and Hall, for Committee of the Council on Education, [1880].

———. "Pan-Hinduism" (letter), *Times,* 7 January 1910, 101.

Buchanan, William James. *Memoirs of Painting, with a Chronological History of the Emportation of Pictures by the Great Masters into England since the French Revolution.* 2 vols. London: R. Ackerman, 1824.

Cennini, D'Andrea Cennino. *The Book of the Art of Cennino Cennini: A Contemporary Practical Treatise on Quattrocento Painting.* Translated by Christiana Jane Herringham. London: George Allen & Unwin, 1899. American edition: *The Art of the Old Masters, as told by Cennino Cennini in 1437 [1397]: How they ground and mixed their Colours, painted their Pictures and Miniatures, tinted their Papers, made their Varnishes, etc. etc. A Reference work for the Artist, Picture Collector and Others.* New York: Francis P. Harper, 1899.

———. *A Treatise on Painting written by Cennino Cennini in the year 1437 [1397]; and first published in Italian in 1821, with an introduction and notes by Signor Tambroni . . .* Translated by [Mary Philadelphia] Merrifield. London: E. Lumley, 1844.

———. *The Craftsman's Handbook: The Italian "Il Libro dell' Arte."* Translated by Daniel V. Thompson, Jr. New York: Dover Publications, 1933.

Clark, Michael J. "The Rejection of Psychological Approaches to Mental Disorder in Late Nineteenth-Century British Psychiatry." *Madhouses, Mad-doctors, and Madmen: The Social History of Psychiatry in the Victorian Era.* Edited by Andrew Scull. Philadelphia: University of Pennsylvania Press, 1981.

Cole, Bruce. *Agnolo Gaddi.* Oxford Studies in the History of Art and Literature. Oxford: Clarendon, 1977.

Coomaraswamy, Ananda Kentish. *Mediaeval Sinhalese Art: Being a Monograph of Mediaeval Sinhalese Arts and Crafts, Mainly as Surviving in the Eighteenth Century, with an Account of the Structure of Society and the Status of the Craftsmen.* Broad Campden, Gloucestershire: Essex House, 1908; 2d ed., with author's corrections, New York: Pantheon Books, 1956.

———. "Oriental Bronzes," *Burlington Magazine* 7 (1910): 86–94.

[Curzon Committee]. *Report of the Committee of Trustees of the National Gallery Appointed by the Trustees to Enquire into the Retention of Important Pictures in this Country and Other Matters Connected with the National Art Collections, with Appendices.* London: H.M. Stationery Office, 1915.

Curzon, George Nathaniel. *Speeches by Lord Curzon of Kedleston, Viceroy and Governor of India, 1898–1901.* Calcutta: Thacker, Spink, 1901.

Eastlake, Charles Lock. *Methods and Materials of Painting of the Great Schools and Masters.* 2 vols. London: Longman, Brown, Green, and Longmans, 1847; New York: Dover Publications, 1969.

Fergusson, James, and James Burgess. *The Cave Temples of India.* 1880. Reprint, Delhi: Oriental Books, 1969.

Forster, E. M. *The Hill of Devi and Other Indian Writings.* Abinger Edition. Edited by Elizabeth Heine. London: Edward Arnold, 1983.

———. *A Passage to India.* Abinger Edition. Edited by Oliver Stallybrass. London: Edward Arnold, 1978.

———. *Selected Letters of E. M. Forster.* Edited by Mary Lago and P. N. Furbank. 2 vols. London: Collins, 1983, 1985; Cambridge: Harvard University Press, 1983, 1985.

[Fry, Roger]. "The Chantrey Bequest," *Athenaeum,* 7 November 1903, 620.

Fry, Roger. *Giovanni Bellini.* London: Unicorn, 1899.

———. "Ideals of a Picture Gallery," *Metropolitan Museum of Art Bulletin* 1 (March 1907): 59.

———. *Letters of Roger Fry.* Edited by Denys Sutton. 2 vols. London: Chatto and Windus, 1972.

———. "The Munich Exhibition of Mohammedan Art," *Burlington Magazine* 17 (1910): 283–90, 327–33.

[———]. "The National Art Collections Fund," *Athenaeum,* 26 September 1903, 452–53.

———. "Tempera Painting," *Burlington Magazine* 7 (1905): 175–76.

Girouard, Mark. *Sweetness and Light: The "Queen Anne" Movement, 1860–1900.* Oxford: Clarendon, 1977.

Goetze, Sigismund. "The Rokeby Velasquez" (letter), *Times,* 18 November 1905, 8.

———. "The 'Venus' of Velasquez" (letter), *Times,* 13 January 1906, 4.

Goloubew, Victor. *Documents pour servir á l'étude d'Ajanta: Les Peintures de la première grotte.* Ars Asiatica 10. Paris: Librairie Nationale d'Art et d'Histoire, 1927.

Guha-Thakurta, Tapati. *The Making of a New "Indian Art": Artists, Aesthetics, and Nationalism in Bengal, 1850–1920.* Cambridge, England: The University Press, 1992.

Havell, Ernest B. "Art Administration in India," *Journal of the Royal Society of Arts* 58 (1909–1910): 273–74.

———. *Essays on Indian Art, Industry, and Education.* Madras: G. Nateson, [1910].

———. *The Ideals of Indian Art.* London: John Murray, 1911.

———. *Indian Sculpture and Painting, Illustrated by Typical Masterpieces with an Explanation of Their Motives and Ideals.* London: John Murray, 1908.

Herringham, Christiana Jane. "Archaeology in India," *Times,* 21 August 1908, 4.

———. "The Caves of Ajanta," *Englishwoman* 9 (1911): 64–71.

———. "The Copies of the Ajanta Frescoes at the Festival of Empire," *Times,* 14 June 1911, 9.

———. "The Frescoes of Ajanta," *Burlington Magazine* 17 (1910): 136–39.

———. Introduction to *Catalogue of an Exhibition of Works by Members of the Society of Painters in Tempera.* London: Baillie Gallery, 1909.

———. Introduction to *Papers of the Society of Painters in Tempera, 1901–1907.* Edited by Christiana Herringham. London: privately printed by Women's Printing Society, 1907.

———. Introduction to *Papers of the Society of Painters in Tempera: Volume I, 1901–1907,* 2d ed. Edited by M. Sargant-Florence. Brighton: Dolphin, 1928.

———. "Notes on Mediaeval Methods." In *The Book of the Art of Cennino Cennini: A Contemporary Practical Treatise on Quattrocento Painting,* by D'Andrea Cennino Cennini. Translated by Christiana Jane Herringham. London: George Allen & Unwin, 1899.

———. Preface to *Catalogue of an Exhibition of Works by Members of the Society of Painters in Tempera.* London: Carfax Gallery, 1905.

———, et al. *Ajanta Frescoes: Being Reproductions in Colour and Monochrome of Frescoes in Some of the Caves at Ajanta after Copies Taken in the Years 1909–1911 by Lady Herringham and Her Assistants, with Introductory Essays by Various Members of the India Society.* London: Humphrey Milford, 1915.

Herringham, Wilmot P. *A Physician in France.* London: Edward Arnold, 1919.

Herrmann, Frank. *The English as Collectors: A Documentary Chrestomathy.* New York: Norton, 1972.

Holmes, C. J. *Self and Partners (Mostly Self): The Reminiscences of C. J. Holmes.* London: Macmillan, 1936.

Houghton, Walter. *The Victorian Frame of Mind, 1830–1870.* New Haven: Yale University Press, 1963.

Hynes, Samuel. *The Edwardian Turn of Mind.* Princeton, N.J.: Princeton University Press, 1968.

Ladis, Andrew. *Taddeo Gaddi: Critical Reappraisal and Catalogue Raisonné.* Columbia: University of Missouri Press, 1982.

Lago, Mary. "Christiana Herringham and the National Art Collections Fund," *Burlington Magazine* 135 (1993): 202–11.

———. *E. M. Forster: A Literary Life.* Basingstoke: Macmillan, 1995; New York: St. Martin's Press, 1995.

———, ed. *Imperfect Encounter: Letters of William Rothenstein and Rabindranath Tagore, 1911–1941.* Cambridge: Harvard University Press, 1972.

Leslie, G. D. *The Inner Life of the Royal Academy with an Account of Its Schools and Exhibitions Principally in the Reign of Queen Victoria.* London: John Murray, 1941.

Lindsay, David Alexander Edward. *The Crawford Papers: The Journals of David Lindsay, Twenty-Seventh Earl of Crawford and Tenth Earl of Balcarres, 1871–1940, during the Years 1892 to 1940.* Edited by John Vincent. Manchester: Manchester University Press, 1984.

———. *Donatello.* London: Duckworth, 1903; New York: Scribner, 1903.

———. *The Evolution of Italian Sculpture.* London: John Murray, 1909.

———. "The Rokeby Velasquez" (letter), *Times,* 16 March 1906, 8.

———. "The Rokeby Velasquez" (letter), *Times,* 21 March 1906, 10.

———, et al. "The Rokeby Velasquez" (letter), *Times,* 9 January 1906, 8.

———, et al. "The Rokeby Velasquez" (letter), *Times,* 24 January 1906, 8.

Lindsay, James Ludovic. *Sketches of the History of Christian Art.* 3 vols. London: John Murray, 1847.

Lipsey, Roger. *Coomaraswamy: His Life and Work.* Bollingen Series 89. Princeton, N.J.: Princeton University Press, 1977.

MacColl, D. S. "The Academy," *Saturday Review* 95 (9 May 1903): 585–87.

———. "The Academy: IV. 'Murder!'," *Saturday Review* 91 (13 June 1903): 766–67.

———. "Art at the Paris Exhibition: I," *Saturday Review* 90 (15 September 1900): 326–27.

———. "Art at the Paris Exhibition: II. Manet," *Saturday Review* 90 (22 September 1900): 358–59.

———. "Art at the Paris Exhibition: III. Rodin," *Saturday Review* 90 (29 September 1900): 358–59.

———. *Confessions of a Keeper, or Culture Is Anarchy.* Glasgow: A. Maclehose, 1931.

———. "Friends of the National Gallery," *Saturday Review* 90 (15 December 1900): 751–52.

———. "The Loss of the Velasquez" (letter), *Saturday Review* 101 (13 January 1906): 43–44.

———. "The 'Magazine of Art' and the Chantrey Bequest" (letter), *Saturday Review* 95 (7 November 1903): 573–74.

———. "The Maladministration of the Chantrey Trust," *Saturday Review* 95 (25 April 1903): 516–17.

[———]. "A National Art Collections Fund," *Saturday Review* 96 (26 September 1903): 393–94.

———. "The Royal Academy and National Art," *National Review* 45 (May 1905): 505–14.

———. "Some Political Matters of Art," *Saturday Review* 95 (7 March 1903): 289–90.

———. "Twenty-One Years of the National Art Collections Fund," *Burlington Magazine* 44 (1924): 175–79.

———, ed. *Twenty-Five Years of the National Art Collections Fund, 1903–1928.* Glasgow: Robert Maclehose with the Glasgow University Press, 1928.

McCarthy, Kathleen. *Women's Culture: American Philanthropy and Art, 1830–1930.* Chicago: University of Chicago Press, 1991.

Merrifield, Mary Philadelphia. *The Art of Fresco Painting, as Practised by the Old Italian and Spanish Masters, with a Preliminary Inquiry into the Nature of the Colours Used in Fresco Painting, with Observations and Notes.* London: published for the author by Charles Gilpin, 1846.

———. *Original Treatises, Dating from the XIIth to XVIIIth Centuries on Arts of Painting in Oil, Miniature, Mosaic, and on Glass; of Gilding, Dyeing, and the Preparation of Colours and Artificial Gems; Preceded by a General Introduction; with Translations, Prefaces, and Notes.* 2 vols. 1849. Reprint, New York: Dover Publications, 1967.

Mitter, Partha. *Much Maligned Monsters: History of European Reactions to Indian Art.* Oxford: Clarendon, 1977.

Müller, Charles. *Cinq mois aux Indes: de Bombay à Colombo.* Paris: E. Floury, 1924.

National Art Collections Fund. *Saved for the Nation: Fifty Years of the National Art Collections Fund.* London: Thames and Hudson, 1935.

Newbolt, Henry. *My World as in My Time: Memoirs, 1862–1932.* London: Faber and Faber, 1932.

Nicolson, Benedict. "Fifty Years of the Burlington Magazine," *Burlington Magazine* 95 (1953): 63–65.

Nochlin, Linda. "Why Have There Been No Great Women Artists?" *Art and Sexual Politics: Women's Liberation, Women Artists, and Art History.* Edited by Thomas B. Hess and Elizabeth C. Baker. Art News Series. New York: Collier Books, 1971.

Nunn, Pamela Gerrish. *Victorian Women Artists.* London: Women's Press, 1987.

Parker, Rozsika, and Griselda Pollock. *Old Mistresses: Women, Art, and Ideology.* New York: Pantheon, 1981.

Phillips, Claude. *Antoine Watteau.* London: Seeley, 1895; New York, Macmillan, 1895.

———. *The Earlier Work of Titian.* London: Seeley, 1897; New York: Macmillan, 1897.

———. *Frederick Walker and His Works.* London: Seeley, 1897.

———. *The Later Work of Titian.* London: Seeley, 1898; New York: Macmillan, 1898.

———. *The Picture Gallery of Charles I.* London: Seeley, 1896; New York: Macmillan, 1896.

Pointon, Marcia. *William Dyce, 1806–1864: A Critical Biography.* Oxford: Clarendon, 1979.

"Proceedings," *Journal of the Royal Society of Arts* 58 (1909–10): 189–90, 273–74.

Robertson, David. *Sir Charles Eastlake and the Victorian Art World.* Princeton, N.J.: Princeton University Press, 1978.

Rothenstein, William. *Men and Memories: Recollections, 1872–1900.* London: Faber and Faber, 1931.

———. *Men and Memories: Recollections, 1872–1938.* Edited and abridged by Mary Lago. London: Chatto and Windus, 1978; Columbia: University of Missouri Press, 1978.

———. *Men and Memories: Recollections, 1900–1922.* London: Faber and Faber, 1932.

———. *Since Fifty: Recollections, 1922–1938.* London: Faber and Faber, 1939.

Ruskin, John. *Works.* Library Edition. Edited by E. T. Cook and Alexander Wedderburn. 39 vols. London: George Allen, 1903–1912.

Scull, Andrew. *The Most Solitary of Afflictions: Madness and Society in Britain, 1700–1900.* New Haven: Yale University Press, 1993.

Spalding, Frances. *Roger Fry: Art and Life.* London: Granada, 1980.

Stevenson, R. A. M. *The Art of Velasquez.* London: George Bell, 1895.

Strachey, Ray. *The Cause: A Short History of the Women's Movement in Great Britain.* London: Virago, 1978.

Tickner, Lisa. *The Spectacle of Women: Imagery of the Suffrage Campaign, 1907–1914.* Chicago: University of Chicago Press, 1988.

Victoria and Albert Museum. *Saved for the Nation: The Achievement of the National Art Collections Fund, 1903–1973.* London: Victoria and Albert Museum, 1973.

[Waverley Committee], H.M. Treasury. *The Export of Works of Art, etc.: Report of a Committee Appointed by the Chancellor of the Exchequer.* London: H.M. Stationery Office, 1952.

Witt, Robert Clermont. *The Art of Collecting.* London: privately printed for the National Art Collections Fund by Shenval Press, 1950.

———. "A Movement in Aid of Our National Art Collections," *Nineteenth Century and After* 54 (1903): 651–59.

———. *The Nation and Its Treasures.* London: Cassell, 1911.

Woolf, Virginia. *Roger Fry: A Biography.* 1940. Reprint, London: Hogarth, 1969.

Yazdani, Ghulam. *Ajanta: The Colour and Monochrome Reproductions of the Ajanta Frescoes Based on Photography, with an Explanatory Text by G. Yazdani and an Introduction by Laurence Binyon.* 4 vols. London: Oxford University Press, 1930–1953.

INDEX